W. Porter

GAME HARVEST MANAGEMENT

Edited by
Samuel L. Beasom
Sheila F. Roberson

A Proceedings of the
Third International Symposium of the
Caesar Kleberg Wildlife Research Institute
College of Agriculture
Texas A&I University
Kingsville, Texas 78363
October 3-6, 1983

International Standard Book Number 0-912229-08-X (Paper)
0-912229-09-8 (Cloth)
Library of Congress Catalog Card Number 84-72724

Copyright 1985 by the Caesar Kleberg Wildlife Research Institute
Printed in the United States of America

Available from:

    Caesar Kleberg Wildlife Research Institute
    Texas A&I University
    Campus Box 218
    Kingsville, TX 78363
    $20 hardbound, $15 soft cover

Example of citing a paper from the Proceedings:

CAUGHLEY, G. 1985. Harvesting of wildlife: past, present, and future. Pages 3-14 *in* S. L. Beasom and S. F. Roberson, eds. Game harvest management. Caesar Kleberg Wildlife Research Inst., Kingsville, Tex.

TABLE OF CONTENTS

INTRODUCTION vii

LIST OF REGISTERED PARTICIPANTS xi

TECHNIQUES FOR ESTABLISHING HARVEST QUOTAS AND MONITORING HARVEST

    HARVESTING OF WILDLIFE: PAST, PRESENT, AND FUTURE—
    Graeme Caughley 3

    SAMPLING PATTERNS AND INTENSITIES FOR HELICOPTER CENSUSES OF WHITE-TAILED DEER—James G. Teer, D. Lynn Drawe, and
    Raymond L. Urubek 15

    AN EVALUATION OF 7 YEARS OF SPOTLIGHT-COUNT DATA ON A COASTAL SOUTH CAROLINA PLANTATION—Gene W. Wood,
    James R. Davis, and George R. Askew 25

    LINE TRANSECT ESTIMATION OF ANIMAL DENSITIES FROM LARGE DATA SETS—C. E. Gates, W. Evans, D. R. Gober, F. S. Guthery,
    and W. E. Grant 37

    UTILIZATION OF AERIAL SURVEY DATA TO SET PRONGHORN HARVEST QUOTAS IN NEW MEXICO—Bruce L. Morrison 51

    EVALUATING KILL QUOTAS FOR DEER USING MINIMAL DATA—
    David Euler and Howard Smith 57

    NEVADA'S USE OF CHANGE-IN-RATIO ESTIMATES TO ESTABLISH DEER HUNTING QUOTAS—Mike Hess 67

    SEX RATIOS AND HARVEST MANAGEMENT: A COMPUTER SIMULATION AND ANALYSIS FOR WHITE-TAILED DEER—Brian Underwood
    and William F. Porter 83

    A GENERALIZED SUSTAINED YIELD TABLE FOR WHITE-TAILED DEER—
    Robert Downing and David C. Guynn, Jr. 95

    CONSTRAINED OPTIMAL EXPLOITATION: A QUANTITATIVE THEORY—
    David R. Anderson 105

    EVALUATIONS OF THE TELEPHONE AND MAIL SURVEY METHODS OF OBTAINING HARVEST DATA FROM LICENSED SPORTSMEN IN
    MONTANA—John D. Cada 117

RESPONSES OF DEER POPULATIONS TO HARVEST STRATEGIES

    INFLUENCE OF REGULATION ON DEER HARVEST—David S. deCalesta 131

    BLACK-TAILED DEER POPULATION REGULATION THROUGH ANTLERLESS HUNTS IN WESTERN WASHINGTON—Kenneth J. Raedeke and
    Richard D. Taber 139

    BUCK PERMITS AS A MANAGEMENT TOOL IN SOUTH TEXAS—Horace
    Gore, William F. Harwell, Michael D. Hobson, and Willbern J. Williams 149

    DEER HARVEST MANAGEMENT, WELDER AND McCAN RANCH, TEXAS—
    Noel E. Adams, Jr. 165

SELECTIVE HARVESTING OF WHITE-TAILED BUCK DEER ON GROTON
PLANTATION IN SOUTH CAROLINA—Carlyle Franklin, Gerald Moore,
and Lewis Rogers 175

DEER POPULATION MANAGEMENT IN NEW YORK: USING PUBLIC INPUT
TO MEET PUBLIC NEEDS—Daniel J. Decker, Tommy L. Brown, and
George F. Mattfeld 185

DEMOGRAPHIC AND GENETIC CHARACTERISTICS OF WHITE-TAILED
DEER POPULATIONS SUBJECTED TO STILL OR DOG HUNTING—
Kim T. Scribner, Michael C. Wooten, Michael H. Smith, and Paul E. Johns 197

MANAGEMENT OF EXOTIC DEER IN CONJUNCTION WITH WHITE-TAILED
DEER—John T. Baccus, Donnie E. Harmel, and William E. Armstrong 213

HARVEST STRATEGIES FOR OTHER MAMMALS

SEX- AND AGE-SELECTIVE HARVEST STRATEGY FOR MOOSE MANAGEMENT
IN SASKATCHEWAN—R. R. Stewart 229

SOCIAL DETERMINANTS OF BLACK BEAR MANAGEMENT FOR THE
NORTHERN CATSKILL MOUNTAINS—Daniel J. Decker,
Robert A. Smolka, Jr., John O'Pezio, and Tommy L. Brown 239

CHARACTERISTICS OF HARVESTED COLLARED PECCARIES IN RELATION
TO RAINFALL PATTERNS IN SOUTHEASTERN ARIZONA—
Lyle K. Sowls and Brian A. Maurer 249

HARVEST STRATEGIES TO CONTROL EXOTIC UNGULATE
POPULATIONS IN NEW MEXICO—Bruce L. Morrison 261

CONSERVATION AND MANAGEMENT PLAN FOR THE MOUNTAIN GAZELLE
IN ISRAEL—Yoram Ayal and Dan Baharav 269

COMMERCIAL HUNTING OF WILD RED DEER IN NEW ZEALAND—
C. N. Challies 279

HARVESTING GAME AT NIGHT IN SOUTH WEST AFRICA—Eugene Joubert 289

RESPONSE OF GAME BIRD POPULATIONS TO HARVEST STRATEGIES

REGULATIONS AND RESTRICTIONS PERTAINING TO BOBWHITE QUAIL
HARVESTS IN THE SOUTHEAST—George A. Hurst and Walter Rosene 301

FEBRUARY HUNTING OF AMERICAN WOODCOCK: BREEDING
IMPLICATIONS—R. Montague Whiting, Jr., Ronald R. George, M. Keith Causey,
and Thomas H. Roberts 309

HARVESTING RED GROUSE IN THE NORTH OF ENGLAND—Peter J. Hudson .. 319

EFFECTS OF CHANGES IN HUNTING REGULATIONS ON BLUE GROUSE
POPULATIONS—Richard W. Hoffman 327

EFFECTS OF CHANGES IN HUNTING REGULATIONS ON SAGE GROUSE
HARVEST AND POPULATIONS—Clait E. Braun and Thomas D. I. Beck 335

THE ADDITIVE EFFECT OF HUNTING MORTALITY ON THE NATURAL
MORTALITY RATES OF GROUSE—A. T. Bergerud 345

ABSTRACTS

INTENSIVE FARM MANAGEMENT OF WAPITI BANDS WITH RELOCATION OF YOUNG MALES INTO NEW HUNTING PRESERVES—G. H. Moore 369

GAME HARVEST MANAGEMENT AS APPLIED TO A GAME RANCHING PROGRAM—Colin E. Rudman 370

CONSERVATION AND MANAGEMENT OF BLACKBUCK AND GAZELLE—S. M. Mohnot 371

A SUMMARY OF NEW YORK'S WILD TURKEY MANAGEMENT PROGRAM SINCE 1950—James Glidden 372

RESPONSE OF GRAY AND FOX SQUIRREL POPULATIONS TO DIFFERENTIAL HARVEST INTENSITIES—Charles E. Davis, Charles S. Smith, Samuel L. Beasom, and Wendell G. Swank 373

HUNTER PARTICIPATION IN THE MANAGEMENT OF A HERD OF TROPHY ELK—John A. Anderson 374

INTRODUCTION

The Game Harvest Management Symposium focused on current knowledge in the establishment of harvest quotas and the response of a wide variety of animals to prescribed harvests. This phase of wildlife management represents one of the most important aspects of the stewardship by wildlife biologists of the wild game populations that they are entrusted to conserve and perpetuate.

This responsibility must be addressed in an objective and professional manner because of the universal concern and respect for wildlife. More and more, questions concerning philosophies are arising from a growing public that does not understand or believe in the hunting of wild animals—be it for food, sport, or profit.

The task of wildlife biologists should not be to impose their own subjective value judgments in this regard. In contrast, their primary responsibility should be to derive objective schemes that permit wise use of our wildlife resources in such a way that species maintenance is insured forever. This responsibility, however, does not permit a "license" to manipulate unwisely and without biological facts.

To adequately fulfill the responsibility of stewardship over wild game populations, biologists must understand the consequences of all outside influences. To this end, this symposium was designed about 1 potentially major influence—hunting. A knowledge of the impacts to and responses of all wild game species populations to varied intensities of hunting or rates of harvest should be, and doubtless some day will be, a requisite to the establishment of hunting seasons or offtake quotas.

From the keynote address by Graeme Caughley through the individual application of harvest prescriptions by other speakers, a wide variety of philosophies and approaches are presented. This is not surprising considering the wide variety of situations that the various studies represent. Hopefully, this publication will "set the stage" for additional research that will further advance our knowledge in this critical area of wildlife management.

Many individuals, too numerous to mention, contributed to the success of this symposium, and we are extremely appreciative of their efforts. The Izaak Walton League of America, Inc. contributed to defray publication costs. The efforts of Andres Garza, Jr., Gail Ivie, Kay Flenniken, David Smith, Kristin Wood, Morgan Richardson, Mike Abbott, and student members of the Wildlife Society and the Biology Club are especially noteworthy and deserve a special thanks. Also, the editorial board, composed of the following individuals, are recognized for their contributions to the quality of the final product:

David R. Anderson
Utah State University

Al B. Brothers
Zachry Ranches, Laredo, Texas

John C. Barron
Texas Parks and Wildlife
  Department

Reginald H. Barrett
University of California, Berkeley

Arthur T. Bergerud
University of Victoria

Lytle H. Blankenship
Texas A&M University

Clait E. Braun
Colorado Division of Wildlife

Sam Brownlee
General Land Office, Texas

John R. Cary
University of Wisconsin

Graeme Caughley
CSIRO, Australia

Robert L. Cook
Shelton Ranches, Kerrville, Texas

D. Lynn Drawe
Rob and Bessie Welder Wildlife
  Foundation

Lester L. Eberhart
Kennewick, Washington

Fern L. Filion
Canadian Wildlife Service

Todd K. Fuller
University of Wisconsin

Charles E. Gates
Texas A&M University

Robert H. Giles, Jr.
Virginia Polytechnic Institute & State
  University

Horace G. Gore
Texas Parks and Wildlife
  Department

William E. Grant
Texas A&M University

Galen E. Green
College Station, Texas

Fred S. Guthery
Texas A&I University

David C. Guynn, Jr.
Clemson University

Dwight E. Guynn
Texas A&M University

Donnie E. Harmel
Texas Parks and Wildlife
  Department

Douglas B. Houston
Olympic National Park, Washington

Volney W. Howard, Jr.
New Mexico State University

Lynn R. Irby
Montana State University

Lloyd B. Keith
University of Wisconsin

William H. Kiel, Jr.
King Ranch, Inc., Kingsville, Texas

Fritz L. Knopf
Colorado State University

Bruce E. Kohn
Wisconsin Department of Natural
  Resources

Edward L. Kozicky
Texas A&I University

Richard J. Mackie
Montana State University

Robert A. McCabe
University of Wisconsin

Bruce L. Morrison
New Mexico Department of Game
  and Fish

Emil A. Mucchetti
Texas A&I University

W. Scott Overton
Oregon State University

Joseph E. Paloheimo
University of Toronto

Michael R. Pelton
University of Tennessee

Rolf O. Peterson
Michigan Technological University

Orrin J. Rongstad
University of Wisconsin

John L. Roseberry
Southern Illinois University

Donald H. Rusch
University of Wisconsin

Kim T. Scribner
Savannah River Ecology Laboratory,
  University of Georgia

Nova J. Silvy
Texas A&M University

Vashti C. Supplee
Arizona Game and Fish Department

Richard D. Taber
University of Washington

Gary C. White
Colorado State University

R. Montague Whiting, Jr.
Stephen F. Austin State University

John D. Williams
Texas A&M University

Don E. Wilson
Texas Parks and Wildlife
  Department

Philip J. Zwank
Louisiana State University

Fred C. Zwickel
University of Alberta

LIST OF REGISTERED PARTICIPANTS

Noel Adams
Welder & McCan Ranch
PO Box T
Woodsboro, TX 78393

Carroll Allen
Georgia Department of Natural Resources
Rt. 1 Box 187
Arnoldsville, GA 30619

Jean A. Allen
Small Woodlot Forestry Research &
  Development Program
North Carolina State University
103 Enterprise Street
Raleigh, NC 27607

David Anderson
Utah Cooperative Wildlife Research Unit
510 Spring Creek Road
Logan, UT 84322

John and Joan Anderson
New Zealand Deerstalkers' Association
Glendonald Albury
New Zealand

Kay Anderson
Sunburst Energies
105 Shore Cliff
Portland, TX 78374

Bill Armstrong
Texas Parks & Wildlife Department
Rt. 1 Box 180
Hunt, TX 78024

Yoram Ayal
3 Ya'el Street
Jerusalem, Israel

John Baccus
Biology Department
Southwest Texas State University
San Marcos, TX 78666

Robert Barbee
Florida Game & Fresh Water Fish Commission
4907 NE 6th Street
Ocala, FL 32674

Delwin Benson
Department of Fishery & Wildlife Ecology
Room 109 Wagar Building
Colorado State University
Fort Collins, CO 80524

A. T. Bergerud
University of Victoria
RR 1
Fulford, British Columbia

Clait E. Braun
Colorado Division of Wildlife
Wildlife Research Center
317 West Prospect
Fort Collins, CO 80526

Timothy A. Breault
Florida Game & Fresh Water
  Fish Commission
551 N. Military Trail
West Palm Beach, FL 33406

George E. Burgoyne, Jr.
Wildlife Division
Michigan Department of Natural Resources
4916 Devonshire Avenue
Lansing, MI 48910

Gary Burke
U.S. Fish & Wildlife Service
Laguna Atascosa National Wildlife Refuge
Box 450
Rio Hondo, TX 78583

John D. Cada
Montana Department of Fish, Wildlife,
  and Parks
Bozeman, MT 59717

L. A. Carter
309 Cape May
Corpus Christi, TX 78412

John Cary
Department of Wildlife Ecology
226 Russell Lab
University of Wisconsin
Madison, WI 53706

Graeme Caughley
CSIRO
Canberra, Australia

C. N. Challies
Forest Research Institute
PO Box 31011
Christchurch, New Zealand

Doug Coates
Range & Animal Science Department
Sul Ross State University
Box C-110
Alpine, TX 79830

Virginia Cogar
Range & Animal Science Department
Sul Ross State University
Box C-110
Alpine, TX 79830

Will E. Cohen
Rt. 3 Box 195
Marble Falls, TX 78654

Bryan Coleman
Valdina Farms
Utopia, TX 78884

Robert Cook
Shelton Ranches
PO Box 1107
Kerrville, TX 78028

Dalton Cross
Biology Department
Southwest Texas State University
San Marcos, TX 78666

David deCalesta
Oregon State University
1765 NW Menlo Drive
Corvallis, OR 97330

Daniel J. Decker
Department of Natural Resources
Cornell University
Ithaca, NY 14853

Eugene Decker
Wildlife Department
Colorado State University
1537 W. 29th Street
Loveland, CO 80537

Robert Downing
114 Lewis Road
Clemson, SC 29631

Lynn Drawe
Welder Wildlife Foundation
PO Drawer 1400
Sinton, TX 78387

Chris Duggan
Range & Animal Science Department
Sul Ross State University
Box C-110
Alpine, TX 79830

David Euler
Wildlife Branch
Ontario Ministry of Natural Resources
Queen's Park
Toronto, Ontario M7A IW3
Canada

Darrell Evans
Stephen F. Austin State University
Box 4207
Nacogdoches, TX 75961

Thomas J. Fillinger
Texas Agricultural Experiment Station
PO Box 362
D'Hanis, TX 78850

R. J. Fischer
U.S. Fish & Wildlife Service
500 NE Multromeh
Portland, OR 97232

Bubba Fowler
Exotic Game Ranch Managers
Rt. 1 Box 130
Rosanky, TX 78953

Carlyle Franklin
Small Woodlot Forestry Research &
  Development Program
North Carolina State University
103 Enterprise Street
Raleigh, NC 27607

William Franklin
124 Science II
Iowa State University
Ames, IA 50011

Mike Fritz
124 Science II
Iowa State University
Ames, IA 50011

Jim Gallagher
1707 Palasota Drive #17
Bryan, TX 77801

Nick Garza
Range Science Department
Texas A&M University
College Station, TX 77843

C. E. Gates
Department of Statistics
Texas A&M University
College Station, TX 77843

A. C. Gilbert
Bass Brothers Enterprises
Texas Exotic Game Ranch
Rt. 1 Box 10
Santo, TX 76472

James Gilbert
Wildlife Division
University of Maine
Orono, ME 04496

Horace Gore
Texas Parks & Wildlife Department
4200 Smith School Road
Austin, TX 78744

Galen Green
Texas A&M University
Rt. 4 Box 375
College Station, TX 77843

Brad Gruver
Department of Range & Wildlife
Texas Tech University
Lubbock, TX 79409

Keith Guthrie
602 Field Street
Taft, TX 78390

David Guynn
Department of Forestry
Clemson University
406 Rockingham Road
Seneca, SC 29678

Robert Hazel
North Carolina State University
305 Lakeside Drive
Garner, NC 27529

Dennis Heisey
Minnesota Department of Natural Resources
Box 7, Centennial Building
St. Paul, MN 55155

James Henson
USDA Soil Conservation Service
PO Box 648
Temple, TX 76501

June Herbst
PO Box 1050
Corpus Christi, TX 78403

Mike Hess
Nevada Department of Wildlife
PO Box 10678
Reno, NV 89520

Richard W. Hoffman
Colorado Division of Wildlife
Wildlife Research Center
317 W. Prospect
Fort Collins, CO 80526

Julie Hogan
Rt. 1 Box 27C
Spicewood, TX 78669

Douglas Houston
National Park Service
816 Mt. Angeles Road
Port Angeles, WA 98362

Peter Hudson
Game Conservancy
Mews House, Askrigg
Leyborn
N. Yorks, England

Neill Hunter
203 Druid Hills Road
Arkadelphia, AR 71923

George Hurst
Mississippi State University
PO Drawer LW
Mississippi State, MS 39762

Larry Ivy
U.S. Fish & Wildlife Service
Rt. 1 Box 151
Tishomingo, OK 73460

Tom Jose
Valdina Farms
Utopia, TX 78886

Eugene Joubert
Nature Conservation
PO 613306
Windhoek, South West Africa

Tom Jurgensen
124 Science II
Iowa State University
Ames, IA 50011

Lloyd Keith
Department of Wildlife Ecology
226 Russell Lab
University of Wisconsin
Madison, WI 53706

Bill Kiel
King Ranch, Inc.
Box 1418
Kingsville, TX 78363

Don Klebenow
Range, Wildlife & Forestry Department
University of Nevada
Reno, NV 89512

Ed Kozicky
817 Southmoor
Godfrey, IL 62035

Joseph Kurz
Georgia Game & Fish Department
270 Washington Street
Atlanta, GA 30303

Richard Lancia
Forestry Department
North Carolina State University
Raleigh, NC 27650

Albert LeCount
Arizona Game & Fish Department
2222 W. Greenway Road
Phoenix, AZ 85023

Forrest Loomis
Illinois Department of Conservation
902 E. Euclid
Monmouth, IL 61462

Larry Marcum
Tennessee Wildlife Resources Agency
Box 40747
Nashville, TN 37204

Kathleen McCoy
Navajo Game & Fish Department
PO Box 1480
Window Rock, AZ 86515

Brian Maurer
Arizona Coop Wildlife Research Unit
University of Arizona
10142 E. Rio de Oro Drive
Tucson, AZ 85749

L. H. Minton
Vaughan Properties
PO Box 1579
Corpus Christi, TX 78403

William Morrill
Rt. 1 Box 1332
Boerne, TX 78006

Bruce Morrison
New Mexico Department of Game & Fish
Villagra Building
Santa Fe, NM 87501

Byron Moser
Oklahoma Department of Wildlife
    Conservation
1801 N. Lincoln Boulevard
PO Box 73152
Oklahoma City, OK 73105

Woodrow Myers
Department of Game
600 N. Capitol
Olympia, WA 98501

Brian O'Kelley
Welder Wildlife Foundation
PO Drawer 1400
Sinton, TX 78387

John O'Pezio
Wildlife Resources Center
New York State Department of Environmental
    Conservation
Albany, NY 12054

Barry and Karen Osborn
Rt. 3 Box 219R
Hamilton, TX 76531

Jeff Pebworth
5908 N. San Bernardo #48
Laredo, TX 78041

Gary Ploch
Patio Ranch
Rt. 1 Box 132
Hunt, TX 78024

Wayne Porath
Missouri Department of Conservation
1110 College Avenue
Columbia, MO 65201

Michael Porter
Samuel Roberts Noble Foundation
PO Box 2180
Ardmore, OK 73402

Lynn Post
Soil Conservation Service
Box 399
Hondo, TX 78861

Kenneth J. Raedeke
College of Forest Resources
University of Washington
Seattle, WA 98195

Dean Ransom, Jr.
226 Russell Lab
University of Wisconsin
Madison, WI 53706

David Reid
Texas Parks & Wildlife Department
3205 12th Street
Bay City, TX 77414

Rory Reynolds
Killam Ranch
PO Box 499
Laredo, TX 78041

Mark Rhodes
Missouri Department of Conservation
University of Missouri
112 Stephens
Columbia, MO 65211

William Richardson
Dresser Industries
PO Box 460
Falfurrias, TX 78355

Orrin Rongstad
Department of Wildlife Ecology
226 Russell Lab
University of Wisconsin
Madison, WI 53706

Gary Rose
Exotic Game Ranch Managers
Rt. 1 Box 130
Rosanky, TX 78953

John Roseberry
Southern Illinois University
Rt. 8
Carbondale, IL 62901

C. E. Rudman
Brandtkoppen
Sapkamma, South Africa 6235

Kim Scribner
Savannah River Ecology Laboratory
Drawer E
Aiken, SC 29801

Keith Sexson
Kansas Fish & Game Commission
832 E. 6th Street
Emporia, KS 66801

William Sheffield
Rt. 4, 54 Triple Bend Road
College Station, TX 77840

Nova Silvy
Department of Wildlife & Fisheries
Texas A&M University
College Station, TX 77843

Randy Simpson
Guajolota Ranch
801 Dawson Drive
Edinburg, TX 78539

Glynnis Newman Smith
Ontario Ministry of Natural
  Resources
RR 1
Beeton, Ontario, Canada

Howard Smith
Ministry of Natural Resources
RR 1
Beeton, Ontario, Canada

Lyle Sowls
Arizona Coop Wildlife Research Unit
214 Biological Sciences East
University of Arizona
Tucson, AZ 85721

Frank Sprague
USDA Soil Conservation Service
Box 648
Temple, TX 76513

Tom Stehn
U.S. Fish & Wildlife Service
PO Box 100
Austwell, TX 77950

Robert Stewart
Box 2647
Melville, Saskatchewan
Canada

San Stiver
Nevada Department of Wildlife
PO Box 10678
Reno, NV 89520

Thad Swann
Rio Paisano Ranch
PO Box 130
Riviera, TX 78379

Richard Taber
University of Washington
2024 23rd Avenue E
Seattle, WA 98112

Tim Taylor
505 NW 38th Street
Hangar 32 South Mecham Field
Fort Worth, TX 76106

Jim Teer
Welder Wildlife Foundation
PO Drawer 1400
Sinton, TX 78387

Kevin Thompson
Texas Tech University
2419 35th Street
Lubbock, TX 79406

Michael Thompson
College of Forest Resources
240 Nutting Hall
University of Maine
Orono, ME 04469

George Tsukamoto
Nevada Department of Wildlife
70 York Way
Sparks, NV 89431

Terry Turney
Box 123
Port Mansfield, TX 78598

Jerry Turrentine
Soil Conservation Service
PO Box 1001
Uvalde, TX 78801

Brian Underwood
CESF, 224 Illick Hall
State University of New York
Syracuse, NY 13210

Raymond Urubek
Welder Wildlife Foundation
PO Drawer 1400
Sinton, TX 78387

Susan Wardroup
Texas Parks & Wildlife Department
PO 206
Hunt, TX 78024

Roy Welch
Southwest Texas State University
PO Box 1548
Canyon Lake, TX 78130

David Whitehouse
Valley View Cattle Company
Rt. 1 Box 68
Athens, TX 75751

Montague Whiting
Stephen F. Austin State University
Box 6109
Nacogdoches, TX 75962

Lamar Windberg
118 Naranjo Avenue
Laredo, TX 78041

Charles Winkler
Texas Parks & Wildlife Department
4200 Smith School Road
Austin, TX 78744

Gene Wood
Clemson University
305 Meeting Street
Georgetown, SC 29440

Greg Yarrow
Stephen F. Austin State University
14072 SFA
Nacogdoches, TX 75962

TECHNIQUES FOR ESTABLISHING HARVEST QUOTAS AND MONITORING HARVEST

HARVESTING OF WILDLIFE: PAST, PRESENT, AND FUTURE

GRAEME CAUGHLEY, CSIRO Division of Wildlife and Rangelands Research, P.O. Box 84, Lyneham, ACT 2602, Australia

Abstract: Modern game harvest management, especially as it is practiced, has many similarities to the philosophies espoused as early as the Eighth Century in Europe. Great advances, however, have been made in theoretical population dynamics, such as in the development of predictive models to simulate perturbation-response relationships. Two harvest models, complete and partial compensation, are defined and tested for appropriateness relative to particular animal species. Mallard (*Anas platyrhynchos*) populations were evaluated with the complete compensation model, and moose (*Alces alces*) populations were evaluated with the partial compensation model.

KEY WORDS: Harvest management, Wildlife harvesting, Compensatory mortality, Compensation models, Mallard, Moose.

This paper reviews the history of wildlife harvesting management, comments on its current problems, and speculates on its future. I thank Jeff Short and Judy Caughley for criticizing a previous draft and F.D.R. Knight for drafting the figures.

THE PAST

We tend to think of wildlife harvesting management as relatively recent, but it has a long history. Its elements had been established in France by the Eighth Century when Charlemagne instituted an elaborate set of game laws. These limited offtake and provided for habitat protection by banning grazing and cultivation in the realm's deer forests (Graham 1973). Under Ghenghis Khan the Mongols restricted hunting to the 4 months of winter; to allow for the escape of a nucleus of survivors, the slaughter at the end of their massive drives always terminated before total annihilation of the animals (Lamb 1927). Ghenghis Khan's grandson, Khubilai, is credited with inventing the supplementary feeding of game (Leopold 1933); he had millet planted around the boundaries of his game reserves. The Mongols conserved wildlife much better than they did people.

The dominant attributes of modern harvesting management come down to us from ancient times: protection of habitat and the proclamation of hunting seasons. Elaborations were to follow.

Persecution of predators, with the aim of reducing non-hunting mortality of game species, did not become widespread until the Eighteenth Century. It was a natural progression from the control of predators of domestic livestock, a means of control in full swing from at least the beginning of recorded history. It explains why there are now no wolves (*Canis lupus*) or brown bears (*Ursus* sp.) in Britain and no present plans to reintroduce them. Hunting licenses and bag limits are very modern; they were unheard of before the second half of the Nineteenth Century. New York State has required a hunting license since 1865 (Leopold 1933), and New Zealand instituted deerstalking licenses in 1867 (Caughley 1983). One of the first formal bag limits was 25 prairie chickens (*Tympanuchus cupido*)/day, enacted by the Iowan legislature in 1878 (Leopold 1933).

In those countries where game is the property of the people rather than of the landowner, the perceived imperatives of wildlife harvesting management had become fixed by 1900. The hunter would be licensed, he would hunt for only part of the year, he would not take too many animals in a single day, and he risked both his immortal soul and a heavy fine if he dared to hunt on Sunday. Add a little predator control and rather less habitat management, and that was about it.

THE PRESENT

Wildlife harvesting management today, in practice as against theory, differs little from what it was in 1900. The major advance is a relaxation of strictures against hunting on Sundays. There is now, however, a much wider gap between what is said and what is done. The wildlife management agencies of all countries claim that the hunting regulations that they so earnestly enforce are based on sound scientific principles and intricate mathematical calculations. In fact, current deliberations leading to harvesting regulations seldom differ in kind from those of the hunting subcommittee of the Mongol Supreme Command in the Thirteenth Century. Decisions on hunting seasons and bag limits are about as arbitrary now as they were then. Research findings contribute little to their formulation. The advice of practicing biologists, if it is sought at all, is largely ignored.

This may seem a harsh judgment and, if true, a scandal. I view it differently. The regulations may appear arbitrary, but in most cases they err on the side of caution. They may not have much scientific basis, but they have an ethical one underpinned by much common sense. A cautious control of offtake, combined with a careful monitoring of indices, may not provide the best of yields. However, it seldom yields catastrophies.

Wildlife biologists can claim that, with few exceptions, wildlife stocks are in as good a shape now as they were 30 years ago. Whaling and fisheries biologists cannot make the same claim. But over that period, wildlife biologists did not make the big decisions on wildlife harvesting. They were made by committees typically including a politician, an industrialist, a government administrator, an *ex officio* lawyer, and the president of the local hunting club. They served us well. We have been luckier than we deserve.

Against that, consider what might have happened if 30 years ago wildlife biologists were solely responsible for setting offtake quotas. They would have accepted the challenge with the certainty that their skill and knowledge were equal to the task, they would have aimed not for safety but for a maximum sustained yield, and they would have used models of population dynamics which, although accepted then, are now viewed as highly dubious. A number of populations would have been overharvested severely before the biologists learned that they did not know as much as they thought they did.

HARVESTING DYNAMICS

The theory of harvesting dynamics is very simple. It has 2 parts:

1. If some animals are taken out of a population the fortunes of the others will be enhanced, and their fecundity and survival will rise to compensate for the removals.
2. If the rate of removal is too high, the population will be unable to compensate and will slide to extinction.

These 2 lemmas have considerable empirical backing. The doubts come with the elaborations. Within that general theory there are divergent views on the form and strength of the compensation that the removals trigger. Is the compensation so absolute that the numbers next year will average the same whether the population is harvested or not (the harvestable surplus model)? Or will the population's compensatory reaction to the removals be insufficient to hold density steady at its unharvested level (the surplus production model)? These 2 confusing names are replaced here with more descriptive tags. The first is the "complete compensation model", the second the "partial compensation model." Both models have a threshold beyond which additional harvesting forces the population to extinction.

The Complete Compensation Model

By this model harvesting does not affect the population's size unless its rate exceeds a threshold, the numbers next year being much the same as those for this year whether or not the population is harvested. Although compensation could conceivably work through fecundity or survival or both, the protagonists of this model have suggested only enhanced survival. They assume that the harvesting of 1 animal saves the life of another. Over a given year the number destined to die is preordained; the manner of the dying is inconsequential.

The origins of this model are obscure. The first comprehensible statement I can find is in Leopold's (1933) Chapter 7. But even there it does not come across cleanly, and Leopold may have had a somewhat different model in mind, for example his statement (1933:171) "often, of course, only a part of the crop [i.e., the maximum sustained yield] is removed as kill, the rest being left as capital accretion. This is the proper policy where a larger breeding stock is desired." This view smacks more of partial compensation than of complete compensation.

Figure 1a diagrams the simplest form of the partial compensation model. Two regions are defined within the space set by harvesting rate against population size. In 1 region the population is harvested to extinction; in the

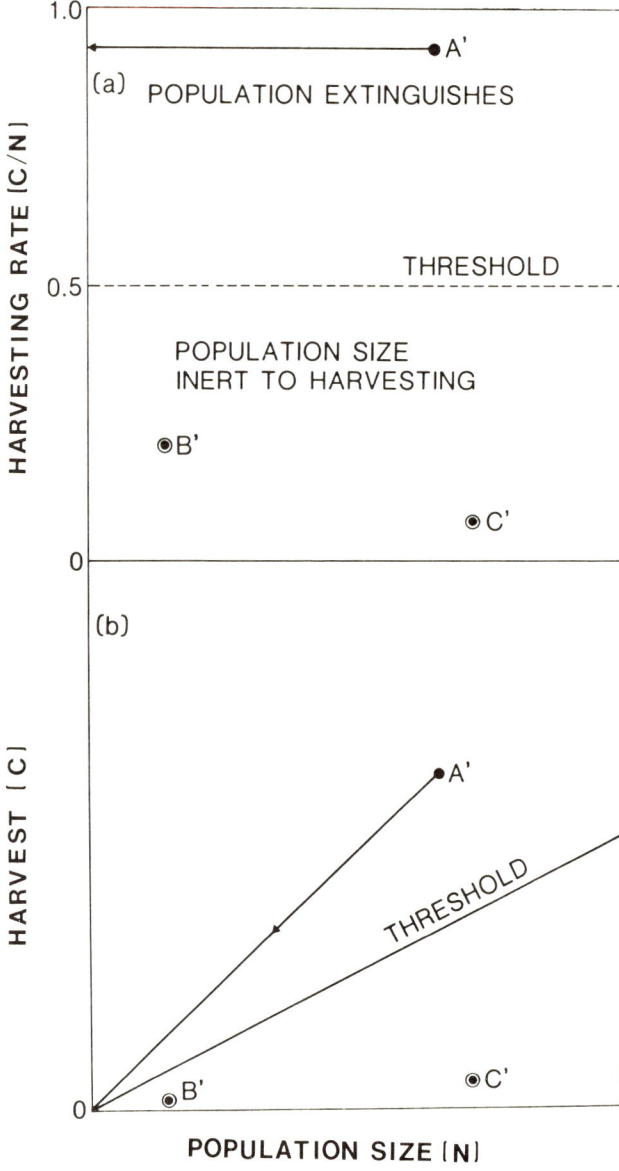

Fig. 1. The simplest form of the complete compensation model. The horizontal line of (a) is a threshold rate of constant harvesting (arbitrarily set at 0.5) above which harvesting forces the population to extinction and below which it has no effect on population size. In (b) the same cross-referenced points are graphed to show the offtake accruing from a constant rate of harvesting.

other the harvesting has no effect. The boundary between them may be horizontal, as in the diagram, or curved, but it may not touch the x axis. Figure 1b relates catch to population size.

The Partial Compensation Model

The essence of the partial compensation model is that harvesting, even light harvesting, reduces the population to below its unharvested density. Since the population is smaller, there are now fewer animals to share food, water, and space. Each animal receives an additional portion of life's necessities, and fecundity and survival rise accordingly. Thus, a potential rate of increase is generated that would become actual if harvesting were terminated. The lower that harvesting pushes the population, the higher the potential rate of increase. When the population declines to a level where potential rate of increase equals the rate of harvesting, the population stabilizes.

This model is the child of the Russian fisheries biologist F. I. Baranov (1918, 1926). He characterized it in these terms: "a fishery, by thinning out a fish population, itself creates the production by which it is maintained" (Baranov 1927). Figure 2a diagrams this model. On axes of harvesting rate against population size, it has 3 regions. In 1 the population is harvested to extinction; in the other 2 the population decreases to equilibrium with harvesting or increases to equilibrium with harvesting. Figure 2b gives the same relationship for catch against population size. The fisheries and whaling literature provide multitudinous elaborations, but these are all recognizable as minor variants of the partial compensation model.

Testing between the 2 Models

We can test whether 1 or the other model applies to a particular species by studying the effect on its density of 2 levels of sustained hunting pressure. If it is desired, 1 level may be set at zero. With both rates of harvesting below threshold, average density will not differ between treatments if the population conforms to the complete compensation model. If the species conforms instead to the partial compensation model, the more heavily harvested population will settle to a lower density than that of the other population. An equilibrating interval is necessary before the effect of the harvesting is evaluated. Ideally, the 2 harvesting pressures should be applied simultaneously to populations similar in all respects except for their different levels of harvest. Alternatively, the experiment may be run on 1 population, the 2 levels of harvesting being applied sequentially.

EXAMPLES

Having touched lightly on the 2 major models of harvesting dynamics, I will now review 2 studies that investigated their validity. The first, on

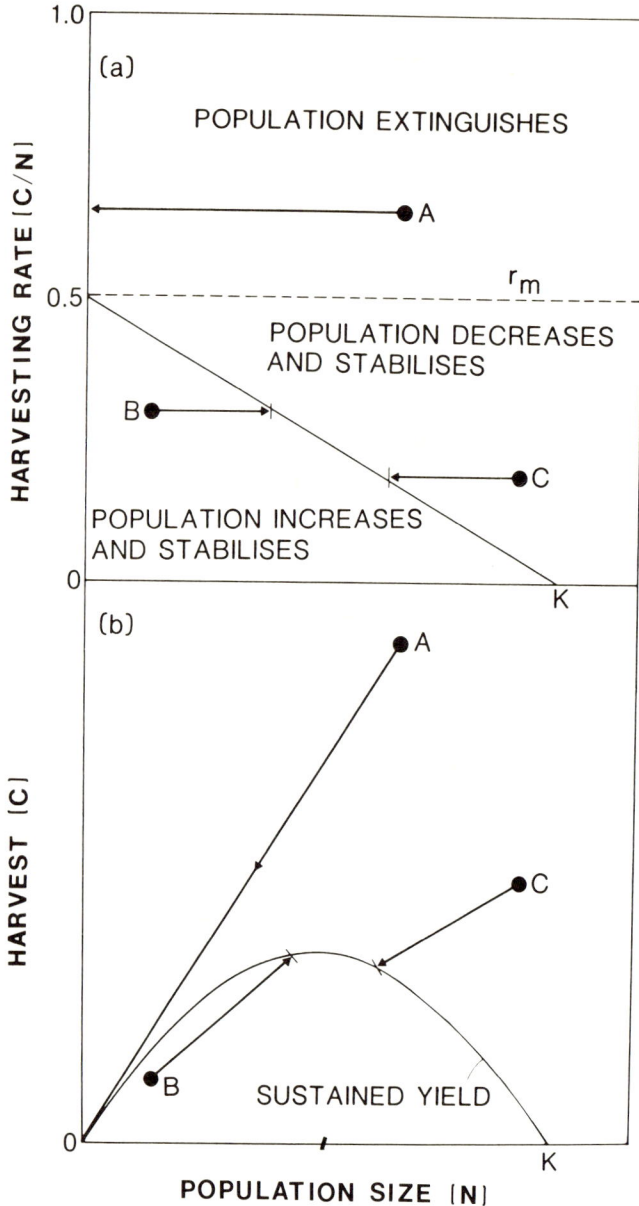

Fig. 2. The simplest form of the partial compensation model. The diagonal of (a) marks the equilibrium harvesting rate for any population size. The vectors show the effect of different initial population sizes and different rates of constant harvesting. These same vectors are diagrammed in (b) for harvest offtake against population size, harvesting rate again being constant.

mallards, leaned towards the complete compensation model. The second looked at moose through the rifle sight of the partial compensation model.

Mallards

Anderson and Burnham (1976) analyzed 11 years of band returns from mallard ducks in North America. Two competing hypotheses were defined regarding the effect of hunting on population survival rate: that hunting mortality is a completely additive form of mortality, and that if annual hunting mortality is below some threshold point, then increased hunting mortality (below the threshold point) is compensated for by a corresponding decrease in other forms of mortality. The second hypothesis is immediately recognizable as the complete compensation model, the first being a statement of what may be termed the "zero compensation model." The analysis is complex; since I have no argument with it, we will take it as read. In brief, a regression of non-hunting mortality rate on hunting mortality rate would, for this example, slope at about -0.24 if the 2 forms of mortality were additive or at -1.0 (this constant is independent of the example) if they were completely compensatory. Anderson and Burnham had a slope of -0.78 (Fig. 3). They then tested that value against those expected by their alternative hypothesis, showing that it differed significantly from -0.24 but not from -1.0. On that basis they rejected complete additivity of hunting and non-hunting mortality and accepted complete compensation.

Their conclusions were reinforced by a second analysis seeking a difference in overall survival rate for years when hunting regulations favored the shooter against years in which his shooting was severely curtailed. No significant difference emerged. Thus, they concluded that variation in hunting pressure had no detectable effect on overall survival rate.

From these 2 results Anderson and Burnham concluded that the complete compensation model applied to mallards, as did its corollary that "mallards cannot be effectively 'stockpiled'. Very restrictive hunting seasons are unlikely to save birds and increase the breeding population the following year" (Anderson and Burnham 1976:40).

I am wary of these conclusions for 2 reasons. First, the authors considered only extreme hypotheses. The value of their first test statistic fell between those expected by each hypothesis, precisely within the domain of the partial compensation model. But Anderson and Burnham did not test that hypothesis. Second, the comparison of overall survival rate between years of restrictive and liberal hunting regulations confounds factors. Presumably, the restrictive regulations of a particular year were a reaction to poor recruitment during that year and perhaps to a presumption that non-hunting mortality was increasing for the same reason, hunting mortality being reduced by regulations to compensate. Liberal regulations may reflect

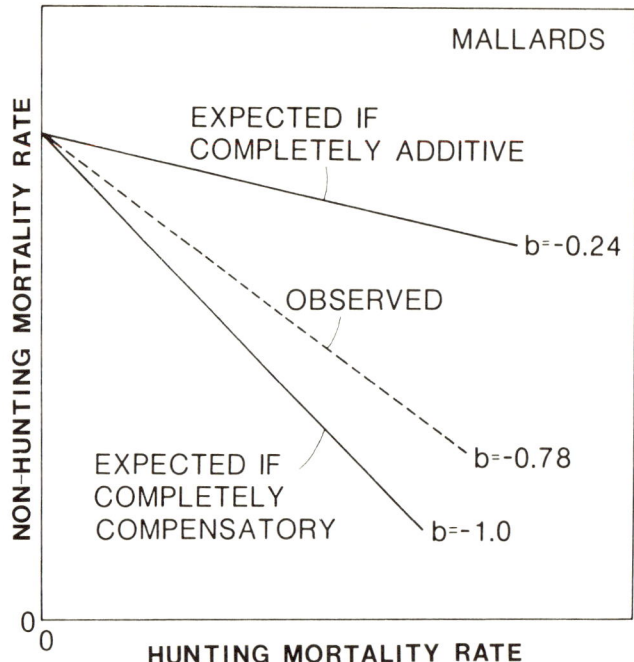

Fig. 3. The trend of non-hunting mortality rate on hunting mortality rate to be expected when the 2 sources of mortality are completely additive or completely compensatory. An observed trend for mallards falls between them. From Anderson and Burham (1976).

the reverse. Another possibility, too frightening to contemplate, is that the regulations were entirely capricious. But only if they were capricious would the analysis be valid. That comparison of survival of ducks between years in which duck hunters were restrained and years in which they were encouraged presupposes that there was no relationship between the severity of the regulations and that of natural mortality.

Moose

Crete et al. (1981) studied the relationship between harvesting rate and density of moose on pairs of areas replicated 3 times. Each of the 6 blocks exceeded 500 km^2. For 5 years 1 element of each pair had been hunted intensively; the other was hunted only lightly. Intensively hunted blocks averaged 6.9 hunter days/km^2/year against 0.12 for the lightly hunted blocks.

The authors reported a strong negative correlation between the density of moose and the intensity with which they had been hunted. Figure 4 shows their data plotted as offtake against density, together with 2 curves I have fitted to them. The parabola representing the logistic form of the partial compensation model is a poor fit. A second form of that model, with peak offtake displaced to the left, is better than the logistic but still not very

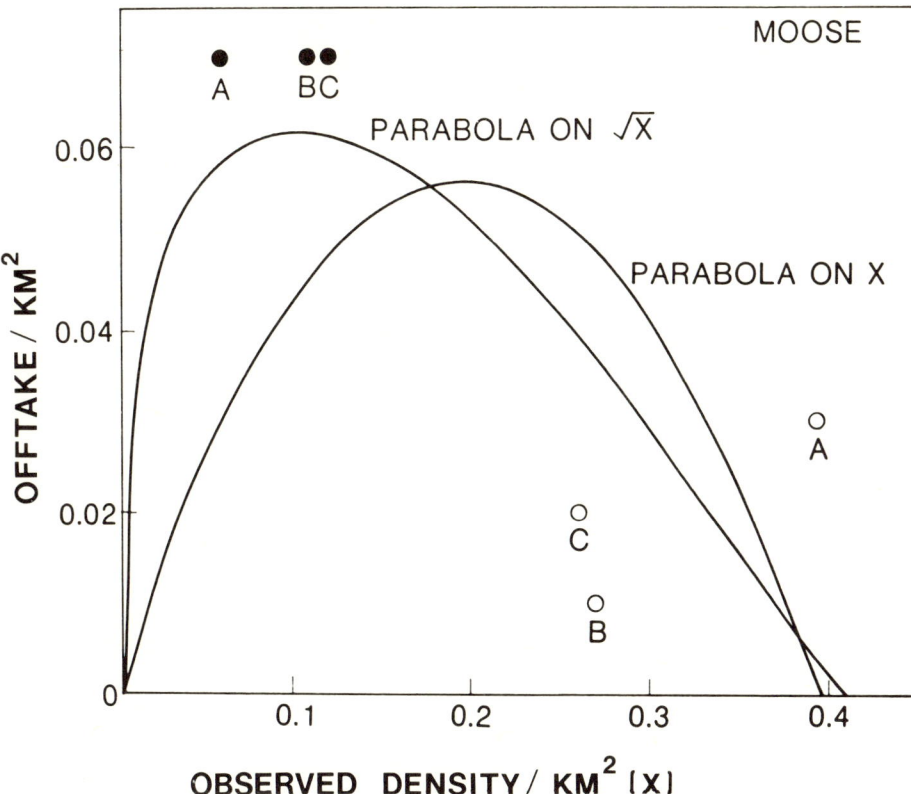

Fig. 4. Crete et al.'s (1981) data on annual harvest of moose against population density. Letters identify paired comparisons. Two curves are fitted to these data: a parabola representing the equilibrium yield of a population conforming to logistic assumptions, and an asymmetrical curve that is another variant of the partial compensation model.

convincing. However, the lack of fit does not need to cause distress because the cluster of high points is biologically impossible. They cannot conceivably represent equilibrium offtake for moose since they average a harvest of 72%/year (an offtake of $0.07/km^2$ from a density of $0.097/km^2$). Clearly something is wrong. The authors were aware of this and offered 3 possible explanations: dispersal between the 2 elements of the paired treatments, inaccurate aerial survey estimates of density, and the "moose populations not being at equilibrium but declining due to overexploitation."

Disperal does not seem to be implicated. Table 2 of Crete et al. shows no clear trends of density towards the boundary separating high from low hunting intensity. The authors were reluctant to believe that their low-level surveys by helicopter underestimated moose density, but similar surveys underestimate white-tailed deer (*Odocoileus virginianus*) (Beasom et al. 1981), and the same may be expected of moose. To bring these points within biological plausibility, the harvest rate has to come down from 72% to below 30%. Since offtake was measured accurately, the density would have had to be underestimated by a factor of 2.5. Although I could believe that for an attempted total count over large areas of mixed coniferous and deciduous forest, I doubt that the pilot and observers would. More than likely the high points represent populations whose density was still adjusting to a high hunting pressure, the density itself being underestimated. Whatever the explanation, this study does not reveal the shape of the offtake-density curve for equilibrium hunting pressure.

Discussion of Examples

Neither of these studies produced conclusions solid enough to be of immediate use in managing the harvesting of mallards or moose. Yet these are 2 of the best studies of wildlife harvesting available to us. Anderson and Burnham's study exemplifies the creative use of rigorous mathematics. Unfortunately, the excellence of their analysis was not matched by the material to which it was applied. They had no control over experimental design, hunting regulations, or hunting intensity; their questions were posed after the data were in. Inevitably, the design was unbalanced and factors were confounded. The sample size of 700,000 does not compensate for these deficiencies.

In contrast, the study by Crete et al. used an experimental design that could well serve as a model for subsequent studies. They got the important things right but were beaten by a detail, probably setting the hunting pressure a little too high in their high intensity hunting treatments. This study records a near miss that can be rectified easily in a subsequent study.

The problem posed by the mallard study is less easily corrected. I suspect that Anderson and Burnham asked the wrong question; the question they asked was imposed by the form of the data available to them. Crete et al. clearly asked the right question, and that question could be asked because the experiment was designed to answer it.

THE FUTURE

As of now we lack the knowledge to manage wildlife harvesting scientifically. We cannot say whether the complete compensation model or the partial compensation model is the appropriate one for more than a handful of species, let alone choose between variants of these. Enough is known of the population dynamics and relationship with resources for the Himalayan thar (*Hemitragus jemlahicus*) (Caughley 1970), African buffalo (*Syncerus caffer*) (Sinclair 1977), and white-tailed deer (McCullough 1979) to be confident that the partial compensation model applies to these species. I suspect that it will ultimately prove appropriate for most large herbivores whose environment is less than violently disruptive. Perhaps some close modification of the complete compensation model will prove more applicable to birds and small mammals. However, these are no more than guesses.

We are faced not by a shortage of models but by a shortage of the data needed to adjudicate between them. We will not get the data if we are content simply to monitor the effects of harvesting whose intensity we do not control. Simulation models employing such undisciplined data, held together by FORTRAN guesses that often outnumber the data, are unlikely to teach us much. Robert May's jibe that most simulation models would benefit from the installation of an on-line incinerator is as true as it is uncivil.

Instead of undisciplined data, we need the sure data of carefully designed and executed experiments of the type Crete and his co-workers attempted. Ideally, these should reveal equilibrium offtake (or the lack of an equilibrium) for at least 3 levels of hunting intensity. It would be technically convenient if 1 of those levels were set at zero. Such experiments would need to be run for at least 2 generations of the harvested species to ensure that offtake had reached equilibrium, if equilibrium is possible, with constant harvesting pressure. At the end of that equilibrating exercise, offtake would be plotted against density, or hunting effort, or the level of a resource, to determine which model was appropriate and the constants of its yield curve. With the results of a few of these experiments at hand, we would be able to make useful comments on how current non-scientific harvesting management might be improved.

Such experiments should be kept simple. One should master the skills of a base hit before advancing to the technology of a home run. The first is not simply a miniaturization of the second. Similarly, the dynamics of across-the board harvesting must be understood before one advances to the refinements of manipulating the distributions of sex and age. To my major point—that wildlife harvesting management will not become scientific until we indulge in some tight experimentation—there is likely to be only muffled disagreement. Opposition would instead emphasize problems and practicalities. Wildlife biologists often complain that they would like to institute long-term experiments on the effect of constant harvesting efforts but that they are restrained from doing so. Their administrators rule that it would conflict with currently accepted management practices and that it would inconvenience the sportsmen. I have little sympathy with this complaint. Biologists get the administrators they deserve and vice versa.

LITERATURE CITED

ANDERSON, D. R., AND K. P. BURNHAM. 1976. Population ecology of the mallard. VI. The effect of exploitation on survival. U.S. Dep. Inter., Fish and Wildl. Serv. Resour. Publ. 128. 66pp.

BARANOV, F. I. 1918. On the question of the biological basis of fisheries. Nauchn. Issled. Ikhthiologicheskii Inst. Izv. 1:81-128. (In Russian. Not seen: quoted in Ricker [1975]).

———. 1926. On the question of the dynamics of the fishing industry. Byull. Rybn. Khoz. 8:7-11. (In Russian. Not seen: quoted in Ricker [1975]).

———. 1927. More about the poor catch of volba. Byull. Rybn. Khoz. 7:7 (In Russian. Not seen: quoted in Ricker [1975]).

BEASOM, S. L., J. C. HOOD, AND J. R. CAIN. 1981. The effect of strip width on helicopter censusing of deer. J. Range Manage. 34:36-37.

CAUGHLEY, G. 1970. Eruption of ungulate populations, with emphasis on Himalayan thar in New Zealand. Ecology 51:54-72.

———. 1983. The deer wars: the story of deer in New Zealand. Heinemann Publishers, Auckland, N.Z. 187pp.

CRETE, M., R. J. TAYLOR, AND P. A. JORDAN. 1981. Optimization of moose harvest in southwestern Quebec. J. Wildl. Manage. 45:598-611.

GRAHAM, A. D. 1973. The gardeners of Eden. George, Allen and Graham. 1935. Unwin Ltd., London, U.K. 246pp.

LAMB, H. 1927. Ghenghis Khan: emperor of all men. McBride and Coy, New York, N.Y. 240pp.

LEOPOLD, A. 1933. Game management. Charles Scribner's Sons, New York, N.Y. 481pp.

McCULLOUGH, D. R. 1979. The George Reserve deer herd: population ecology of a K-selected species. Univ. Michigan Press, Ann Arbor. 271pp.

RICKER, W. E. 1975. Computation and interpretation of biological statistics of fish populations. Fish. Res. Board Can. Bull. 191. 382pp.

SINCLAIR, A. R. E. 1977. The African buffalo—a study of resource limitation of populations. Univ. Chicago Press, Chicago, Ill. 355pp.

SAMPLING PATTERNS AND INTENSITIES FOR HELICOPTER CENSUSES OF WHITE-TAILED DEER

JAMES G. TEER, Rob and Bessie Welder Wildlife Foundation, P.O. Drawer 1400, Sinton, TX 78387

D. LYNN DRAWE, Rob and Bessie Welder Wildlife Foundation, P.O. Drawer 1400, Sinton, TX 78387

RAYMOND L. URUBEK, Rob and Bessie Welder Wildlife Foundation, P.O. Drawer 1400, Sinton, TX 78387

Abstract: The precision of deer censuses conducted by helicopter on transect and quadrat sampling units at varying sampling intensities was examined over a 4-year period. Quadrats gave lower estimates of numbers in 3 of the 4 years and had higher variance terms. Using transects, population estimates were similar to the 100% coverage when estimates from a 50% or a 33% coverage were used. Similar results were obtained with quadrat counts. A series of permanently marked transects counted year after year can yield reliable data on deer numbers and trends.

KEY WORDS: Helicopter census, Sampling patterns, White-tailed deer, Sample variability, Census variability, Census coverage.

The white-tailed deer (*Odocoileus virginianus*) is the most numerous big game animal in Texas. From a herd numbering around 3 million animals (Harwell and Gore 1982), more than 300,000 are harvested in most years (Boydston and Harwell 1983). About 150,000, or roughly 33% of the annual harvest, are taken from the 9,712,500 ha of densely populated deer range of the Edwards Plateau and Central Mineral Basin. About 50,000 are harvested each year in the Rio Grande Plains, commonly called the "brush country", of south Texas. This 8,093,700-ha range is a flat brushland made up of large cattle ranches. Almost all of the trophy deer from Texas listed in Boone and Crockett Club records are taken in the Rio Grande Plains (Nesbitt and Wright 1981). Although some deterioration in quality (antler development and body size) has occurred in the past 3 decades, the Rio Grande Plains is still the region where hunters choose to hunt for trophy bucks. Because of the decline in deer quality, the deer herd has been the object of special management efforts by the Texas Parks and Wildlife Department. Their strategy has been to limit buck kill to permit bucks to achieve maximum potential growth and to encourage the kill of antlerless deer (females of all ages and buck fawns) and spike bucks to reduce herd density (Hobson et al. 1979). Many ranches practice this strategy. A great stimulus to manage deer for trophy animals in south Texas and elsewhere was provided by the popular book *Producing Quality Whitetails* (Brothers and Ray 1975).

Hunting leases in south Texas bring up to $24/ha (Henson et al. 1977) that goes directly to the rancher. It is not unusual for ranchers to provide trophy hunting of deer for up to $3,000/animal (see Teer and Forrest 1968,

Burger and Teer 1981, and Teer et al. 1983 for descriptions of commercial hunting in Texas and the United States). Without question, the value of wildlife through commercial hunting systems has been an important impetus for the landowner to produce and manage wildlife in Texas.

Because of the value of game, many landowners contract for censuses of their ranges. They census their herds to establish harvest quotas to meet some goal of management and to obtain information about the herd for marketing hunting leases. Censuses are most often conducted by helicopter, and frequently complete counts are made on contiguous transects to determine density, sex, and age composition of the herd.

Extension biologists of the Texas Parks and Wildlife Department and private consultants provide deer management plans to ranchers. The census is the essential element of management plans, and ranchers pay for these services because deer and other wildlife are economically valuable to them in commerical hunting systems. They pay for only the helicopter rental costs when extension biologists of the Texas Parks and Wildlife Department provide the surveys and management plans. Consultant fees vary with ranch size and amount of time the consultants spend gathering information on deer and other wildlife.

Cost of helicopter rental has increased over the years. Hourly rental costs range between $200 and $250/hour with additional charges of about $0.62/km for "roading" the helicopter on a trailer to the ranch. Most helicopter companies charge a minimum of 3 hours flying time. Because censuses are often conducted as complete coverage of the ranches, costs for censusing large ranches may range upwards to $2,000 and higher. These are substantial outlays, but the service provided by biologists, private and public, is increasing in south Texas.

In this paper we examine the precision of white-tailed deer censuses conducted by helicopter on transect and quadrat sampling units at varying sampling intensities. The objectives of the study were to determine if deer censuses made on quadrats yielded results similar to deer censuses made on transects and to determine if sampling intensity (sample size) could be reduced from complete coverage (100% sample) to reduce costs without losing precision in the estimates.

Many students at the Welder Foundation participated in the study by assisting in marking transects and quadrats and in serving as roving markers at the ends of transects during the census. For their assistance we are most grateful. A special note of thanks is due James E. Cox, foreman, for his assistance. This is Welder Wildlife Foundation Contribution No. 276.

STUDY AREA

The study was conducted on the 3,157-ha Rob and Bessie Welder Wildlife Foundation Refuge in San Patricio County, part of the Coastal Bend Region of Texas. Deer numbers on the refuge have fluctuated rather closely around a mean density of about 40 deer/km^2 (Welder Wildlife Foundation, unpubl. data, Kie et al. 1978). The herd is unhunted, so the deer tend to have a short flight distance (about 30 m) in comparison to deer in hunted herds, and the herd has a buck:doe composition of about 1 buck:2 does. Many bucks are in the trophy class with antler spreads greater than 70 mm. The herd has been studied by many students doing advanced degrees in wildlife ecology and management and, thus, is one of the best-known herds in the region (Knowlton 1964, White 1966, Drawe 1968, Cook et al. 1971, Hirth 1977, Kie et al. 1980).

Vegetation on the refuge consists of 4 major types with open-to-dense brushland interspersed with open grassland and dense riverine habitat (Drawe et al. 1978). Vegetation is denser on the refuge than the average habitat in the Rio Grande Plains because soils are fertile, and rainfall averages about 89 cm/year or about 25 cm higher than most of the south Texas brush country.

The refuge has a cow-calf operation with a stocking rate of an animal unit/5 ha under 2 rotation grazing systems compared to continuous, year-long grazing. It is operated as a working ranch but with better livestock and range management than is ordinary for the region.

METHODS

The refuge is gridded on the cardinal points in a pattern of 400-m intervals (Fig. 1). The resulting 16.2-ha quadrats or blocks are marked on all corners with concrete markers, not visible from the air, and 2-m steel posts that are visible from the air. The grid has about 200 quadrats and 59 north-south lines used as flight lines in our study.

A census was flown in January or February in each year from 1980 through 1983. At this season deciduous, woody vegetation has shed its leaves, and ground cover is at its lowest ebb; thus, visibility of deer is greater than at any other season of the year. Censuses were conducted on the transects and quadrats on the same or consecutive 2-day periods. North-south flight lines were marked on the ground with ribbon flagging placed on the 2-m grid stakes. The grid lines served as the center of the transects. A 2-3-m length of white butcher paper was placed on the west corners of each quadrat used in the sample. A pickup truck was moved from transect to transect on the south ends of the transects to assist the pilot in maintaining his flight lines. Fences, roads, windmills, streams, and other physical features of the landscape were also used to keep on course. The longest transect was 4.0 km; the shortest was about 0.8 km.

Transects were flown at an altitude of 25 m at an air speed of 25-35 knots depending on wind speed (Fig. 2). Two observers sitting to the right of the pilot in a Bell 47-G4A helicopter counted deer in the transects.

Since the grid pattern was established on 400-m intervals, complete coverage of the refuge was accomplished by using 200-m widths of transects and by flying the 2 transects in each 400-m interval (Fig. 1). For example,

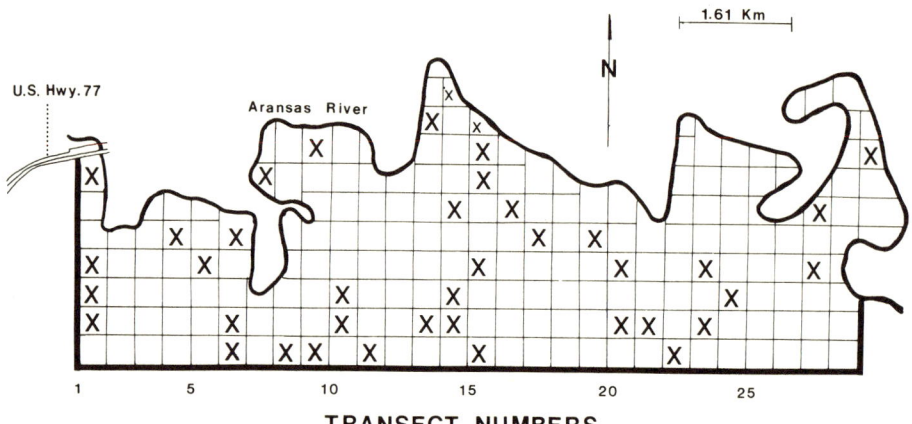

Fig. 1. The sampling scheme for aerial censuses of white-tailed deer on the 3,157-ha Welder Wildlife Foundation Refuge consisted of 59 north-south flight lines and 39 16.2-ha quadrats. Flight lines and west corners of quadrats were marked with 2-3-m lengths of butcher paper and by colored flagging on 2-m steel posts.

the north-bearing transects were flown on the grid lines, and the south-bearing transects were flown between the grid lines. The entire refuge was censused in 2 of the 4 years in this manner. In 1982-83, because of the pilot's inability to hold on course in crosswinds, only the grid lines were flown; thus, the coverage amounted to only 50% of the deer range. The person at the right window was responsible for counting animals on the 100

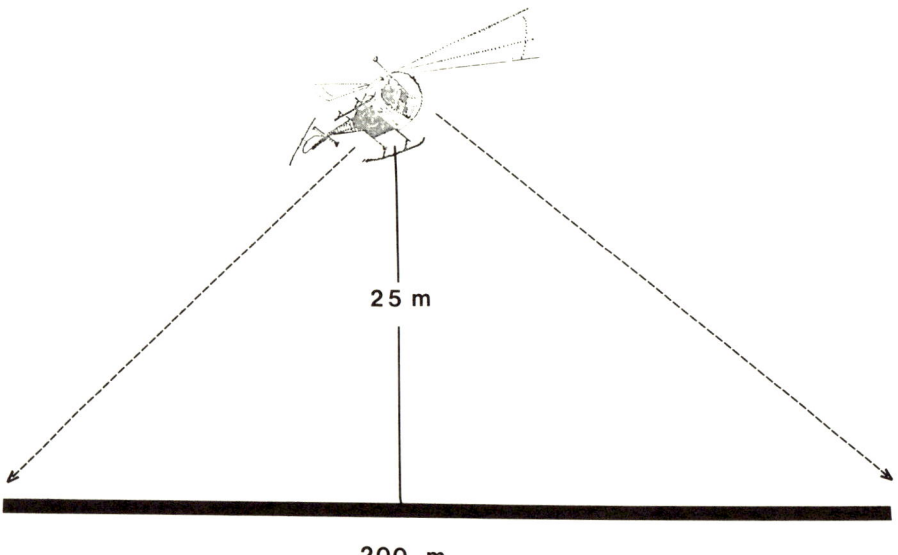

Fig. 2. The censuses were flown in a Bell 47-G4A helicopter at 25-35 knots at 25-m altitude. A 200-m strip, 100 m on each side of the aircraft, was censused.

m to his right. The observer in the middle and the pilot counted animals on the 100 m to their left.

Caughley's (1977) descriptions were used to calculate population estimates and variances of the estimates in systems where the area was sampled without replacement as follows:

$$\hat{Y} = RZ$$

$$SE(\hat{Y}) = \sqrt{\frac{N(N-n)}{n(n-1)} (\Sigma y^2 + R^2 \Sigma z^2 - 2R \Sigma yz)}$$

where

$\hat{Y}$ = population estimate,

y = number of animals in a given unit of size z,

z = area of transect,

n = number of transects,

Z = total area under survey,

$$R = \frac{\Sigma y}{\Sigma z},$$

$$\bar{z} = \frac{Z}{n},$$

$$N = \frac{Z}{\bar{z}}.$$

By and large our samples were small, the largest data set being 57 units, but these represented total coverage of the area. Sample sizes were reduced as smaller subsets from these 57 units were drawn to test effects of sample sizes in transect and quadrat censuses on estimates of the population and variances of the estimates. For example, when a sample of 20 sampling units was pulled from the 57 transects, 33% of the area was included in the sample.

RESULTS

Transects vs. Quadrats

Results of censuses conducted on transects and quadrats were different in 3 of the 4 years of study (Table 1). Differences ranged as high as 23%, and

Table 1. Population estimates of white-tailed deer on the 3,157-ha Welder Wildlife Foundation Refuge obtained from transect and quadrat sampling systems having relatively comparable numbers of sampling units (n).

Year	Sample size (n-ha)		N deer		Standard error ($SE_{\hat{y}}$)	
	Transects	Quadrats	Transects	Quadrats	Transects	Quadrats
1980	30-1,538	39-631	998	769	86	125
1981	29-1,504	39-631	1,145	954	93	155
1982	29-1,437	39-631	870	673	77	135
1983	29-1,437	39-631	1,041	1,060	85	182

in all 3 years the quadrats gave lower estimates of numbers. Variances ($SE_{\hat{y}}$) were larger for quadrat censuses in every case.

The number of quadrats in the sample was lower than the number of transects (29 vs. 39), and differences in sample sizes likely account for the larger variance terms for estimates gained from the quadrat censuses.

Although quadrat sizes were constant, areas of transects varied with their length. To determine if areas of the sampling systems (ha in the samples) had an effect on estimates and variance terms, we compared censuses in which sizes were similar. To make the comparison, 12 transects were randomly selected from the array of 57 transects and compared with estimates obtained from the 40 quadrats (Table 2). This exercise resulted in sample sizes near 647 ha for quadrats and transects. In this comparison, population estimates and variance terms were much more erratic than when number of units was controlled; number of sampling units was more important than acreages within the total samples.

Intensities of Sampling

Fifty-seven transects were flown to obtain complete coverage of the Welder Wildlife Refuge. The transects varied in area because transect lengths differed, but their widths were held constant. From the total of 57 transects, we randomly pulled samples of 28, 20, and 12 transects and calculated estimates of the population and variance terms for each sample (Table 3). Population estimates were not too different except when sample size was 12. Variance terms increased as sample sizes decreased. Similar results were

Table 2. Population estimates of white-tailed deer on the 3,157-ha Welder Wildlife Foundation Refuge obtained from transect and quadrat sampling systems having relatively comparable area in the sampling units.

Year	Sample size (n-ha)		N deer		Standard error ($SE_{\hat{y}}$)	
	Transects	Quadrats	Transects	Quadrats	Transects	Quadrats
1980	12-652	39-631	784	769	123	125
1981	12-652	39-631	1,137	954	224	155
1982	12-602	39-631	854	673	187	135
1983	12-602	39-631	881	1,060	147	182

Table 3. Population estimates ($\hat{Y}$) and standard error of the estimate ($SE_{\hat{y}}$) of white-tailed deer on the Welder Wildlife Foundation Refuge, as obtained on transects at 4 intensities of sampling by helicopter.

Year	57 Transects (100%)[a]	28 Transects (50%)	20 Transects (33%)	12 Transects (12%)
1980	1,018±24	998±86	1,013±126	783±123
1981	872±27	1,145±93	832±140	1,137±224
1982		870±77	991±106	854±187
1983		1,041±85	953±143	881±147

[a] Percentages are the amounts of the 3,517 ha in the samples.

obtained with quadrat censuses (Table 4). Estimates of population numbers were reasonably close except when sample size was reduced to 10 quadrats, and variance increased as sample sizes decreased in all samples.

DISCUSSION

In making estimates of numbers or density of a population, unless there is a known population with which census results can be compared, accuracy of estimates can seldom be quantified. Precision of an estimate is determined by calculating a variance term for the estimate. A standard error for the estimate provides information about repeatability of the sampling effort and provides the manager with some measure of confidence in estimates of population levels and fluctuations from 1 census to the next. We measured precision and not accuracy in our studies.

Our transects had lower variance terms than quadrats at almost all levels of sampling intensity, and thus, we propose to use transects in sampling of deer from aerial platforms. However, it appears that the degree of sampling need not be as large as commonly used. A sample as small as 33% of the total deer range may be about as useful as 100% coverage. Variance terms of smaller samples were somewhat larger but not large enough to justify the increased costs of helicopter rental.

We do not know how accurate our estimates are. However, they vary within reasonable limits and track reasonably well with estimates of recruitment, mortality, and environmental perturbations (weather patterns, predator levels, grazing pressures of domestic livestock, range conditions, etc.) that influence herd dynamics from year to year.

Table 4. Population estimates ($\hat{Y}$) and standard error of the estimate ($SE_{\hat{y}}$) of white-tailed deer on the Welder Wildlife Foundation Refuge, as obtained on transects at 3 intensities of sampling by helicopter.

Year	39 Quadrats (20%)[a]	20 Quadrats (10%)	10 Quadrats (5%)
1980	769±125	907±172	585±238
1981	954±155	1,287±241	917±339
1982	673±135	692±153	624±306
1983	1,060±182	1,131±251	1,070±314

[a] Percentages are the amounts of the 3,517 ha in the samples.

As Caughley (1974:921) stated, "most efforts at refinement (of census efforts) have been aimed at raising the precision of the estimates by combining impeccable survey design, high sampling intensity, intricate stratification, and powerful methods of analysis." In our surveys we were particularly careful to standardize procedures and take into account weather factors, behavior of deer during time of census (whether they were active or lying down), differences in visibility of deer in different vegetative types, and differences in visibility of various sex and age classes. In an operational census, we can only guess at some of the bias.

Aside from these factors, the most important problem with which we have dealt has been keeping the helicopter on the transect, especially when even slight crosswinds cause the aircraft to drift. The pilot "crabs" the aircraft to correct for drift, and the correction is often too little or too much. The pilot's experience in keeping on the line obviously is important. Short transects in rangelands with distinct landscape features are helpful, but when contiguous transects are flown, a few meters to either side causes transects to overlap. However, the error caused by wandering from the transects is not large. If the aircraft wanders as much as 800 m off a 3.2-km-long transect, the increase in area amounts to 7.0 ha (Table 5). At 200 m the increase in area of the transect is almost negligible. As a matter of fact, there is far more error in missing deer by simply not seeing them than from increasing the length of a transect through wandering. In 2 of the 4 censuses conducted in this study, we abandoned efforts to do complete counts because we could not hold our course in crosswinds of 16-24 kph.

We favor sampling systems of counting deer rather than complete counts because of the cost and also because deer are chased onto adjoining transects when 100-m-wide strip counts are made in a contiguous design. We sometimes encounter herds as large as 30-40 deer and as many as 10-15 small groups of deer on a 3.2-km transect. To record in memory the number and direction the deer flee as the aircraft proceeds along its flight path is difficult. Inevitably, some are counted again on the next transect if they run in the direction in which the census progresses. Conversely, if transects are kept short, i.e., 0.8 km or less, a good pilot and experienced counters can keep the amount of double-counting to a minimum and within tolerable limits. However, short transects cost more and may not be practical in large surveys. For example, helicopter time involved in counting 0.8-km vs. 1.6-km transects would increase simply because the number of turns is doubled.

We conclude that aerial counts of deer should be made on transects using sampling systems rather than counts on contiguous transects. Transects should be spaced at least 0.8-km apart when transect widths are 200-m wide, and sample sizes should include at least 20-30% of the area being censused. Size of ranch or deer range and relative density of deer in the various ecological elements of the habitat should be taken into account. Stratification of the sampling effort can reduce variability in estimates if differences in deer densities are large (Siniff and Skoog 1964, Jolly 1969,

Table 5. Effects of wandering of an aircraft from the center of a transect on counts of white-tailed deer.

Distance aircraft wandered from center of transect (m)	Increase in length of transect (m)	Increase in area of transect (ha)	Increase in number of deer/transect[a]
200	25	0.4	0.15
400	130	1.8	0.60
800	380	7.0	2.29

[a] The average number of deer/3.2-km transect in the study was 16.3.

Kufeld et al. 1980). In operational censuses, especially on ranches as small as 2,000 ha, stratified random sampling may not be possible or even desirable because of costs of aircraft rental, lack of information on deer density in ecological types, and variability in visibility of deer in various densities of vegetative cover. In large blocks of deer range, such sampling schemes should be given careful consideration because deer densities do change between soil and vegetative types and in land-use patterns of the region.

We have found a series of transects marked on a map and used year after year to yield reliable population parameters and trends for ranch populations. Standardization of census procedures and comparisons of census results with other observations of population and environmental conditions are useful in interpreting census results. Despite not knowing how accurate census results are, trends are evident and useful in management of herds and habitat.

LITERATURE CITED

BOYDSTON, C., AND F. HARWELL. 1983. Big game harvest regulations (white-tailed deer harvest surveys). Tex. Parks and Wildlife Dep. Fed. Aid Proj. W-109-R-6. Job 4. 139pp.

BROTHERS, A., AND M. E. RAY, JR. 1975. Producing quality whitetails. Wildlife Services, Laredo, Tex. 1st printing. 246pp.

BURGER, G. V., AND J. G. TEER. 1981. Economic and socioeconomic issues influencing wildlife management on private lands. Pages 252-278 in Wildlife management on private lands. Wisc. Chapter, The Wildlife Society, Madison.

CAUGHLEY, G. 1974. Bias in aerial survey. J. Wildl. Manage. 38:921-933.

———. 1977. Sampling in aerial survey. J. Wildl. Manage. 41:605-615.

COOK, R. S., M. WHITE, D. O. TRAINER, AND W. C. GLAZENER. 1971. Mortality of young white-tailed deer fawns in south Texas. J. Wildl. Manage. 35:47-56.

DRAWE, D. L. 1968. Mid-summer diet of deer on the Welder Wildlife Refuge. J. Range Manage. 21:164-166.

———, A. D. CHAMRAD, AND T. W. BOX. 1978. Plant communities of the Welder Wildlife Refuge. Welder Wildl. Found. Contrib. 5, Ser. B, rev. 37pp.

HARWELL, W. F., AND H. G. GORE. 1982. White-tailed deer population trends. Tex. Parks and Wildl. Dep. Fed. Aid Proj. W-109-R-5. Job 1. 78pp.

HENSON, J., F. SPRAGUE, AND G. VALENTINE. 1977. Soil Conservation Service assistance in managing wildlife on private lands in Texas. Trans. North Am. Wildl. and Nat. Resour. Conf. 42:264-270.

HIRTH, D. H. 1977. Social behavior of white-tailed deer in relation to habitat. Wildl. Monogr. 53. 55pp.

HOBSON, M., R. L. COOK, AND W. F. HARWELL. 1979. Webb County buck permit experiment. Tex. Parks and Wildl. Dep. Special Report, Fed. Aid Proj. W-109-R-2. Job 2. 20pp.

JOLLY, G. M. 1969. Sampling methods for aerial censuses of wildlife populations. East Afr. Agric. For. J. 34 (special issue):46-49.

KIE, J. G., M. WHITE, AND F. F. KNOWLTON. 1978. Effects of coyote predation on population dynamics of white-tailed deer. Proc. Welder Wildlife Foundation Symposium. Welder Wildl. Found. Contrib. B-7. 1:65-82.

———, D. L. DRAWE, AND G. SCOTT. 1980. Changes in diet and nutrition with increased herd size in Texas white-tailed deer. J. Range Manage. 33:28-34.

KNOWLTON, F. F. 1964. Aspects of coyote predation in south Texas with special reference to white-tailed deer. Ph.D. Thesis. Purdue Univ., Lafayette, Ind. 189pp.

KUFELD, R. C., J. H. OLTERMAN, AND D. C. BOWDEN. 1980. A helicopter quadrat census for mule deer on Uncompahgre Plateau, Colorado J. Wildl. Manage. 44:632-639.

NESBITT, W. H., AND P. L. WRIGHT. 1981. Records of North American big game. Boone and Crockett Club, Alexandria, Va. 8th ed. 409pp.

SINIFF, D. B., AND R. O. SKOOG. 1964. Aerial censusing of caribou using stratified random sampling. J. Wildl. Manage. 28:391-401.

TEER, J. G., AND N. K. FORREST. 1968. Bionomic and ethical implications of commercial game harvest programs. Trans. North Am. Wildl. Conf. 33:192-204.

———, G. V. BURGER, AND C. Y. DEKNATEL. 1983. State-supported habitat management and commercial hunting on private lands in the United States. Trans. North Am. Wildl. and Nat. Resour. Conf. 48:445-456.

WHITE, M. 1966. Population ecology of some white-tailed deer in south Texas. Ph.D. Thesis. Purdue Univ., Lafayette, Ind. 215pp.

AN EVALUATION OF 7 YEARS OF SPOTLIGHT-COUNT DATA ON A COASTAL SOUTH CAROLINA PLANTATION

GENE W. WOOD, Belle W. Baruch Forest Science Institute of Clemson University, Georgetown, SC 29442

JAMES R. DAVIS, Belle W. Baruch Forest Science Institute of Clemson University, Georgetown, SC 29442

GEORGE R. ASKEW, Belle W. Baruch Forest Science Institute of Clemson University, Georgetown, SC 29442

Abstract: Five methods were employed to calculate indices to white-tailed deer (*Odocoileus virginianus*) population density along a 28-km spotlight-count route on Hobcaw Barony. Eight counts were made during the first 3 weeks of December in each of 7 years. Although there were some differences in the indicated magnitudes of change, all methods evaluated appeared to respond to a substantial change in the deer population caused by an epidemic of epizootic hemorrhagic disease. Weather patterns also appeared to substantially affect movement activity and, therefore, detectability of animals. Of the methods tested, the Hanson method (using 1-km plots) was most suitable for the purpose of documenting significant population changes in our situation because it offered an expression of variance that incorporated all data from all surveys in 1 year.

KEY WORDS: Deer population index, Spotlight counts, Transect sampling, Sample variability, Game management.

An intelligent attempt to balance an animal population with its environment requires an understanding of the population's dynamics. Hunted populations of cervids lend themselves well to population models because the amounts of information that usually can be gathered from harvested animals will yield adequate values for most model parameters. In situations where no harvesting is permitted, but where the manager is expected to have some knowledge of, at least, change in herd size, indices related to sightings of animals or animal signs must be relied upon.

Two characteristics of these indices are of primary importance. First, changes in the estimated index value are related to actual changes in the population. In most situations this relationship is assumed to be directly proportional. Validation of this assumption is, in most cases, impractical if not impossible.

Second, the index estimate must have some minimum level of precision; i.e., the variance must be low enough to detect what the manager has set as the minimum level of change that he believes to be significant for his purposes. Variance, of course, can be lowered in part by adhering closely to sound, standardized data-gathering procedures. The rest is left to how well the index technique fits the detectability of the animal in its environment.

The information reported here resulted from the necessity to find an index technique that could be applied to an unhunted herd of white-tailed deer on a 7,000-ha plantation in coastal South Carolina. Spotlighting along existing roads was the only practical method of gathering field data. This method resulted in a need to find a population index-estimation model that would accommodate spotlight-count data and would satisfy the need to develop evidence of important herd size changes should they occur.

STUDY AREA

The work reported here was conducted on Hobcaw Barony, a 7,000-ha plantation located about 3 km east of Georgetown, South Carolina. It is at the end of a peninsula known as the Waccamaw Neck and is bounded to the west and south by Winyah Bay and to the east by the Atlantic Ocean. About 3,000 ha is under forest cover; 3,000 ha is saltmarsh; and 1,000 ha is freshwater, brackish marshes, and abandoned ricefields.

About 61% of the forest is in pine stands with 22% in loblolly pine (*Pinus taeda*), 21% in longleaf pine (*P. palustris*), and 18% in mixed pine. Pine-hardwood stands make up 20% of the forest cover, and upland hardwoods account for 11%. Cypress-gum (*Taxodium-Nyssa*) stands account for 5% of the area and open fields for 3%. The area has about 128 km of roads that provide excellent access to all upland areas.

METHODS

Field Procedure

Figure 1 is a map of Hobcaw Barony showing the 28-km route taken for each spotlight count. The particular roads composing the route were chosen because they represented all upland habitats on the plantation in approximate proportion to their relative area. In addition, these particular roads were passable in a 2-wheel drive pick-up under all weather conditions.

A total of 8 spotlight counts were made in each of 7 years from 1976 to 1982. Counts were made during the first 3 weeks of December each year. A maximum of 3 counts was made in any 1 week. There were no restrictions on whether counts were on contiguous nights. Moon phase was not a factor in scheduling sampling dates. Rainy and foggy conditions were avoided because of impaired visibility.

Counts were made by 2 crews having designated starting points on the route each night at 1900 hours. Each crew traveled about 50% of the route and alternated sections each night. Each crew contained 2 spotters with 35,000-candlepower spotlights. Only personnel experienced in spotlighting deer were used as counters.

Upon spotting a deer, the counters alerted the driver to stop. The spotter then reported whether the deer was antlered, antlerless, or unknown. A person with a flashlight then was sent to the location in which the deer was standing. The sighting distance then was determined by focusing a range-

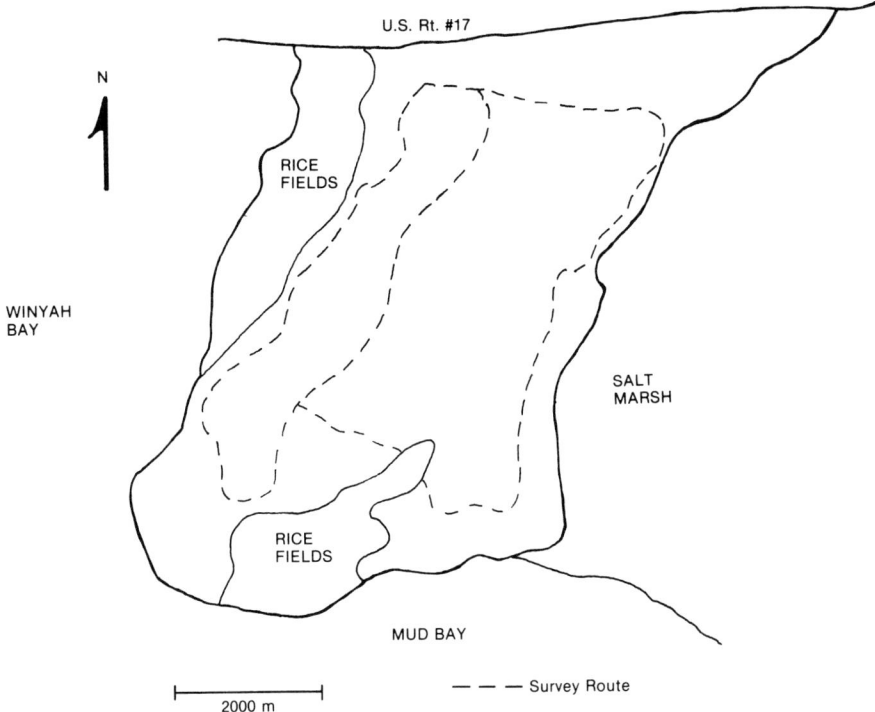

Fig. 1. Map of Hobcaw Barony and survey route used in annual spotlight counts on a coastal South Carolina plantation.

finder on the flashlight. The angle that the line of sighting made with the centerline of the road was determined with a hand compass. The driver also recorded his position on the route to the nearest 0.16 km from the route's beginning point.

Index Calculations

Three methods were used to calculate population index estimates for the upland portion of the plantation. The first method of estimation will be referred to as the Eberhart-Gross, and it was based on the lateral distances that the animals were sighted from the route line. It yielded an index to the size of the deer population in the area defined by the length of the route times twice the mean perpendicular distance from the road to the spotlighted individuals. This method was described by Gross et al. (1974) and was a modification of Eberhart (1968). The calculation was as follows:

1. The angle of sighting (Q) was taken from the route data.
2. The sighting distance (R) was taken from the route data.
3. The lateral distance (W) was calculated by W=R (sine Q).
4. A curve was plotted with number of animals sighted (n) over lateral distances (W).

5. Area under the curve (A_w) was the probability that an animal within the width of the route would be sighted.
6. $N = n/A_w$ where N was the number of animals estimated to be in the spotlighted area.

The second method was based on sighting distances (R). Hayne (1949), Gates (1969), and Gross et al. (1974) have described the method. It differed from Method 1 in 3 ways: it had a survey-area size factor, the route width was based on sighting distances, and the method of determining the probability of sighting was completely different. In addition, we used a variant of this method, substituting perpendicular distance for sighting distance (Gates et al. 1968). The method was as follows:

1. Sighting distance (R) was taken from the route data.
2. Survey area (A) was 3×10^7 m² (total area of deer habitat on Hobcaw Barony expressed in meter units to coincide with route length [L] and R units).
3. Probability (P) of observing an animal in the survey area was:
$$P = 2L/\lambda A$$
where λ was a constant determined by;
$\lambda = (2n-1)/\Sigma R$,
n = number of animals observed.
4. Population (N) of the censused area then was found by
$$N = n/P$$

The third method was based on repeated surveys with numbers of animals being spotted separated by the segment of the route in which they were seen. We experimented with both 1-km- and 2-km-segment size-classes. This method was a modification of Hanson (1968) and yielded a population index estimate of deer numbers along the route. The index numbers were converted to an expression of density along the route by dividing the population by an area equal to the route length times twice the mean perpendicular distance for all sightings on all surveys for that year. Calculations were as follows:

1. Probability (P) of seeing a deer that occurred in the census area was
$$P = 1 - (S_{i+1}/S_i)^{\frac{1}{2}}$$
where S_i = number of deer seen on i^{th} survey and S_{i+1} the number seen on the next survey. For a series of n surveys then
$$P = 1 - \left[\frac{S_2 + S_3 + S_4 \cdot S_n}{S_1 + S_2 + S_3 \cdot S_{n-1}} \right]^{\frac{1}{2}}$$
2. Number of animals (N) in the census area was found by
$$N = s/P$$
where s was the mean number of animals sighted on n surveys.

RESULTS AND DISCUSSION

Eberhart-Gross Index

The Eberhart-Gross index to the population along the spotlight route was calculated for the years 1976-80 (Table 1). In 3 of those 5 years, the mean index value for 8 nights substantially exceeded that of the other 2 methods and their variants. The ratios of the highest index value for a single night to the lowest in a given year were well within the range of the same comparisons for the other index methods. However, when the estimated trends were compared, the Eberhart-Gross indicated a substantial drop in population density in 1978, whereas the other indices suggested no substantial change.

The large percentage increase in the index from 1978 to 1979 followed by a substantial decrease from 1979 to 1980 were comparable in direction of population density change that the other methods indicated. However, the magnitude of change that the Eberhart-Gross indicated was substantially different from the other methods and their variants.

It was important here, however, to see all of the methods responding to what we knew to be a high rate of mortality and debilitation that resulted from a serious outbreak of epizootic hemorrhagic disease (EHD) in early fall 1980. The main problem with the Eberhart-Gross method applied to spotlight-count data was that it assumed a completely random distribution of deer along the center of the route. The calculation of probability of sighting was based entirely on this assumption (Table 2). A basic portion of this assumption was that the animal exercised no avoidance behavior when it detected man's presence. Probability of sighting then is theoretically regulated entirely by visibility along the route.

The theoretical curve from which sighting probability is obtained indicated that the highest number of deer will be seen along or close to the center of the route because they are most visible here. Actually, very few deer were seen close to the center of our route. Instead of a plot with number of sightings over route width yielding a smooth curve with a negative slope, the actual plot revealed a peak at about 40-m width and something more like the theoretical geometry of the expected curve from that point.

Burham et al. (1980) recommended that instead of plotting distance of each animal from the center of the transect to construct the curve, one should draw a bar graph using numbers of animals sighted in distance classes. Then a curve could be constructed through the centers of the bars. We used their suggestion in calculating the data reported here. However, because of the seemingly erratic behavior of the index in comparison to the other methods and skepticism of the method of calculating the probability of sighting, use of this index was discontinued after 1980.

Table 1. Comparison of results from 5 estimators of indices to deer density along a 28-km route on a coastal South Carolina plantation.

		Estimated density (deer/40 ha)				
		Gates		Hanson		
Year	Parameter	Sighting-distance method	Perpendicular-distance method	1-km plot	2-km plot	Eberhart-Gross
1976	Mean	5.9	8.9	10.4	7.3	11.9
	Range	2.5-9.2	2.7-18.1	6.9-13.4	4.3-10.4	5.2-19.5
	±2 SE's			0.4	0.4	
1977	Mean	7.0	9.3	12.4	8.9	12.1
	Range	4.1-8.9	5.0-13.6	8.9-15.8	6.7-11.9	9.1-16.1
	±2 SE's			0.5	2.1	
1978	Mean	6.8	8.9	12.5	8.8	9.4
	Range	3.0-11.1	3.2-13.3	9.7-18.2	5.4-11.8	5.0-14.2
	±2 SE's			1.4	3.4	
1979	Mean	11.6	14.0	16.9	12.9	23.7
	Range	8.8-13.8	9.4-17.3	14.9-19.1	10.3-19.1	16.4-29.4
	±2 SE's			0.3	4.2	
1980	Mean	8.1	10.2	13.2	9.2	18.5
	Range	3.0-14.5	3.6-17.3	10.4-15.7	6.5-11.8	8.7-31.2
	±2 SE's			0.4	6.2	
1981	Mean	6.1	9.3	13.0	8.1	
	Range	3.8-10.2	4.7-15.7	9.7-15.1	5.9-9.8	
	±2 SE's			3.9	6.1	
1982	Mean		8.4	14.9	9.1	
	Range		0.4-12.8	12.8-17.2	6.9-11.6	
	±2 SE's			3.7	5.9	

Gates Index

The Gates index was calculated using the sighting distance to determine the route's mean width and then using the perpendicular distance from the route center line to the deer to calculate the width. Presumably, with the sighting-distance approach, the animal would begin escape behavior as soon as it detected the presence of an observer, irrespective of the observer's position relative to it. In determination of the perpendicular-distance variant of this method, it is assumed that the animal's position relative to the center of the route on which the observer was traveling had nothing to do with the observer's presence.

The sighting-distance approach seemed most appropriate where deer were frequently exposed to gunfire that could be associated with vehicles. They would be expected to flush at about the same distances, given the same cover, irrespective of the observer's position. However, the perpendicular-distance method seemed appropriate for our situation because our deer rarely tried to escape the spotlights and had no apparent fear of vehicles.

The perpendicular-distance variant, of course, yielded higher density index values simply because the same number of sightings was on a smaller calculated route area (Table 1). The magnitudes of indicated change were

Table 2. Comparison of probability-of-sighting factors used in 5 deer density index estimates applied to spotlight-route data from a coastal South Carolina plantation.

		Probability of sighting a deer (%)				
		Gates estimator		Hanson estimator		
Year	Parameter	Sighting-distance method	Perpendicular-distance method	1-km plot	2-km plot	Eberhart-Gross
1976	Mean	7.2	5.2	37.1	54.2	33.1
	Range	5.9-9.9	3.2-9.4	18.4-54.2	20.2-72.3	
	±2 SE's			3.4	3.8	
1977	Mean	6.6	5.0	37.0	51.4	37.4
	Range	5.6-8.3	3.6-6.6	27.7-47.2	35.0-70.8	
	±2 SE's			1.8	2.4	
1978	Mean	6.2	4.8	34.1	46.9	45.2
	Range	5.5-7.6	3.7-7.1	12.5-52.0	24.1-65.0	
	±2 SE's			2.9	3.7	
1979	Mean	5.7	4.7	42.0	55.9	30.0
	Range	4.5-7.0	3.7-5.9	25.7-55.3	24.1-72.5	
	±2 SE's			2.2	3.7	
1980	Mean	5.3	4.2	36.8	53.1	26.3
	Range	3.8-6.8	2.7-5.1	14.9-56.5	25.7-76.4	
	±2 SE's			3.1	4.1	
1981	Mean	6.8	4.6	34.5	54.6	
	Range	4.9-8.1	3.2-6.0	22.3-53.3	34.0-72.6	
	±2 SE's			2.6	3.3	
1982	Mean		5.3	33.5	54.2	
	Range		3.8-7.1	18.7-48.2	37.0-80.2	
	±2 SE's			2.4	3.1	

very similar for both approaches. The real difference was in the range from highest to lowest estimated index values among 8 nights within any given year. The ratio of the highest to the lowest value for the perpendicular approach always considerably exceeded that of the sighting-distance approach and probably indicated lower precision of the latter.

The wider range could have been related to the method of obtaining the perpendicular-distance estimate. The observers read their compasses under poor light conditions and often made a mental calculation of the angle of sighting. In 1982, however, advantage was taken of the deer's lack of fear of the vehicle and spotlights. At each sighting, the vehicle moved to a point where the line of sight from observer to animal was perpendicular to the road centerline. There was no indication in the field that this tactic should have caused a problem. However, the index calculations for 1982 had the widest range of any in the 7 years. A complicating factor in judging this was the abnormally warm weather combined with a continuing influence of EHD in the herd during this survey period. Examination of the range in probabilities of sighting did not indicate that these values had a wider range in 1982 than in any previous year except 1976 (Table 2).

A comparison between the probability of sighting based on the sighting-distance approach with the perpendicular-distance approach shows lower values for the latter because of the smaller value for route width calculated by the perpendicular distance. The low probabilities-of-sighting values calculated by the Gates method are much lower than those calculated by the other 2 methods. This is because the Gates calculation is relative to sighting a deer on the 3,000-ha survey area, whereas the other methods are restricted entirely to sightings and measurements along the survey route.

Hanson Index

Table 1 shows the Hanson index calculations for deer density using 1-km and 2-km plots. It was interesting that the 2-km plot gave index estimates comparable in size and trend to the Gates perpendicular-distance approach. This, in part, resulted because both index estimates were for a route area equal to the route length times twice its width based on perpendicular distance to the sighted animals. In addition, it was our perception of the Hobcaw herd that its density was realistically in the range of these 2 indices.

Although the 1-km plot gave considerably higher index estimates, with the exception of 1976, it consistently had a lower variance as standard errors in Table 1 show. Herein lies the value of the Hanson method; it combined all of the information from all surveys in 1 year to produce 1 estimate of the index and calculated a standard error of that estimate. Whereas the 2-km plot was producing what we thought might be a more realistic index value relative to the actual population density, the 1-km plot was producing a far more precise estimate.

The accuracy of the indices in approximating the actual deer densities on the area probably never will be known, but with this method, using the 1-km plot, we can make a valid probability statement about changes in density along the survey route which we believe to be representative of the survey area.

As would be expected, the probability of sighting was higher for 2-km plots than for 1-km plots (Table 2). Unexpected, however, was the disproportionate increase that came from doubling plot size. Relative increases ranged from approximately 33 to 62% with an average of 46% for the 7 years.

Figure 2 and Table 3 show the relative importance of the number of survey nights used in the Hanson index calculation. In 1979, the population was high and apparently healthy, and seasonally cool temperatures prevailed during the survey period. In that year, precision in the Hanson index method might have been about as good if we had used only 3 surveys among the 8 that were used. This result was also reflected in the probability-of-sighting evaluation (Table 4).

In 1980, when EHD hit the herd, it took all 8 surveys to get the precision that might have been obtained with only 3 surveys in 1979. In 1982, EHD was still at a high infection rate in the herd, although the population indices suggested that some stability had been obtained. However, the temperatures during the 1982 survey period were unseasonably warm as they

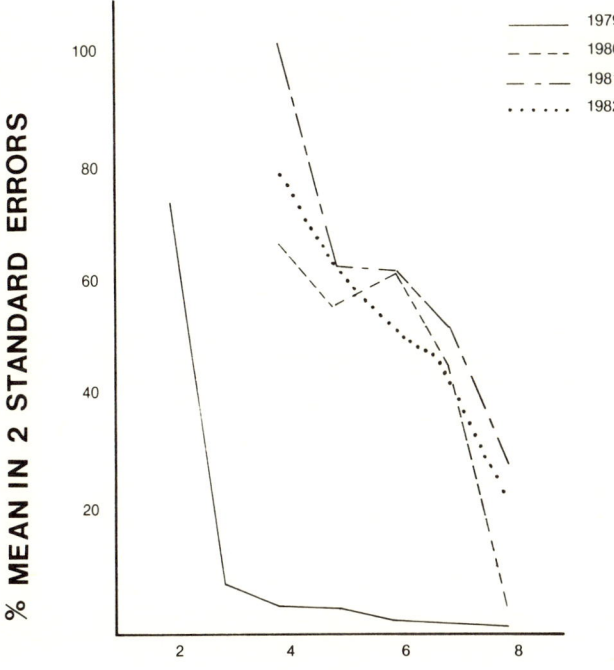

FIG. 2. Change in precision of the Hanson index estimate (1-km plots) with number of survey nights utilized by survey year for a deer population in South Carolina.

had been throughout the fall months that year. It was our belief that these abnormally high temperatures greatly decreased all wild animal activity on Hobcaw during this survey period relative to that in other years. Low activity appeared to contribute to erratic counts among plots along the route as well as among nights which, of course, greatly increased the variance term.

Table 3. Change in precision (expressed as a percentage of the mean in 2 standard errors) of the estimated probability of sighting in the Hanson index, with changes in number of survey nights utilized by survey year, for a deer population in South Carolina.

	Year			
N survey nights	1979	1980	1981	1982
2	119.4	92.8	100.5	13.4
3	6.0	23.1	29.2	18.8
4	18.5	21.6	19.5	15.9
5	10.4	8.0	14.7	14.8
6	5.9	12.4	10.2	9.9
7	5.7	10.5	8.3	8.4
8	5.3	36.0	4.9	9.2

Table 4. Comparison of results of Hanson-method estimates, using 1-km and 2-km plots, for deer on a coastal South Carolina plantation.

	Index estimates			2 SE's[b] of estimate			Probability of sighting			2 SE's of probability		
Year	1-km plot	2-km plot	Ratio[a]	1-km plot	2-km plot	Ratio	1-km plot	2-km plot	Ratio	1-km plot	2-km plot	Ratio
1976	78.9	55.4	0.70	2.9	3.1	1.07	0.335	0.542	1.62	0.024	0.038	1.58
1977	90.9	65.3	0.72	3.8	15.5	4.08	0.345	0.514	1.49	0.026	0.024	0.92
1978	88.1	62.0	0.70	9.5	23.7	2.49	0.368	0.469	1.27	0.031	0.037	1.19
1979	117.4	89.5	0.76	2.1	29.3	13.95	0.419	0.559	1.33	0.022	0.037	1.68
1980	90.9	56.0	0.69	2.2	38.0	17.27	0.267	0.531	1.99	0.096	0.041	0.43
1981	86.7	54.1	0.62	25.8	41.0	1.59	0.371	0.546	1.47	0.018	0.033	1.83
1982	109.8	67.6	0.62	27.7	43.6	1.57	0.371	0.543	1.46	0.034	0.031	0.91

[a] Ratio of 2-km plot:1-km plot.
[b] Standard errors.

Antlerless to Antlered Ratios

Spotlight counts have been used frequently to estimate buck:doe ratios. We were unable to separate mature does from fawns of the year in December and could only record antlered and antlerless animals and those in which no determination of this type could be made (Table 5). There were 1,878 deer sightings in the 7 years of work, but approximately 48% of these were unclassified.

The antlerless:antlered ratios steadily increased throughout the study period, although the reason for this has not been documented. The dramatic increases since 1980 may have been in part due to the continuing EHD infection. Observations of several deer in pens on Hobcaw Barony suggested that rutting bucks may be more susceptible to EHD infection than other deer. If this is the case, there may have been some selection against bucks that would disproportionately lower the probability of them being sighted.

Timing of Spotlight Counts

In developing a population density index, all rules that apply to sampling for an actual population estimate should be followed, but the interpretation is more limited because of certain recognized limitations in the data. One such rule is that every individual should have an equal opportunity of being counted. In the situation that we have described for Hobcaw Barony, we know that this is not true because our sampling is not random. We have recognized that limitation and restricted ourselves to index estimates.

Proper comparisons of 1 year with another can only be made when the type of field sampling that we did is also systematic in timing. Wood and Davis analyzed 3,600 radio-telemetry locations of 5 does and 4 bucks on Hobcaw Barony and found large differences among seasons and between sexes in movement activity throughout the year. For example, movements for both sexes were at their lowest in late August to early September and

Table 5. Changes in recognition of antlered and antlerless classes of deer on a coastal South Carolina plantation.

Sightings	Year							Overall
	1976	1977	1978	1979	1980	1981	1982	
Total	226	267	240	399	235	237	274	1,878
% antlered	18.60	15.40	12.50	13.30	15.30	13.90	11.70	14.20
% antlerless	32.70	20.60	27.50	38.60	47.70	49.80	46.70	37.60
% unknown	48.70	64.00	60.00	48.10	37.00	36.30	41.60	48.10
Antlerless: antlered ratio	1.76	1.34	2.20	2.91	3.11	3.58	4.00	2.65

at their highest in late October through mid-November. Since probability-of-sighting is a measure of detectability and the amount of movement affects detection, population indices estimated for these 2 periods in the same year would not be comparable even though the actual population sizes would probably not be different.

CONCLUSIONS

After 7 years of experience at collecting and analyzing deer spotlight-count data on Hobcaw Barony, we believe that the Hanson method (using 1-km plots) is very suitable for yielding a population index suitable for detecting significant population changes. The most important aspect of this method is that it integrates data from a number of surveys and provides 1 estimate with a variance for all data combined. The other methods tested singularly provided estimates with variance terms for each survey.

LITERATURE CITED

BURNHAM, K. P., D. R. ANDERSON, AND J. L. LAAKE. 1980. Estimation of density from line transect sampling of biological populations. Wildl. Monogr. 72. 202pp.

EBERHART, L. L. 1968. A preliminary appraisal of line transects. J. Wildl. Manage. 32:82-88.

GATES, C. E. 1969. Simulation study of estimators for the line transect sampling method. Biometrics 15:317-328.

———, W. H. MARSHALL, AND D. P. OLSON. 1968. Line transect method of estimating grouse densities. Biometrics 24:135-145.

GROSS, J. E., L. E. STODDART, AND F. H. WAGNER. 1974. Demographic analysis of a northern Utah jackrabbit population. Wildl. Monogr. 40. 68pp.

HANSON, W. R. 1968. Estimating the number of animals: a rapid method for unidentified individuals. Science 16:675-676.

HAYNE, D. W. 1949. An examination of the strip census method for estimating animal populations. J. Wildl. Manage. 13:145-157.

LINE TRANSECT ESTIMATION OF ANIMAL DENSITIES FROM LARGE DATA SETS

C. E. GATES, Department of Statistics, Texas A&M University, College Station, TX 77843

W. EVANS, New Mexico Department of Game and Fish, State Capitol, Santa Fe, NM 87503

D. R. GOBER, 1319 Shafter, San Angelo, TX 76901

F. S. GUTHERY, Department of Range and Wildlife Management, Texas Tech University, Lubbock, TX 79409[a]

W. E. GRANT, Department of Wildlife and Fisheries Sciences, Texas A&M University, College Station, TX 77843

Abstract: This study examines the statistical properties of several large line transect data sets involving animals. It discusses "heaping", i.e., a great excess of observations at 0, 5, 10, etc. units of measurement. This study shows that such heaping must be taken into account when estimating densities, even with nonparametric estimation, and when fitting the distribution of sighting distances to common, nonincreasing parametric distributions. Computer simulation showed that the Fourier series estimator is robust against heaping of right angle distances, whereas the polynomial estimator is substantially biased upward. Data from 5 large data sets showed that when class intervals exceed the shoulder width, densities of all estimators examined here, except the Fourier series, are negatively biased relative to densities from ungrouped data. Analysis of 2 very large data sets showed that final estimates of density did not differ whether computed from number of animals sighted or from the number of sightings expanded by the average number of animals/sighting, but that variances must be calculated from the number of sightings. Examination of random subsets of these data showed that line transects should have 100 or more sightings to make meaningful goodness-of-fit tests to several parametric distributions. The 3 largest data sets, in general, did not fit any of the 4 parametric distributions. However, grouping of the data from the largest data set (n=3,573) on the irregularly spaced heap points of right angle distances (arising from heaping of sighting angles and distances) improved the goodness-of-fit tests markedly in 3 of the 4 distributions attempted.

KEY WORDS: Line transect, Animal densities, Heaping, Data grouping, Goodness-of-fit tests, Simulation.

In the line transect (LT) method of sampling wildlife populations, an observer attempts to estimate the unknown population size, and hence density, by moving a distance, L, across a tract of area, A, in non-intersecting lines or transects. The observer counts the number, n, of animals sighted for each species being investigated and records 1 or more of the following statistics at the time of sighting: radial distance from the observer to the animal at the time of sighting, right-angle distance from the animal sighted to the observer's path, and angle of sighting as measured from the observer's path to the point at which the animal is first sighted.

Many line transect data sets are available, but few have hundreds of sightings and even fewer have thousands of them. We have several large data sets collected in 3 ecological regions of Texas on a variety of species. The

[a]Present address: Caesar Kleberg Wildlife Research Institute, College of Agriculture, Texas A&I University, Campus Box 218, Kingsville, TX 78363.

objective of this paper is to examine the statistical properties of large line transect data sets. In particular, we will examine:

1. The problem of "heaping" of distance observations at rounded intervals (0, 5, 10 m, etc.).
2. The effects on density estimates of grouping right-angle distances into intervals of different widths.
3. Use of the number of sightings vs. the number of animals to estimate density.
4. The effects of sample size on the goodness-of-fit of data to parametric distributions.

Data were analyzed using the August 1983 version of LINETRAN (Gates 1980), which describes most of the estimators used herein. The Fourier series estimator is described by Burnham et al. (1980).

MATERIALS AND METHODS

Coastal Bend Study Area

Evans (1975) collected data on the flushing behavior of white-tailed deer (*Odocoileus virginianus*) on the Rob and Bessie Welder Wildlife Refuge near Sinton, San Patricio County, Texas. Fourteen linear transects totaling 16 km in length were established in June 1970 on a restricted randomized sampling design. The study area was divided into 5 blocks of about equal size. Transects were assigned to the blocks at a density of 1.6 km of transect/ 2.56 km^2. Randomly selected grid monuments served as starting points. Cardinal directions of the transect from starting points were selected randomly, and transects followed gridlines.

Transects 1.6-km long were preferred and established when selected gridlines were sufficiently long. Transects 0.8-km long were established when selected gridlines crossed block boundaries within less than 1.6 km from the starting point. Routes were marked with yellow vinyl flagging at maximum intervals of about 50 m.

Transects were walked within 1 hour after sunrise or before sunset. When the wind was blowing, the observer walked at some angle into the wind. Otherwise, the observer walked with the sun at his back. Counts were not made on days of extreme weather conditions or restricted visibility. No counts were made when wind velocity exceeded 38 kph.

Positional measurements were made to locate the detected deer with respect to the observer and the transect. The distance between the deer and the observer at the moment of detection was estimated with a Range-O-Matic rangefinder. The observation angle was measured to the nearest 10° with a protractor. The observer searched a 180° field of view extending 90° on both sides of the transect. Binoculars were not used. Other facts recorded included size of the group in which the deer was observed.

Trans-Pecos Study Area

Gober (1979) collected data on the flushing behavior of black-tailed jackrabbits (*Lepus californicus*) and cottontails (*Sylvilagus* spp.) on private ranches northeast of Alpine, Texas near the confluence of Pecos, Brewster, and Jeff Davis counties. Study areas were situated between the Glass and Davis mountains on a portion of the Pecos Plains within the Coyanosa Draw Drainage System.

Three permanently marked transects were established in a north-south direction across a pasture in each of 3 study areas. Parallel transects within a pasture were separated by about 0.8 km. The total number of times that transects were walked during 1975, 1976, and 1977 were 114, 137, and 210, respectively. Transects were walked a similar number of times on each study area in each sampling period. About 1,500 km of transects were walked during the study. Transect length varied from 2.7 to 4.5 km, depending on the size of the pasture sampled. In 1975-76, sampling was conducted on 3 study areas during 5 periods. In 1977, sampling was conducted on 3 study areas during 7 periods. Transects were walked about 1-2 hours before sunset in all years; in 1976-77, transects also were initiated at sunrise.

Observations on transects included the species (and number) of lagomorphs seen and the corresponding flushing angles and radial flushing distances. A mean perpendicular distance from the transect line was calculated for each observation.

Rio Grande Plain Study Area

The data were gathered in Zavala County, Texas, during January-July 1975 and 1976 (Guthery 1977). The study area had dense brush (over 5,700 stems/ha), mostly 1-2 m tall, on rolling terrain.

Linear transects 0.32-km apart were established systematically in 2 pastures, flagged with plastic tape, and cleared of brush to facilitate travel. The north-south transects included 4 1.8-km long and 5 1.6-km long. Counts started at about sunrise and at 2-3 hours before sunset. Each transect was walked 4 times/month.

The number, radial flushing distance, and flushing angle were recorded for each individual or group of black-tailed jackrabbits, cottontails, white-tailed deer, scaled quail (*Callipepla squamata*), or bobwhites (*Colinus virginianus*) flushed. The flushing angle was estimated to the nearest 5° with reference to a compass imprinted on field data forms. Distances were paced to the nearest meter, except for white-tailed deer that flushed in excess of 50 m. In these cases the radial distance was estimated visually to the nearest 5 m.

RESULTS

Heaping

Heaping or clumping of distance measurements occurs when certain values are over- and adjacent values are under-represented. Radial distances from the Trans-Pecos Study Area had excess frequencies at 5, 10, 15, 20, 25, 30 m, etc. (Fig. 1). This characteristic of the data set is not necessarily a failing of the observer, since beyond 50 m or so, a human probably cannot estimate better than the nearest 5 or 10 m. Heaping at distances less than 20 m is clearly indicative of incomplete training. Figure 2 shows data for the same species in terms of the right-angle distances rounded to the nearest integer. Because the right-angle distances were computed from the radial distances and the sighting angles, the "clumping" is still present, but less pronounced than with radial distances (Fig. 1), except for the excess of observations at 0 m.

What can be done about heaping once it exists? A first thought was to "smooth" the data; data smoothing techniques are well accepted statistical tools in time-series work. However, in the present case, we wished to preserve the total count, so a modified technique (5-point moving average) was used as follows:

$$f_i = \sum_{j=i-2}^{i+2} f_j/5 \text{ for } 2 < i < k-2$$

where f_i is the frequency for the ith distance (f_1 is the frequency for the 0 class). The lower end points are given by:

$$f_1 = (3f_1 + f_2 + f_2 + f_3)/5$$
$$f_2 = (f_1 + 2f_2 + f_3 + f_4)/5$$

Similar definitions hold for the upper end points.

Thus, smoothing has helped somewhat but does not appear to be the final solution (Fig. 3). Gates et al. (1968) suggested that distances with excess observations at 5, 10, 15 m, etc. could be grouped readily into 5-m increments with observations at the heaping joints equally divided between adjacent intervals. This method seems to work well (Fig. 4). Here one obtains a near-classical distribution of sighting distances. Actually, variable width classes were used here, with 10 m from 0 to 150 m and 60 m from 150 to 300 m. The estimated densities (jackrabbits/km^2) with 95% confidence intervals were, using the Hayne method:

Data Set	*n*	*Density*
Original data	3,573	82.2 ± 6.3
5-point moving average	3,573	95.8 ± 11.4
Grouped into 5-m intervals	3,573	87.6 ± 6.5

Thus, the grouping into 5-m intervals preserves the original density estimates better than the 5-point moving average even though there is no

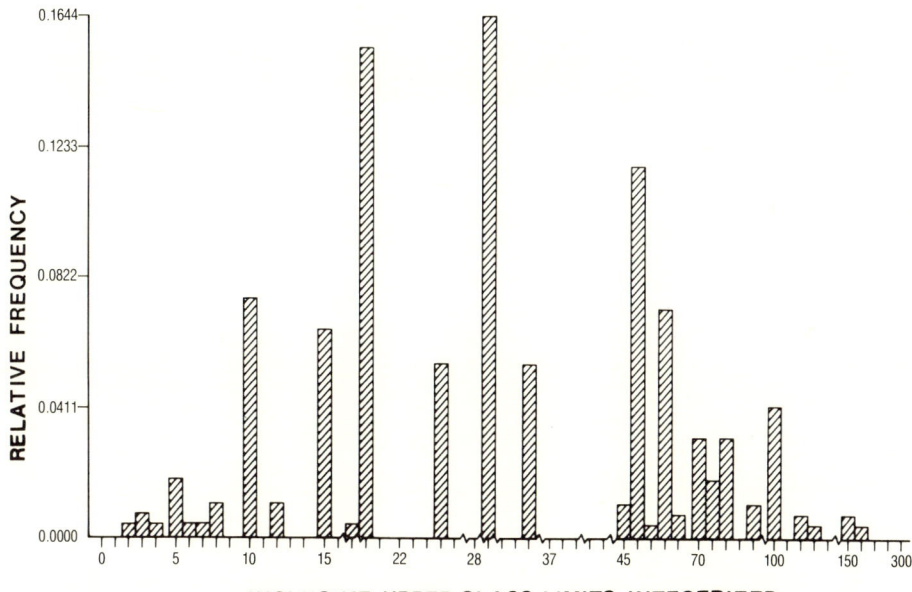

Fig. 1. Observed radial distance sightings for 3,573 jackrabbits (Gober 1979) (maximum frequency = 523).

significant difference. On the other hand, one could draw the conclusion that there was "much ado about nothing" as the density estimate did not change much from using the badly clumped data.

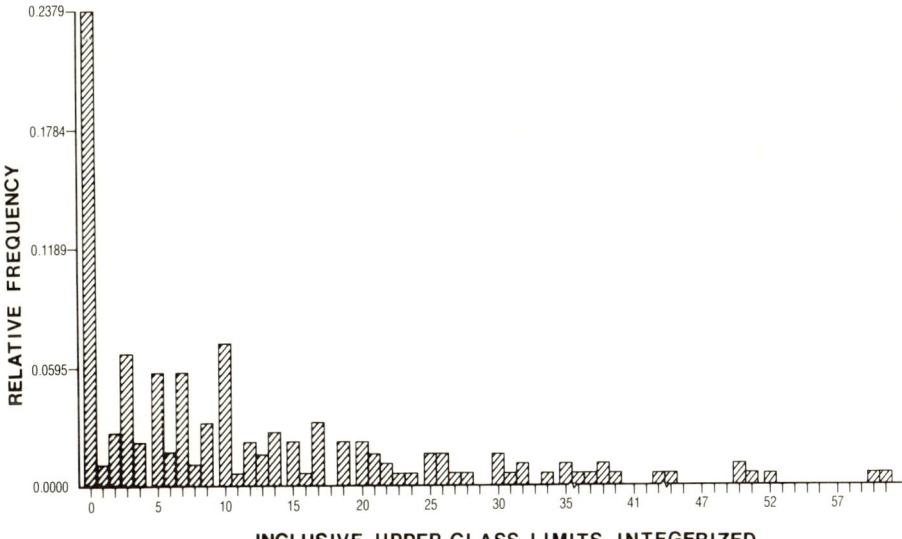

Fig. 2. Observed right-angle distance sightings for 3,573 jackrabbits (Gober 1979) (maximum frequency = 850).

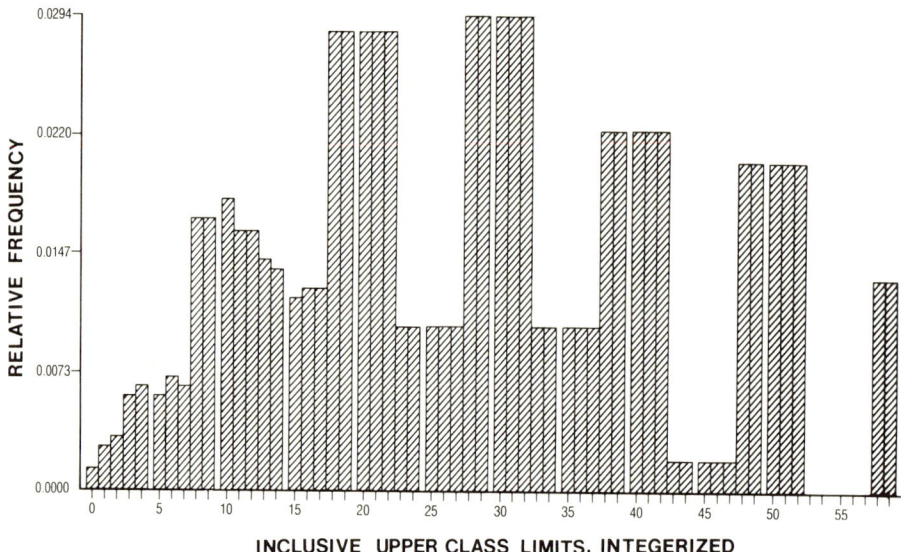

Fig. 3. Jackrabbit radial distances for 3,573 sightings after using a 5-point moving average algorithm (Gober 1979) (maximum frequency = 104.8).

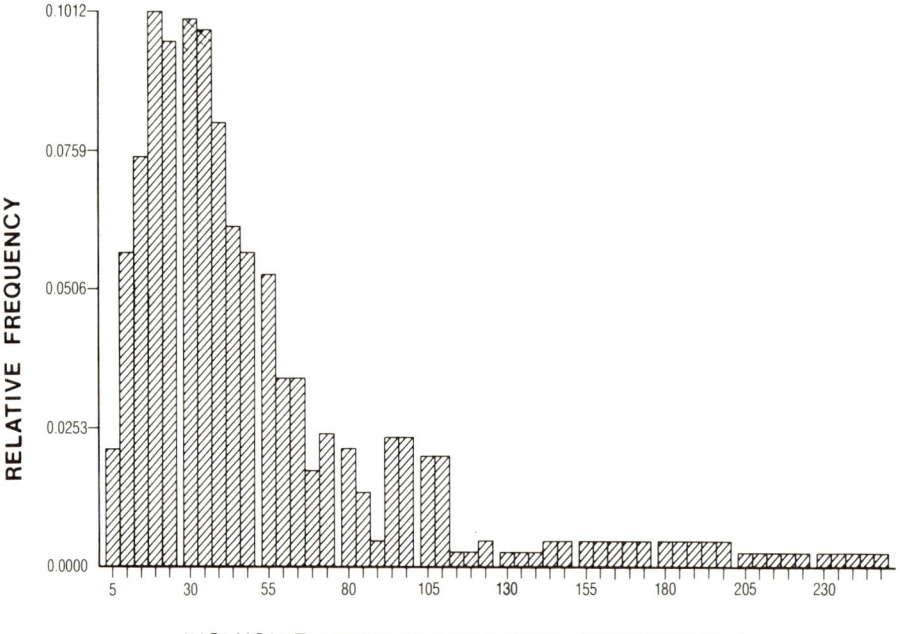

Fig. 4. Jackrabbit radial distances of 3,573 sightings after grouping at the points of heaping (Gober 1979) (maximum frequency = 361.5).

Post-survey Grouping Effects

Table 1 shows the effect on point estimates of density of post-survey grouping of data into the 2-, 3-, 4-, and 5-m increments, except for white-tailed deer where 2, 5, 10, and 15 m were used (a "1" indicates ungrouped data). The right-angle distances were computed from the sighting angles and distances and rounded to the nearest integer. As expected, the effect of grouping is most dramatic on the Kelker Index. The densities differed dramatically by the different intervals for all species. The density for the 1-m interval cannot be calculated here because the Kelker Index requires grouping (Technically, the data *have* been grouped, even in 1-m intervals, and thus the estimators could be calculated. But because of the very large heaping effects observed at $X=0$, such density estimates are ridiculously high). The story's moral is that the observer should be certain all animals can be seen to the specified width before using this estimator. The Eberhardt-Cox estimator, like the Kelker Index, is highly dependent on the particular grouping of right angle distances used. It also tends to give higher estimates than all the other estimators for small interval width, except occasionally the generalized exponential. The spline estimator (Gates 1979) was developed for the situation in which all animals are sighted for some distance from the line; in fact, in such cases with broad-shouldered detection functions, it will not only estimate the density, but it will also estimate the distance at which fall-off in detectability occurs. With narrow-shouldered data the spline estimator tends to give the same density estimates as the Kelker Index.

Burnham et al. (1980) introduced the concept of "shoulder" with reference to sets of perpendicular line transect data sets. The shoulder represents the interval nearest the line transect within which all animals are seen. A "narrow" shoulder and a "broad" shoulder mean that there are relatively narrow widths and relatively broad widths within which all animals are seen. A good example of a broad-shouldered data set is that of the duck-nest data of Anderson and Posphala (1970). If any data set is grouped into intervals whose interval width exceeds the width of the shoulder, there must be a decrease in density estimated from the resulting grouped data as the data in the shoulder are "averaged down" with values beyond the shoulder. Thus in the data sets shown in Table 1, we have grouped beyond any possible shoulder; this accounts for the general trend of the first 3 estimators to decrease with interval width. Now that we have disposed of the 3 special-purpose nonparametric estimators, let us examine the remaining 4. The generalized exponential is the only parametric estimator shown (in the original 7); the other 3 estimators—Fourier series, polynomial, and quadratic—are nonparametric and require no assumptions of particular distributions. Also, in theory, none of these 4 estimators should vary with interval size; the densities should randomly vary as interval size increases. Note in Table 1 that there is variability in density estimates and a general

Table 1. Effect of grouping on estimation in densities. Numbers are density estimates in individuals/km. Intervals are in m. Data from Guthery (1977).

Estimator	White-tailed deer (N=521)				
	Interval				
	1	2	5	10	15
Kelker		12.5	10.4	8.1	7.5
Eberhardt-Cox		16.4	12.7	9.5	9.1
Spline	18.1	12.5	10.4	8.1	7.5
Generalized exponential		10.5	9.7	8.9	8.3
Polynomial	9.4	10.6	9.8	8.8	8.5
Quadratic	8.4	11.3	10.0	9.0	8.8
Fourier	9.0	7.3	7.3	7.3	8.3

Estimator	Cottontail (N=540)				
	Interval				
	1	2	3	4	5
Kelker		97.0	80.2	67.6	57.8
Eberhardt-Cox		122.8	107.8	93.8	81.6
Spline	72.8	97.0	80.2	67.6	57.8
Generalized exponential	226.9	139.6	109.2	90.0	68.8
Polynomial	80.0	109.0	95.2	61.2	57.6
Quadratic	76.2	113.2	104.2	102.5	98.6
Fourier	106.6	98.2	98.3	86.9	75.4

Estimator	Scaled quail (N=550)				
	Interval				
	1	2	3	4	5
Kelker		38.0	32.7	26.9	23.1
Eberhardt-Cox		47.6	42.8	34.5	28.7
Spline	28.5	38.0	32.7	26.9	23.1
Generalized exponential	22.7	21.7	21.9	21.0	20.1
Polynomial	22.4	31.6	28.4	25.7	26.4
Quadratic	21.4	35.7	32.5	29.5	27.1
Fourier	24.8	13.4	17.1	22.9	22.8

Estimator	Bobwhite (N=1,262)				
	Interval				
	1	2	3	4	5
Kelker		86.1	82.3	76.0	71.6
Eberhardt-Cox		97.5	95.8	89.6	87.9
Spline	75.0	86.1	82.3	76.0	71.6
Generalized exponential	152.4	120.1	111.9	102.7	93.9
Polynomial	77.2	90.3	89.6	86.1	82.5
Quadratic	77.3	94.2	93.3	90.6	88.7
Fourier	87.4	82.9	87.7	88.0	83.7

decrease in density with interval size, the Fourier series estimator showing, in general, less change with increasing interval size.

The Fourier series estimator is programmed to use exact methods (Burnham et al. 1980) with grouped data, whereas the other 3 methods use approximate methods. However, we believe the main reason for the general decrease in density exhibited by the polynomial, quadratic, and generalized exponential estimators and the variability of the Fourier series estimator is heaping, particularly at 0. The Fourier series estimator is regarded as one of the best available.

In order to study the effect of heaping on the more general (nonparametric) estimators utilized here, a computer simulation program was developed. In this simulation program, the data were generated by the generalized exponential distribution, with parameters "half-way" between the half-normal and the exponential distributions (parameters $\alpha = 1.5$, $\beta = 53$). Distances were randomly drawn from a population with a true density of 1.8 animals/square unit. The randomly generated distances, using the rejection method, were rounded to the nearest unit. The densities were determined by both the polynomial and Fourier series estimators, and the entire process was repeated a minimum of 449 times. The average n for each replicate run was approximately 175.

The algorithm used to simulate heaping is as follows: distances from 0 to 45 units were heaped at 5-unit increments while distances above 45 units were heaped at 10-unit increments. There is, of course, some overlap, between 45 and 50 units.

First:

$X' = 5(INT[(dist + 2.5)/5.0])$ for dist ≤ 46.25

$X' = 10(INT[(dist + 5.0)/10.0])$ for dist > 46.25

Then: $X = X'$ if $u_i < (1 - X''/10)$

$= FLOAT (INT[dist + 0.5])$ if $u_i \geq (1 - X''/10)$,

where

$u_i =$ (pseudo) random uniform number,

$X'' = |X' - dist|$,

dist = distance from the line transect to a sighted animal.

Verbally, the algorithm specifies that all distances between 0 and 45 are converted to the nearest integer divisible by 5, and between 50 and the largest observed value are converted to an integer divisible by 10. Then either the heaped value or the original distance is used. The closer the true value is to the heaped value, the more likely it is that the heaped value will be used. Thus, if dist = 26, the probability is $1 - |26 - 25|/10 = 0.9$ that 25 will be used. Examination of such generated data sets reveals excellent examples of heaping. The average computed densities ($\bar{X} \pm 1$ SE) are:

	Estimator	
Ungrouped data	*Polynomial*	*Fourier*
No heaping	1.814 ± 0.014	1.808 ± 0.007
	(450 runs)	(1,350 runs)
Heaping allowed	3.344 ± 0.028	1.799 ± 0.006
	(900 runs)	(1,800 runs)

The simulations without heaping show that both the polynomial and Fourier estimators are unbiased as expected, with the Fourier series estimator having a slightly lower standard error (because d.f. are essentially infinity, conservative 95% confidence intervals can be obtained by multiplication of the standard errors of the means by 2). When heaping is allowed, the Fourier series remains, somewhat surprisingly, unbiased. The polynomial estimator is badly biased (86% too large) by the heaping, undoubtedly due entirely to heaping at zero. The Fourier series estimator, fortuitously, cannot rise fast enough near the origin, while the polynomial not only can but does. These results are impressive, indicating not only robustness of the Fourier series estimator against heaping of observed right angle distances but also that grouping at the heap points is not necessary. There is, however, one word of caution here. The simulated heaping was done on the right angle distances *per se*. Suppose (as is true for most of our data sets) heaping occurs on the *sighting* angles and distances which are subsequently converted to right angle distances. It is not clear if the Fourier series estimator will be as robust against that form of heaping.

Sighting vs. Number of Animals

Normally, when the observer first sights the target species, he records the distance and angle to the center of the group if more than 1 individual is observed. The question naturally arises as to whether it is better statistically to estimate the density of individuals by estimating densities of sightings and then expanding that to density of individuals by the average number of animals/group or to calculate the density of individuals directly, simply by counting n_i animals, all assumed at the same distance at the ith sighting. We have analyzed 2 large data sets both ways using the Fourier series estimator and have recorded the relevant information in Table 2. For either the jackrabbit or cottontail data of Gober (1979), we see that it makes little difference as far as density is concerned which method is used because the density of individuals computed either way is very similar. However, we cannot overemphasize that the number of sightings must be used to get the correct variance. This is made clearer by reference to item D in Table 2 where the variance of the estimated density of individuals is obtained by utilizing the variance of a product. As is seen the variance of the product is substantially larger than the variance of density based on individuals.

Table 2. Estimation of density of individuals vs. density of sightings. Numbers in table are Fourier series estimates of individuals/km^2 or sightings/km^2 followed by 95% confidence intervals. Data are from Gober (1979).

	Species	
Item	Jackrabbit	Cottontail
A. Density (individuals)	179.8 ± 10.3	152.5 ± 18.4
B. Density (sightings)	156.5 ± 15.2	148.5 ± 26.0
C. Individuals/sighting	1.2018 ± 0.0097	1.0377 ± 0.0086
D. Product (B × C)	188.1 ± 18.3	154.1 ± 27.0
E. N sightings	3,573	1,327
F. N individuals	4,294	1,377

Effects of Sample Size on Goodness-of-Fit Tests

Another advantage of having available large data sets is that random subsamples can be taken from those data sets, and the statistical properties of the subsamples can be examined. We can look at tests of goodness-of-fit to several distributions that correspond to non-increasing detectability curves (Ramsey 1979). Four of these parametric distributions are considered here: the half-normal distribution, the gamma distribution, with $\alpha = 1$ (i.e., the exponential distribution), the generalized exponential distribution, and the gamma distribution with parameters α and β. We have investigated the effect of sample size by sampling at random from several data sets previously mentioned; the subsamples themselves were then tested for goodness-of-fit (Stephens 1974) to the 4 distributions mentioned above. Table 3 shows the results of these tests. Analysis of the original Gober jackrabbit data set showed that the data did not fit any of the 4 distributions ($P \leq 0.01$). When the data were assigned randomly to 10 subsamples (with an average of 357.3 sightings each) and when tests of goodness-of-fit were made to those subsamples, all goodness-of-fit tests agreed with the original sample except for the 2-parameter gamma where 1 of 10 subsamples indicated a good fit to that distribution. The Gober (1979) cottontail and the Evans (1975) white-tailed deer data sets, with 1,327 and 1,078 sightings, respectively, had even better agreement between the goodness-of-fit tests for the original data set and the 10 random subsamples. The average subsample sizes were about 133 and 108, respectively. However, when the total sample size is in the 500's, with the average subsample size in the 50's, agreement between the original and subsample tends to degenerate. While the Guthery (1977) cottontail data subsamples agree with the original closely, the Guthery (1977) scaled quail and white-tailed deer data sets showed some drastic discrepancies between the original sample and the subsamples. For the generalized exponential distribution, the Guthery scaled quail showed that the data did not fit in 3 of the 10 subsamples, whereas the original showed a good fit. In the Guthery white-tailed deer data set, there was almost a complete reversal on both the exponential distribution and the 2-

Table 3. Effect of sample size on tests of goodness-of-fit to various distributions. Data are from Evans (1975), Gober (1979), and Guthery (1980).

Data type	Half-normal			Exponential (1, β)			Generalized exponential			Gamma (α,β)		
	NS	*	**	NS	*	**	NS	*	**	NS	*	**
Jackrabbit (Gober 1979) (N=3,573)												
Original	0	0	1	0	0	1	0	0	1	0	0	1
10 subsamples	0	0	10	0	0	10	0	0	10	1	2	7
Cottontail (Gober 1979) (N=1,327)												
Original	0	0	1	0	0	1	0	0	1	1	0	0
10 subsamples	0	0	10	0	0	10	0	0	10	10	0	0
White-tailed deer (Evans 1975) (N=1,078)												
Original	0	0	1	0	0	1	0	0	1	0	0	1
10 subsamples	0	0	10	0	0	10	0	0	10	0	1	9
Scaled quail (Guthery 1977) (N=550)												
Original	0	0	1	1	0	0	1	0	0	1	0	0
10 subsamples	2	4	4	9	1	0	7	2	1	10	0	0
Cottontail (Guthery 1977) (N=540)												
Original	0	0	1	1	0	0	1	0	0	1	0	0
10 subsamples	0	1	9	10	0	0	10	0	0	10	0	0
White-tailed deer (Guthery 1977) (N=521)												
Original	0	0	1	0	0	1	0	0	1	0	1	0
10 subsamples	0	0	10	9	0	1	5	3	2	9	0	1

NS = Non-significant, $P > 0.05$.
* = $0.01 < P < 0.05$.
** = $P < 0.01$.

parameter gamma, with 9 of 10 subsamples showing a good fit, whereas the original showed that the data did not fit. Similarly for the same data set, 5 of the 10 subsamples showed a good fit for the generalized exponential, whereas the original sample did not fit that distribution. Thus, a sample size of 100 sightings or more is necessary to measure with any assurance whether data sets do or do not fit these distributions. Many published data sets have many fewer observations than 100. The results also strengthen the argument for using non-parametric estimators with small data sets.

We wish to emphasize that in Table 3 neither the Gober jackrabbit data nor the Evans white-tailed deer data fit *any* of the 4 distributions examined. Indeed, the goodness-of-fit tests were rejected at the $P \leq 0.01$ level. Similarly, the Gober cottontail data failed to fit 3 or 4 distributions, only the 2-parameter gamma gave a good fit. With an excess of 1,000 sightings, the power of such tests is high, and it is conceivable that such large data sets cannot be shown to fit any common distribution. However, because heaping has played such a critical role elsewhere in this paper, we supposed it could play such a role here. Thus we have grouped the Gober jackrabbit data of Table 3 on the presumed heap points (which arose from heaping of sighting angles and distances). Obvious heaping points are at 3, 5, 7, and 10 m, of necessity unequal intervals (Fig. 2). These grouped data were then fitted to the same 4 distributions, giving startlingly different results. While the goodness-of-fit to the half-normal became significant, $0.01 < P \leq 0.05$, instead of highly significant, $P \leq 0.01$, the other goodness-of-fit tests indicated good fits to the 2 gamma distributions and the generalized expotential, $P > 0.05$, instead of $P \leq 0.01$. In summary, since the influence of heaping is so pervasive in the statistics concerned with line transects, we recommend that observers measure distances carefully, if possible, or at least be carefully trained to avoid heaping in estimating distances or angles. If that is not possible, the data should be carefully examined by plotting the ungrouped data (such as was done in Fig. 1 and 2), then grouped on the heap points with 50% of the observations going into each of the adjacent classes, and finally analyzed by exact nonparametric procedures for grouped data, such as the Fourier series estimator (Burnham et al. 1980). In other words, automatic computer analysis of line transect data sets does not appear possible, at least without a very sophisticated code.

CONCLUSIONS

Smoothing of radial distances heaped at 5-m integers had no appreciable effect on density estimates calculated with Hayne's method, generally regarded as the estimator of choice if radial distances are used to estimate density (Burnham et al. 1980). The slightly modified 5-point moving average is not helpful in estimating densities with heaped data.

The sensitivity of density estimators to grouping intervals for right-angle distances varied. The Kelker Index and Eberhardt-Cox and spline estimators were highly sensitive, giving poor estimates as interval width increased. The only parametric estimator shown, the generalized exponential, and the quadratic and polynomial nonparametric estimators showed a downward trend with increasing interval width. The Fourier series estimator correctly showed no tendency to either change with increasing interval width.

Heaping, an excess of observations at distances exactly divisible by 5 or 10, is critical in estimating densities. There is evidence that heaping influences all estimators except possibly the Fourier series. We demonstrated by computer simulation that the Fourier series is unbiased against heaping of right angle distances, and the polynomial estimator is badly biased with such heaping.

Where multiple animals can be observed in a single sighting, densities may be calculated from either sightings or animals, but to calculate the correct variance, sightings must be used.

A sample size of 100 sightings or more is necessary to measure with any assurance whether data sets with a large amount of heaping do or do not fit parametric distributions. Grouping on the heap points drastically changes the results of goodness-of-fit tests to several candidate distributions of right angle flushing distances.

LITERATURE CITED

ANDERSON, D. R., AND R. S. POSPHALA. 1970. Correction of bias in belt transect studies of immotile objects. J. Wildl. Manage. 34:141-146.

BURHAM, K. P., D. R. ANDERSON, AND J. L. LKE. 1980. Estimation of density from line transect sampling of biological populations. Wildl. Monogr. 72. 202pp.

EVANS, W. 1975. Methods of estimating densities of white-tailed deer. Ph.D. Thesis. Texas A&M Univ., College Station. 185pp.

GATES, C. E. 1979. Line transect and related issues. Pages 71-154 *in* R. M. Cormack, G. P. Patil, and D. S. Robson, eds. Sampling biological populations. Satellite program in statistical ecology. International Cooperative Publ. House, Fairfield, Md.

———. 1980. LINETRAN, a general computer program for analyzing line transect data. J. Wildl. Manage. 44:658-661.

———, W. H. MARSHALL, AND D. P. OLSON. 1968. Line transect method of estimating grouse population densities. Biometrics 24:135-145.

GOBER, D. R. 1979. Factors affecting domestic sheep losses to predators in Trans-Pecos Texas. Ph.D. Thesis. Texas A&M Univ., College Station. 119pp.

GUTHERY, F. S. 1977. Efficacy and ecological effects of predator control in South Texas. Ph.D. Thesis. Texas A&M Univ., College Station. 50pp.

RAMSEY, F. L. 1979. Parametric models for line transect surveys. Biometrika 66:505-512.

STEPHENS, M. A. 1974. EDF statistics for goodness of fit and some comparisons. J. Am. Stat. Assoc. 69:730-737.

UTILIZATION OF AERIAL SURVEY DATA TO SET PRONGHORN HARVEST QUOTAS IN NEW MEXICO

BRUCE L. MORRISON, New Mexico Department of Game and Fish, Villagra Building, Santa Fe, New Mexico 87503

Abstract: New Mexico has the fifth largest pronghorn (*Antilocapra americana*) population in the United States. In terms of revenue to the Department of Game and Fish, it ranks third behind mule deer (*Odocoileus hemionus*) and elk (*Cervus elaphus*). To ensure perpetuation of this important resource, extensive aerial surveys and rigid harvest quotas are used for proper management of pronghorn populations. In 1966, surveying procedures were developed for all major pronghorn populations. Pronghorn management units are flown on a rotational basis every third year to obtain population estimates. All population surveys are conducted between 1 April and 31 May of each year with fixed-wing aircraft. Fawn-crop surveys are conducted in all major management units beginning 10 July of each year. After sex and age ratios and fawn survival for each herd unit is determined upper limits for harvest quotas are established, then divided into harvest quotas for each ranch in the management unit. Harvest quotas are set to maintain a ratio of 1 buck:5 does. Past hunter-harvest data determines the final number of permits needed to achieve the desired harvest.

KEY WORDS: Pronghorn, Harvest quotas, Aerial surveys, Management units, New Mexico, Permit system.

Over 26,000 pronghorns inhabit New Mexico (Morrison 1982). Approximately 80% of these are found on the state's eastern plains; the remaining 20% occupy scattered habitats in western New Mexico. Every year over 3,500 sportsmen pursue this game animal during the fall hunting seasons. Only deer and elk attract more hunters (Kirkpatrick 1965). The pronghorn represents a substantial source of income to the New Mexico Department of Game and Fish (NMDGF). Thus, the proper management of this resource is not only important from an economic standpoint, but it is essential if we are to perpetuate this animal for the enjoyment of future generations.

METHODS

In 1966, biologists from the NMDGF conducted extensive surveys and divided the state into pronghorn management units (D. Brown, pers. commun.). Each unit represented pronghorn herds that freely interchanged members at various times of the year. Topographical features that impeded pronghorn movement and other barriers that prohibited interchange of herd members were chosen as unit boundaries whenever possible. Units were further divided into subunits for the purpose of aerial surveys of individual pronghorn herds. There are 48 pronghorn management units in New Mexico with each divided into 1 or more subunits.

Various pronghorn survey methods were also tested. The technique determined to give the most accurate data was the strip-census method which used an airplane. This technique was tested by conducting concurrent counts by airplane and by ground observers in vehicles and then comparing the results. The aerial strip-census results were consistently within 5% of the ground observations (J. Johnson, pers. commun). NMDGF conducts 2 types of population surveys each spring, a 33% and 100% population count. Certain units were surveyed more frequently for biological, political, or budgetary reasons. The basic survey was the 33% population survey; that is, a unit was flown in a north-south direction on flight lines approximately 2.5-km apart. All pronghorns observed within 0.8 km to the west of the aircraft were counted and classified as to sex and age. When necessary, the aircraft was moved from its normal flight path to obtain accurate count and classification data. At the end of the survey, the count by sex and age was multiplied by 3 for a total population estimate. In units where a more accurate count was desired or where topographical features prohibit an accurate 33% survey, a 100% survey was conducted. For this survey, the units were flown on north-south flight lines 0.8-km apart with all pronghorns counted and classified. The final count was used for the unit population estimate. In July of each year, a third type of survey, the annual fawn crop survey, was conducted; areas in selected units were flown where concentrations of pronghorn were known to occur. To obtain the yearly fawn crop for a unit, a minimum sample of 100 does and associated fawns was counted. All surveys were flown at a height of about 60 m above ground level.

When the population surveys were completed, district conservation officers and area game managers met to determine the number of permits to allocate for each unit. Bag limits were set after fawn-crop surveys were completed. Harvest quotas were determined by analyzing data from the current year's population surveys, past hunter harvest, historic fawn crops, and climatic factors. Rather than using a predetermined formula to evaluate the data, the knowledge and experience of our field biologists was used to analyze the information. If the most recent population surveys indicated a ratio of 1 buck:4 or 5 does, the herd composition was deemed proper. In this case, harvest quotas were set to allow hunters to remove the predicted surplus. Surpluses were determined by looking at previous fawn crops and hunter harvest and setting permit numbers accordingly. In years following a drought, the permits were reduced to compensate for the reduced fecundity of the doe segment and the additional natural mortality. During years following above-average rainfall, the harvest quotas were increased to take advantage of additional animals available for harvest. If the surveys did not indicate the desired sex ratios, the harvest quotas were adjusted. If the sex ratio was 1 buck:less than 4 does, the harvest quota was increased to remove surplus bucks. If the sex ratio was 1 buck:more than 5 does, the harvest quota was decreased. These quota increases and decreases were made only if population counts indicated that they would not be detrimental to the herd. In the case of a large population count and a buck:doe ratio above that desired, the bag limit might be either sex to bring the ratios down. If the July fawn-crop surveys indicated a high recruitment rate, the bag limit might also be either sex to take advantage of surplus animals.

After the quotas were set for each unit, they were further divided into quotas by ranch. The number of ranches assigned quotas was determined by contacting each landowner in the unit whose ranch contained the acreage and pronghorn numbers to support a harvest. Each rancher was given the opportunity to sign a yearly Pronghorn Hunt Agreement that contained information as to land status, ownership, location, and permit numbers for each ranch. The number of permits for each ranch was determined by allocating the permits on a basis of the ranch acreage in comparison with the total acreage to be hunted in that unit combined with the percentage of the pronghorns inhabiting each ranch, compared with the total population estimate on all hunted ranches. The permits of each ranch were divided into 2 types—landowner and public. The land status of each ranch determined how many permits were landowner or public. The percentage of deeded land contained in the ranch determined the percentage of the permits allocated to the landowner; the remaining ones were public permits. These were issued on a lottery system to successful applicants who were selected by computer. These applicants had to meet a mid-July deadline for submitting a completed application form, the proper license fee, and a $3.00 processing fee. Unsuccessful applicants received a refund of their license fee. To obtain a landowner permit, the hunter had to negotiate with a landowner for an authorization to purchase a pronghorn license. These numbered authorizations were issued to each landowner at the time he signed the Pronghorn Hunt Agreement. Some landowners give these authorizations to family and friends, whereas others charged as high as $1,500 for them. Whoever obtained an authorization also purchased a pronghorn license from the NMDGF.

RESULTS

The establishment of pronghorn harvest quotas through the use of aerial-survey data required reliance upon field biologists. Once data from the surveys were available, the biologists were directed to recommend a harvest quota and bag limit for each unit. For example, during the 1980 surveys (100%) in Pronghorn Management Unit 36, 150 bucks and 450 does were counted; the buck:doe ratio was 1:3. The fawn crop for the unit averaged 59.4% over the past 5 years. Assuming a low mortality in the population, there was the potential for 267 new pronghorns being added to the population during the next year. The second assumption was that sex ratios at birth would be equal. Although this was not true every year, it was believed to average out over a period of years. The 267 new pronghorns then represented a potential for 283 bucks and 583 does and a buck:doe ratio of

1:2.1. With 583 does, 116 bucks were required for a buck:doe ratio of 1:5. This meant a surplus of 167 bucks available for harvest. After subtracting 25% to account for natural mortality and potential bias in observations, 125 bucks could be safely harvested without harming the herd. Hunter success in this unit averaged 78.4% over the past 5 years. To achieve the desired harvest of 125 bucks, 159 permits were allocated. Mortality factors affecting the doe segment of the population were not considered. In New Mexico, doe mortality was extremely variable; therefore, taking a few more years to achieve the proper ratios was deemed more desirable than potentially causing major fluctuations by under- or overestimating doe mortality. The 1981 survey in this unit indicated a buck:doe ratio of 1:3.5. After going through the above exercise with the new data, 150 permits were allocated for the 1982 hunt. Post-hunt surveys conducted in this unit indicated a buck:doe ratio of 1:4.1. There were 145 permits allocated for the recently completed 1983 hunt. This unit was surveyed on a 100% basis for 3 consecutive years because of concerns over the effect of a new highway near the area. Usually 3 years are required before results of the quota manipulations are noted and adjustments made in them. Thirty-two of New Mexico's 48 pronghorn management units now have buck:doe ratios between 1:4 and 1:5.5. Various factors prohibit the achievement of proper ratios in some of the units and are a source of constant frustrations to department biologists. In Unit 31 the desired ratio was almost achieved, changing from a 1 buck:12 doe ratio in 1977 to a 1 buck:8 doe ratio in 1980, until numerous small landowners discovered that they could sell antelope authorizations. Due to political pressure, the department was forced to allocate from 1 to 3 permits to each landowner, thereby exceeding the desired quota. Luckily, the unit has an abundance of pronghorn, and the population was not overharvested. In future years, an attempt will be made to manipulate the increased permits to again start working toward a 1:5 ratio.

The most vital part of the entire system is the aerial surveys. Potential bias in aerial survey results have been studied by numerous authors (Jolly 1969, Caughley 1974, LeResche and Rausch 1974, Caughley et al. 1976). The majority of these studies concerned species that inhabited areas where vegetation affected sightability of the animal. Caughley et al. (1976) determined that sightability declined with increasing aircraft speed, height above ground, and transect width during studies on the red kangaroo (*Megaleia rufa*), a species that occupies a habitat similar to pronghorn. To reduce this bias, NMDGF flew all surveys at a fixed speed and height and maintained a set transect width. Utilizing the same observers and pilot each year further reduced survey bias. The normal 3-year break was compensated for by using a 25% reduction factor in the calculations used for determining the final harvest quota for each unit. Without data from aerial surveys, harvest quotas could not be manipulated to achieve the desired ratios. The inherent biases in survey data were corrected for as much as possible, and the resultant quota manipulations have achieved the desired result over the majority of New Mexico's pronghorn range. Once the proper ratios are achieved in a unit, continued monitoring of the pronghorn populations and manipulation of the harvest quotas should maintain the ratios. The application of this system in New Mexico should prevent the overexploitation of the resource and guarantee quality pronghorn hunting in New Mexico's future.

LITERATURE CITED

CAUGHLEY, G. 1974. Bias in aerial survey. J. Wildl. Manage. 38:921-933.

———, R. SINCLAIR, AND D. SCOTT-KEMMIS. 1976. Experiments in aerial survey. J. Wildl. Manage. 40:290-300.

JOLLY, G. M. 1969. Sampling methods for aerial censuses of wildlife populations. E. Afr. Agric. For. J. 34 (special issue):46-49.

KIRKPATRICK, T. O. 1965. The economic and social values of hunting and fishing in New Mexico. Univ. New Mexico Bureau of Business Res., Albuquerque. 94pp.

LERESCHE, R. E., AND R. A. RAUSCH. 1974. Accuracy and precision of aerial moose censusing. J. Wildl. Manage. 38:175-182.

MORRISON, B. L. 1982. New Mexico state report. Proc. Biennial Pronghorn Antelope States Workshop 10:28-29.

EVALUATING KILL QUOTAS FOR DEER USING MINIMAL DATA

DAVID EULER, Wildlife Branch, Ontario Ministry of Natural Resources, Queen's Park, Toronto, Ontario M7A 1W3, Canada

HOWARD SMITH, Wildlife Branch, Ontario Ministry of Natural Resources, Queen's Park, Toronto, Ontario M7A 1W3, Canada

Abstract: In 1980, after many years of any-deer hunting seasons, a Selective Harvest System was instituted in Ontario. Deer managers had previously controlled the kill through hunting-season length; however, that proved inadequate for proper management. The Selective Harvest System controls the kill by limiting the number of antlerless permits available to hunters. Often deer managers in Ontario have to set antlerless kill quotas without knowledge of the parameters they would most like to know. Reliable population estimates are not available, non-hunting mortality cannot be determined, and the percentage of the population removed by hunters is generally unknown. The only possible approach in this situation is to set quotas of antlerless kill by monitoring the harvest sex ratio. Although this is not a precise technique, if antlerless permits are issued so that females do not exceed 30% of the total animals killed, the chances of overharvesting deer in Ontario are acceptably low under normal winter conditions. If the goal is to increase the herd, keeping the kill at about 15% female is a realistic target.

KEY WORDS: Deer harvest, Kill-quotas, White-tailed deer, Hunting impacts, Harvest sex ratio, Controlled harvest, Population model.

For about 30 years prior to 1980, Ontario had any-deer hunting regulations throughout most of its deer range (Fig. 1). One white-tailed deer (*Odocoileus virginianus*) of either sex was allowed/hunter. In addition, hunters were permitted to use dogs to hunt these animals in most areas of the province. Manipulation of the hunting-season length controlled the kill; shorter seasons usually, but not always, meant fewer animals killed. This technique was reasonably satisfactory, except when severe winters reduced herd numbers. Following hard winters, the hunter kill was sometimes too high to permit herd stability or growth because it was difficult to gather evidence and convince the decision-makers soon enough to shorten the next hunting season. Difficult winters in 1971-72, combined with heavy hunting pressure, reduced the population to much less than the habitat could carry. Under this system the herd was unable to recover, and it was necessary to institute some basic changes in hunting regulations. In 1980, the harvest strategy was changed to an antlerless permit system, much like in other jurisdictions. The kill of antlered animals is not controlled, but a limited number of permits for antlerless deer is issued to hunters.

Calculation of kill quotas is a significant problem in the current system. Much of the data that would be useful for this purpose are unavailable. For many managers population size is usually unknown. The hunter-kill is not necessarily representative of the herd age structure (Coe et al. 1980), and

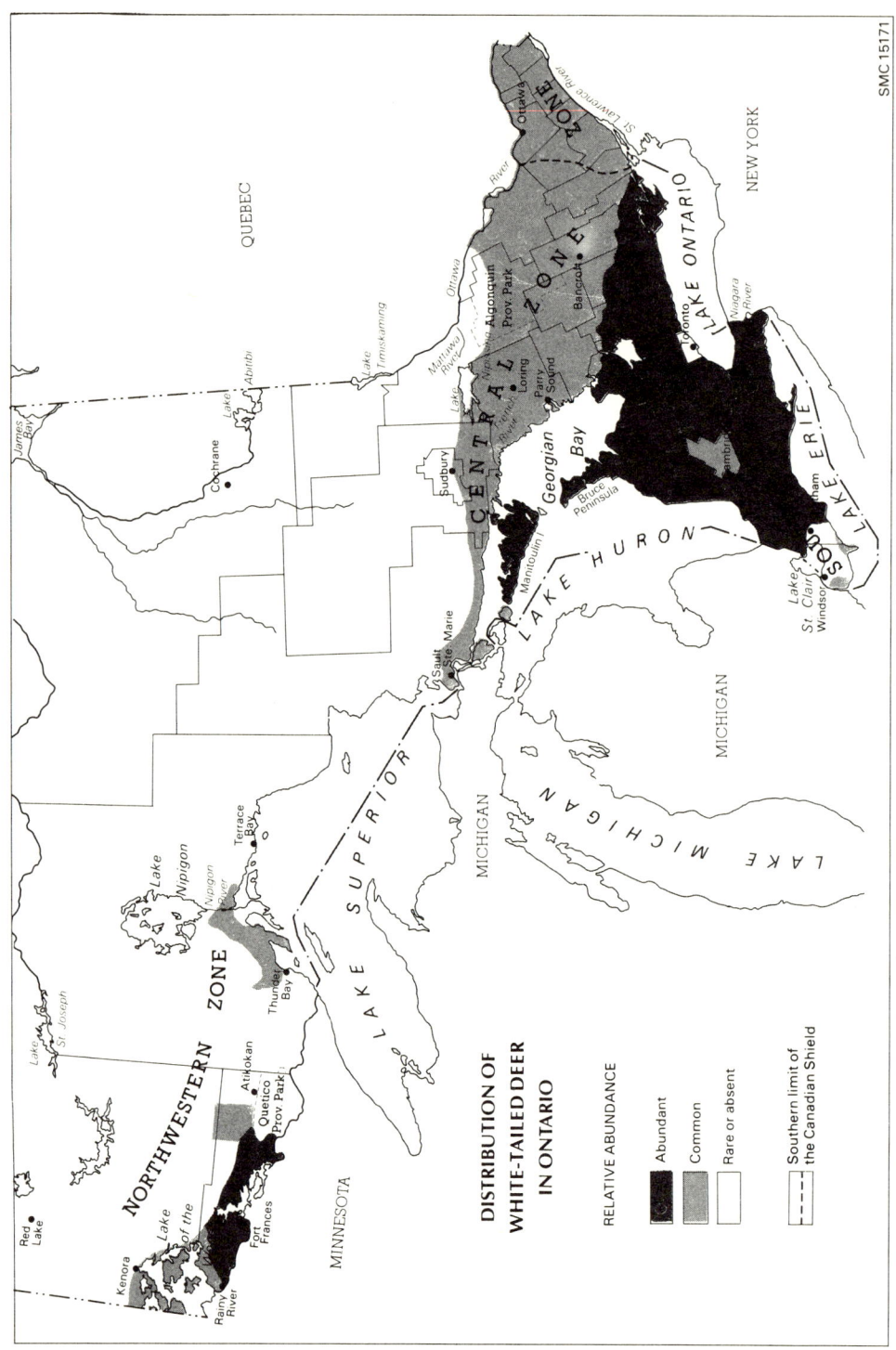

Fig. 1. Distribution and gross relative abundance of white-tailed deer in Ontario.

hunter effort expended/animal killed has not provided enough guidance to determine the relative size of the herd.

Kill/unit effort is sensitive to many factors, such as weather, herd size, hunter numbers, and probably several others as well; and the relationship between hunter effort and population size is not well understood. Pellet surveys are available for estimating herd size (Neff 1968, Ryel 1971); however, they are expensive to conduct. Further, many field managers doubt the validity of this technique and resist applying it. Aerial surveys have been attempted many times with few positive results. In the mixed conifer-deciduous forests of Ontario, the animals are not visible from the air, and many are missed in aerial surveys.

Even though managers do not have all the information they would like, they must still issue a limited number of antlerless permits to control the kill. They need to have a rational basis for that estimate. Tools useful in setting quotas include population modeling and population reconstruction (Walters and Gross 1972, Meddin and Anderson 1979, Williams 1981). For these tools to be helpful, information about non-hunting mortality is usually necessary. Downing's (1980) technique, for example, requires a reasonable estimate of losses to causes other than hunting. In many cases this type of information is unavailable.

Another approach when data are scarce is to set the kill quota based on the sex ratio in the harvest. Haynes and Gwynn (1977) and Paloheimo and Fraser (1981) provide some ideas that form the basis for a quota-setting technique. Downing (1981) has also reviewed some of the problems with harvest-sex-ratio techniques.

This paper evaluates how sex ratio in the harvest is useful in setting kill quotas under management conditions present in Ontario.

RATIONALE

For animals with a differential vulnerability to hunting, e.g., moose (*Alces alces*) and black bear (*Ursus americanus*) (Paloheimo and Fraser 1981, Fraser et al. 1982), the male:female sex ratio by age in the harvest can be used to estimate the percentage of the population killed by hunters. This estimate is a useful technique, particularly with black bears in Ontario, which are very sensitive to hunting pressure. A problem with this technique, however, is that some indication of non-hunting mortality or an independent estimate of population size should be made to evaluate the impact of the hunting on the population. If an estimate is unavailable, experimental manipulation of the kill is needed to evaluate the impact of hunting on the herd, a technique that is often impossible because of the need to maintain steady recreational hunting and the time delay in getting results.

Haynes and Gwynn (1977) demonstrated that it is possible to maintain a stable deer population with a harvest heavily biased to males. This is true if input into the population is about 1:1 male to female, the percentage of females killed in the standing herd is not excessive, 1 male can impregnate more than 1 female, and non-hunting mortality is not excessive. McCullough (1979) recounts that natality of these animals is adjusted in response to mortality and habitat condition so that a male-biased harvest is useful when the herd is below carrying capacity. He suggests that when the herd is at or above carrying capacity, any-deer hunting is as useful as a male-biased system because the deer adjust their reproductive rate to compensate for the hunting losses.

In the mathematical approach taken by Haynes and Gwynn (1977), the overall non-hunting mortality is set at 26%/year for all deer ages and sex classes. This constant is useful in illustrating the idea and in producing the equations that demonstrate how a stable population can exist under a biased sex harvest. Managers dealing with populations affected by predation, weather, and many other factors know that the mortality is not equal in all age classes and that it varies considerably each year.

An evaluation of Haynes and Gwynn's technique, based on a variety of typical Ontario non-hunting mortality and natality patterns, is helpful to managers thinking about using this technique. Such an evaluation assists in understanding the impact on the population by establishing a desirable harvest sex ratio. Models are useful for this purpose because mortality and natality can be controlled and the impacts of the strategy assessed.

METHODS

In this paper the technique of setting antlerless harvest quotas using only harvest data is examined with the aid of the computer model ONEPOP (Walters and Gross 1972, Gross et al. 1973).

Since non-hunting mortality rates for white-tailed deer vary with winter severity, a composite of rates for severe, moderate, and easy winters was used in the model. Rates were based on manager judgment and research information (e.g., Verme 1969) from a variety of areas (Table 1). The real rates are unknown, but those given here represent the best and most conservative judgments available for Ontario.

Other input to the model (Table 2) was derived from data collected by field managers and from relevant literature. Accuracy checks and measurements of precision of these data are often not possible because the expense and difficulty of collecting it presents substantial obstacles. The purpose of this technique, however, is to provide a method of establishing effective quotas when only best estimates are available.

RESULTS AND DISCUSSION

Figure 2 represents the results of modeling the Ontario situation. This graph, in the same format used by Haynes and Gwynn, indicates the combinations of hunting mortality rates that produce various proportions of females in the kill. In addition, the rates of fawn recruitment needed to

Table 1. Typical non-hunting mortality rates for white-tailed deer in Ontario (expressed as a percentage of animals alive at the beginning of the period).

Age class	Severe winter		Moderate winter		Easy winter	
	Spring-summer	Winter	Spring-summer	Winter	Spring-summer	Winter
Male:						
(1) fawns	75	52	40	27	17	12
(2) yearlings	10	30	5	15	2	7
(3) adults	10	20	5	10	2	5
(4) adults	10	20	5	10	2	5
(5) adults	10	20	5	10	2	5
(6) adults	10	20	5	10	2	5
(7) adults	10	20	5	10	2	5
(8) adults	10	30	5	15	2	7
(9) 10	100	100	5	100	2	100
Female:						
(1) fawns	70	50	35	25	15	10
(2) yearlings	10	30	5	15	2	7
(3) adults	10	20	5	10	2	5
(4) adults	10	20	5	10	2	5
(5) adults	10	20	5	10	2	5
(6) adults	10	20	5	10	2	5
(7) adults	10	20	5	10	2	5
(8) adults	10	30	5	15	2	7
(9) 10	100	100	5	100	2	100

produce stability are represented. Tables 3-5 show more explicitly the parameters of the population for 1 point on the F=0.40 line on the graph. The F-value represents the percentage of the kill that is female.

All points on the F-curves represent conditions where stability in the population is achieved at the specific non-hunting mortality rates, hunting mortality, and fawn production rates noted. In these simulations stability refers to a relatively close adherence to a given population size. When using the graph to evaluate a quota-setting strategy, the manager must first determine the fall hunt fawn:doe ratio. In Ontario, the fawn:doe ratio over the long term is about 1 fawn:doe (1.5 years or older) in the fall hunt. A safe line on the graph for Ontario then corresponds to the line reading 1.0

Table 2. Data input to the model as used in ONEPOP simulations for white-tailed deer in Ontario.

Initial age structure	1	2	3	4	5	6	7	8	9
N males	195	71	63	20	12	5	3	2	1
N females	195	80	121	59	58	42	22	34	17
Wounding loss	6% of the harvest lost to wounding								
Male:female fetal ratio	52:48								
Mortality sequence	Non-hunting mortality rates listed in Table 1 were applied in the sequence; easy, easy, severe, severe, moderate, easy, moderate; to reflect a typical sequence of Ontario winters								

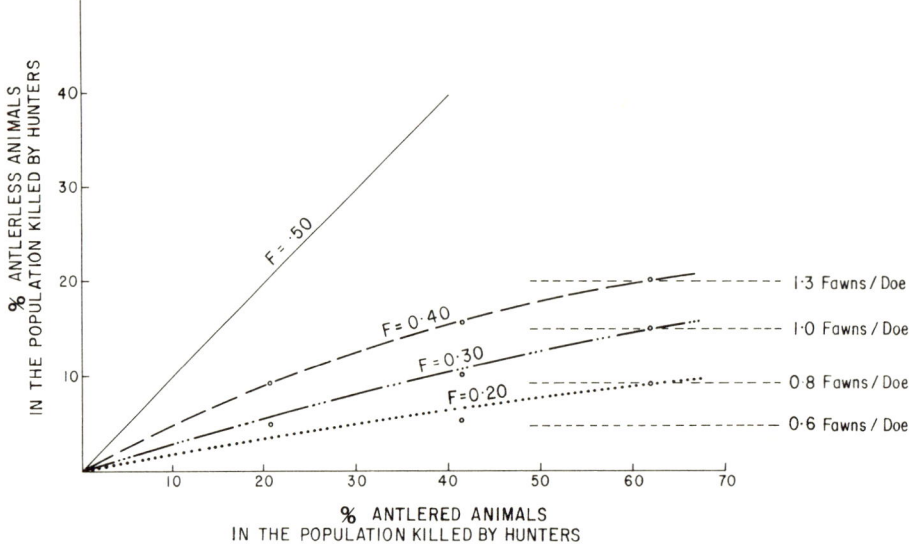

Fig. 2. A population of deer is stable when the percentage of antlered animals killed, the percentage of antlerless animals killed, and the corresponding reproductive rate meet at any point on 1 of the lines on the graph. Tables 1 and 2 show non-hunting mortality rates and other population parameters. The percentage of the harvest comprised of female deer equals F, and the reproductive rate is measured as a fawn:doe ratio in the hunt.

fawns/doe. Any point under this line is a safe area. That is, as long as fall recruitment rates average about 1.0 fawns/doe, then several combinations of antlered and antlerless kill rates are possible without causing the herd to decline. Up to 60% of the antlered deer can be killed, for example, if the antlerless kill rate stays less than about 15%.

By monitoring the kill alone, managers may not know exactly where they are on the graph. However, if there is a harvest sex ratio of 30% female, then at least they are somewhere on the F=0.30 line. The probability that the antlered kill is higher than about 60% in Ontario is very low. Deer density in much of the central and northern Ontario range is relatively low, and the hunting pressure is relatively light; thus hunters seldom take more than 40-50% of the herd's antlered deer.

Within these limits, a manager can then feel comfortable that hunting is not causing the herd to decline. In some cases, a harvest of 40% females would also be acceptable; however, more risk is associated with that kill level because a kill of more than 40% of the antlered population and more than 15% of the antlerless population could occur and would probably result in a decline of the herd.

If the percentage of antlered kill increases to values in excess of 60%, the risk of overharvest increases. The lines on the graph, however, are

Table 3. Deer population size at the beginning, prehunt, post-hunt, and the end of the year under conditions in which F = 0.40, as simulated by the computer model ONEPOP.

Year	Start	Prehunt	Posthunt	End	% change[a]
1969	1,000	925	738	669	
1970	1,364	1,239	993	889	36
1971	1,745	1,014	782	532	28
1972	1,090	618	486	336	−38
1973	706	550	443	357	−35
1974	727	660	529	476	3
1975	937	740	582	464	29
1976	917	835	663	601	−2
1977	1,170	1,067	842	761	28
1978	1,470	862	660	446	26
1979	901	515	403	285	−39
1980	597	465	374	307	−34
1981	628	571	458	413	5
1982	813	642	505	406	30
1983	804	732	581	525	−2
1984	1,022	931	735	661	27
1985	1,277	749	573	388	25
1986	784	448	350	248	−39

[a] Difference between start populations in each 2 years.

asymptotic; thus, the risk does not increase without limit. By simply reducing the harvest sex ratio target from 0.30 to 0.25 or slightly lower, the risk of hunting causing a herd decline is slight.

Table 4. Totals and percentage of antlered and antlerless deer harvested under conditions in which F = 0.40, as simulated by the computer model ONEPOP.

Year	N antlered animals in the harvest	% antlered population in the harvest	N antlerless animals in the harvest	% antlerless population in the harvest
1969	73	42	103	14
1970	84	42	147	14
1971	120	42	98	13
1972	60	42	64	13
1973	36	42	65	14
1974	45	42	78	14
1975	68	42	81	14
1976	67	42	96	14
1977	91	42	120	14
1978	109	42	81	13
1979	54	42	52	13
1980	31	42	55	14
1981	39	42	68	14
1982	58	42	70	14
1983	58	42	84	14
1984	80	42	105	14
1985	95	42	70	13
1986	47	42	45	13

Table 5. Totals and percentages of males and females harvested and in the harvest under conditions in which F = 0.40, as simulated by the computer model ONEPOP.

Year	N males in harvest	% male population in harvest	N females in harvest	% female population in harvest	% harvest which is female
1969	102	30	74	13	42
1970	138	28	93	13	40
1971	140	35	78	13	36
1972	73	34	51	13	41
1973	56	28	44	13	44
1974	74	28	50	13	41
1975	93	31	55	13	37
1976	102	29	61	13	38
1977	135	29	76	13	36
1978	125	36	64	13	34
1979	64	34	41	13	39
1980	48	28	37	13	43
1981	63	28	43	13	41
1982	81	31	48	13	38
1983	89	29	53	13	37
1984	118	29	66	13	36
1985	109	36	56	13	36
1986	56	34	36	13	39

The most serious disadvantage of this approach is that, if the harvest ratio is kept at 30% female and if the percentage of the herd killed is low, the resource is underharvested. This built-in bias to err on the conservative side puts the herd's welfare above the hunter's. For the manager who has very little data, this approach works quite well.

CONCLUSION

Clearly, a technique for developing and evaluating harvest quotas from harvest data only is relatively simplistic. However, for a manager faced with the everyday reality of inadequate data, this technique provides another tool to assist in quota-setting and evaluation. Even though a system using quotas based on harvest sex ratios cannot indicate how much or how fast a herd will decline or grow, it can ensure the manager that the probability of a decline due to hunting is minimal.

LITERATURE CITED

COE, R. J., R. L. DOWNING, AND B. S. MCGINNES. 1980. Sex and age bias in hunter-killed white-tailed deer. J. Wildl. Manage. 44:245-249.

DOWNING, R. L. 1980. Vital statistics of animal populations. Pages 247-267 in S. D. Schemnitz, ed. Wildlife management techniques manual, 4th ed. The Wildlife Society, Washington, D.C.

―――. 1981. Deer harvest sex ratios: a symptom, a prescription, or what? Wildl. Soc. Bull. 9:8-13.

FRASER, D., J. F. GARDNER, G. B. KOLENOSKY, AND S. STRATHEARN. 1982. Estimation of harvest rate of black bears (*Ursus americanus*) from age and sex data. Wildl. Soc. Bull. 10:53-57.

GROSS, J. E., J. E. ROELLE, AND G. L. WILLIAMS. 1973. Program ONEPOP and information processor: a systems modeling and communications project. Colo. Coop. Wildl. Res. Unit, Colorado State Univ., Fort Collins. 327pp.

HAYNES, D. W., AND J. V. GWYNN. 1977. Percentage does in total kill as a harvest strategy. Trans. Northeast. Deer Study Group Meeting 13:1-16.

McCULLOUGH, D. R. 1979. The George Reserve deer herd: population ecology of a K-selected species. Univ. Michigan Press, Ann Arbor. 271pp.

MEDDIN, D. E., AND A. E. ANDERSON. 1979. Modeling the dynamics of a Colorado mule deer population. Wildl. Monogr. 68. 77pp.

NEFF, D. J. 1968. The pellet-group count technique for big game trends, census, and distribution: a review. J. Wildl. Manage. 32:597-614.

PALOHEIMO, J. E., AND D. E. FRASER. 1981. Estimation of harvest rate and vulnerability from age and sex data. J. Wildl. Manage. 45:948-958.

RYEL, L. A. 1971. Evaluation of pellet group surveys for estimating deer populations in Michigan. Ph.D. Thesis, Michigan State Univ., East Lansing. 237pp.

VERME, L. J. 1969. Reproductive patterns of white-tailed deer related to nutritional plane. J. Wildl. Manage. 33:881-887.

WALTERS, C. J., AND J. E. GROSS. 1972. Development of big-game management plans through simulation modeling. J. Wildl. Manage. 36:119-128.

WILLIAMS, G. L. 1981. An example of simulation models as decision tools in wildlife management. Wildl. Soc. Bull. 9:101-107.

NEVADA'S USE OF CHANGE-IN-RATIO ESTIMATES TO ESTABLISH DEER HUNTING QUOTAS

MIKE HESS, Nevada Department of Wildlife, P.O. Box 10678, Reno, NV 89520

Abstract: In 1976, a full-quota deer-hunting system was initiated in Nevada. Hunter quotas in 30 of 34 hunting units were based on individual change-in-ratio (CIR) population estimates. The CIR estimator used included a simple annual model designed to fit the data that could realistically be collected. Independent analysis of Nevada's estimate technique conducted in 1978 identified that the estimates were sensitive to variations in all data inputs. The identification of sources of bias and the improvement of sampling techniques have represented a continuous process since that analysis. Herd composition was collected using helicopters; recent annual state-wide samples averaged 70,000 deer. Mandatory-response hunter questionnaires with a recent average annual return rate of 95% provided the harvest input. With minor modifications, the original estimate-quota program is still being used. Apparent population-estimate accuracy varies between units and years, based on comparisons of observed herd composition changes resulting from harvest removal and on subsequent population estimates. Units that encompass several distinct deer populations, units with poorly delineated migrations, and units with low deer densities present the most difficulty in making consistently accurate estimates. The post-hunting-season buck ratio, the estimated number of yearlings recruited, and the rate of hunter success represent the criteria used to determine quotas. Buck ratios, buck antler-point class observed in the harvest, and hunter success have risen since the implementation of the quota system. Despite the severe limitation of hunting opportunity that the full quota system imposes, a recent hunter poll found that Nevada hunters strongly support it.

KEY WORDS: Assumptions, Census, Change-in-ratio, Estimate, Model, Nevada, *Odocoileus hemionus*, Population, Quota.

The mule deer (*Odocoileus hemionus*) population declines noted throughout the western United States during the last decade (Julander and Low 1976) became most apparent in Nevada through reductions in harvest and hunter success. The hunter success rate for bucks fell to a low of 11% in 1975 under unrestricted buck-only hunting with some antlerless quotas. Public dissatisfaction with this relatively poor hunting success precipitated the 1976 adoption of a full-quota deer hunting system that restricted hunter numbers by specific management units. Prospective hunters were required to apply for deer tags that were issued through a drawing process. Tag quotas were established in 30 of 34 hunting units based on deer population estimates derived by using a modification of the Selleck-Hart (1957) CIR technique. Estimated population size, the estimated number of yearlings recruited into the population preceding the hunting season, the desired post-season buck ratio, and recent hunter success rates were the parameters used when developing the specific annual quotas for each unit.

This paper summarizes survey and inventory work funded by the Nevada Federal Aid in Wildlife Restoration Project W-48-R and the Nevada

Department of Wildlife. George Tsukamoto, Sam Millazzo, and Jim Jeffress contributed significantly during the surveys and analyses. John King reviewed the paper and provided invaluable comments during writing.

DEVELOPING THE CIR MODEL

Several separate management programs and research investigations were synthesized into Nevada's CIR estimator model. Nevada's deer management areas or hunting units that were established in the early 1950's were originally defined using county lines. Trapping-and-marking studies were conducted during 1950-70 to identify deer herd (population) boundaries (Gruell and Papez 1963). Management unit boundaries were then continuously modified to conform with population movements as marked-deer observations were accumulated. Some deer populations were relatively sedentary, making only altitudinal movements seasonally within the same mountain system, whereas other populations made large movements crossing wide valleys between distinct seasonal ranges that occurred in separate mountain systems. Management unit boundaries evolved that reflected most identified seasonal deer population migrations. Harvest data were collected by management unit using both a 10% hunter questionnaire system and a deer-tag, return-card system. Post-hunting-season population composition censuses were conducted from the ground for most large deer populations beginning in the late 1950's. Both buck:doe and fawn:doe ratios were collected. Annual spring censuses to obtain fawn:adult ratios as a method of estimating over-winter fawn mortality were being conducted for most herds by the early 1970's.

Nevada initiated a research project in 1973 to compare helicopter-census with traditional ground-census techniques (Tsukamoto 1977). Additional major objectives included improving composition sample reliability and determining optimum census timing. This project was still in progress when the quota hunt system was adopted; however, early results were instrumental in development of the CIR estimator model. The Ruby-Butte study, which resulted in the marking of 2,535 deer, allowed a comparison of the Lincoln mark-recapture method and the Selleck-Hart CIR to estimate deer populations (Papez 1976). Studies in the Pinenut Range during the late 1960's had shown that population trends could be tracked over time using the Sellect-Hart CIR (S. Millazzo, pers. commun.). Each of the preceding management developments or studies contributed to Nevada's CIR usage.

The basic Selleck-Hart CIR formulas used in Nevada were:

$$\frac{B - A}{K - A} = \text{decimal fraction of base population killed (does)}$$

and

$$\frac{K (B - A)}{B (K - A)} = \text{decimal fraction of ratio population killed (bucks)}$$

where

B = prehunt bucks/100 does,

K = bucks/100 does in kill,

A = post-hunt bucks/100 does.

However, the collection of consistently reliable prehunt buck:doe ratios was found impractical, even using intensive helicopter surveys. Although the rut was approaching during that sampling period, the behavioral segregation of the sexes was still sufficiently noticeable that sex ratio samples varied widely. Robinette et al. (1977) reported similar results for ground census of Utah mule deer for prehunt buck:doe ratios. Rather than continuing to collect prehunt buck ratios, an estimated ratio derived from a simple annual model that used the preceding post-hunt buck ratio and the spring fawn:adult ratio was substituted.

This adjustment is similar to the "1 sample" CIR method discussed by Seber (1973:347). Essentially, the model accounts for population removals and additions occurring between hunting seasons. The model is described as follows:

Step 1: CIR is used to estimate prehunt adult population (year 1). The post-hunt buck:doe ratio and reported kill are taken from census data. Estimated unreported kill and crippling losses are added to reported kill for the CIR input. The prehunt buck ratio is estimated from the preceding year's post-hunt buck ratio and the spring fawn:adult ratio.

Step 2: Hunt mortality, including reported kill (from hunter-return cards), estimates of unreported kill, and crippling loss, is subtracted from prehunt adult population estimate (year 1) to yield a post-hunt adult population estimate.

Step 3: Winter fawn mortality rate is estimated by comparing post-hunt and spring fawn:adult ratios. Ratios are obtained from censuses. Estimated winter fawn mortality rate is used to prorate estimates of winter adult mortality (by sex). Estimated winter adult mortality is deducted from the post-hunt adult population estimate yielding a spring adult population estimate.

Step 4: Spring adult population estimate and spring fawn:adult ratio are used to calculate a spring fawn population estimate. The spring fawn population estimate is added in a 1:1 sex ratio to the spring adult population estimate (by sex). No further adjustments are made for additions or removals; this estimate is a prehunt adult population estimate. Quotas and prehunt buck ratio are prepared based on this estimate.

Step 5: Following the hunt and post-season census, Step 1 can now be repeated using CIR to prepare a prehunt adult population estimate (year 2). After spring census the remaining sequence through Step 4 is repeated.

Step 5, which is the subsequential equivalent of Step 1, was included in the model description to demonstrate that 2 separate prehunt population estimates are developed within the model (Steps 4 and 5). The CIR calculations in Step 5 depend on the prehunt buck ratio derived from Step 4, but the kill and post-season buck ratio are obtained from independent surveys. The Step 5 estimate represents an excellent feedback for both the Step 4 estimate and the CIR inputs. This CIR-model system was standardized in 1975 with final revisions completed in 1977 (Tsukamoto and Millazzo, unpubl. data).

ESTABLISHING QUOTAS

The political climate in Nevada that resulted in the adoption of the deer hunting quota system is simply characterized. Nevada deer hunters lacked confidence in the state's past harvest management policies and demanded a more conservative approach. Particularly at the onset, the quota system was intended as an ultra-conservative strategy. The basic rationale that governed establishing quotas was that harvest would not interfere with any potential deer population increase. In developing quotas, all deer managers used 2 guidelines: the buck quota was intended to result in a harvest that did not exceed 75% of the estimated number of yearling bucks recruited into the herd from the preceding year's fawn cohort, and the post-hunt buck ratio would be maintained at or above 20 bucks:100 does. Token doe harvests were proposed initially, but public sentiment did not favor their adoption.

An allowable buck harvest (ABH) was developed using the population estimate that would meet both the recruitment and buck ratio guidelines. The quota then was calculated using a recent average hunter success rate for the unit involved. Assuming the estimate was accurate and the quota resulted in a harvest equivalent to the ABH, a post-hunt buck-ratio objective was predicted. Most managers eventually selected buck-ratio objectives that were higher than the guidelines.

In those management areas where deer densities were too low for collection of meaningful herd composition data, quotas were set that were intended to maintain average harvest levels, and only harvest was monitored.

STATISTICAL ASSESSMENT OF THE CIR-MODEL

The Nevada Department of Wildlife contracted with the University of Nevada at Reno in 1977 to evaluate the statistical precision of the CIR estimates and to recommend improvements in sampling and estimation techniques. The contract was completed in 1978 (Alldredge et al. 1978). The most germane findings of this evaluation were as follows:

1. Several CIR's were compared (Kelker 1940, Riordan 1948, Selleck and Hart 1957, and Paulik and Robson 1969). Given the same input data, equivalent estimates were obtained.

2. The sensitivity of the Selleck-Hart CIR was tested by holding all inputs but 1 constant and by varying the remaining input through a range of values. The CIR was found to be very sensitive to changes in all inputs except antlerless removal. This inferred insensitivity to doe removal has resulted in a cautious approach to antlerless harvests.
3. Estimates derived from field census inputs were tested for statistical variance, using the "propagation-of-error-method" or "delta method" as recommended by Paulik and Robson (1969:13). The statistical variance of the CIR estimates was found to be extremely wide. For example, in Nevada Management Unit 014 (the Granites), which was considered to have the best data base because of longer experience with intensive helicopter census, the 1978 prehunt adult population estimate was 912 animals with a standard deviation of 302.55 and an 80% confidence interval of ± 387. Much of this imprecision was identified as inherent to the CIR method since the variance in input samples has a cumulative effect.

Several recommendations were made for improving the CIR estimates. The continued use of Selleck-Hart was recommended because all CIR methods tested yielded equivalent results; Nevada was most familiar with Selleck-Hart. Although on occasion oversampling could be occurring during the spring composition censuses, for the most part larger population-ratio samples would improve the precision and accuracy of the estimates. Two-stage and inverse sampling strategies were suggested as possible improvements. More importantly, the degree of conformity to the assumptions of both the CIR and of Nevada's model should be improved wherever possible. Caughley (1977) outlined the implicit assumptions for CIR's:

1. The 2 classes are equally available at each survey.
2. There is no natural mortality between surveys.
3. There is no recruitment or immigration between surveys.
4. All removals and additions are recorded.

Because Nevada's method does not take a direct measure of buck:doe ratios before the hunting season, but accounts for additions and removals outside the hunt, Alldredge et al. (1978) identified new assumptions and proposed modifications of others:

1. Natural mortality is proportionally sex independent.
2. Immigration and emigration are proportionally sex independent.
3. Natality is sex independent.
4. Yearling survival is sex independent.
5. Crippling loss can be estimated or is negligible.
6. Doe kill can be estimated or is negligible.
7. Unreported kill can be estimated or is negligible.
8. Herd units are identifiable during periods of data collection.

The investigators felt that the basic assumption of "identifiable units" was the most critical and recommended that every effort be made to ensure that sampling on seasonal ranges dealt with a single population. In addition, research to determine levels of crippling loss were recommended.

SAMPLE AND ESTIMATE IMPROVEMENT

Continuous efforts to enlarge samples and reduce biases have been made since using the CIR to establish quotas. The original deer population-delineation work provided a good basis for meeting the new CIR assumption of identifiable units with a few exceptions. Several large management areas involving migratory herds were redefined in 1977 to guarantee that composition samples and harvests conformed to the known movement patterns of the populations. Certain deer migrations are not fully documented at present, and future trapping efforts using telemetry follow-up are planned.

Composition census work has received the greatest attention since adopting the quota system. Most of the original data used in estimating populations were derived from ground samples. Comparisons between ground and helicopter samples in Nevada found that the aerial samples were statistically more precise and were more representative of an entire population (Tsukamoto 1977). In the latter circumstance, helicopter surveys revealed considerable spatial variation in population sex and age structure, even in seemingly homogeneous habitats with continuous animal distributions. This variation appeared similar to that recently described for some white-tailed deer (*Odocoileus virginianus*) populations (Dapson et al. 1979). The helicopter survey reduced the chance of bias by facilitating the sampling of all population segments. Initially, because helicopter surveys could not be scheduled in all management areas, some flexibility in application of CIR was necessary to permit the use of several years' averages or intuitive inferences where actual population ratios were lacking or considered unreliable. As more helicopter time became available, game biologists collected relatively reliable data for the CIR input, and the use of average or intuitive data declined appreciably. Aerial surveys were scheduled for increasingly more management areas between 1975 and 1977. By 1978, all major deer populations were routinely surveyed by helicopter as soon as possible following the close of deer season and again in the late winter-early spring.

For the past few years, an approximate combined total of 600 hours of helicopter census has been expended annually during the 2 census periods. During the post-hunt survey, roughly 35,000 deer are classified for age and sex, whereas about 40,000 are classified for age in the spring. Recently, adjustments in survey schedules have been made to take better advantage of annual weather patterns and to allow survey of migratory herds before major movements.

Nevada's harvest-data-collection system has improved since the implementation of quota hunting. Deer-hunter-return cards presently represent the primary method of collecting harvest data. Before 1979, although return of these cards was mandatory by regulation, the rate of returns averaged only 60% because penalties for non-return were not enforced. New regulations that provided for the revocation of big-game hunting privileges during the next successive open season for failure to return a properly completed report card boosted the return rate to 95% in 1979. That reporting rate has been maintained to the present. During 1981-82, individual hunter-return reports have been compared with field observations of success and harvested-animal class in an attempt to measure unreported kills and hunter accuracy in reporting. Preliminary results indicate that despite a high return rate unreported kills may be as high as 15% in a given year. This comparison of observed vs. reported success will be continued for several more years.

Although the major emphasis since 1976 has been placed on improving sampling techniques, a research effort was started to determine the rates and causes of deer mortality from factors other than hunting; however, samples obtained were too small to draw legitimate inferences (Stiver 1978). Further research was impractical because of economic restrictions. The recent focus has shifted from applied research to a thorough review of mule deer management literature for estimates of mortality rates and to a substantiation of CIR model assumptions. The assumptions involving natality, mortality, and dispersal, which presume sex independency, may not be totally valid based on work by Robinette et al. (1957), Anderson et al. (1974), Robinette et al. (1977), and Verme (1983). All of the preceding investigations demonstrated sex differential rates in deer population parameters. Widely differential rates of yearling survival would invalidate the state's assumption of a 1:1 sex ratio that is a critical parameter since preseason buck ratios are not collected. More significantly, the estimated rates of crippling loss that Nevada has used in the CIR are minimal, particularly in view of research findings by Welch (1975) and Robinette et al. (1977). Any change in hunting-related buck mortality produces a directly proportional change in the CIR estimate.

DISCUSSION

The effectiveness of Nevada's CIR-model system to track deer population changes in order to establish annual hunt quotas varies on an individual management-unit basis. Considering the many variables that can influence the state-wide situation, perhaps the best means of examining relative effectiveness is to compare 2 units, 1 where the system works well and another where results have been less successful. The 2 units selected for this comparison occur adjacent to each other in extreme northwestern Nevada. Unit 011, which is actually comprised of 3 separately described units (011, 012, and 013) but which is managed as an entity with a commonly shared estimate and quota, is bordered by both California and Oregon. The second unit, 014, lies immediately south of Unit 011, which borders it on both the northwest and the northeast. Both units were included in a pilot full-quota hunt in 1975, 1 year before state-wide adoption; regular helicopter census was initiated in 014 in 1973 and in 011 in 1976. The 2 units differ markedly in topography and in the nature of the existing deer populations.

Unit 011 encompasses about 6,051 km^2 in area with elevations ranging from 1,432.6 m to nearly 2,407.9 m. The topography consists predominantly of high plateaus and rims interspersed with rolling mountains. Deer habitat is extensive but is considered of poor to medium quality. Deer are widely distributed with densities being relatively low except at the higher elevations. Two, and possibly 3, distinct summer populations may occur, but seasonal ranges and migrations are poorly understood. Winter immigration from California, Oregon, and other Nevada units has been suggested, but this has never been documented. Some winter emigration into California by summer resident deer may occur, but again no documentation exists.

In contrast, Unit 014, containing approximately 2,082 km^2, is about 33% of the size of 011. The Granite Mountains, a narrow, rugged mountain range typical of the Great Basin, rise from an elevation of 1,188 m at their base to slightly over 2,743 m on the highest peaks. Deer habitat is limited in extent but is medium to excellent in quality. Deer seasonal ranges are well-documented primarily because Unit 014 was selected as 1 of the study areas for the aerial sampling investigations and was surveyed intensively by helicopter at least biannually beginning in 1973. No evidence of immigration or emigration has been reported or observed.

Both areas are easily surveyed from the air since dense vegetative cover is limited in distribution. However, Unit 011 is more difficult to sample adequately despite a larger estimated deer population because of wider distribution, lower densities, and poorly understood migrations. During the past 7 years, post-hunt census samples in Unit 011 have averaged 529.6 deer (357-751), with an average survey flight time of 7.3 hours (5.6-8.8). By comparison, Unit 014 samples have averaged 739.7 deer (607-954) for the same years, with an average survey time of 4.2 hours (3.1-6.4). Figure 1 compares the average deer/hour figures for all post-hunt flights conducted in the 2 units. Experience of the observers in the unit, weather, and many other factors may influence these censuses, but the risk of collecting biased samples is obviously greater in Unit 011 than in Unit 014.

The population estimates that have been prepared for the 2 units since the start of the quota system demonstrate this greater chance for error. Comparisons of 3 differing sets of CIR estimates prepared for units 011 and 014 are presented in Figures 2 and 3, respectively. Two of the series of estimates for each unit are taken from the original CIR model estimates that were used to develop the hunt quotas. These represent the Step 4 (model-

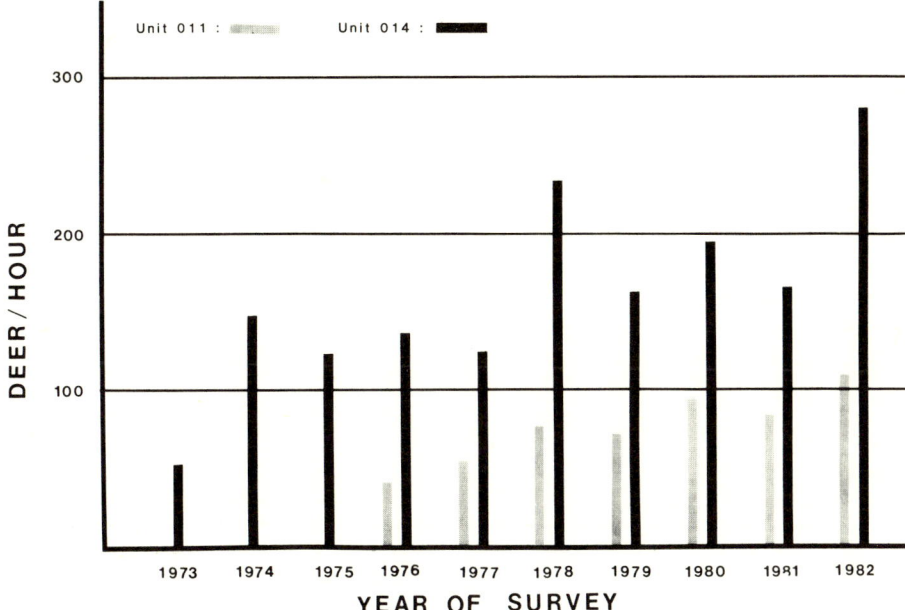

Fig. 1. Deer/helicopter survey hour in 2 management units in Nevada.

derived) and Step 5 (CIR) estimates. The third series of estimates in each figure is analogous to the Step 5 estimates but differs from them because only reported harvest (as opposed to expanded kill with added estimates of crippling loss) and ratios obtained from raw survey data (as opposed to substitutions of averages or intuitively based ratios intended to smooth estimates) are used as inputs.

Statistically, the estimates that yielded quotas were judged to be highly successful in tracking the Unit 014 deer population. Correlation coefficients comparing each of the 3 sets of estimates obtained in Unit 014 indicate good correlation in 2 of the 3 comparisons. One ratio substitution to affect smoothing was used in Unit 014 estimates; the correlation between the Step 5 estimate and the actual data estimate ($r = 0.794$) is strong (Crovelli 1973). The strong correlation between the Step 4 estimate and the Step 5 estimate ($r = 0.795$) indicates that the model-derived estimate is relatively successful in simulating actual changes in the population that the ratio changes indicated. The correlation between the Step 4 estimate and the actual data estimate is only moderate ($r = 0.591$), primarily as a result of the wide difference between the 2 initial-year (1975) estimates.

Similar comparisons of the Unit 011 sets of estimates show considerable variation from the correlations seen in Unit 014, as can be predicted by simply examining Figure 2. Little correlation is evident either between the actual data estimate and the Step 4 estimate ($r = -0.262$) or the actual data estimate and the Step 5 estimate ($r = 0.279$). Relatively strong correlation

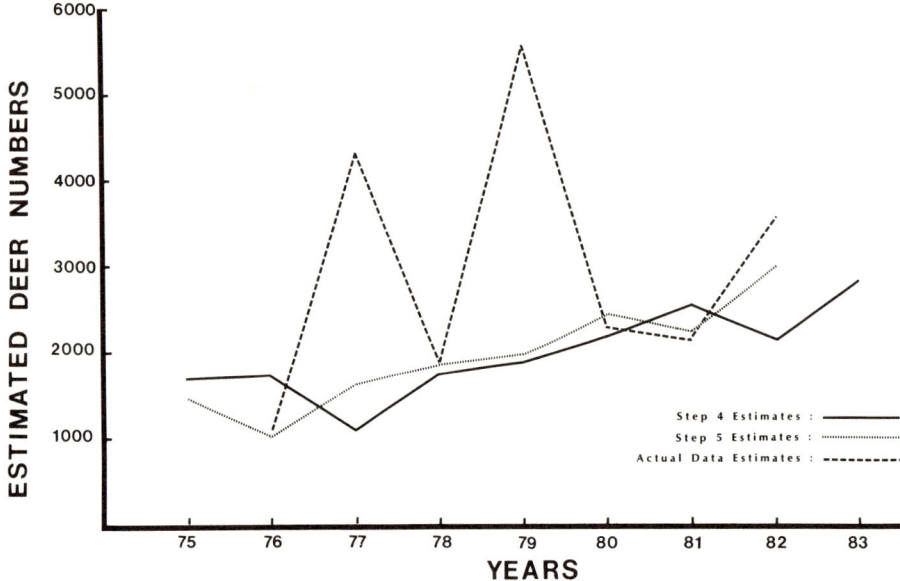

Fig. 2. Prehunt adult deer population estimates for Management Unit 011 in Nevada.

between the Step 4 and Step 5 estimates (r = 0.772) suggests that considerable smoothing occurred, which was in fact the case. Although the smoothing was justifiable from a management perspective (to prevent unreasonable gyrations in the quotas), the validity and accuracy of the smoothed estimates become questionable, particularly when the actual data estimate and the Step 5 estimate correlate so poorly.

Comparisons of the desired management objectives that the harvest quotas were intended to achieve and the actual results that were reported by hunters following the hunt yield some insight into the accuracy of the estimates, whether smoothed or not. Figure 4 presents the intended harvests and the reported harvests by year for units 011 and 014. The coefficients of correlation between intended and reported harvests are strong for both units, r = 0.862 for Unit 011 and r = 0.938 for Unit 014. These correlations between intended and reported harvest are similar to those documented by Lang and Wood (1976) for antlerless quotas in Pennsylvania; however, these types of correlations, when considered by themselves, could be interpreted merely that harvest can be predicted by quota size under given circumstances. The effect of the removal must also be examined to judge the relative accuracy of the estimator that was the basis for the quotas. Figure 5 compares the observed post-hunt buck ratios, and their respective 90% confidence intervals, with the expected post-hunt buck ratios that the quotas were intended to achieve. Using chi square to test the null hypothesis (P=0.01) that quotas based on the Step 4 estimates are sufficiently accurate to achieve expected post-hunt buck ratios, units 011 and 014 post-hunt buck

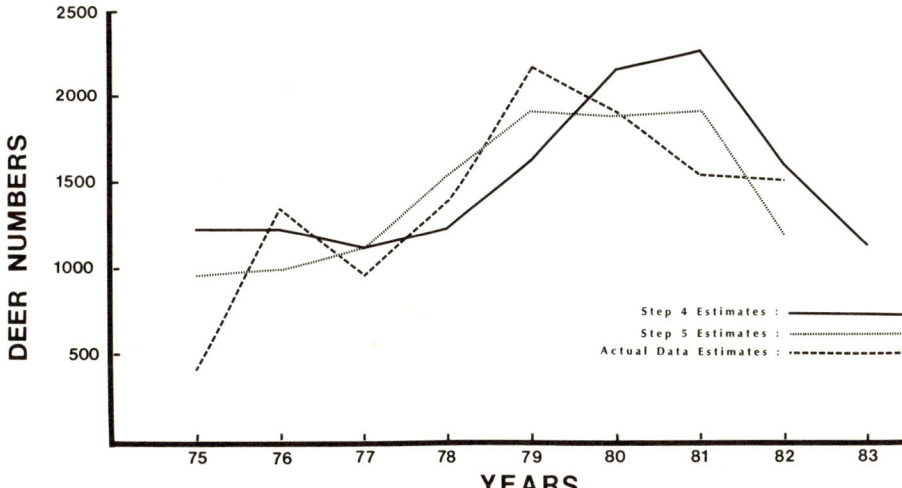

Fig. 3. Prehunt adult deer population estimates for Management Unit 014 in Nevada.

ratios allow acceptance of the null hypothesis. The acceptance of the Unit 011 results should clearly be tempered with the knowledge that the estimates were manipulated. However, the chi square result does appear to confirm that the smoothed Step 4 estimates track the Unit 011 population better than the actual data estimates. In theory, the larger quotas that would have resulted from the actual data estimates would have resulted in a greater disparity between expected and observed post-hunt buck ratios. Furthermore, the biases in the input data that were collected in Unit 011 are relatively large.

Seemingly inconsistent with the preceding evaluation, the best test of accuracy for the Unit 011 estimate would have been to have harvested heavily and to have affected a large change in the post-hunt buck ratio. Although this concept is nearly impossible to convey to conservative hunters and even to some game managers, the self-correcting nature of sustained CIR-based removals represents their greatest strength. If the estimates even roughly track the deer population, a much larger-than-expected removal should be easily detected in the post-hunt buck ratio.

A comparison of units 011 and 014 reaffirms the conclusion that conformity of the CIR method to its implicit assumptions is critical. Although the CIR model and the quotas are relatively successful in Unit 011, the level of uncertainty is higher than in Unit 014. The lack of definite knowledge regarding distinct populations and their seasonal movement patterns hinders the collection of representative-ratio samples. Superimposed on this "identifiable unit" problem, deer densities in Unit 011 are low enough that more intensified survey efforts would be necessary to reduce the sample biases. The expense of more intensified efforts in Unit 011 needs to

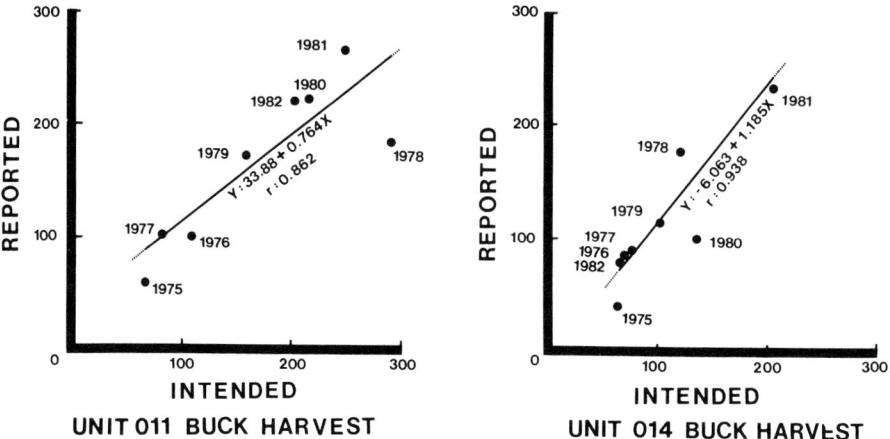

Fig. 4. Linear regression lines comparing intended and reported harvest of mule deer in Nevada.

be weighed carefully against the anticipated management gains that might accrue.

The effectiveness of the CIR model and quota system in the majority of Nevada's deer units falls between those levels seen in units 011 and 014. In a few instances where the assumptions are even more poorly met or densities are extremely low, Nevada is less successful in simulating the deer population than in Unit 011. Most interstate deer populations, although numbers are usually large, are poorly tracked because management emphasis varies between states.

The quota system imposed severe restrictions on Nevada deer hunters. Most obvious was the limitation in hunter opportunity. During the 6 years (1970-75) preceding the quota system, annual tag sales averaged 47,060 compared to an average of 23,441 for the comparable period after quota (1976-81); this latter figure represents a 50% reduction in hunter opportunity (Hess 1982). In addition, those hunters who were successful in drawing a tag in the deer lottery were restricted to hunting within a relatively small area. Conversely, a number of benefits to the hunter have resulted from the system. Buck ratios have risen throughout the state, although this rise is masked in the larger herds because of antlerless harvests that occurred before the quota. The age class of available bucks has also increased since the reduction in hunting pressure. Most significantly, hunter success that averaged 19% for buck hunters during the 1970-75 period increased to an average 42% during 1976-81 after adoption of the quota. In certain units success rates have reached and have been maintained in excess of 75%.

With the relatively large numbers of hunters unsuccessful in drawing tags each year (over 13,000 in each of the past 2 years) Nevada has attempted to be more responsive to the deer hunting desires of the public. To that end

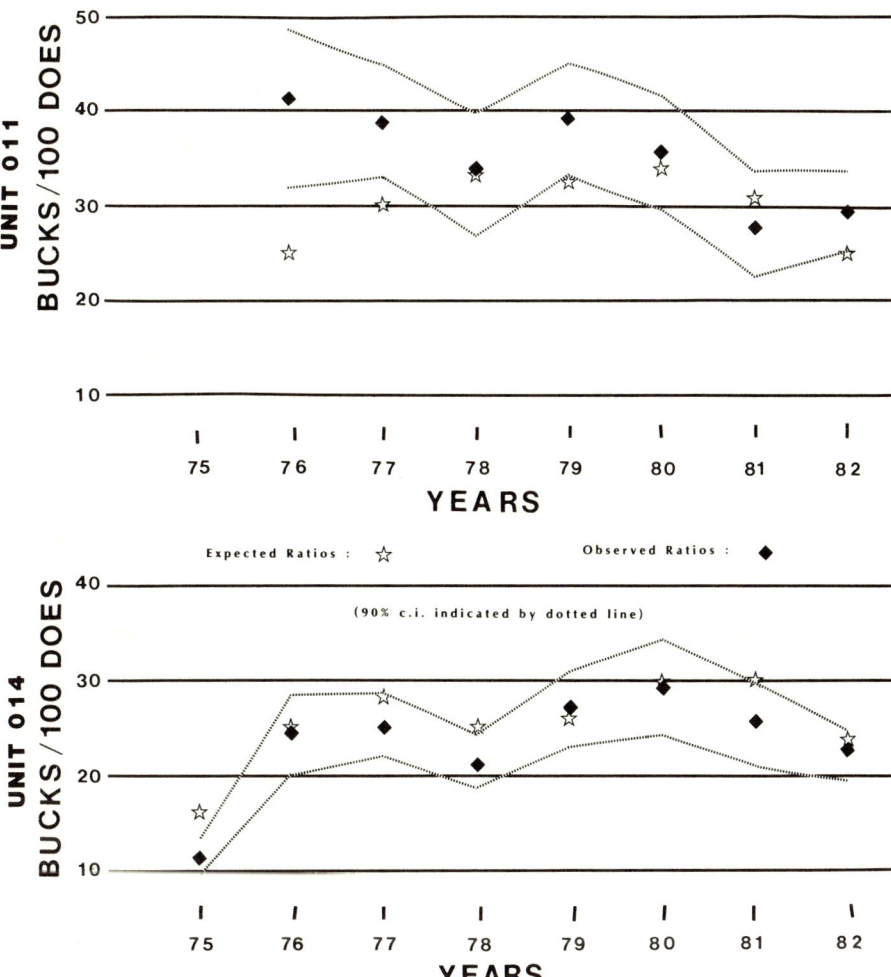

Fig. 5. Expected and observed post-hunt buck ratios in Nevada.

a random poll of hunters was conducted during the fall of 1982. Many questions in the poll dealt with the present deer management strategies.

The responses to 3 questions seem to best typify hunter attitudes, questioning bias aside. Seventy-nine percent said yes to the question: "Do you support a deer management program that attempts to match harvest levels to individual herd production?" Seventy-eight percent replied no to the question: "Would you favor more deer tags being issued knowing that hunter success and the point class of available bucks would eventually decline?" The third question asked: "Do you have confidence in the Nevada Department of Wildlife's wildlife population estimates program?" A total of 51% responded yes, 10% responded no, 20% were skeptical, and 19% had no opinion. While the responses to these 3 questions indicated hunters' attitudes, they were also interpreted as an endorsement of the quota system and the CIR estimates.

CONCLUSION

Although CIR's are generally recognized as 1 of the few techniques available for estimating population numbers (Davis and Winstead 1980:245) and their usage has been relatively widespread for limited situations, such as unit harvest estimations (Aney 1974), CIR applications for large-scale management programs are not well-documented. Pennsylvania's antlerless harvest program (Shope 1978) represents a significant exception. Of interest, Pennsylvania's and Nevada's CIR applications closely parallel one another although the deer species involved, the data collection methods, and the eventual management objectives differ significantly.

Based on Nevada's experience with CIR to establish deer hunting quotas for the past 8 years, the technique is an extremely useful management tool. Although it is inherently statistically imprecise, the CIR accuracy is related directly to a particular application's compliance with the basic assumptions. Despite possible inexactness in some assumptions, Nevada's CIR model is sufficiently accurate with present data collection levels that hunting quotas can be established that are commensurate with annual population changes.

LITERATURE CITED

ALLDREDGE, J. R., P. T. TUELLER, AND S. DEAN. 1978. Evaluation of methods used in determining deer population trends. Nev. Dep. Fish and Game. Job Final Report, P-R Proj. W-48-9. Study RI-A. Job 1. 12pp.

ANDERSON, F. M., G. E. CONNOLLY, A. N. HALTER, AND W. M. LONGHURST. 1974. A computer simulation study of deer in Mendocino County, California. Oregon State Univ. Agric. Exp. Sta. Tech. Bull. 130. 72pp.

ANEY, W. W. 1974. Estimating fish and wildlife harvest, a survey of methods used. Proc. Annu. Conf. West. Assoc. Fish and Game Comm. 54:70-99.

CAUGHLEY, G. 1977. Analysis of vertebrate populations. John Wiley & Sons, New York, N.Y. 234pp.

CROVELLI, R. A. 1973. Principles of statistics and probability. Prindle, Weber and Schmidt, Boston, Mass. 307pp.

DAPSON, R. W., P. R. RAMSEY, M. H. SMITH, AND D. F. URBSTON. 1979. Demographic differences in contiguous populations of white-tailed deer. J. Wildl. Manage. 43:889-898.

DAVIS, D. E., AND R. L. WINSTEAD. 1980. Estimating the numbers of wildlife populations. Pages 221-245 in S. D. Schemnitz, ed. Wildlife management techniques manual. 4th ed. The Wildlife Society, Washington, D.C.

GRUELL, G. E., AND N. J. PAPEZ. 1963. Movements of mule deer in northeastern Nevada. J. Wildl. Manage. 27:414-422.

HESS, M. 1982. Mule deer hunting under a statewide quota system. Proc. Annu. Conf. West. Assoc. Fish and Game Comm. 62:394-407.

JULANDER, O., AND J. B. LOW. 1976. A historical account and present status of mule deer in the West. Pages 3-35 in G. W. Workman and J. B. Low, eds. Mule deer decline in the West, a symposium. Utah State Univ., Logan.

KELKER, G. H. 1940. Estimating deer populations by a differential hunting loss in the sexes. Proc. Utah Acad. Sci., Arts and Letters. 17:65-69.
LANG, L. M., AND G. W. WOOD. 1976. Manipulation of the Pennsylvania deer herd. Wildl. Soc. Bull. 4:159-166.
PAPEZ, N. J. 1976. The Ruby-Butte deer herd. Nev. Dep. Fish and Game. Biol. Bull. 5. 61pp.
PAULIK, G. J., AND D. S. ROBSON. 1969. Statistical calculations for change-in-ratio estimates of population parameters. J. Wildl. Manage. 33:1-27.
RIORDAN, L. E. 1948. The sexing of deer and elk by airplane in Colorado. Trans. North Am. Wildl. Conf. 13:409-428.
ROBINETTE, W. L., J. S. GASHWILER, J. B. LOW, AND D. A. JONES. 1957. Differential mortality by sex and age among mule deer. J. Wildl. Manage. 21:1-16.
——, N. V. HANCOCK, AND D. A. JONES. 1977. The Oak Creek mule deer herd in Utah. Utah State Div. Wildl. Resour. Publ. 77-15. 148pp.
SEBER, G. A. F. 1973. The estimation of animal abundance and related parameters. Hafner Press, New York, N.Y. 506pp.
SELLECK, D. M., AND C. M. HART. 1957. Calculating the percentage of kill from sex and age ratios. Calif. Fish and Game. 43:309-316.
SHOPE, W. K. 1978. Estimating deer populations using CIR procedures and age structure data and harvest management decision making from CIR estimates. Trans. Annu. Conf. Northeast. Deer Study Group 14:28-35.
STIVER, S. J. 1978. Mule deer mortality and reproductive capability. Nev. Dep. Fish and Game. Job Final Report, P-R Proj. W-48-9. Study RI-B. Jobs 1 and 2. 30pp.
TSUKAMOTO, G. K. 1977. Evaluation of methods used in determining deer population trends. Nev. Dep. Fish and Game. Job Prog. Report, P-R Proj. W-48-7. Study RI-A. Job 1. 52pp.
VERME, L. J. 1983. Sex ratio variation in *Odocoileus*: a critical review. J. Wildl. Manage. 47:573-582.
WELCH, R. D. 1975. Mule deer crippling loss surveys, New Mexico. Proc. West. States Mule Deer Workshop. Silver City, N.Mex. 5:6-13.

SEX RATIOS AND HARVEST MANAGEMENT: A COMPUTER SIMULATION AND ANALYSIS FOR WHITE-TAILED DEER

BRIAN UNDERWOOD, Adirondack Ecological Center, State University of New York, College of Environmental Science and Forestry, Syracuse, NY 13210

WILLIAM F. PORTER, Adirondack Ecological Center, State University of New York, College of Environmental Science and Forestry, Syracuse, NY 13210

Abstract: Harvest statistics represent the largest population data base available to deer managers. Consequently the ratio of bucks:does in the harvest is widely used to determine antlerless deer kill quotas in harvest management programs. We address several aspects of a sex-ratio-based harvest management program through computer-aided sensitivity analyses and simulations. Model variables are age-specific natality, fawn sex ratio, fawns/adult female in the harvest, and adult male and female removals. The model is most sensitive to the level of adult female harvest and least sensitive to adult male removals. Harvest simulations show the relative influence of stochastic elements on population size. Harvest sex ratios alone are not reliable symptoms of population welfare. However, when combined with indexes to recruitment and population size, harvest sex ratios can be useful for prescribing future management.

KEY WORDS: Deer, Sex ratios, Harvest quotas, Computer simulation.

White-tailed deer (*Odocoileus virginianus*) populations in the northeastern United States have increased dramatically since the turn of the century. For many state wildlife agencies in this region, the control and maintenance of deer numbers have proven to be a formidable challenge. White-tailed deer harvests in New York alone have exceeded 150,000 animals in recent years.

Harvest statistics represent the largest population data base available to deer managers and have become popular for setting annual antlerless deer kill quotas. Several eastern states have adopted deer management programs in which the sex ratio of harvested animals plays an important role in the determination of future management prescriptions (Lang and Wood 1976, Burke and Winkel 1977, Hayne and Gwynn 1977, Dickinson 1982). Deer biologists in New Jersey, New York, and Pennsylvania have based their models on the original work of Severinghaus and Maguire (1955). Additionally, Dickinson (1982) has presented the mathematical basis for using certain harvest sex ratios for the determination of antlerless deer kill quotas. However, Downing (1981) has noted that misinterpretation of harvest sex ratios can occur unless care is taken in the application of this technique.

Our objectives are to address several of the key assumptions, applications, and important considerations of the sex-ratio models developed by Severinghaus and Maguire (1955) and Dickinson (1982). Through computer simulation we will define the driving variables used in the sex-ratio model and explore the effect of each variable on the dynamics of the model.

We are indebted to Kent A. Gustafson, State University of New York, College of Environmental Science and Forestry, for his computer programming expertise and input into this endeavor. We also thank Nathanial R. Dickinson, New York State Department of Environmental Conservation, for reviewing an early draft of this manuscript.

BACKGROUND INFORMATION

The relationship between the number of deer harvested and the number of deer in the prehunt (late summer) population is expressed in the equation (after Severinghaus and Maguire 1955):

$$\frac{AF}{AM} = \frac{M}{F} \cdot \frac{1}{X} \qquad \text{Eq. 1}$$

where

AF = number of adult females in the late summer population,
AM = number of adult males in the late summer population,
M = level of adult male removal (%) in the fall harvest,
F = level of adult female removal (%) in the fall harvest,
X = sex ratio (males:females) among fawns.

The number of adult females to be removed/adult male in the harvest (AF/AM HR) is equal to the ratio of females:males at birth:

$$AF/AM\ HR = \frac{1}{X} \qquad \text{Eq. 2}$$

Application of this harvest ratio can result in a stationary population size if the following assumptions are met:

1. The legal harvest is the most important cause of mortality, or other losses occur equally across sexes and age classes.
2. The sex ratio among fawns at birth and at recruitment is essentially equal.
3. Harvested deer represent a random sample of the prehunt population.

METHODS

Through a series of computer simulations, we examined selected aspects of sex-ratio-based models in deer harvest management applications. Computer programs were developed that calculated late summer populations, numbers of deer harvested by sex and age (adults and fawns), and post-hunt populations (Table 1). These algorithms were based on formulas provided in Severinghaus and Maguire (1955) and Dickinson

Table 1. Hierarchy of calculations performed in 2 computer programs that simulate white-tailed deer harvests based on a sex-ratio model (after Dickinson 1982).

1. Calculate adult females/adult male in the late summer population.
2. Separate adult females into age classes according to the percentage of adult female removal.
3. Assign reproductive rates (age-specific natality).
4. Calculate the number of fawns.
5. Assign the fawns a sex according to the sex ratio.
6. Harvest the adult male deer.
7. Harvest the adult females according to the AF/AM HR.
8. Remove the appropriate number of fawns/adult female in the harvest.
9. Determine the post-hunt population size.

(1982). Model variables were age-specific natality, fawn sex ratio, fawns/adult female in the harvest, and adult male and female removals (Table 2).

Two modeling approaches were developed, deterministic and probabilistic. The deterministic model included fixed variable values; to examine the sensitivity of the deterministic model, each variable was changed over a reasonable range of input values, while leaving all others at initial conditions. Observations of the number of individuals in each sex and age class and the time required for population recruitment to balance with the harvest were noted.

Two variables were selected for probabilistic modeling. Age-specific reproduction and percentages of adult male removal were permitted to vary in a probabilistic manner. These particular variables were chosen because we felt they most directly reflected factors affecting both population and harvest sizes (e.g., deer range quality and weather). Variants for each variable were derived by multiplying the standard deviation (SD) of the variable by a coefficient (between 0.0 and 4.0) and adding that product to the mean of the variable (Table 3). Selection of coefficients took 2 forms.

Table 2. Model variables and initial values for 2 computer programs that simulate white-tailed deer harvests based on a sex-ratio model (after Dickinson 1982).

Variable name	Initial value[a]	Variants[b]	
		$\bar{X}$	SD
% adult male removal[c]	80	80	5
% adult female removal	40		
Fawn sex ratio (♂:♀)	1.25:1.00		
Fawns/adult female in harvest	0.60		
Age-specific natality[d]			
Yearlings	0.30	0.30	0.037
2 years	1.40	1.40	0.125
3+ years	1.90	1.90	0.041

[a] All initial values after Dickinson (1982).
[b] Variants were derived from the means and standard deviations for each variable of interest. Variants were selected within a range of ± 4 standard deviations of the mean.
[c] Best estimate (after Dickinson 1982).
[d] Modified from Hesselton and Jackson (1974).

Table 3. Selection probabilities and relative frequencies of coefficients used to derive variants in a probabilistic model of white-tailed deer harvests.

Mean standard normal[a] deviation	Probability of[b] selection	Freq/1,000
0.00	0.07966	80
0.20	0.07808	78
0.40	0.07355	74
0.60	0.06658	67
0.80	0.05790	58
1.00	0.04839	48
1.20	0.03887	39
1.40	0.02999	30
1.60	0.02224	22
1.80	0.01585	16
2.08	0.01649	16
2.68	0.01088	11
3.00	0.00135	1
4.00	0.00135	1

[a] Represent positive and negative deviations around the mean ($\bar{X}=0$) under the standard normal curve.
[b] In the second form of selection, all coefficients had equal probability of selection.

The first form produced variants very near the specified mean of the variable by selecting coefficients in the lower extreme of possible values. The second form selected coefficients at random and, consequently, variants could differ greatly from year to year. Means and standard deviations for the 2 variables were derived from the literature or approximated when information was lacking (Table 2).

The first form of selection of values for reproduction and male removal was used in an attempt to mimic an average year while maintaining some likelihood of disturbance every 5-10 years. The second form was used for comparative purposes. Both programs were designed to simulate the manner in which sex ratio models are employed. All simulations were run for 100 consecutive years each to demonstrate trends in harvests. For each iteration, the model displayed the realized adult male removal (%), the assumed adult female removal (%), the applied AF/AM HR, the realized age-specific reproduction, and the ideal AF/AM HR (the ratio that should have been used to attain a stationary population size).

The probabilistic simulations were classified as uninterrupted or interrupted. Uninterrupted simulations were run without updating the AF/AM HR (i.e., the same AF/AM HR was used from year to year). Interrupted simulations were updated annually by changing the AF/AM HR to the ideal ratio calculated post-hunt the previous season. All simulations and analyses started with 100 adult males in the late summer population.

RESULTS

Statements regarding stationary population sizes herein coincide with Dickinson's use of stable populations. Both terms refer to the number of deer, not population age structures (Caughley 1977).

Sensitivity Analysis

Variable adult male harvests do not disrupt the stationary nature of the late summer population size (Fig. 1). The number of adult females in the late summer population is calculated from a known adult male harvest level. Because recruitment is solely dependent upon the level of adult female removal and the fawn sex ratio, a change in adult male removal alone affects only the initial late summer population size (see Eq. 1).

The model is most sensitive to adult female removals (Fig. 2). A 20% adult female removal results in a 3-fold increase in the late summer population size after 20 years. Overharvests result from adult female removals greater than 40%. For example, a 25% increase above the initial level of adult females harvested causes a 50% decline in the late summer population 8 years after the first harvest (Fig. 1).

Finally, changes in age-specific reproduction have substantial effects on total late summer population sizes (Fig. 3). A 26% increase in total mean fawn production (all age classes) causes the late summer population to increase nearly 1.5 times the initial population by the sixth harvest. The elimination of the fawn age class (1-year old at parturition) from the reproductive effort and a reduction in natality for older females (from 1.40 to 1.00 for 2-year-old females, and from 1.90 to 1.50 for 3+-year-old females) results in a late summer adult male population nearly 50% its initial size 5 years after the first harvest.

Harvest Simulations

In uninterrupted simulations, an AF/AM HR of 0.80 was used year after year to demonstrate the range of population fluctuations. Variants for the 2 variables rarely exceeded ± 2 SD in the first probabilistic form, and fluctuations rarely exceeded ± 15% of the initial population size (Fig. 4). When the level of adult male removal and age-specific reproduction were permitted to vary within a wider range of values (second probabilistic form), fluctuations frequently exceeded ± 25% of the initial late summer population size.

Interrupted simulations revealed that short-term population fluctuations were dampened considerably (Fig. 5). However, a downward trend in late summer population size was readily apparent when longer simulations were run. While population extinctions never occurred in the first probabilistic model over the 100-year period, 1 of every 10 simulations using the second form of value selection resulted in a population extinction. Nearly all

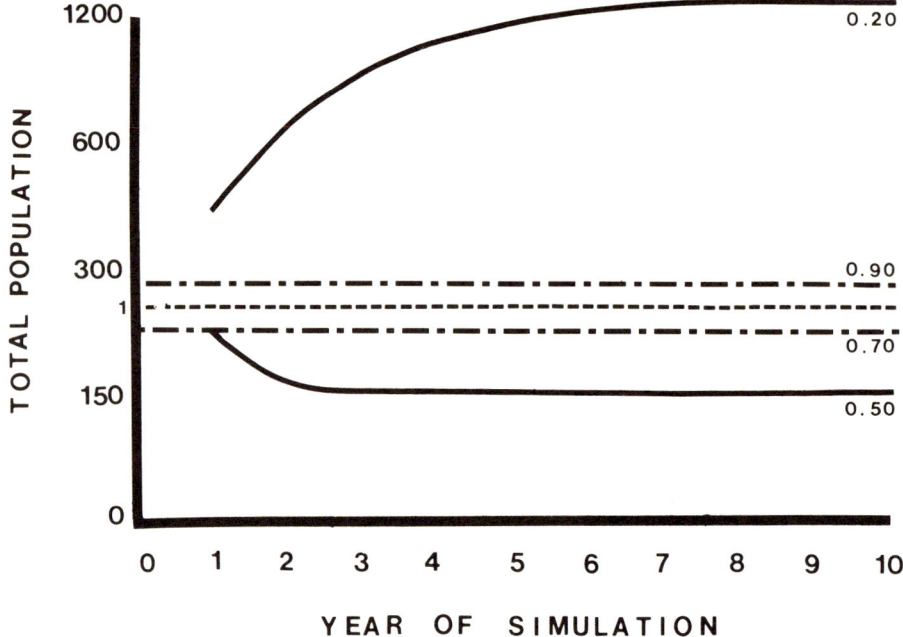

FIG. 1. White-tailed deer population response to simulated harvest. The solid line represents the proportion of adult female removal, and the broken line represents the proportion of adult male removal. The dashed line, marked 1, represents the stationary population size at initial conditions.

second-form probabilistic simulations ultimately produced late summer population sizes of 20 individuals or less over the 100-year period.

DISCUSSION

Sensitivity Analysis

Variables that cause large changes in model outputs over a reasonable range of input values are those that should be quantified with the greatest reliability. The deterministic model is most sensitive to the harvest of adult females. If the survival of adult females is significantly influenced by factors other than hunter harvest, then an attempt at quantifying or at least identifying other losses is important. This is especially crucial if those losses "drain" certain age classes within the female segment of the population. If mortality from causes other than the legal harvest can be partitioned so that all mortality is included, then the AF/AM HR can be adjusted accordingly (Dickinson 1982). If other mortality factors cannot be identified or otherwise accounted for, the AF/AM HR cannot be adjusted in an objective manner.

Changes in the fawn sex ratio can influence the population dynamics of a deer herd (McCullough 1979, Verme 1983) (Fig. 2). Although it is important to be aware of the circumstances that contribute to these changes, it is unlikely that populations in which harvest is consistent and well

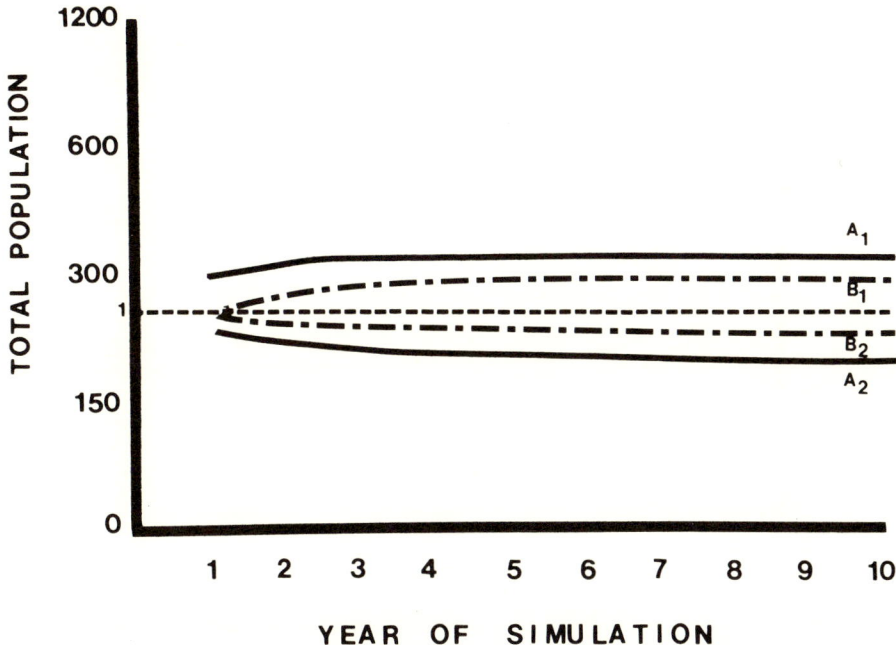

Fig. 2. Ten-year simulation of white-tailed deer harvest. The solid line represents 2 levels of fawn sex ratio: $A_1 = 1.00:1.00$, and $A_2 = 1.50:1.00$. The broken line represents 2 levels of fawns/adult female in the harvest: $B_1 = 40/100$, and $B_2 = 80/100$. The dashed line, marked 1, represents the stationary population size at initial conditions.

regulated experience major fluctuations in the fawn sex ratio. Significant fluctuations may occur in previously unhunted populations exposed to major herd reductions, heavily exploited populations, under-exploited populations, or populations exposed to large increases in food and cover requirements (McCullough 1979, Verme 1983). Fluctuations in the number of fawns harvested/adult female in the harvest are more likely to be dynamic. However, this variable does not dramatically influence the deterministic model (Fig. 2).

An increase in population productivity has a considerable impact on the growth of a deer herd (Fig. 3). Our model suggests that the incidence of fawn breeding is particularly important when evaluating deer herd dynamics. This observation supports findings from other research on deer population dynamics (Hesselton et al. 1965, McCullough 1979, Woolf and Harder 1979).

Harvest Simulations

The AF/AM HR that is actually applied in a particular year results from 2 stages of development. The first stage is the initial calculation of the harvest sex ratio performed immediately after a harvest. The second stage is the adjustment of the calculated ratio to accommodate changes in model

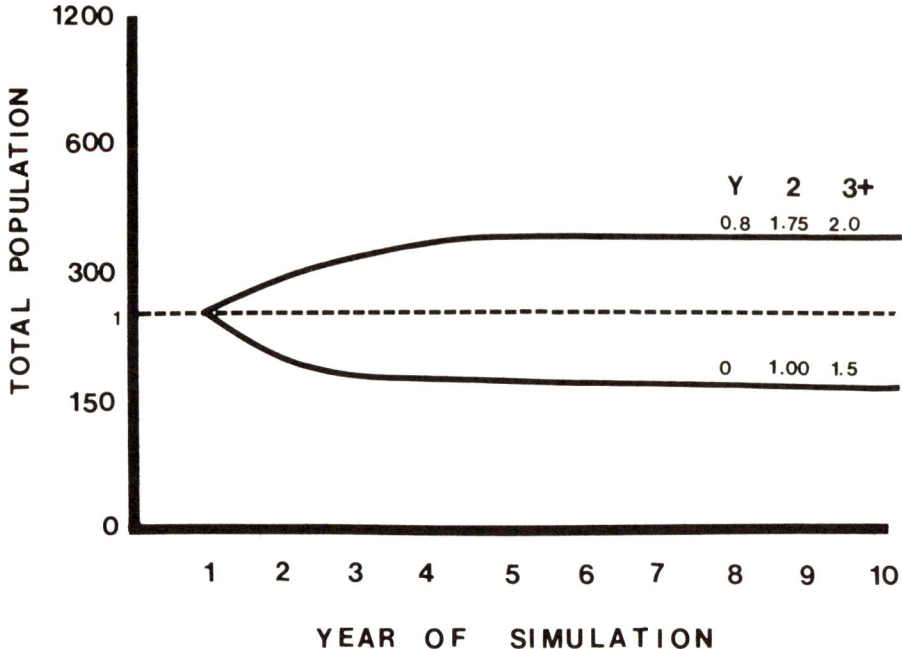

Fig. 3. Ten-year simulation of white-tailed deer harvest. This graph displays 2 levels of age-specific natality. The dashed line, marked 1, represents the stationary population size at initial conditions. Ages represent age at parturition.

variables or management objectives between posthunt 1 year and prehunt the very next year. For example, the manager may wish to decrease the AF/AM HR by some factor to compensate for poor recruitment due to an unusually severe winter. Figure 5 represents the application of AF/AM HR's from stage 1 development but not stage 2. Our ability to predict the values for age-specific natality and level of adult male removal is not adequate to demonstrate the stage 2 development of AM/AF HR's. Experience refines the manager's ability to anticipate changes in model variables from 1 year to the next. With variable adult male harvests and changing female reproductive rates, the application of a stage 1 AF/AM HR is not sufficient for proper herd regulation (Fig. 5).

Assuming that our probabilistic model adequately depicts a realistic range of population responses to changes in adult male removal and age-specific natality, we can expect the total late summer population to fluctuate as much as ± 15% within a 10-year period given a constant AF/AM HR of 0.80 (Fig. 4). In these contexts, 15% of 260 deer is almost trivial. However, 15% of 500,000 deer is a very different perspective. The appealing aspect of probabilistic approaches to population modeling is that the unrealistic constancy of the deterministic models and the extremes of purely random models are avoided.

In the interrupted simulations (Fig. 5), the probability of a harvest larger than the annual recruitment is always greater than the probability of an

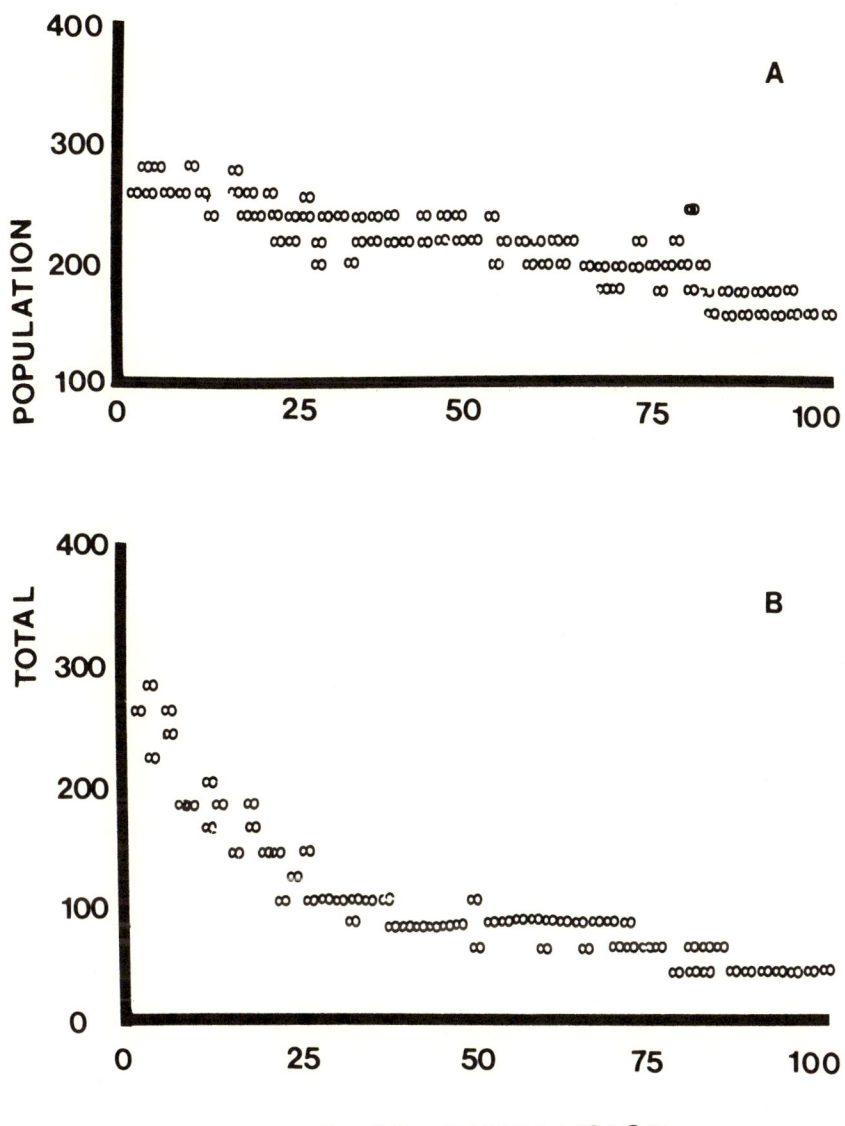

Fig. 4. One-hundred-year simulation of white-tailed deer harvests. Variants for adult male removal (%) and age-specific natality were derived from a restricted range of possible values (A) and a wide range of possible values (B). An adult female:adult male harvest ratio of 0.80:1 was used throughout the simulation (uninterrupted simulation; AF/AM HR=0.80).

underharvest within the range of variants for adult male removal and age-specific natality. However, if the updating of the AF/AM HR is delayed to every other year or longer, the population escapes overharvest and increases for several years before declining to low numbers. The longer the interval between updates, the more dramatic the population increase and subsequent decline.

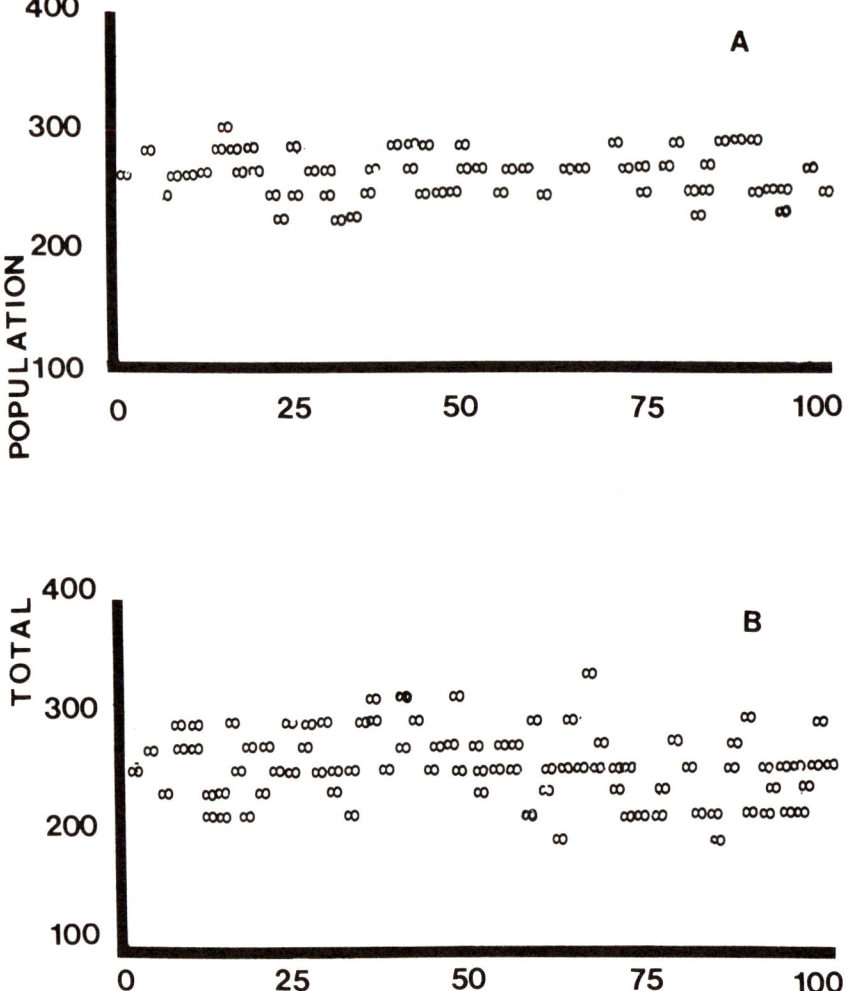

Fig. 5. One-hundred-year simulation of white-tailed deer harvests. Variants for adult male removal (%) and age-specific natality were derived from a restricted range of possible values (A) and a wide range of possible values (B). The adult female:adult male harvest ratio that was applied in each year was that which was calculated post-hunt the previous season (interrupted simulation).

A Management Example

A common misconception among managers is that shifts in the harvest sex ratio directly reflect changes in the sex structure of the prehunt population. Downing (1981) lists 6 possible scenarios that may explain an increase in the proportion of does to bucks in the harvest sex ratio.

Differential vulnerability, weather, hunting pressure, hunter success, and the combined effects of these variables make the proper interpretation of harvest sex ratios nearly impossible. It is apparent that the harvest sex ratio *alone* is of little diagnostic value. Caughley (1974) states a similar argument concerning the interpretation of harvest age ratios. It is the number of deer of each sex and age class that is important (Downing 1981).

The sex-ratio-based system described by Dickinson (1982), and others like it, makes reference to both population size and recruitment. For example, managers in New York implement a system in which 2 major indexes to population welfare are monitored. The first is an index to the late summer population size (Buck Kill Index) and the second is an index to natality (mean yearling male antler beam diameter; see Severinghaus and Moen 1983). The Buck Kill Index aids the manager in reconstructing the approximate size of the prehunt population. Mean yearling antler beam diameters transpose into reproductive rates for fawns, yearlings, and older deer via regression equations.

These 2 indexes, combined with information on hunting pressure and hunting success, provide the manager with a practical method of calculating antlerless deer quotas and have proven highly successful in areas where antlerless deer management is actively pursued (Dickinson 1982). In some management units, the response resolution has approached ±5% of the targeted goal. There is a 1-year lag time before the harvest data reflect changes in management practices, however (Lang and Wood 1976). This is caused by the *a posteriori* nature of this harvest management program.

Assumptions and Special Considerations

The assumption that hunter harvest accounts for most of the deer mortality is probably reasonable in areas that receive relatively constant hunting pressure and show good hunter success from year to year. If that condition is met, there is evidence that suggests that losses to severe winter weather may be minimal (McCullough 1979). The assumption that losses occur equally across age classes is considerably more tenuous, however. The Severinghaus and Maguire (1955) equation is dependent upon concurrent random sampling of each sex of the adult population. Because differential vulnerability between sexes and age classes is nearly always the rule, considerably more effort and money must be expended to achieve truly random samples. This is virtually impossible within the budgetary framework of most management agencies. However, in management units that receive moderate hunting pressure, a random sample of the adult population may be approximated if most deer are shot when encountered, regardless of their sex. Moreover, objective adjusting of the AF/AM HR requires that all mortality be accounted for, especially among the female segment of the population.

CONCLUSIONS

Harvest sex-ratio-based models can be useful management tools if applied correctly. In nearly all instances, ratios are *meaningless* unless they translate to numbers of deer harvested relative to the number in the prehunt population. Recruitment and other important population vital statistics must be quantified for sound management decision making. Indexes to natality and population size provide managers with relatively inexpensive, yet informative alternatives to the stringent data requirements of most sex ratio models.

LITERATURE CITED

BURKE, D., AND R. P. WINKEL. 1977. Deer harvest strategies in New Jersey. Pages 5-9 *in* H. Gillam and S. Coleman, eds. Proc. Joint Northeast-Southeast Deer Study Group Meeting, Boston, Mass.

CAUGHLEY, G. 1974. Interpretation of age ratios. J. Wildl. Manage. 38:557-562.

―――. 1977. Analysis of vertebrate populations. John Wiley & Sons, New York, N.Y. 234pp.

DICKINSON, N. R. 1982. Basis for using selected sex ratios in the harvest for deriving quotas for harvesting antlerless deer. N.Y. Fish and Game J. 29:75-89.

DOWNING, R. L. 1981. Deer harvest sex ratios: a symptom, a prescription, or what? Wildl. Soc. Bull. 9:8-13.

HAYNE, D. W., AND J. V. GWYNN. 1977. Percentage does in total kill as a harvest strategy. Pages 117-127 *in* H. Gillam and S. Coleman, eds. Proc. Joint Northeast-Southeast Deer Study Group Meeting, Boston, Mass.

HESSELTON, W. T., C. W. SEVERINGHAUS, AND J. E. TANCK. 1965. Population dynamics of deer at the Seneca Army Depot. N.Y. Fish and Game J. 12:17-30.

―――, AND L. W. JACKSON. 1974. Reproductive rates of white-tailed deer in New York. N.Y. Fish and Game J. 21:135-152.

LANG, L. M., AND G. W. WOOD. 1976. Manipulation of the Pennsylvania deer herd. Wildl. Soc. Bull. 4:159-165.

MCCULLOUGH, D. R. 1979. The George Reserve deer herd: population ecology of a K-selected species. Univ. Michigan Press, Ann Arbor. 271pp.

SEVERINGHAUS, C. W., and H. F. MAGUIRE. 1955. Use of age composition data for determining sex ratios among adult deer. N.Y. Fish and Game J. 2:242-245.

―――, AND A. N. MOEN. 1983. Prediction of weight and reproductive rates of a white-tailed deer population from records of antler beam diameters among yearling males. N.Y. Fish and Game J. 30:30-38.

VERME, L. J. 1983. Sex ratio variation in *Odocoileus*: a critical review. J. Wildl. Manage. 47:573-582.

WOOLF, A., AND J. D. HARDER. 1979. Population dynamics of a captive white-tailed deer herd with emphasis on reproduction and mortality. Wildl. Monogr. 67. 53pp.

A GENERALIZED SUSTAINED YIELD TABLE FOR WHITE-TAILED DEER

ROBERT L. DOWNING, 114 Lewis Road, Clemson, SC 29631
DAVID C. GUYNN, JR., Department of Forestry, Clemson University, Clemson, SC 29631

Abstract: The sustained yield table that McCullough (1979) presented for the George Reserve white-tailed deer (*Odocoileus virginianus*) herd in Michigan was modified to develop a generalized sustained yield model applicable to unfenced areas that employ long buck-only and short either-sex hunting seasons. The generalized model seems most applicable where habitat composition, soil, weather, and other density independent factors allow deer to reach their full biological potential. This paper presents a method to adapt the table to areas where poor habitat does not allow deer to reach their full potential. In spite of the dramatic differences in management between the George Reserve and more typical areas, there is remarkable agreement between their sustained yield tables. The broad range of densities over which yield remains high and the forgiving nature of effort-regulated hunting explains much of the success of past deer management. The threshold of fawn breeding may be indicative of optimum density.

KEY WORDS: Sustained yield, Yield table, Population model, White-tailed deer, *Odocoileus virginianus*.

Caughley (1977), McCullough (1979), Savidge and Ziesenis (1980), and Fowler and Smith (1981) have recently summarized the concepts of sustained yield management. McCullough (1979) assembled data for the George Reserve white-tailed deer herd in Michigan and presented a unique table that demonstrated how reproduction, mortality, and population structure interact to affect sustained yields (SY). Although the table was conceptually quite useful, many deer herd managers are reluctant to apply these results because the George Reserve was harvested differently and experienced fewer non-harvest losses than unfenced, less protected areas. We have relied on McCullough's work, other pertinent literature, and our own experience to construct a yield table that may be applicable to many deer herds that are harvested in the normal, buck-predominating manner. We offer advice for adapting the table to areas having poor habitat or other limiting factors, and for optimizing yield with other considerations, such as hunter effort and satisfaction, to achieve a better balance between biological and human needs.

METHODS

McCullough's (1979:118) table was modified by expressing population sizes as relative population density (percentage of maximum sustainable density), population composition as percentages, and reproduction and mortality as rates rather than as numbers (Table 1). These modifications make it possible to compare the vital statistics of deer in areas of different size or quality

Table 1. Yield table for the George Reserve, Michigan, white-tailed deer herd, revised from McCullough (1979).

Density N^a or % maximum (Geo. Res. N)	Posthunt population composition			Embryos/ fawn ♀ N	Embryos/ adult ♀ N	Total N embryos	Fawn sex ratio % ♂	Non-harvest mortality		Rate of increase[b] %	Total SY
	Adult and yearling ♂ %	Fawn ♀ (8 month) %	Adult ♀ (20+ month) %					Adult %	Fawn %		
(17.6) 10	48	27	25	1.44	1.90	8.9	53	0	0	89	8.9
(35.2) 20	48	21	31	1.19	1.81	16.1	53	0	0	81	16.1
(52.8) 30	48	20	32	0.89	1.70	21.6	53	0	0	72	21.6
(70.4) 40	48	20	32	0.59	1.60	25.4	53	0	0	64	25.4
(88.0) 50	48	19	33	0.29	1.49	27.3	53	0	0	55	27.3
(99.0) 56.2	48	19	33	0.10	1.43	27.7	53	0	0	49	27.7 (MSY)
(105.6) 60	48	18	34	0.04	1.37	28.2	53	0	3	45	27.2
(123.2) 70	48	16	36	0	1.21	30.9	53	1	16	36	25.2
(140.8) 80	48	12	40	0	1.01	32.3	53	3	30	25	20.3
(158.4) 90	48	9	43	0	0.79	30.9	53	6	43	13	12.1
(176.0) 100	48	5	47	0	0.55	26.0	53	11	57	0	0.2

[a] N yearlings and adults in an area capable of supporting 100 deer.
[b] If no harvest taken.

where relative population density is more comparable than other expressions of population size or density. In Table 2, we expressed harvest and non-harvest losses by age and sex. Separate rates of non-harvest mortality are needed where the various sex-age classes are harvested at different rates because hunting often compensates for non-harvest losses; thus, non-harvest mortality rates may be unequal by sex and age if harvest rates are unequal. McCullough had little need to present non-harvest losses by sex because the harvest was non-selective and because few non-harvest losses were recorded.

We used slightly higher adult ($\geq$ 24 months of age) reproductive rates than McCullough because of the evidence (McDowell 1970, Harder 1980) that many deer herds had higher reproductive rates than the George Reserve herd demonstrated. We dropped the reproductive rate of 0.55 fawns/doe at maximum density extrapolated by McCullough because we knew of no other reports of adult reproductive rates below 0.9. McCullough found a better correlation between reproductive rates and doe density than with total density suggesting the influence of niche separation by sex. The bucks-only hunting that we employed (at 90% relative density in our model) caused adult doe density to be higher at 90% density than at 100%. Undecided about whether to let reproductive rates change with total density or with doe density, we compromised by assuming the same reproductive rate at both the 90 and 100% relative densities.

We used fawn reproductive rates that were considerably lower than those McCullough reported. The highest fawn reproductive rate measured at the George Reserve was 0.73 embryos/doe at a relative density near 35%. We chose a maximum rate of 0.9 fawns/doe because it was the highest rate we had seen reported (1.21 embryos/pregnant doe, with only 74% pregnant = 0.9 [Haugen 1975]). We agreed with McCullough that fawns rarely breed at densities above 60%.

McCullough did not vary the fawn sex ratio with density because the regression was statistically different from zero only at the 94% confidence level. Nevertheless, he stated that the trend was clear, and the relationship could not be ignored. Other work, especially the analysis by Verme (1983), convinced us that male fawns are likely to predominate at high densities, whereas females generally predominate at low densities. We used a similar range of fawn sex ratios in our generalized sustained yield model.

The most important departure of our model from McCullough's was the manner in which the deer were harvested. The George Reserve was harvested non-selectively, whereas most states with which we are familiar have prolonged seasons for antlered bucks only. Buck-only hunting was the only harvest we modeled at the 90% relative density because many herds have been managed in this manner, and all of the SY can be removed by harvesting bucks only. Lower densities were modeled using a 70% harvest of antlered bucks and as much antlerless harvest as needed to stabilize density. Although differential vulnerability of fawns and does has not been

Table 2. Generalized sustained yield table for the white-tailed deer.

Density % maximum or N^a	Fawning season population composition					Total N fawns born	Fawn sex ratio % ♂	Non-harvest losses (Mortality + dispersal)			Rate of increase[b] %	Sustainable yield			
	Adult and yearling ♂ %	Yearling ♀ (12 month) %	Adult ♀ (24+ month) %	Fawns/ yearling ♀ N	Fawns/ adult ♀ N			Adult ♂ %	Adult ♀ %	Fawns %		Adult ♂[c] N	Adult ♀ N	Fawns N	Total N
10	34	33	33	0.9	2.0	9.6	42	2	4	10	82	2.3	3.0	2.9	8.2
20	34	31	35	0.8	1.9	18.3	44	3	5	12	76	4.6	5.6	5.0	15.2
30	34	29	37	0.7	1.8	26.1	46	4	6	14	69	6.9	7.5	6.3	20.7
40	34	26.5	39.5	0.5	1.7	32.2	48	5	7	16	62	9.0	8.8	6.7	24.5
50	33.5	24	42.5	0.3	1.6	37.6	50	6	8	18	54	11.0	9.5	6.7	27.2
60	33	21.5	45.5	0.1	1.5	42.2	52	7	9	22	47	12.9	9.3	5.8	28.0 (MSY)
70	31.5	19.5	49	0	1.4	48.0	54	8	10	29	40	14.2	8.6	4.8	27.6
80	28.5	16.5	55	0	1.2	52.8	56	9	12	38	30	14.5	6.4	2.9	23.8
90	23	12	65	0	0.9	53.6	58	10	15	52	14	12.8	0	0	12.8
100	48	8	44	0	0.9	39.6	58	23	15	52	0	0	0	0	0

[a] N yearlings and adults in an area capable of supporting 100 deer.
[b] If no harvest taken.
[c] Buck harvest is a constant 70%.

accurately measured (see Coe et al. 1980), we chose to harvest fawns at only 70% as high a rate as adult does, a differential often revealed when a population is reconstructed (Downing 1980).

We found it difficult to estimate "typical" rates of non-harvest loss because few such losses have been measured. The rate of non-harvest loss for maximum density was most easily chosen because, by definition, it must "balance" reproduction. The very low rates of non-harvest loss at the lower densities represent the biological potential of white-tailed deer where density independent factors, such as soil and climate, are not limiting. However, non-harvest losses were never assumed to be zero, as McCullough reported, because few herds are enclosed and as well protected as the George Reserve. Initial (spring) population composition was obtained by trial and error as dictated by whether each trial composition, under the influence of the assumed reproductive and mortality rates, remained stable year after year.

RESULTS AND DISCUSSION

Although our generalized model (Table 2) represents a vastly different situation than McCullough's, the 2 models offer remarkably similar messages for managers. In both, maximum sustained yield (MSY) was achieved at similar densities. They also demonstrate a broad-topped peak or "plateau" of SY within 85-90% of MSY that spans a considerable range of densities, from 40 to 70% at George Reserve and from 40 to 80% in Table 2. This characteristically wide margin of error, so to speak, may explain the wide-ranging success of deer management programs. Once buck-only hunting, typified by the 90% density (Table 2), was abandoned and harvesting significant numbers of does and fawns (80% density and below) was begun, reproduction was stimulated and non-harvest mortality was reduced to the extent that herds were remarkably tolerant of all but the most extreme mismanagement. For example, a herd inadvertently reduced to 30% density has a SY that is almost 75% of MSY. This concept of a broad "plateau" of yields near mid-density should apply to all deer herds and to many other species as well, even though reproductive and mortality rates vary considerably.

We lack confidence in the applicability of our table to low density deer herds because few such herds have been intensively studied. Furthermore, there are areas with poor habitats where high reproductive rates, such as those used with the lower relative densities in the generalized model, have never been recorded. Seemingly, the full biological potential of the white-tailed deer cannot be achieved on such sites.

The generalized model can be modified to better approximate conditions where a density independent factor, such as poor habitat, will not allow deer herds to reach their full biological potential. For example, suppose that the highest reproductive rate, recorded at low density, on a particular site is 0.7 fawns/doe for yearlings and 1.8 fawns/doe for adults, corresponding to statistics observed at the 30% relative density level in Table 2. Reproductive rates consistent with the 2 lowest relative densities (10 and 20%) seem unobtainable so the remaining 8 steps of the table must be stretched over the entire range of densities at 12.5% (100÷8) intervals (Table 3). This "poor habitat" model results in lower sustained yields at all densities, as expected, but otherwise it is similar to the generalized model. MSY is achieved at the 62.5% density, and there is a "plateau" of yields within 80% of MSY that spans the range from 37.5 to 75% relative densities.

Table 2 also may not seem appropriate where poaching, predation, and accidental deaths are prevalent. However, Table 2 may apply if such losses are considered part of the sustainable yield. Unfortunately, the loss of an unknown portion makes the remainder of the yield, the legal harvest, difficult if not impossible to prescribe accurately.

Assuming that errors in prescribing an appropriate harvest are inevitable, let us consider what mechanisms are available to compensate for these mistakes. As Caughley (1977) pointed out, if population density is above the point where MSY is achieved, constant (fixed) harvests less than MSY but inappropriate for the density will cause density to self-correct slowly toward an appropriate balance with yield. Therefore, populations above MSY density are generally stable. On the other hand, populations at or below MSY density are inherently unstable—a series of constant harvests greater than SY will soon extirpate the population, whereas constant harvests less than SY will cause density to swing rather abruptly across the yield curve to the appropriate density on the opposite side.

However, the above comparisons of the relative stability of the 2 arms of the yield curve do not take into account the regulatory effect of changing deer density and the accompanying changes in hunter efficiency. Holsworth (1973) presented data showing that hunting efficiency declined proportionately with declining deer density, and we used these data (Table 4) to compute the hunter effort required to remove each SY in Table 2. Even though Holsworth's data were based on either-sex hunting and our SY's are predicted on a combination of either-sex and buck-only hunts, we feel the comparisons between densities are useful. The fact that hunter effort continues to increase below 60% relative density, even though yield declines, suggests a self-limiting mechanism. A limit imposed on hunter effort may be all that is needed to prevent the population from declining excessively. We simulated a typical "mistake" by prescribing 25% more hunter effort than is actually required to remove MSY and found that this extra effort caused the population to slowly decline and stabilize in about 15 years at 44% relative density. The yield at this level was reduced only 8.6% from MSY.

In contrast, if the manager had prescribed that a constant *number* of deer be removed, and the number chosen was mistakenly 25% higher than MSY, the population would have been extirpated in only 5 years. This comparison between prescribing constant hunter effort and prescribing a

Table 3. Mathematics involved in stretching the higher 8 steps of Table 2 over the entire range of densities, simulating the "poor habitat" limitation on a white-tailed deer's biological potential.

10-step density	8-step density	SY multiplier	10-step SY	8-step SY
30	12.5	12.5/30 = 0.417	20.7	8.6
40	25.0	25/40 = 0.625	24.5	15.3
50	37.5	37.5/50 = 0.750	27.2	20.4
60	50.0	50/60 = 0.833	28.0	23.3
70	62.5	62.5/70 = 0.893	27.6	24.6
80	75.0	75/80 = 0.937	23.8	22.3
90	87.5	87.5/90 = 0.972	12.8	12.4
100	100.0	100/100 = 1.000	0	0

constant number for removal demonstrates that the constant number should be avoided because it is not forgiving of mistakes at or below densities yielding MSY.

We suspect that hunter efficiency does not decline in proportion to the decline in deer density under special conditions where cover is sparse and heavily used by both deer and hunters, where tracking snow allows the hunter to maintain contact with deer, and where dogs are used to drive deer past the hunter. Deer density should be constantly monitored and hunter effort should be cautiously prescribed in such situations, but we cannot visualize a situation where the hunter-effort prescription would be more sensitive to error than a prescription calling for a constant number of deer to be harvested. When in doubt, prescriptions should be based on hunter-days, not numbers of deer.

CONCLUSIONS

Even though deer populations are forgiving of mistakes in the amount of effort prescribed during harvests, the manager must have a management objective (such as to harvest MSY) and endeavor to confirm that a

Table 4. Hunter effort required to harvest deer at various deer densities, based on data from Holsworth (1973).

% density	Kill/hour (densities)	Table 2 SY	Hunter effort to take SY (hours)	Hunter effort/ deer (hours)
10	0.06 (10-20)	8.2	136.7	16.7
20	0.12 (20-30)	15.2	112.2	7.4
30	0.18 (30-40)	20.7	99.6	4.8
40	0.24 (40-50)	24.5	87.5	3.6
50	0.30 (50-60)	27.2	78.2	2.9
60	0.36 (60-70)	28.0	68.2	2.4
70	0.42 (70-80)	27.6	58.7	2.1
80	0.48 (80-90)	23.8	45.6	1.9
90	0.54 (90-100)	12.8	23.2	1.8
100	0.60 (100+)	0		

population consistent with this objective is being maintained. The fact that there is a broad "plateau" of yields near MSY amply demonstrates that the yield itself is a very insensitive and, therefore, poor indicator of population status. The most sensitive indicator seems to be the incidence of breeding by fawns which has its threshold at about the same density that produces MSY. Fawn breeding can be monitored by looking at fawn reproductive tracts in mid-winter or by noting lactation rates or *corpora albicantia* in yearling does each fall. Fawn breeding seems sensitive to density changes at 60% relative density and below (Table 2). However, fawn breeding may not occur at high densities and, therefore, becomes extremely insensitive if the herd reaches a higher (70% and above) relative density. Therefore, density must be kept at 60% density or below if fawn breeding is being relied on to monitor changes. Less sensitive density indicators, such as adult reproductive rate or percentage of fawns in the harvest, must be monitored if the objective is to maintain the population at 70% density or above.

Hunter satisfaction, as well as yield, should be considered in developing harvest strategy (Hendee 1974, McCullough and Carmen 1982). The number of hunters encountered (Decker et al. 1980) and perception of population size (McCullough and Carmen 1982), both important aspects of hunter satisfaction, may be enhanced by reducing hunting effort and maintaining higher deer densities. For example, the data in Table 4 indicate that 14% fewer hunters will kill only 1.4% fewer deer if the population is maintained at 70% density, rather than at 60%. This lower density of hunters and higher density of deer may be more important to hunters than the slight loss in the number and quality of the deer harvested.

The generalized sustained yield model described in this paper must be viewed as a starting point. Proper management requires local documentation that the population is responding as expected and that the assumed rates of reproduction and mortality are valid for the area in question. Managers should cautiously gain experience with their herds and their hunters that will eventually supersede dependence on any standard yield table. Hopefully, the concepts developed here will make that experience easier to interpret and put into perspective.

LITERATURE CITED

CAUGHLEY, G. 1977. Analysis of vertebrate populations. John Wiley & Sons. New York, N.Y. 234pp.

COE, R. J., R. L. DOWNING, AND B. S. MCGINNES. 1980. Sex and age bias in hunter-killed white-tailed deer. J. Wildl. Manage. 44:245-249.

DECKER, D. J., T. L. BROWN, AND R. J. GUTIERREZ. 1980. Further insights into multiple-satisfactions approach for hunter management. Wildl. Soc. Bull. 8:323-331.

DOWNING, R. L. 1980. Vital statistics of animal populations. Pages 247-268 *in* S. D. Schemnitz, ed. Wildlife management techniques manual, 4th ed. (rev.) The Wildlife Society, Washington, D.C.

FOWLER, C. W., AND T. D. SMITH. 1981. Dynamics of large mammal populations. John Wiley & Sons. New York, N.Y. 477pp.

HARDER, J. D. 1980. Reproduction of white-tailed deer in the North Central United States. Pages 23-35 *in* R. L. Hine and S. Nehls, eds. White-tailed deer population management in the north central states. N. Cent. Sec. The Wildlife Society, Urbana, Ill.

HAUGEN, A. O. 1975. Reproductive performance of white-tailed deer in Iowa. J. Mammal. 56:151-159.

HENDEE, J. C. 1974. A multiple-satisfaction approach to game management. Wildl. Soc. Bull. 2:104-113.

HOLSWORTH, W. N. 1973. Hunting efficiency and white-tailed deer density. J. Wildl. Manage. 37:336-342.

MCCULLOUGH, D. R. 1979. The George Reserve deer herd: population ecology of a K-selected species. Univ. Michigan Press, Ann Arbor. 271pp.

———, AND W. J. CARMEN. 1982. Management goals for deer hunter satisfaction. Wildl. Soc. Bull. 10:49-52.

MCDOWELL, R. D. 1970. Photoperiodism among breeding eastern white-tailed deer (*Odocoileus virginianus*). Trans. Northeast. Fish and Wildl. Conf. 27:19-38.

SAVIDGE, I. R., AND J. S. ZIESENIS. 1980. Sustained yield management. Pages 405-410 *in* S. D. Schemnitz, ed. Wildlife management techniques manual, 4th ed. (rev.) The Wildlife Society, Washington, D.C.

VERME, L. J. 1983. Sex ratio variation in *Odocoileus*: a critical review. J. Wildl. Manage. 47:573-582.

CONSTRAINED OPTIMAL EXPLOITATION: A QUANTITATIVE THEORY

DAVID R. ANDERSON, Utah Cooperative Wildlife Research Unit, Utah State University, UMC 52, Logan, UT 84322[a]

Abstract: This paper reviews the quantitative theory of modeling and sustained harvest optimization of exploited animal populations. A case is made for stochastic models that are dynamic in time, assume no specific steady state, and allow birth and death rates to depend on environmental variables and population density. If the environmental variables are allowed to be stochastic and Markovian, then this general model admits most other models as special cases. Optimal harvest strategies must be based on control or feedback equations. This fact not only dictates the necessity of annual surveys to assess the state variables, but it also allows optimal decisions to be based on these observed states rather than on a predicted or expected state. The recursive theory of stochastic dynamic programming is the only realistic approach to determining optimal harvest strategies. It allows optimization with a variety of complicated constraints on state and decision variables and permits a complex return function. Some comparison is made between this approach and the deterministic and zero-order systems.

KEY WORDS: Dynamic programming, Exploitation, Harvest, Markov, Maximum sustained yield, Optimal, Stochastic, Strategies.

Optimal exploitation programs in wildlife and fisheries management involve a great many complexities. The word "exploitation" refers to hunting, fishing, trapping, or control programs. The general optimal yield problem falls into a branch of applied mathematics concerned with making optimal decisions in the face of uncertainty. The focal point of optimal harvest management concerns sequences of decisions (strategies) that are optimal toward a specified objective. The decisions concern the optimal number of animals to harvest, whereas the objective is optimal sustained exploitation. Constraints may be imposed on the optimal strategy; these may be imposed on the decisions to be made or on the value of the state variables.

The result of a particular decision affects the state of the population the following year (particularly the age and sex structure, production rates, and non-hunting mortality rates). Therefore, sequences of related decisions must be considered in developing a valid optimal harvest strategy. In reality, sequences of decisions (strategies) must also recognize the randomly varying environmental variables and the complex ways that population dynamics are related to these environmental variables (Reed 1978).

Exploited animal populations can be considered under the general framework of what is termed "multistage decision processes." The derivation of optimal strategies for such problems falls into the recursive methodology termed "stochastic dynamic programming."

[a]Present address: Colorado Cooperative Fish and Wildlife Research Unit, Colorado State University, Fort Collins, CO 80523.

The objective of this paper is to suggest some state-of-the-science approaches for optimal harvesting programs. Techniques are available, in principle, to cope realistically with the complexities often encountered (see Amidon and Akin 1968 and Martin and Ek 1981 for examples in other natural resource management fields).

The term "strategy" is used for decision rules in stochastic formulations of harvesting programs, whereas "policy" refers to (unlikely) deterministic processes (Kaufman 1967:104). In either case, a decision D_t is made each year t, and the objective is how to make this an optimal decision $D°$ with respect to a sustained yield objective.

OPTIMAL STRATEGIES

Most previous efforts in optimal harvest management have relied on relatively simple deterministic models of population dynamics (see Reed 1978). The calculus was used frequently to find an optimum point (e.g., the population size at which reproduction rate is maximized, as in the logistic model). Environmental variables were rarely considered except as an unchanging constant (e.g., the constant K in a logistic model). Neither constraints nor the sequential or multistage nature of the process were considered. The result was a policy that was quite unrealistic and of little use in actual exploitation problems.

Optimal harvesting programs typically involve non-biological complexities and constraints. These may involve political or economic realities that have a bearing on the biological aspects of harvesting a population. Finally, natural resource agencies and managers feel a moral responsiblity to employ an extra measure of conservation in harvesting programs. That is, they wish to underharvest rather than overharvest if an error is committed.

Multistage Decision Processes

A major complexity deals with the sequential nature of the dynamics of exploited animal populations. A decision in year t affects the state of the population in year $t+1$. Most papers on harvesting programs ignore this critical aspect (e.g., Watt 1968 notes that many optimal decisions are optimal if used only once). Figure 1 shows a multistage system where the state of the system X_t changes through time.

A decision D_t is to be made at each year t, based on the state of the system X_t. A return r_t is expected. The return then alters the state of the system the following year X_{t+1} (Fig. 2). Stochastic components enter through the vector k_t. The important point is that the effect of the decision made at time t alters the state of the system at time $t+1$. For each possible decision D_t, the state of the system the following year X_{t+1} will change (Fig. 3).

Stochastic components enter in several places in decision processes. A decision may not result in precisely the desired number harvested, only the probability of various realized results may be known. The environment or

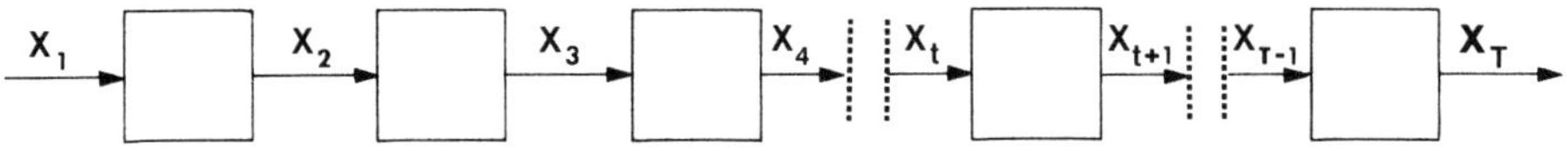

$$X_{t+1} = W_t(X_t, D_t, k_t)$$

Fig. 1. Multistage process showing the state of the system X_t changing through time. W_t is the vector of equations that transform the state variables through time.

other components may be stochastic. Optimal exploitation must rely on realistic models of the dynamics of the population and its changing environment. This reveals the obvious need for stochastic dynamic population models.

An optimal harvesting strategy is a set of rules for optimal decision making in the face of uncertainty. In year t the resource manager observes the state of the system X_t, usually based on the results of extensive surveys. He makes a decision $D°$ whose effect is known, at least probabilistically. The result of this decision alters the state of the system the following year X_{t+1}. In general, the value of X_{t+1} actually observed the following year $(t+1)$ is rarely the same as that expected at time t (after all, it is a stochastic process). However, in year $t+1$ it must be possible to make another optimal decision $D°$ based on the observed state of the system X_{t+1}. The theory of dynamic programming allows such optimal strategies to be derived. The result is a rule $D° = g(X_t)$ allowing optimal decisions to be made as a

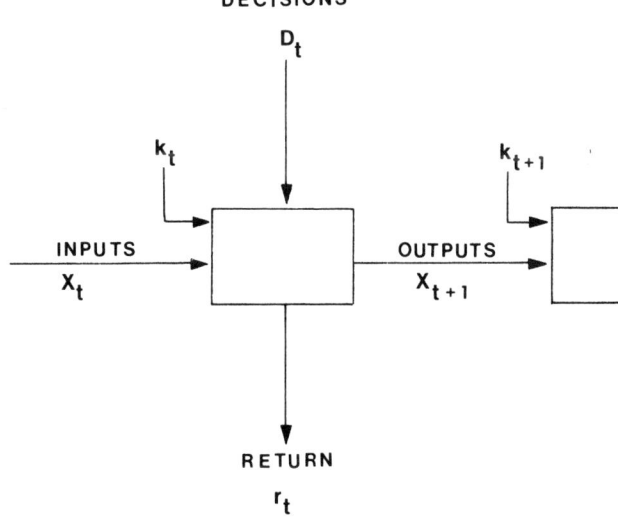

Fig. 2. Year t in a multistage decision process. The state of the system at time $t+1$ (partially shown) is the result of the decision D_t made at time t. A return r_t is realized from the decision; however, this may be known in advance only probabilistically. Stochastic components affecting the state variables, X_t to X_{t+1}, and the uncertainty in the return r_t enter through the vector k_t.

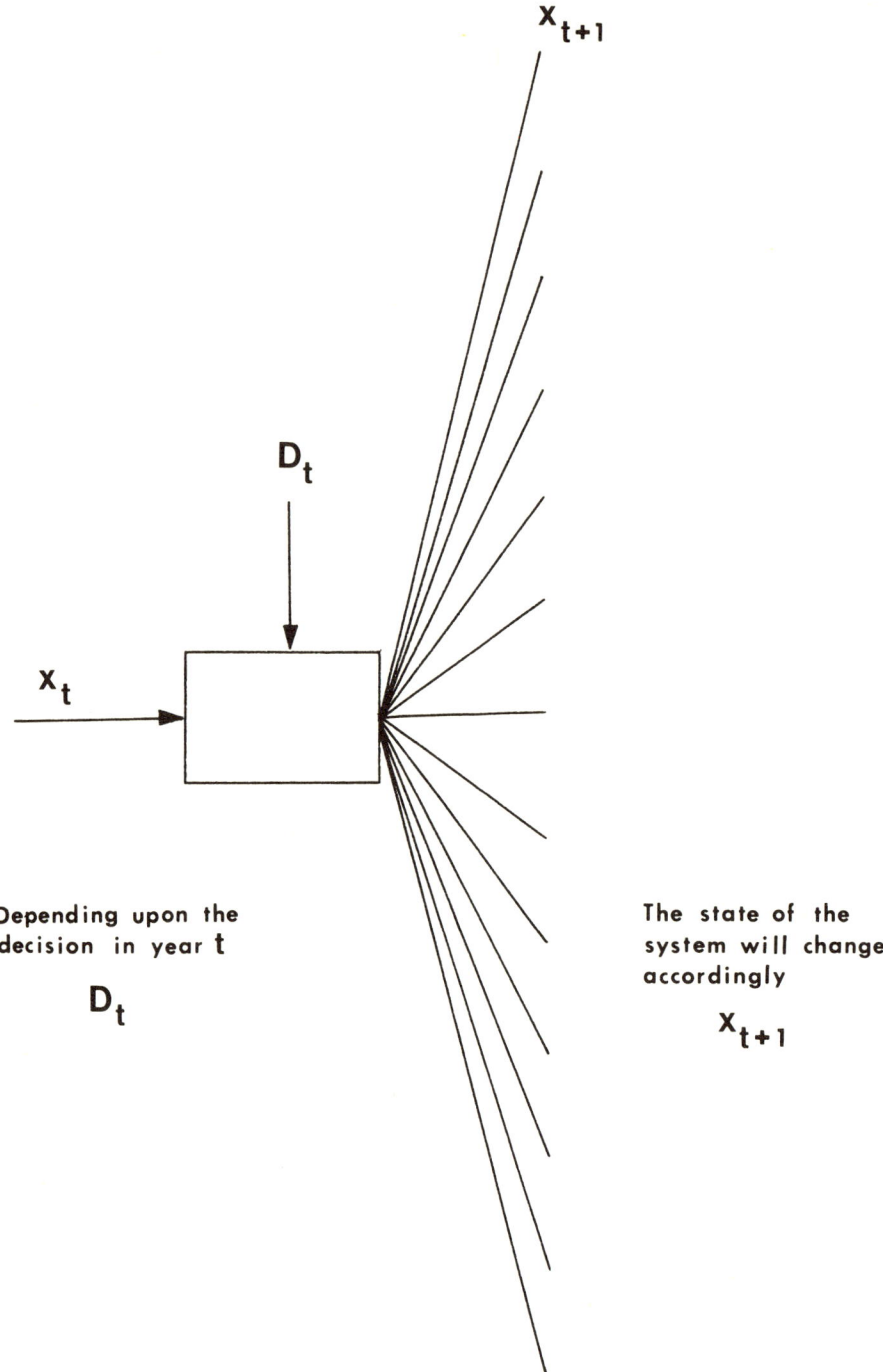

Fig 3. A decision in year t has an effect on the state of the system the following year X_{t+1}. Depending on the decision D_t in year t, the state of the system will change according to the transformation equations W_t. In an optimal exploitation strategy, a decision $D°$ is sought each year such that harvest is optimized on a sustained basis.

function of the observed state of the system in year t, X_t (not on what was expected the previous year[s]). This optimal rule follows from Bellman's (1957:83) *Principle of Optimality*: "An optimal policy has the property that whatever the initial decisions are, the remaining decisions must constitute an optimal policy with regard to the state resulting from the first decision."

Desired Properties of an Optimal Exploitation Strategy

A biologically realistic optimal exploitation strategy should have the following properties: be globally optimal with respect to the objective function specified; allow a variety of imposed constraints on D_t and X_t (e.g., the undesirability of closing the resource to exploitation for, say, p years); reflect the uncertainty in r_t as a function of D_t and X_{t+1} as a function of X_t; allow for frequent differences in the observed size of the population and the state of the environment in year $t+1$, compared to what was expected (predicted) for year $t+1$; allow optimal decisions D_t° to be based on the observed state of the system (X_t), regardless of what was expected (an information feedback loop—e.g., $D_t^{\circ} = g[X_t]$, where $g[\cdot]$ is some function); ergodic in the sense that the optimal decision is independent of the year (e.g., $D_t^{\circ} = D^{\circ} = g[X_t]$).

Paramount in importance is that an information feedback loop is an integral component of the optimal strategy. This feedback loop is lacking in zero-order systems and optimization techniques, such as linear and nonlinear programming. Points 4 and 5 are at the focus of this matter and can be conceptualized by the following example. Consider a florist who expects to sell 200 potted plants next month (June). He, therefore, orders 200 plants to arrive before June 1. In fact, he sells only 30 plants during June—far from the expected value of 200. If he still expects to sell 200 plants the following month (July), he would be foolish to order an additional 200 plants to arrive before July 1. The key point is this: the florist should be able to observe the state of his inventory (X_t) each month and base his decision as to the number of plants to order on the actual number of plants he has ($X_{t+1}=170$), not on the number expected or predicted a period earlier at time t, ($E[X_{t+1}]=0$). Obviously, $D^{\circ}=30$ plants, not 200. This is a key point and an essential aspect of multistage stochastic decision processes.

Zero-Order Systems

Optimal policies for multistage deterministic processes can be derived using linear and nonlinear programming methods (see Hillier and Lieberman 1967 for explanation of these techniques). Davis (1967) used linear programming, although he terms it dynamic programming, and Lomnicki (1972) used nonlinear programming to derive optimal harvest policies.

In stochastic decision processes, the use of linear and nonlinear programming is not appropriate because these methods apply only to what are termed zero-order systems. They provide the optimal decision sequence D_1°, $D_2^\circ,...D_t^\circ$ "all at once." Given X_1 and D_1, then the remaining decisions are based on only the expected values of the state variables $E(X_2)$, $E(X_3),...E(X_T)$ (see Thompson et al. 1977). However, it is unlikely the state of the system at time 2 is as was expected (e.g., $X_2 \neq E[X_2]$). Of course, this objection also applies to future years.

In contrast, stochastic dynamic programming allows D_t° to be based on the observed state of the system. Because of the *Principle of Optimality*, the remaining decisions D_{t+1}, D_{t+2}, etc. still constitute an optimal strategy.

POPULATION MODEL

Model Building

Consider modeling the exploitation problem using the following general formulations:

Let
   X_t = a vector of ℓ state variables at time t,
     $i=1,...j$ the population size by age and sex,
     $i=j+1,...\ell$ the relevant, dynamic environmental variables affecting birth and death rates or decisions affecting the harvest decisions,
   W_t = a vector-valued function (with ℓ elements) which transforms the state variables through time; i.e., $X_{t+1} = W_t X_t$.

W_t will not be restricted in form or complexity; it can be nonlinear, piecewise, or whatever to allow realism. Most important is that W_t can be stochastic and incorporate random variables k_t (a vector) with specified probability distributions.

The state variables X_t and transformation equations W_t are very general, and essentially all discrete population models are special cases of this formalism (see Reed 1974 and Beddington and May 1977). The population model should critically detail the effect of exploitation on production and survival rates. Naive models should be avoided and emphasis placed on a realistic model of the dynamics of the exploited population and its interaction with the dynamic environment. Model building may be facilitated by using comprehensive theory and modeling packages developed in recent years in other fields of science and engineering (Åstrom et al. 1965, Åstrom 1970, Bard 1974).

The optimal harvest strategy is derived numerically from the population model. Obviously, the model must be sound and supported by the data, which usually implies the availability of long-term empirical data on the relevant features of the population and its environment. The investigator must hypothesize realistic functional relationships, critically test their appropriateness, and properly estimate the parameters of the model.

It is imperative that the birth and death processes are modeled separately. In particular, the total death rate must be known as a function of the number harvested and the state of the system:

$$\hat{h}_1(D_t, X_t)$$

where: $\hat{h}_1$ is a function estimated from past time series data. The production rate must be known as a function of population density for a given state of the environment:

$$\hat{h}_2(D_t, X_t)$$

where $\hat{h}_2$ is an estimated function derived from past time series data.

The availability of adequate data will continue to be a serious limitation. Optimal exploitation strategies are dependent upon a realistic model of the population dynamics. Collection and proper analysis of the relevant data are expensive tasks but are absolutely essential for rational, much less optimal, management of animal resources.

Anderson (1975) presented an example of an age-specific population model where the production rate was allowed to be a function of population density and an environmental variable. The environment was Markovian (serially correlated in time with an important stochastic component). The total annual death rate was allowed to be a function of the harvest (i.e., related to the decision D_t) and hypothesized to be compensatory or additive. Many other population models can be considered special cases. For example, the environment may be stochastic but not serially correlated.

Naive Models

Much work has appeared in the literature on harvest policies based on deterministic models. Many of these are not very useful because the models are unrealistic. In particular, a great many papers are based on the age-specific Leslie (1945) model. Not only is this simple model deterministic, but it assumes exponential growth, hardly a likely condition.

Other work has focused on the simple logistic model and used calculus to determine the population size at which productivity is maximized. Even though this may serve as an interesting textbook example, it is far from a useful method in real-world problems involving exploited animal populations.

OPTIMIZATION THEORY

The development of optimal exploitation of dynamic animal populations in stochastic environments lies in the field of dynamic programming that Bellman (1957) developed. Interested readers can gain insight into this very general optimization approach by reviewing books by Bellman and Dreyfus (1962), Aris (1964), and Nemhauser (1966).

The resource manager must make a decision each year D_t. This often concerns the number of animals to harvest that year (e.g., the decision to harvest 200,000 deer). Of course, he attempts to make an optimal decision D_t^* so that the longterm yield is both optimal and sustained. From this decision, some return is realized.

The Return Function

A return function r_t must be defined for each year. This is the return resulting from a particular harvest decision in year t. The return is a function of the state of the population and its environment X_t.

A simple return function at year t is the number of animals harvested, $r_t = D_t$. However, more realistically, D_t is a function of X_t, and r_t is not known with certainty. Therefore, the expected return resulting from a decision made in year t is, letting $\bar{r}_t = E(R_t)$ for notational simplicity:

$$\bar{r}_t = \sum_{k_t} p_t(k_t) \cdot r_t(X_t, D_t, k_t)$$

where $p_t(k_t)$ is the probability density function of the random variable k_t, which reflects the concept that the actual return r_t is a weighted average in a sense.

A major advantage of dynamic programming is that realistic return functions can be employed. Two examples will illustrate some alternatives.

$$r_t = D_t - \alpha(\text{Prob}[N_t < \beta]), \text{ where } \alpha > 0.$$

This equation represents a return function whereby strategies are more conservative as α increases. Increasing α would penalize decision sequences that might allow the size of the population

$$(N_t = \sum_{i=i}^{j} X_{ti})$$

to decrease below some threshold population level β. Of course, decisions less than a_t or greater than b_t may also be excluded from consideration.

A second example might be $r_t = D_t e^{\delta t}$, where δ relates to principles of economic discounting and is an instantaneous annual "interest" rate (see Clark 1976). The return function can be deterministic or stochastic, simple or complex, and functions of X_t. Considerable realism can be modeled in the return function r_t (see Lord 1973).

Constraints

A wide variety of equality and inequality constraints can be imposed to recognize certain limitations of the exploitation process (e.g., biological, social, or political realities). A natural resource manager may not wish to consider an exploitation season where less than 7.3 million kg are expected to be harvested (e.g., $D_t > 7.3$ million kg). This constraint may be forced due to economic infeasibility for small catches. The decision D_t may be constrained by constants or complicated functions and may vary from year to year.

Constraints may also be imposed on future values of the population. In general, we can express the value of X_{t+1} as $W_t(X_t, D_t, k_t)$. It may be appropriate to consider exploitation strategies so that $X_{t+1} > a$ where a is a lower bound selected for some biological, social, economic, or political reason. If large populations cause economic or ecosystem damage, constraints such as $X_{t+1} < b$ may have merit in constraining the optimal exploitation strategy. Equations may be used to replace a and b (above) if the constraints are not simple constants. Complex constraints do not result in computational difficulties in deriving strategies via stochastic dynamic programming.

If r_t is optimized over a T-year process, the final decision is obviously to harvest all the animals remaining at time T. Such a final decision is hardly ethical and calls for a constraint on the final population size.

Stochastic Dynamic Programming

For each year, r_t is the expected return from a decision made as a function of the state of the system X_t. The expression $f_1(X_1)$ will be used to denote the T-year optimal return. Bellman (1957) formulated the fundamental recursion equations (also see Nemhauser 1966:155) as:

$$\overline{f}_t(X_t) = \max_{D_t} \sum_{k_t} p_t(k_t) Q_t(X_t, D_t, k_t), \quad \text{for } t=T,...1$$

where

$$Q_t(X_t, D_t, k_t) = r_t(X_t, D_t, k_t) + \overline{f}_{t+1}(W_t[X_t, D_t, k_t]), \quad \text{for } t=T-1,...1,$$

$$Q_T(X_T, D_T, k_T) = r_T(X_T, D_T, k_T).$$

The theory of stochastic dynamic programming and a large, modern computer allow $\overline{f}_t(X_t)$ to be found. More importantly, one is interested in $D_t^\circ = D_t^\circ(X_t|k_t)$, the optimal decision for X_t given the realization of the stochastic component at stage t. This expression will be shortened to the expression $D^\circ = g(X_t)$. The optimal decision rule, the function $g(X_t)$, can be easily derived from the sequence of tabled values of $\overline{f}_t(X_t)$.

Dynamic programming is an extremely efficient method for determining optimal strategies when it is compared to an exhaustive search of all alternatives. Nemhauser (1966:78) provides an example of a deterministic case involving 10 years T, 100 values of the state variables X, and 100 values of the decision variable D. The dynamic programming policy was found in 20 sec on an outdated computer (IBM 7094), whereas direct enumeration would require 10^{48} sec (Nemhauser comments that the age of the earth is postulated to be something less than 10^{17} sec). The combination of the power of the dynamic programming algorithm and modern, digital computers allows the solution of many realistic optimization problems.

Application

The application of the dynamic programming solution is typically simple as the optimal decision is a function of the observed state of the system; i.e., $D^\circ = g(X_t)$. The optimal strategy is essentially a feedback loop in that an optimal decision is made annually, based on the observed state of the system X_t. The function $g(X_t)$ can be shown as a graph (Fig. 4) or table. Anderson

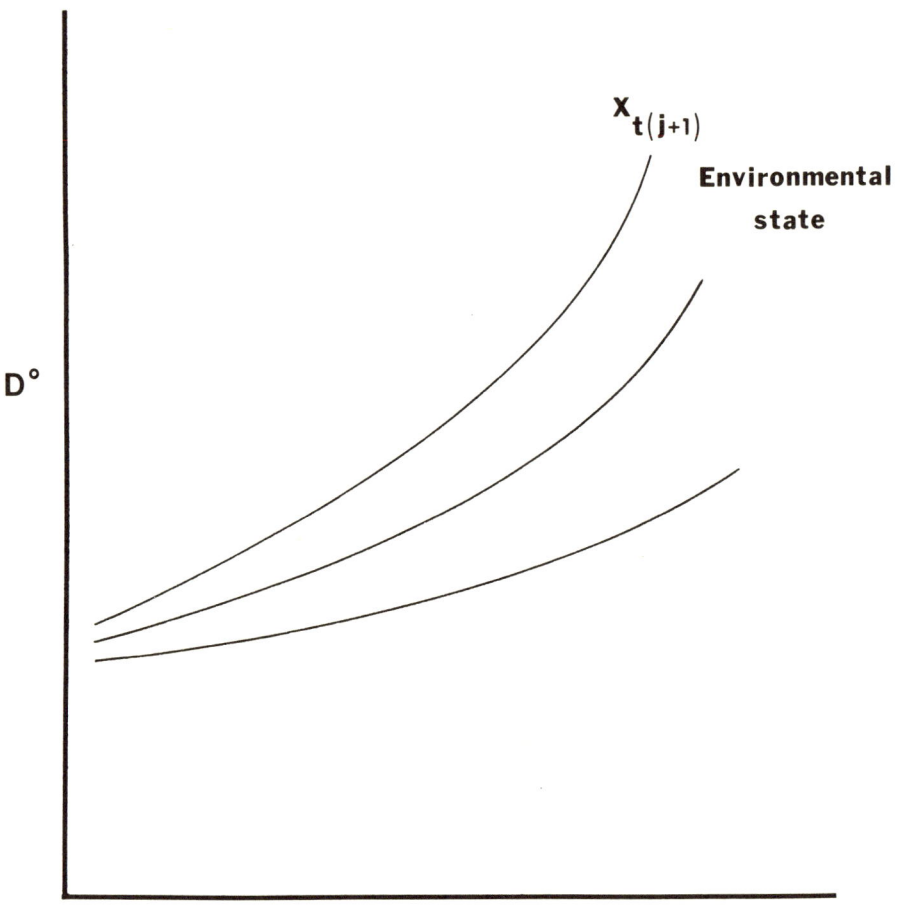

Fig. 4. A hypothetical optimal decision function, $D° = g(X_t)$. Each year, the state of the system is assessed and an optimal decision $D°$ is made based on the decision strategy derived from the use of stochastic dynamic programming.

(1975) and Walters (1975) provide examples and additional discussion. Walters and Hilborn (1976) provide an application of adaptive dynamic programming to the optimal exploitation problem. This theory, also due to Bellman (1961), allows the model and optimization to be updated each year as additional data become available.

DISCUSSION

Stochastic dynamic programming is an extremely general optimization theory and is useful in deriving optimal exploitation strategies. The theory can be applied to realistic harvesting problems, and complex constraints can be imposed on the state variables and decisions to reflect biological, social, economic, or political realities. The solution is not tied to simple deterministic population models or zero-order systems. Dynamic programming provides an objective, realistic theory for optimal harvest management.

Computer simulation is used to evaluate and compare strategies, but it cannot be used to derive them (Lobdell et al. 1972, Roseberry 1979). Simulation can also be employed to explore the sensitivity of the optimal decisions, $D° = g(X_t)$, to various components of the model (e.g., functional forms or parameter values). Certain types of sensitivity studies can be done with dynamic programming (Nemhauser 1966:66-67).

Realistic optimal strategies are dependent upon a realistic model. Every effort must be made to develop a quality model. A responsible manager needs the ability to incorporate new findings into a harvesting program. Frequently, new data are available on the key variables each year, new constraints may arise, and a need may exist to explore the effect on these, or major research programs may provide important new insights into population dynamics. Furthermore, optimal decisions must be based on the values of the observed state variables each year X_t. Annual surveys are required to provide this information, which allows $D°$ to be based on the actual value of X_t rather than on what was expected the previous year, $E(X_{t+1})$.

Although linear and nonlinear programming are useful in optimizing deterministic or zero-order systems, they are not applicable for solving real-world optimization problems involving exploited biological populations. Once the optimal decision $D_t°$ has been made, based on observation of X_t, an allocation problem often remains. Here, particularly, social and economic factors are often involved. A realistic and comprehensive approach to the allocation problem involves nonlinear programming. Judge and Takayama (1970) have discussed this in relation to animal exploitation problems.

SUMMARY

Somewhere between no exploitation and excessive exploitation there is a point, dependent on the year and state of the population and its environment, where allowable exploitation is optimal on a sustained basis. Stochastic dynamic programming provides the theoretical framework for deriving optimal exploitation strategies for real-world populations. A realistic model of the dynamics of the population and its environment is required. The optimization may be constrained in several useful ways to reflect various realities. A large computer is required to derive optimal harvest strategies.

LITERATURE CITED

AMIDON, E., AND G. AKIN. 1968. Dynamic programming to determine optimum levels of growing stock. For. Sci. 14:287-291.

ANDERSON, D. R. 1975. Optimal exploitation strategies for an animal population in a Markovian environment: a theory and an example. Ecology 56:1281-1297.

ARIS, R. 1964. Discrete dynamic programming. Blaisdell Publ. Co., New York, N.Y. 151pp.

ÅSTROM, K. J. 1970. Introduction to stochastic control theory. Academic Press, New York, N.Y. 323pp.

———, T. BOHLIN, AND S. WENSMARK. 1965. Automatic construction of linear stochastic dynamic models for stationary industrial processes with random disturbances using operating records. IBM Nordic Laboratory, Tech. Paper TP 18:150. 143pp.

BARD, Y. 1974. Nonlinear parameter estimation. Academic Press, New York, N.Y. 341pp.

BEDDINGTON, J. R., AND R. M. MAY. 1977. Harvesting natural populations in a randomly fluctuating environment. Science 197:463-465.

BELLMAN, R. 1957. Dynamic programming. Princeton Univ. Press, Princeton, N.J. 342pp.

———. 1961. Adaptive control processes: a guided tour. Princeton Univ. Press, Princeton, N.J. 255pp.

———, AND S. E. DREYFUS. 1962. Applied dynamic programming. Princeton Univ. Press, Princeton, N.J. 363pp.

CLARK, C. E. 1976. Mathematical bioeconomics: the optimal management of renewable resources. John Wiley & Sons, New York, N.Y. 352pp.

DAVIS, L. S. 1967. Dynamic programming for deer management planning. J. Wildl. Manage. 31:667-679.

HILLIER, F. S., AND G. J. LIEBERMAN. 1967. Introduction to operations research. Holden-Day, San Francisco, Calif. 639pp.

JUDGE, G. G., AND T. TAKAYAMA. 1970. Price and allocation over space. Pages 79-95 in A. D. Scott, ed. Economics of fisheries management: a symposium. Inst. of Anim. Resour. Ecol., Univ. British Columbia, Vancouver.

KAUFMAN, A. 1967. Graphs, dynamic programming and finite games. Academic Press, New York, N.Y. 479pp.

LESLIE, P. H. 1945. On the use of matrices in certain population mathematics. Biometrika 33:183-212.

LOBDELL, C. H., K. E. CASE, AND H. S. MOSBY. 1972. Evaluation of harvest strategies for a simulated wild turkey population. J. Wildl. Manage. 36:493-497.

LOMNICKI, A. 1972. Planning of deer population management by non-linear programming. Acta Theriol. 17:137-150.

LORD, G. E. 1973. Characterization of the optimum data acquisition and management of a salmon fishery as a stochastic dynamic program. Fish. Bull. 71:1029-1037.

MARTIN, G. L., AND A. R. EK. 1981. A dynamic programming analysis of silvicultural alternatives for red pine plantations in Wisconsin. Can. J. For. Res. 11:370-379.

NEMHAUSER, G. L. 1966. Introduction to dynamic programming. John Wiley & Sons, New York, N.Y. 256pp.

REED, W. J. 1974. A stochastic model for the economic management of a renewable animal resource. Math. Biosci. 22:313-337.

———. 1978. The steady state of a stochastic harvesting model. Math. Biosci. 41:273-307.

ROSEBERRY, J. L. 1979. Bobwhite population responses to exploitation: real and simulated. J. Wildl. Manage. 43:284-305.

THOMPSON, W. A., W. G. WELLINGTON, E. B. VERTINSKY, AND E. M. MATSUMURA. 1977. Harvesting strategies, control styles and information levels: a study of planned disturbances to a population. Res. Popul. Ecol. 18:160-176.

WALTERS, C. J. 1975. Optimal harvest strategies for salmon in relation to environment variability and uncertain production parameters. J. Fish. Res. Board Can. 32:1777-1784.

———, AND R. HILBORN. 1976. Adaptive control of fishing systems. J. Fish. Res. Board Can. 33:145-159.

WATT, K. E. F. 1968. Ecology and resource management. McGraw-Hill Book Co., New York, N.Y. 450pp.

EVALUATIONS OF THE TELEPHONE AND MAIL SURVEY METHODS OF OBTAINING HARVEST DATA FROM LICENSED SPORTSMEN IN MONTANA

JOHN D. CADA, Montana Department of Fish, Wildlife, and Parks, Bozeman, MT 59717

Abstract: The Montana Department of Fish, Wildlife, and Parks has periodically determined game harvests and hunting success since 1941 and on an annual basis via postal questionnaires since 1958. These surveys monitored 10 species of big game, 11 of upland game birds, and 5 of waterfowl. In 1980, upland-game-bird hunters were surveyed by the telephone and mail methods for comparison purposes. Significant differences were observed between the harvest, hunter days, and bird harvest/day estimates generated by the 2 methods. Estimates from the results obtained by the telephone method of days afield and harvests by species for upland-game-bird hunters were 8 and 4% greater, respectively, than those obtained by the mail survey method. However, estimates of birds harvested/day were 3.1% less for the telephone method. Comparisons of response rates, reduction of bias errors, public acceptance, and others are discussed. Cost comparisons showed that the department saved $24,582 (48%) the first year by conducting the survey by telephone. Further refinements of telephone survey in 1982 resulted in additional increases in contact rate and cost savings.

KEY WORDS: Mail survey, Survey methods, Telephone survey, Wildlife harvest surveys.

Reliable estimates of game harvests, hunter success, and hunter days afield (effort) are necessary for effective game management programs, regardless of the method used to formulate and implement such programs. With few exceptions one of the most efficient ways of collecting reliable harvest information is through region- or state-wide automated surveys.

Although the Montana Department of Fish, Wildlife, and Parks (MDFWP) has been satisfied with the accuracy and completeness of the comprehensive state-wide mail survey, the high overall costs of the project generated interest in looking for ways some monetary savings could be made while maintaining the accuracy of the mail survey. Thus, beginning in 1978, an effort was made not only to evaluate the existing survey method but also to consider an alternative way of accomplishing the survey by a more economical method. This report is a compilation of those efforts.

METHODS

Since 1941, the MDFWP has periodically determined game harvests and hunting success and on an annual basis via postal questionnaires since 1958 (Mussehl and Howell 1971). The resident portion of the state-wide mail survey was terminated in 1980. These surveys monitored 10 species of big game, 11 of upland game birds, and 5 of waterfowl. Samples of licensed sportsmen were selected from the conservation license and license-tag computer files. Sample rates for general resident and nonresident licensees were designed to obtain questionnaire returns from 25% of the license population. This level had been determined previously to obtain a sufficient sample of licensees from the least-hunted hunting units in Montana. Until 1982, all special hunting licensees, except antelope (*Antilocapra americana*), were sampled at the 100% level, which was much higher than necessary for statistical purposes but was done to obtain other information, such as number, age, and sex of observed animals.

Antelope hunters, as other special license holders, were restricted to specific hunting units, and sample sizes were only as large as were necessary for statistical reliability. Harvest questionnaires were sent via data-mailers as soon after the close of the general season as was possible. Until 1980, reminders were sent to nonrespondents generally 4-6 weeks after the initial mailout. Reminders have not been used since.

Data on returned questionnaires were keypunched at the Computer Division, Montana Department of Administration; incomplete or uncoded data on questionnaires were corrected whenever possible and then keypunched. Upland-game-bird data on returned questionnaires were keypunched and then edited manually before processing. Data were then compiled and processed according to prepared programs. Results were then distributed for analysis.

Based on the 1980 telephone survey comparison in 1981-82, the MDFWP conducted the entire resident portion of the state-wide harvest survey by telephone. No alterations in sampling procedures, the analysis programs, or questionnaires were required. However, questionnaires were no longer required to be of the data-mailer type. The lists of sportsmen to be interviewed were supplied to interviewers on mailing labels sorted by last name and by zip code. Each label contained the license type, sportsman's name and address in 1980-81, and telephone number in 1982. In 1981, the interviewer looked up the telephone numbers. All telephoning was done by contracting with trained telephone interviewers using MDFWP phones for long-distance calls and private phones for local calls. Approximately 125 telephone interviewers were strategically located throughout 40 telephone exchanges in Montana so that the number of long-distance calls would be minimal. However, during this study the long-distance calls made using WATS lines were done between 1745-2145 hours and Sundays-Thursdays when there were no telephone charges. Telephone interviewers were paid for each completed questionnaire (interview).

RESULTS

Mail Survey Sample Rates

Mail survey comparisons were made using statistics from the last 3 years that the entire state-wide harvest survey was conducted by a mail survey (1978-80). During the first 2 of these years, the mail survey was accomplished in 2 waves (initial and reminder). First-wave mailings for

1978-79 were 111,613 and 135,462 harvest questionnaires, respectively (Table 1). This represented an initial sampling rate of 41% of the deer and elk (*Cervus elaphus*) license holders and varying rates for the remaining license types. In 1980, the reminder wave was dropped from the survey, and the sample size for deer and elk as well as some of the other general surveys was increased to 60% to accommodate for the lack of reminders. Thus, the initial mailing in 1980 was the highest of the period (162,302 harvest questionnaires).

Mail Survey Response Rates

The response rates for the initial waves of the surveys, after waiting 4-6 weeks in 1978 and 6-10 weeks in 1979-80, ranged from 50% in 1978 to 57% in 1980. When the reminder responses were included, the final response rates in 1978-79 were 66 and 69%, respectively (Table 1). Thus, with the 2-wave survey, the initial sample was broken into 3 categories of respondents: initial respondents (50%), reminder respondents (13%), and non-respondents (37%).

Response rates for special license types averaged 18% higher than general license types (Table 1). In fact, the return rates for specials averaged about 4% higher than the general license returns did with reminders. This trend was apparently the result of the higher interest level of the special permit holders. Response rates within license type groups were 17% higher for the initial wave than for the reminder wave. Thus, the cost/return for the second wave would be greater than for the first.

Table 1. Summary of terrestrial wildlife harvest questionnaire mailings in Montana, 1978-80.

Survey type	Initial wave				Reminder wave			Total returned	
	Mailed		Returned		Mailed	Returned			
	N	%	N	%	N	N	%	N	%
Deer-elk									
1978	51,176	41	23,925	47	24,921	8,151	33	32,076	63
1979	56,850	41	28,192	50	27,165	8,959	33	37,151	65
1980	77,517	60	39,138	50				39,138	50
Specials[a]									
1978	19,845	58	12,972	65	6,796	3,516	52	16,488	83
1979	22,754	73	15,159	67	7,410	3,280	44	18,439	81
1980	28,608	64	21,206	74				21,206	74
Other[b]									
1978	40,592	32	18,830	46	20,205	6,768	34	25,598	63
1979	55,858	38	30,997	56	24,721	8,216	33	38,213	68
1980	56,176	60	32,755	58				32,755	58
Total									
1978	111,613	39	55,727	50	51,922	18,435	36	74,162	66
1979	135,462	43	74,348	55	59,296	20,455	35	93,803	69
1980	162,302	61	93,099	57				93,099	57

[a] Special deer, elk, moose, sheep, mountain goat, and antelope hunters restricted to 1 hunting district.
[b] Includes general archery, black bear, waterfowl, game bird, and turkey.

In general, the response rates for the harvest survey have been very high when compared with response rates of most other mail surveys (Warwick and Lininger 1975).

Mail Survey Response Evaluations

In 1978, hand calculations were used to compare harvest success-rate estimates for initial wave responses with the combined responses of the initial and reminder wave (Table 2). For all species categories, harvest success estimates declined when combined results were used. In 1979, the response evaluation was incorporated into the harvest analysis (Table 3). As in the previous year, all harvest estimates declined when reminder information was included. However, the greatest deviation of success estimates based on sample sizes over 1,000 responses was 4.4% for archery and 4.3% for elk. Based on this modest difference and the expense and delay required by a reminder mail survey, the reminder wave was not conducted in 1980.

Detailed analysis of the questionnaire responses by weekly periods for deer and elk surveys showed that, usually, 90+% of the responses were accounted for by the fourth or fifth week following the initial questionnaire mailing (Table 4). In most cases there was no significant change in success estimates after the third week. This was true of the reminder returns as well.

Comparison of Mail Survey and Telephone Survey Results

In 1980, the game bird survey was conducted by telephone and by mail. The purpose was not only to test the feasibility of conducting the survey

Table 2. Percentage of difference in 1978 harvest estimates between the initial mail survey and the combination of the initial and reminder surveys.

License type/ species	% change	N return[b] questionnaires analyzed	% sample responding
General			
Archery	−4	3,021	70
Deer and elk	−10	19,302[c]	63
Upland game bird	−6	13,155	63
Special			
Antelope	−3	5,826	84
Bighorn sheep	−14	866	84
Deer	−4	2,995	81
Elk	−2	5,254	84
Moose	−1	593	94
Mountain goat	−8	439	89
Turkey (S)[a]	−12	1,443	79
(F)	−7		

[a]S=spring, F = fall.
[b]Reminder questionnaires that kept dribbling in past the reminder cutoff were used in this analysis but not in the computer harvest estimate. These numbers were small and had little effect on the results.
[c]A large number of general-season deer and elk questionnaires were unaccounted for and may have biased the estimated change.

Table 3. Comparisons of the calculated hunting success statistics from data obtained only by the initial survey with the combined data obtained by the initial and reminder surveys for the various game seasons held in Montana, 1979.

License type species	Initials				Initials and reminders				Deviation
	N^a responses	Hunters		% successful hunters	N responses	Hunters		% successful hunters	% change
		N^b	$(\%)^c$			N	$(\%)$		
General									
Deer	26,864	24,231	(90.2)	46.8	33,342	29,847	(89.5)	45.7	2.4
Elk	20,606	16,144	(78.2)	12.1	25,367	19,624	(77.4)	11.6	4.3
Black bear	7,767	4,357	(56.1)	13.5	9,414	5,239	(55.7)	13.4	0.7
Upland game bird	10,333	6,781	(59.0)	89.0	12,681	8,132	(64.1)	88.6	0.5
Waterfowl	8,839	2,690	(33.0)	83.0	11,141	3,307	(29.7)	82.0	1.2
Turkey	1,257	978	(77.8)	43.8	1,398	1,061	(75.9)	43.6	0.5
Archery	2,678	2,370	(88.5)	11.9	3,116	2,740	(87.9)	11.4	4.4
Special									
Deer B	1,951	1,678	(86.0)	59.2	2,224	1,892	(85.1)	58.3	1.5
Deer A	2,064	1,579	(76.5)	45.7	2,359	1,794	(76.0)	45.3	0.9
Elk	4,667	4,275	(91.6)	36.6	5,213	4,741	(90.0)	35.9	1.9
Moose	503	496	(98.6)	74.2	533	526	(98.7)	73.8	0.5
Sheep	826	594	(71.9)	21.2	926	661	(71.4)	19.8	7.1
Goat	363	339	(93.4)	61.7	384	357	(93.0)	59.7	2.3
Antelope	4,877	4,166	(85.4)	71.3	6,325	5,329	(84.3)	70.0	1.9

[a] N license holders responding.
[b] N license holders who hunted.
[c] % responding license holders who hunted.

Table 4. State-wide game harvest questionnaire response rates and calculated hunting success for weekly periods following initial and reminder survey mailings for 3 typical 1979 hunting seasons in Montana.

License type	Week	Initial mailing				Reminder mailings			
		Responses			Success	Responses			Success
		N	%	Cumulative %	Cumulative %	N	%	Cumulative %	Cumulative %
Elk	1	426	2.1	2.1	14.9	3	0.1	0.1	33.3
	2	12,022	58.3	60.4	11.7	1,565	32.9	32.9	8.4
	3	4,309	20.9	81.3	12.2	1,843	38.7	71.6	8.6
	4	1,731	8.4	89.7	12.1	615	12.9	84.6	8.9
	5	818	4.0	93.7	12.0	333	7.0	91.6	8.9
	6	263	1.3	95.0	12.1	133	2.8	94.6	9.1
	7	226	1.1	96.1	12.1	120	2.5	96.9	9.2
	8	204	1.0	97.1	12.1	0	0.0	96.9	9.2
	9	163	0.8	97.8	12.1	118	2.5	99.3	9.1
	10	444	2.2	100.0	12.1	31	0.7	100.00	9.1
Deer	1	555	2.1	2.1	46.9	3	0.0	0.0	33.3
	2	16,140	60.1	62.1	47.1	2,268	35.0	35.1	40.1
	3	5,300	19.7	81.9	47.4	2,437	37.6	72.7	40.5
	4	2,208	8.2	90.1	47.0	814	12.6	85.2	40.7
	5	933	3.7	93.8	46.8	415	6.4	91.6	40.6
	6	360	1.3	95.1	46.8	183	2.8	94.5	40.6
	7	280	1.0	96.2	46.8	162	2.5	97.0	40.7
	8	251	0.9	97.1	46.8	0	0.0	97.0	40.7
	9	206	0.8	97.9	46.8	154	2.4	99.4	40.8
	10	572	2.1	100.0	46.8	42	0.6	100.0	40.8
Special elk	1	0	0.0	0.0	0.0	0	0.0	0.0	0.0
	2	2,927	62.7	62.7	36.4	231	42.3	42.3	30.4
	3	803	17.2	79.9	36.4	167	30.6	72.9	30.1
	4	343	7.3	87.3	36.5	53	9.7	82.6	30.1
	5	154	3.3	90.6	36.3	45	8.2	90.8	30.1
	6	93	2.0	92.6	36.3	17	3.1	94.0	29.0
	7	47	1.0	93.6	36.2	7	1.3	95.2	29.1
	8	176	3.8	97.3	36.4	14	2.6	97.8	29.1
	9	35	0.7	98.1	36.6	0	0.0	97.8	29.1
	10	89	1.9	100.0	36.6	12	2.2	100.0	29.2

by telephone but also to obtain a general comparison of the results. The upland-game-bird survey was selected because of its intermediate size and because it was the most complicated and lengthy survey conducted statewide.

Each survey was based upon an independent and exclusive sample of 1980 game-bird license holders. The surveys were conducted simultaneously and resulted in 6,754 and 5,559 questionnaire responses from the telephone and mail methods, respectively.

Comparisons of harvest estimates for upland game birds by region and by species, statewide, suggest that the telephone survey estimates were 4% higher than the mail survey (Tables 5 and 6). Comparisons of total harvest

Table 5. Montana harvest estimates for upland game birds by region as estimated by the results of the mail and telephone survey methods, 1980.

Region	Harvest			Hunter days			Birds harvested/day		
	Mail	Telephone	Difference %	Mail	Telephone	Difference %	Mail	Telephone	Difference %
1	26,192	28,738	+10	41,213	43,008	+5	0.64	0.67	+4.7
2	24,974	23,318	−6	34,843	40,429	+16	0.72	0.58	−19.4
3	38,903	44,577	+15	42,423	50,940	+20	0.92	0.88	−5.3
4	101,116	115,817	+15	87,616	100,057	+12	1.15	1.16	+0.9
5	34,260	41,469	+21	33,816	40,029	+18	1.01	1.04	+3.0
6	49,575	47,318	−5	37,955	41,578	+10	1.31	1.14	−13.0
7	33,066	29,612	−10	32,797	33,666	+3	1.01	0.88	−12.9
Total[a]	308,086	330,848	+4[b]	310,663	349,705	+8[c]			
State[a]	316,937	330,848		323,360	349,705		0.98	0.95	−3.1[d]

[a] Mail survey totals do not include some returned mail surveys that did not have region of kill indicated.
[b] Paired t-test, $P = 0.8835$.
[c] Paired t-test, $P = 0.00516$.
[d] Paired t-test, $P = 0.06168$.

Table 6. Comparisons of Montana's 1980 upland-game-bird harvest estimates by resident hunters as derived from telephone and mail survey methods.

Species	Telephone	Mail	% change
Pheasant	95,927	94,640	+1.4%
Sharp-tailed grouse	75,073	68,930	+8.9%
Sage grouse	33,326	32,716	+1.9%
Hungarian partridge	45,441	45,258	+0.4%
Mountain grouse	74,010	69,747	−6.1%
Chukar partridge	1,043	699	+49.0%
Total	330,848	316,937	+4.4%[a]

[a] Paired t-test, $P = 0.03941$.

at the regional level showed no significant difference between the 2 methods; however, the difference by species at the state-wide level was significant at $P = 0.03941$.

Results from the telephone method consistently produced higher days-afield estimates for all regions and averaged 8% greater ($P=0.005165$) at the state-wide level (Table 5). When the number of days required to harvest each bird was compared, a 3.1% smaller estimate was made by the telephone method ($P=0.06168$).

Since the 1981-82 surveys were conducted by telephone entirely, there was no further opportunity to compare differences between the 2 methods. However, when harvest results for 1978-80 and 1981-82 were compared, there was no apparent change in trends that could be attributed to survey method (Cada 1981, 1983).

Cost Comparisons

In 1980, for the upland-game-bird-survey test, the mail-method cost including printing and postage was $3,038 for 5,598 returned questionnaires. The telephone-method cost including printing and telephone interviewer charges was $2,445 for 6,701 completed questionnaires. Base costs return were $0.365 and $0.543 for telephone and mail, respectively. Based on 1980 data, a 33% cost savings occurred by using the telephone.

Cost comparisons made since then were based on 1979-80 mail survey statistics, 1981-82 telephone survey statistics, and 1981 telephone and postage rates. The salary of the project supervisor was not included.

The estimated cost savings based on the numbers of questionnaires completed by the telephone survey each year were $24,582.10 and $20,217.18 in 1981 and 1982, respectively (Tables 7 and 8). However, the cost difference between the telephone method in 1981 and 1982 and the 2-wave (reminder) mail survey was $31,071.97 and $25,156.81, respectively. Based on these data, the 1982 telephone method was 48 and 53% less costly than the 1- and 2-wave mail survey methods, respectively.

Table 7. Known and estimated costs for the mail survey based upon 1979-81 mail survey statistics and 1981 postage rates.

	1979-80 (2 wave)			1980-81 (1 wave)		
	N	Postage rate	Cost	N	Postage rate	Cost
Questionnaires mailed	194,758	$0.17	$33,108.86	162,302	$0.17	$27,591.34
Questionnaires returned	93,803	$0.25	$23,450.75	93,099	$0.25	$23,274.75
Data-mailer printing (est.)	200,000		$12,000.00	170,000		$10,000.00
Supervisor/diem (est.)			$200.00			$200.00
Total Cost			$68,759.61			$61,066.09
Cost/returned questionnaire			$0.73			$0.65

An additional annual cost savings, regardless of sample size, occurred as a result of the reduced costs of keying conservation-license data for the telephone survey. Since telephone numbers were substituted for addresses on the data file, the cost savings/keyed conservation license was $0.01 in 1982. Approximately 215,000 conservation licenses were keyed in 1982, resulting in a savings of $2,150.

Telephone Survey Contact Rates

Contact rates for the telephone survey for the deer and elk surveys averaged 58 and 62% in 1981 and 1982, respectively (Table 9). The increase in 1982 was likely the result of the telephone numbers being obtained from the conservation license file rather than manually from the telephone book. Although these statistics appear to be similar to the return rates of the previous mail survey, they are not. The sportsmen not contacted by the telephone survey were not given the opportunity to respond, whereas nonrespondents to the mail survey were in fact sportsmen who were contacted by a mail questionnaire but chose not to respond. The percentage of individuals contacted by the telephone survey who refused to answer the questions was less than 1%.

Table 8. Known and estimated costs for the telephone survey method, 1981-83.

Parameters	1981-82	1982-83
N questionnaires completed	84,284	64,151
Costs		
Interviewer payments	$29,178.00	$20,335.87
Telephone charges	$0.00	$0.00
Printing	$600.00	$600.00
Supervisor/diem (est).	$930.00	$930.00
Total	$30,708.20	$21,865.87
Calculated cost/questionnaire	$0.36	$0.34

Table 9. Contact rate comparisons for Montana's 1981-82 deer and elk harvest surveys, telephone method.

Species	Year	Initial sample		Questionnaires completed	
		N	%	N	%
Deer	1981	40,610	29	23,022	57
	1982	33,039	22	20,173	61
Elk	1981	27,546	32	16,483	60
	1982	18,828	20	11,797	63
Combined	1981	68,156	30	39,195	58
	1982	51,867	21	31,970	62

General Comparisons—Telephone vs. Mail

Some major differences between the 2 surveys were observed but not necessarily documented with quantitative data. One major benefit observed in the telephone survey was the lack of questionnaire editing required before keypunching the data to computer files. Since the interviewers were trained to properly fill out the questionnaire, the cases of in-valid hunting districts, missing data, and illegibility were greatly reduced. Also, the interviewers were able to explain a question the respondent may have had concerning the questionnaire, thus reducing the possibility of confusion on the respondent's part.

One of the surprising results of the telephone survey was its public acceptance. Many respondents want to provide more information concerning their hunting activities than was required by the survey questionnaire.

Although both surveys provide an avenue for making comments, the telephone interviewers could determine whether a written response was necessary and, in some cases, could answer the question to the respondent's satisfaction. Often the respondent simply wanted to make a comment that would be heard by the department.

The telephone survey method is not without its problems. There is a possibility that a few telephone interviewers either knowingly or unknowingly could produce a series of errors on all or most of the questionnaires for a certain locale. This problem would then bias the results for that area to a major degree when the interviewer was the only one covering that locale. This is a problem that can be prevented by better training and spot checking each interviewer's questionnaires.

The greatest weakness of the telephone survey is that it is new to most wildlife agencies and that refinement will occur as more experience is obtained. The mail survey has been used long enough so that many logistical problems have been solved.

DISCUSSION

Montana's experience with large mail and telephone surveys provided an opportunity to evaluate some essential elements of the survey process.

The effectiveness of the initial sample for mail surveys as demonstrated by response rates was influenced as much by the characteristics of the license population as by the method of survey. The information collected in this study showed special license holders on a single-wave mail survey in Montana responded at a higher rate than the general license holders with a 2-wave (reminder) survey. The implications here are that these kinds of factors must be considered when attempting to calculate an initial sample size sufficiently large to produce the desired population response.

Although this study and others (Strickland 1979, Couling and Smith 1980) have demonstrated that estimates computed from only initial questionnaire mailings tend to be inflated, analysis of the difference by a single-reminder wave was shown to be small. Based upon the 4% inflation rate found in Montana, it was determined that the extra cost and delay necessary to conduct the reminder wave was not worth it. However, this determination does not suggest that the real bias error is minor. If the nonrespondents had had the same hunting success as the reminder respondents, then the differences for deer and elk hunting success estimates would have been 8.4 and 12.4%, respectively, based on Montana's 1979 harvest data and nonresponse rates. In 1978, Wyoming Game and Fish conducted a telephone follow-up survey of nonrespondents to their mail harvest survey and found their estimates based on the 1-wave mail survey had to be adjusted downward 12 and 20% for their deer and elk harvest estimates, respectively, when the telephone survey information was included in the analysis (Strickland 1979). The magnitude of the bias error that one might expect in a mail survey would be related to the degree of bias and to the percentage of nonrespondents in the sample (Filion 1978).

This study showed that most of the harvest questionnaires are returned by the fourth week of questionnaire mailing, and harvest estimates changed very little after the third week. However, this analysis was made at the state-wide level and not at the hunting-unit level. Montana has approximately 200 districts that share these data; thus, a few late returns at the hunting-district level can make an important contribution to the realized sample size for some hunting units.

The telephone survey, while maintaining or improving the accuracy of the survey process, has a definite cost advantage over the mail survey. However, the cost savings was the result of the large size of the survey and the ability to circumvent telephone charges. In 1983, the long-distance calls will be charged because of a policy change in the WATS line rate charge. Since 30% of the telephone interviews must be made long-distance, the cost difference between the 2 survey methods in the future will be less, until postage rates change.

Even without the monetary savings, there are significant benefits of the telephone method—the high degree of public acceptance and the reduced sources of errors.

LITERATURE CITED

CADA, J. D. 1981. Statewide wildlife harvest surveys. Mont. Dep. Fish, Wildl. and Parks. P-R Proj. W-104-R-17. Job 1. 26pp.

———. 1983. Statewide wildlife harvest surveys. Mont. Dep. Fish, Wildl. and Parks. P-R Proj. W-104-R-19. Job 1. 22pp.

COULING, L., AND G. E. J. SMITH. 1980. Impact of a postcard follow-up on harvest survey returns. Can. Wildl. Serv., Prog. Notes 113. 9pp.

FILION, F. L. 1978. Increasing the effectiveness of mail surveys. Wildl. Soc. Bull. 6:135-141.

MUSSEHL, T. W., AND F. W. HOWELL. 1971. Game management in Montana. Mont. Fish and Game Dep. 238pp.

STRICKLAND, D. 1979. Annual report of big game harvest, 1978. Wyo. Dep. of Game and Fish. P-R Proj. W-27-R-32. Proj. Objective 1. Job 1. 158pp.

WARWICK, D. P., AND C. A. LININGER. 1975. The sample survey: theory and practice. McGraw-Hill Book Co., New York, N.Y. 344pp.

RESPONSES OF DEER POPULATIONS TO HARVEST STRATEGIES

INFLUENCE OF REGULATION ON DEER HARVEST

DAVID S. DeCALESTA, Department of Fisheries and Wildlife, Oregon State University, Corvallis, OR 97331

Abstract: For 25 years the Oregon Department of Fish and Wildlife has conducted a special hunt for black-tailed deer (*Odocoileus hemionus columbianus*) on a small (47 km^2) refuge in northwest Oregon. Altering opportunity on the refuge for hunters to harvest deer of any sex and age class and competition with regular deer seasons on adjacent forestland resulted in predictable changes in the number of hunters and the number of deer killed on the refuge. As restrictions on type of deer legal for harvest were loosened and competition with regular deer seasons lessened, the number of hunters and deer harvest on the refuge increased and vice-versa. Densities of hunters and deer harvest consistently were significantly lower on forestland adjacent to the refuge.

KEY WORDS: Black-tailed deer, Harvest strategies, Harvest intensity, Hunter density, Special hunts.

Under some circumstances local deer populations may become larger than desired. On the Crab Orchard National Wildlife Refuge (CONWR) in Illinois, white-tailed deer (*Odocoileus virginianus*) density approached the point where it was detrimental to deer and resident goose (*Branta canadensis*) flocks (Roseberry et al. 1969). In eastern Pennsylvania the number of deer reached such levels that losses of agricultural crops were unacceptable to local farmers (Thomas 1954). A practical solution to high deer populations has been to increase the deer harvest by increasing hunting pressure (Eadie 1954). Behrend et al. (1970) noted that antlerless deer (does and fawns) had to be harvested if significant reduction in local deer herds was to result from increased hunting pressure. Thomas et al. (1976) determined through hunter interviews that the number of deer hunters in specified areas decreased with increased distance of these areas from trails, camping or parking sites, and roads.

Thus, special hunts designed to increase harvest of local deer herds should be sufficiently liberal to provide for a large kill of antlerless and antlered deer and should provide easy access to hunting areas. If such special hunts were held when regular deer season was not open (or finished) one would expect they would attract a greater number of hunters than if held when regular season was open.

There are no known studies that evaluated the effectiveness of manipulating special hunts to increase hunter numbers and deer harvest. Examination of the results of a special hunt for black-tailed deer on the McDonald Forest Game Refuge (MFGR) in western Oregon provides an example of hunter and harvest responses to harvest regulations favoring special hunts.

In 1953, the Oregon Game Commission organized a special deer hunt on the MFGR located in western Oregon in the Coast Range foothills. The hunt was designed to evaluate the effects of sustained heavy hunting pressure on black-tailed deer populations. Other objectives were to provide relief from deer browsing damage on Douglas-fir (*Pseudotsuga menziesii*) seedlings and to give an opportunity for students from Oregon State University to gain experience in handling deer in a checking station situation (Sturgis 1977). Since its inception, the hunt has been conducted on weekends only, for 1-4 weekends.

For the first 6 years of the hunt, MFGR was perceived as having an unexploited deer herd, and hunter interest was high, providing the initial stimulus for heavy hunting pressure. Seasons were restrictive, however, as bow hunting only was allowed.

Beginning in 1959, the hunt was made more attractive by allowing hunters to hunt with firearms for antlerless as well as antlered deer. Unsuccessful hunters holding permits to hunt for antlerless deer in the adjacent Alsea Unit were allowed to hunt 1-3 weekends in MFGR. In addition, unsuccessful hunters without Alsea Unit permits often were allowed a few (1-3) weekends to hunt antlerless deer. Some, or all, of these days occurred after the general deer season closed, making MFGR one of the few remaining places unsuccessful deer hunters could hunt.

The objectives of this paper were to determine if changes in MFGR harvest regulations resulted in expected responses in hunter density and harvest within MFGR and if hunter density and deer harvest were higher on MFGR than on the adjacent Alsea Unit forestland, which was open for regular season deer hunting.

METHODS

Study Areas

MFGR is comprised of 2 tracts of forestland (Fig. 1) totalling 47 km^2. The lower tract (McDonald Forest) is a narrow ridgeline running SW-NE. The upper tract (Paul Dunn Forest) is the northern face of a ridgeline running NW-SE.

MFGR is surrounded on 3 sides (N, S, and E) by open farmland and rural residential development. The area between the 2 tracts is open farmland and a rural residential development. Both tracts are bordered by commercial forestland on the west. Elevation ranges from 152 to 661 m. Road density is 3.6 km road/km^2 forestland.

The adjoining 5,025-ha Alsea Unit extends from the floor of the Willamette Valley (70 m) westward to the crest of the Coast Range Mountains (1,250 m). The Alsea Unit, like MFGR, is characterized by clearcuts interspersed within regenerating stands of Douglas-fir. Ownership is split among the U.S. Forest Service, the Bureau of Land Management, and commercial holdings. Road density is 2.2 km road/km^2 forestland.

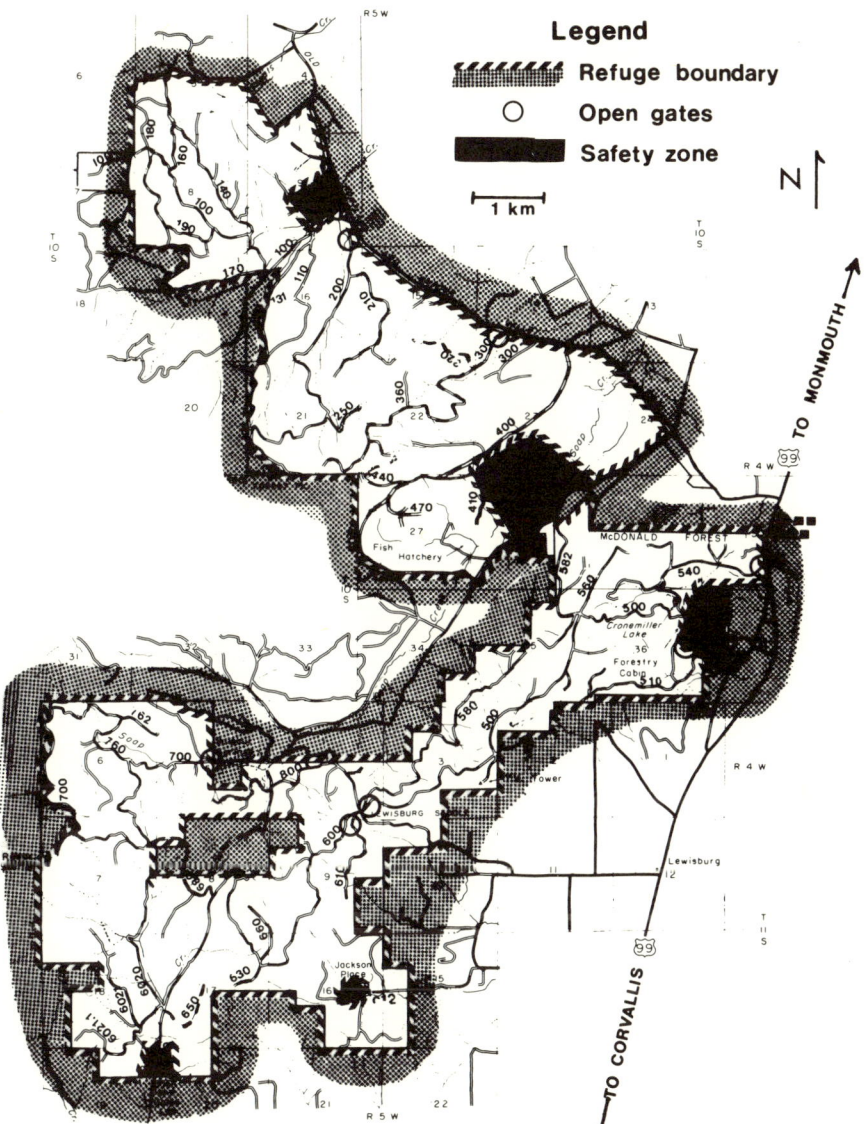

Fig. 1. Map of McDonald Forest Game Refuge in Western Oregon.

Concentration of Hunters/Harvest

The ultimate test of the effectiveness of special hunts is whether they result in high densities of hunters and harvest. The effectiveness of the MFGR special hunt was tested by comparing hunting pressure (hunter days/km^2) and harvest (deer kill/km^2) on MFGR with those on the Alsea Unit. A paired-t test was utilized to test the null hypothesis that hunter days and harvest on MFGR were equal to or less than on the Alsea Unit.

Response of Hunter Numbers and Harvest to Regulation Change

Linear regression analysis was used to determine strength of any relationships between dependent variables (hunter numbers and harvest) and independent variables (percent overlap of MFGR hunt with competing deer seasons, and season length on MFGR for harvest of antlerless deer). The null hypothesis was that no such relationships existed.

The influence of deer harvest regulations in MFGR might be influenced by the status of the state's 2 deer subspecies. Many hunters prefer the larger mule deer (*O. h. hemionus*) of eastern Oregon than the black-tailed deer of western Oregon. Prior to 1965, mule deer and black-tailed deer seasons were identical; hunters could hunt both and, if unsuccessful, could hunt for blacktails on MFGR. For the 1966-74 deer seasons hunters could hunt both subspecies and blacktails on MFGR, but season lengths were different. This resulted in a mule deer season overlap with the MFGR season that differed from overlap with the black-tailed-deer season. After 1976, hunters could hunt only for mule deer or black-tailed deer but not both. Thus, mule deer seasons after 1975 presented additional competition with the MFGR season for hunters, as mule deer hunters no longer were eligible to hunt black-tailed deer on MFGR.

RESULTS AND DISCUSSION

Hunter Concentration and Harvest

Average length of hunting season was significantly less ($P<0.001$) for MFGR (6.8 days) than for the Alsea Unit (29.7 days), but there were significantly more ($P<0.001$) hunter days/km^2 for MFGR (57.3) than for the Alsea Unit (19.9) (Table 1). On a hunter/km^2/day basis, there were 9.3 hunters for MFGR as opposed to 0.6 for the Alsea Unit. This difference was mirrored by the harvest; 5.6 deer were harvested/km^2 for MFGR as opposed to 0.9 deer/km^2 for the Alsea Unit ($P<0.001$). On a deer-harvested/km^2/day basis, 0.8 deer were harvested from MFGR and 0.03 from the Alsea Unit. Hunter success rate (harvest/hunter day) was significantly higher ($P<0.01$) on MFGR than on the Alsea Unit (Table 1), probably reflecting the influence of much heavier hunting pressure on MFGR.

Hunter and Harvest Response to Liberal Season Regulations

As expected, the deer harvest was highly correlated with hunter numbers (r=0.84), $P<0.01$). This confirmed the assumption underlying the basis for special hunts designed to reduce deer numbers (that increases in hunter numbers brought about by regulation will be associated with higher deer harvest).

Hunter numbers and deer harvests were significantly correlated (r values ranged from 0.37 to 0.87, Table 2) with degree of overlap of the MFGR season with the regular black-tailed deer season and with length of season

Table 1. Comparative harvest statistics, McDonald Forest Game Refuge (MFGR) vs. the Alsea Hunt Unit, western Oregon.

Area	Season (days)	Hunter days/km^2	Harvest/km^2	Harvest/hunter day
MFGR	6.8 ± 1.0[a,b]	57.3 ± 30.2[b]	5.6 ± 2.6[b]	0.09 ± 0.03[c]
Alsea	29.7 ± 5.7	19.9 ± 7.4	0.9 ± 0.3	0.07 ± 0.03

[a] Mean values ± SD reported.
[b] Mean values in columns significantly different at $P<0.001$.
[c] Mean values in column significantly different at $P<0.01$.

in which MFGR antlerless deer could be hunted without a permit. Hunter numbers and deer harvests were not significantly ($P>0.05$) correlated with overlap of the MFGR season with the mule deer season (Table 2), indicating that the mule deer season ostensibly had little effect on MFGR hunt statistics. However, correlation coefficients were higher when calculated for the 1959-74 and 1976-82 periods, respectively, than for the entire period (1959-82). The major difference between the 2 periods was mule deer season interaction with MFGR season; for the 1959-74 period unsuccessful mule deer hunters could hunt on MFGR, and for the 1976-82 period they could not.

Regression analysis indicated that hunter density and deer harvests were inversely and significantly ($P<0.05$) related to length of season for Alsea Unit antlerless deer permits in MFGR. As number of days Alsea Unit permit holders could hunt in MFGR increased, hunter density and deer harvest declined. Number of days Alsea Unit permit holders could hunt antlerless deer in MFGR was inversely and significantly ($P<0.05$) related to

Table 2. Correlation coefficients for dependent and independent variables for the 1959-82 deer hunting seasons on the McDonald Forest Game Refuge in western Oregon.

Independent variables	Dependent variables	
	Hunter N/km^2	Deer harvest/km^2
Length antlerless season[a]		
1959-82	0.62[e]	0.37
1959-74	0.78[e]	0.87[e]
1976-82	0.70[d]	0.64
% overlap black-tailed deer[b]		
1959-82	0.49[d]	0.42[d]
1959-74	0.84[e]	0.84[e]
1976-82	0.64	0.74[d]
% overlap mule deer[c]		
1959-74	0.30	0.03

[a] Length antlerless season = N days hunters could harvest antlerless deer without a permit.
[b] % overlap black-tailed deer = % MFGR season that overlaps with black-tailed deer season.
[c] % overlap mule deer = % MFGR season that overlaps with mule deer season.
[d] Correlation coefficient significant at $P<0.05$ level.
[e] Correlation coefficient significant at $P<0.01$ level.

number of days antlerless deer could be hunted in MFGR without a permit. For MFGR hunts when Alsea Unit permits were available (1953-77), regulations specified that antlerless deer could first be hunted only by holders of Alsea Unit permits (0-3 weekends) and then by any hunter (no permit required) on following weekends (Table 3).

Apparently, opportunity to hunt for antlerless deer without need for a permit in MFGR was a greater attractant than hunting with an Alsea Unit permit. When number-of-days hunters could hunt without a permit for antlerless deer were greatest (and number-of-days holders of Alsea Unit permits would hunt were low) hunter density and deer harvest were greatest, and vice-versa. Potential attractiveness of the MFGR hunt to holders of Alsea Unit permits was confounded by the inverse relationship between number of days allocated for Alsea Unit permit hunting and hunting with no permit required.

Examination of extremes in hunter density and deer harvest values supported the notion that regulation influenced harvest (Table 3). Highest hunter density (144.4 hunter days/km^2) and deer harvest (11.7 deer/km^2) occurred in 1970 when the MFGR season was most liberal (highest number of days of antlerless harvest permitted), when the MFGR hunt was held after other deer seasons had closed (no overlap), and when unsuccessful black-tailed and mule deer hunters could hunt MFGR. Lowest hunter densities and deer harvests occurred in 1974 and 1976 when the MFGR season was most restrictive (hunting antlerless deer without a permit not allowed) and competition with other deer seasons was greatest (100% overlap with black-tailed deer season in 1974 and loss of mule deer hunters as potential hunters after 1975).

The sizeable year-to-year fluctuations in hunter response to changes in harvest regulations recurred consistently over a long span of time, providing additional evidence that hunters were capable of detecting and reacting to changes in harvest regulations that altered the attractiveness of the MFGR hunt (Table 3).

The 2 independent variables (percentage of overlap between black-tailed deer and MFGR seasons and number of days allowed for antlerless harvest without a permit) most highly correlated with hunter densities and deer harvest ($P<0.01$). That they were significantly correlated with each other ($r=0.84$), however, precluded use of both variables in a multiple linear regression analysis.

Minimum competition with regular black-tailed deer seasons (0.0% season overlap) was achieved on a number of occasions in the past for MFGR, and the associated upper limits of hunter density and harvest were established. However, number of days when antlerless deer could be hunted without a permit was not expressed over a full range of possible values. The past upper limit of 6 days could easily be exceeded with the reasonable expectation that hunter density and deer harvest would attain higher numbers than achieved in the past. Thus, increases in deer harvest designed

Table 3. Deer harvest summary for the McDonald Forest Game Refuge, in western Oregon 1959-82.

Year	Kind and length of seasons (days)		% season overlap		Hunter days /km^2	Deer kill /km^2
	Any deer with permit	Any deer without permit	Black-tailed deer	Mule deer		
1959	4	2	75	a	35.6	4.7
1960	4	4	50	a	67.5	9.7
1961	4	4	50	a	62.2	8.1
1962	4	4	50	a	62.0	5.6
1963	2	6	25	a	91.6	9.6
1964	4	4	50	a	79.5	8.1
1965	4	4	50	a	57.9	4.9
1966	6	2	75	50	48.4	4.7
1967	4	4	25	0	61.2	6.5
1968	4	4	50	50	57.3	5.5
1969	0	2	75	25	50.5	4.3
1970	0	6	0	0	144.4	11.7
1971	2	4	25	0	100.2	8.2
1972	6	2	75	0	32.9	1.9
1973	4	2	67	0	69.1	6.8
1974	6	0	100	0	31.3	1.4
1975	No season					
1976	6	0	67	100[b]	14.8	1.2
1977	4	2	67	100	25.5	3.5
1978	0	6	33/33[c]	100	25.9	2.3
1979	0	6	0/33	100	47.3	4.1
1980	0	6	0/0	100	87.1	6.5
1981	0	6	0/0	100	87.9	4.8
1982	0	6	0/0	100	68.9	4.0

[a] Mule deer and black-tailed deer seasons identical, and hunters could hunt for both subspecies.
[b] Beginning with the 1976 deer season, hunters could hunt only mule deer or black-tailed deer. Thus, the MFGR season competed 100% with the mule deer season for hunters after 1975.
[c] First figure represents % overlap of MFGR season with regular deer season. Second figure represents % overlap of MFGR season with end-of-season any-deer hunt in Alsea Unit.

to reduce deer numbers below the level where economic crop loss occurs are most likely to be achieved by increasing length of antlerless seasons than by reducing competition for hunters with other deer seasons. Management schemes incorporating reduction of competition and maximization of number of days of antlerless hunting likely will produce the greatest increases in hunter density and harvest, as occurred in MFGR.

The magnitude of hunter response to changes in harvest regulations on MFGR may have been heightened by the ready access to hunting. MFGR is comprised of long, thin ridges with an extensive, interconnecting system of well-maintained all-weather gravel roads. Road density is 1.6 × higher than in the Alsea Unit. There are many access roads (Fig. 1), and MFGR lies adjacent to a major north-south highway. Lastly, there are 4 major metropolitan areas within 80 km of MFGR. Because of its high degree of accessiblity, MFGR may not be representative of other areas where high deer harvest is desired.

MANAGEMENT IMPLICATIONS

The MFGR hunt may not be representative of the majority of special hunts designed to increase deer harvest and reduce local deer population densities. Access to the forest was extremely high, and the hunt was well established.

The CONWR hunt (Roseberry et al. 1969) provided a dramatic example of how regulation can stimulate high hunting pressure and harvest; for the 10-day hunt, total hunting pressure was 67.0 hunters/km^2, and harvest was 18.8 deer/km^2. The hunt provided access to a deer herd previously unhunted, it occurred when all other deer seasons were over, and it allowed unsuccessful hunters 1 last chance to harvest a deer; antlerless deer were legal game, and access was good.

Both hunts do, however, indicate the ability of management to increase hunting pressure and harvest when regulations make the hunt attractive. Such hunts require considerable planning and administration by game management agencies to inform the hunting public and to conduct the hunt. Whether such agencies are willing or able to expend the time and manpower to hold several such hunts/year is unknown. Potential competition among these hunts could reduce hunting pressure and harvest below targeted levels. The ultimate success of special hunts conducted concurrently to reduce local deer herds is dependent on answers to the above questions and the degree of hunter access to hunt sites.

LITERATURE CITED

BEHREND, B. F., G. F. MATTFELD, W. C. TIERSON, AND J. E. WILEY, III. 1970. Deer density control for comprehensive forest management. J. For. 68:695-700.

EADIE, W. R. 1954. Animal control in field, farm, and forest. The MacMillan Co., New York, N.Y. 257pp.

ROSEBERRY, J. L., D. C. AUTRY, W. D. KLIMSTRA, AND L. A. MEHRHOFF, JR. 1969. A controlled deer hunt on Crab Orchard National Wildlife Refuge. J. Wildl. Manage. 33:791-795.

STURGIS, H. 1977. The McDonald Forest deer hunt. Oregon Wildl. 32:1-4.

THOMAS, D. W. 1954. An economic analysis of deer damage to farm crops and income from deer hunters, Potter and Monroe counties, Pennsylvania. 1951. Ph.D. Thesis. Pennsylvania State Univ., State College. 396pp.

THOMAS, J. W., J. D. GILL, J. C. PACK, W. M. HEALY, AND H. R. SANDERSON. 1976. Influence of forestland characteristics on spatial distribution of hunters. J. Wildl. Manage. 40:500-506.

BLACK-TAILED DEER POPULATION REGULATION THROUGH ANTLERLESS HUNTS IN WESTERN WASHINGTON

KENNETH J. RAEDEKE, College of Forest Resources, University of Washington, Seattle, WA 98195

RICHARD D. TABER, College of Forest Resources, University of Washington, Seattle, WA 98195

Abstract: Black-tailed deer (*Odocoileus hemionus columbianus*) damage to conifer seedlings on private lands in western Washington rises sharply with winter deer density at about 24 deer/ km^2 on recent clearcuts. To lessen damage, a cooperative (landowner, state, university) study obtained data on winter deer density, experimental antlerless hunts, and results for deer population density and productivity. Antlerless harvests resulted in an increase in deer productivity, producing a greater potential deer harvest, but requiring additional herd control to reduce seedling damage.

KEY WORDS: Black-tailed deer, Population regulation, Density, Sport hunting, Antlerless harvests, Conifer damage.

Black-tailed deer are abundant in western Washington, wintering below about 475 m. Foothill deer winter range, with the snowy Cascade Mountains above and the centers of human settlement below, is mostly in production-forest dominated by Douglas-fir (*Pseudotsuga menziesii*). Much of the deer winter range is owned by large timber companies. Under current intensive management, clearcut harvest blocks are quickly planted with evenly spaced 2-year-old seedlings. In addition, areas dominated by red alder (*Alnus rubra*) are cleared and planted with Douglas-fir. Each block of seedlings is managed to produce a harvestable stand of even age, uniform dimension, and wood quality after a rotation period of 50-70 years. However, black-tailed deer eat a moderate amount of Douglas-fir, perhaps 10-15% of the diet by preference, in winter (Brown 1961). Under conditions of heavy deer density and competition for alternative forage, and when occasional winter snows cover the ground, the deer eat more Douglas-fir (Hines 1963). Small conifer seedlings are vulnerable to browsing damage by deer only until the terminal bud is over about 1 m from the ground, but this takes 1 or more years from planting; this interval, early in forest succession, is the same period during which the deer congregate in the clearcuts to feed. Severe damage to seedlings necessitates an expensive replanting that may, in turn, be damaged by deer. Even when replanting is successful, production time has been lost and the stand is of uneven age.

The intensity of winter seedling damage is related to the number of foraging deer/unit area (Fig. 1). Management to lessen damage, then, aims to reduce winter deer density. Seasonal movements of deer complicate the situation. Often there is a resident population on the winter range and a migratory population that arrives early or late in response to annual snow accumulation patterns on the higher summer range.

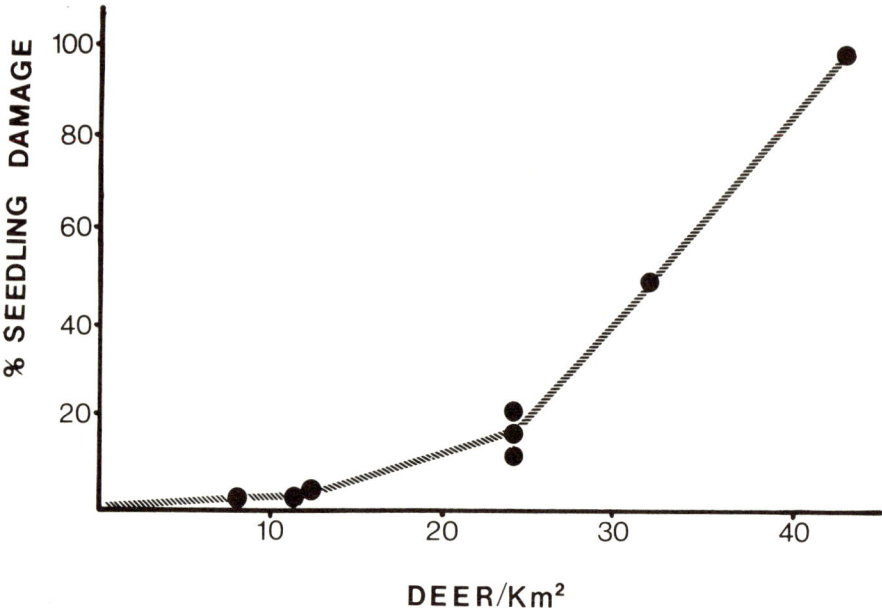

Fig. 1. The relationship between deer density and conifer seedling damage in the Douglas-fir forests of the Pacific Northwest, based on Amaral (1978) and Hines (1963).

The landowner experiencing deer damage is free to protect his seedlings from the deer, which is expensive, but not to reduce the deer population himself. Responsibility for the deer population rests with the Washington Department of Game, which manages deer population levels through regulation of recreational hunting. The basic annual bag limit of deer is 1 antlered buck/licensed hunter, but for management units on which deer population regulation is desired, permits for antlerless deer may be issued through a public drawing.

The present report covers a cooperative study shared by the St. Regis Company, the Washington Department of Game, and the authors to design and test a management plan for reducing deer damage to conifer seedlings on the Kapowsin Tree Farm (KTF).

The specific objectives of the present study were: to assess the relation of deer harvest intensity to deer winter population density; to assess the relation of deer winter population density to deer productivity; and to develop an adaptable, acceptable, cost-effective program of deer herd management.

METHODS

Study Area

The study was conducted between 1980 and 1984 on KTF, a controlled-access production forest of 681 km^2 abutting Mt. Rainier National Park on the west. KTF supports a deer population of about 1,500 (R. H. Taylor, pers. commun.). Deer summering below 457 m are resident, but those summering higher are driven down by winter snows to join the resident deer on a winter range of about 227 km^2. Annual variations in onset of winter storms, total snow pack, and time of snow-melt cause variations in season and duration of winter range use by the migratory portion of the deer herd.

Access to the extensive KTF road system is controlled, so that numbers of hunter-days and deer harvested can be obtained, and harvested deer can be examined.

Estimation of Deer Densities

The deer densities in the winter foraging areas within the study area were estimated using line transect methods as described by Gates et al. (1968). With this method, the deer density (D) was estimated by traveling a distance (L) across a tract of land in non-overlapping transect lines. The number of deer sighted (n) was recorded, together with the right-angle distance (x) from the deer to the transect line at the time of first sighting.

The Gates model is based on the assumption that the probability of sighting a deer decreases exponentially with an increase in the distance from the transect and that the probability of sighting a deer on the transect line is 1.0. The formula for calculating deer density is:

$$D = \frac{(n-1)}{L(\bar{X}i)}$$

where $\bar{X}_1$ is the average of all the right-angle distances in the census. One assumption of this method is that the transects are located randomly throughout the sample area. This proved to be impractical, and it was necessary to use the road system of the study area as the sampling framework. All suitable spur roads within the census area were included in the study. The census route for each area was standardized and followed in the same pattern each time. Minor variations in the route occurred when some roads were not passable. The transects were approximately 20 km in length and required 3-4 hours to complete, depending on the number of deer encountered.

Censuses were conducted regularly throughout the cycle of fall hunting seasons. A minimum of 3 night-counts were made before the start of the general buck hunt, 3 more after the general hunt and before the antlerless season, and 3 more after the antlerless season, with the last census conducted in late January or early February.

Censusing was restricted to the early evening, from 1800 to 2200 hours when the deer were most observable (Progulske and Duerre 1964), on nights without strong winds which tend to reduce deer activity.

Two people were required for the census work; 1 used a spotlight on the passenger side, the other drove the vehicle and recorded the data. For each deer sighted, the time, distance along the transect (based on the odometer in the vehicle), sex and age composition, and right-angle distance were recorded. The right-angle distance was measured with a range-finder when conditions permitted and estimated visually the other times.

Different variations of the road-transect-count methods were considered. Harestad and Jones (1980) suggested simple counts of deer divided by the distance driven. However, this would not be suited to comparisons between years when sighting conditions changed with forest succession. Burnham et al. (1980) have proposed more sophisticated methods, based on angle of initial sighting and distance to the animal. Whereas their methods are superior for determination of absolute abundance, this study required only estimation of relative abundance for comparisons over time. The added complications were not considered to be justified for the needs of the study.

Monitoring the Deer Harvests

The deer harvest on the study area has been monitored routinely since 1959. Since all hunters entering the area must pass through controlled access gates, data on number of hunters, hunter-days, deer harvested, sex and age of deer harvested, and antler development have been recorded. Since the initiation of the antlerless hunts in 1979, condition of the deer also was recorded, in addition to the collection of reproductive tracts. A condition index of Kistner et al. (1980), based on levels of body fat reserves, was used to evaluate condition. The index is based on the amount of fat on the pericardium, heart, brisket, omentum, kidney, and rump area.

Determination of Deer Reproductive Rates

Deer reproductive rates, measured as the number of fetuses/doe, were determined through the examination of reproductive tracts collected from deer harvested in the antlerless hunts in late fall. Tracts were collected from all hunters exiting the area and preserved for later sectioning. The number of embryos, crown-rump length, and sex of embryos were recorded.

RESULTS

Deer Harvests and Population Response

The deer harvest data for the period 1979-83, when antlerless deer were harvested, are summarized in Table 1. In 1979 and 1981, the permits were valid for either sex of deer; in the other years, the special permits were valid for antlerless deer only. The 1979 permit hunt was held on 27 and 28 October. In 1980, the seasons were held in January. From 1981 to 1983, the permit season was held in early December.

Hunter success was lower in those years when either-sex permits were issued. Hunters apparently elected to wait for an antlered deer and passed up opportunities to harvest antlerless deer.

Table 1. Deer harvest data from the Kapowsin Tree Farm, Washington, for the period 1979-83. Data from both the permit season and regular season are included.

Year	Permits	Females			Males			Total
		Adults	Yearlings	Fawns	Antlered	Antlerless	Fawns	
1979	200[a]	55	18	9	189	0	9	282[b]
1980	150	59	17	11	143	5	8	238
1981	300[a]	66	18	17	122	4	21	248
1982	225	64	13	27	96	4	24	228
1983	400	118	51	33	136	7	27	372

[a] Either-sex permits in 1979 and 1981, antlerless in all other years.
[b] Includes 2 fawns of unknown sex.

Although precise estimates of the total deer population in the study area were not available, we estimated the percentage of the population that was harvested. Taylor (pers. commun.) estimated that the deer population in the study area numbered 1,600 deer in 1979 and 1980, based on hunter return data. Deer population estimates for the remaining years were estimated by using the fall deer density estimates as a correction factor. Based on these data, harvest rates have varied from 14.9% in 1980 to a high of 27.1% in 1983 (Table 2).

Population Control

Based on the data from the initial 2 years of the study, we concluded that the antlerless deer harvests had been effective in reducing deer population numbers (see Table 2). Fall deer densities were estimated to have declined 29.8% from 1980 to 1981. However, subsequent analysis of the data from the past 2 years, and data from the surrounding deer management unit, leads to different conclusions.

Several items of circumstantial evidence suggest that the antlerless deer harvests were, at best, only a minor factor in the deer decline. First, the estimated harvest rate for 1980 was only 14.9%, compared to an estimated decline of 29.8%. Second, a similar decline was recorded for the surrounding

Table 2. Deer harvest rates on the Kapowsin Tree Farm, Washington, from 1979 to 1983.

Parameter	1979	1980	1981	1982	1983
Population estimate[a]	1,600	1,600			
Fall deer density[b]		31.5	22.1	23.3	27.1
% change[c]			−29.8	+9.7	+11.9
Calculated population estimate	1,600	1,600	1,112	1,231	1,377
Total deer harvest	282	238	247	233	373
% harvested	17.6	14.9	22.0	18.9	27.1

[a] Based on R. H. Taylor (pers. commun.).
[b] Deer/km^2 in the Beane Creek Drainage.
[c] % change from the previous year's density estimate.

deer management unit where there were no antlerless deer harvests. Deer numbers were reported to have declined from 11,750 to 10,000 (8.9%) in Game Management Unit 478 over the same period (Washington Department of Game, unpubl. data). Third, continued higher deer harvests and estimated deer harvest rates in the subsequent years have not resulted in any comparable decline in the deer population. In fact, all indicators (e.g., hunter success rates, antlered deer harvests, and census results) suggest that the deer population has actually increased since 1981. The hunts may have only dampened the deer population recovery after the decline in 1980-81.

Seasonal Movements of Deer

A series of transects taken through fall and winter on the same clearcut areas typically shows a trend of increasing deer population density (Fig. 2). The seasonal increase in deer density is presumably due to an influx of migrants. Its timing varies from year to year. On the basis of present knowledge, we could schedule a herd-reduction (antlerless deer) hunt in mid-December and be confident that both the resident and migratory deer subpopulations would be reduced.

Density-Carrying Capacity Relations Reflected in Deer Condition

The relative level of nutrition of the individual deer reflects the condition of the population in relation to the carrying capacity of the environment. When deer are crowded onto winter foraging areas above the current carrying capacity of the habitat, the average level of nutrition will be sub-optimal. Sub-optimal nutrition is reflected in the condition of the individual deer (Cowan and Wood 1955).

Winter undernutrition will delay the rate of growth in juveniles and, hence, the age of sexual maturation. Adult females, if they have not recovered from winter undernutrition by the following fall, will experience a sub-optimal ovulation rate and, hence, fecundity (Klein 1969, Crouch 1981, Short 1981). Results for the period 1979-82 indicate that anterless hunts have been followed by an increase in deer productivity (Fig. 3).

From this we predict that an annual increase in the harvest of antlerless deer in winter hunts will result in an increase of males harvested in the regular fall hunting season because of the increase in production and survival of male fawns to yearling age and beyond. This increase in the harvestable crop of males should continue year after year until the female component of the herd has reached its optimal level of physical condition and its biotic potential for reproduction.

DISCUSSION

The information received in this report has been obtained in support of the development and execution of a series of annual herd management plans aimed at reducing winter deer damage to conifer seedlings to a

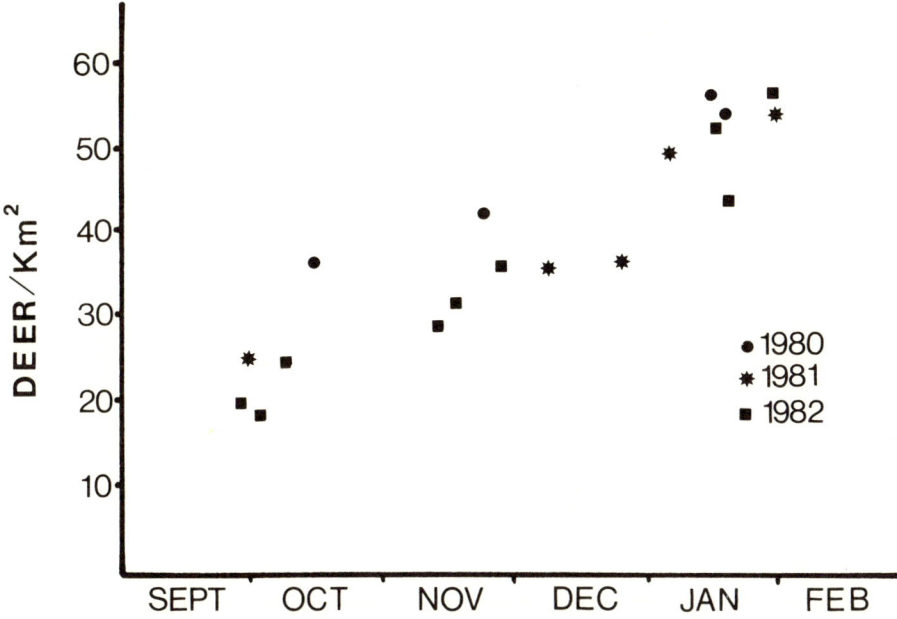

Fig. 2. Seasonal change in deer densities on the Kapowsin Tree Farm, Washington, from late summer to winter, based on line transect census techniques.

tolerable level through controlled public hunting. Some of the major variables that have been identified are: varying winter conditions, which affect the timing of migratory deer movement onto the winter range; changes in the physical condition and productivity of deer associated with changes in winter population pressure; and annual seedling damage in deer winter concentration areas. The overall object of the sequence of annual deer management plans would be to have each annual harvest take place at the right time and attain the correct deer kill to keep winter deer density in 0-10-year-old clearcuts below 24 deer/km^2.

Timing of the antlerless deer hunt is important, since the hunt should take place shortly after most of the early winter influx of migratory deer has occurred. This would cause an early reduction in winter deer concentration and would provide hunters with deer in better physical condition than they would be later. Since the timing of migration varies from year to year depending on the snow accumulation pattern on the summer range, there should be a parallel annual variation in the timing of the antlerless harvest. Three kinds of evidence bear on the question of when the main migratory movement has been made:

1. During the regular fall buck season, the effects of an early winter and early migration will be noted in a higher-than-average rate of hunter success (deer harvested/100 hunter-days afield) and a higher-than-average total buck harvest.

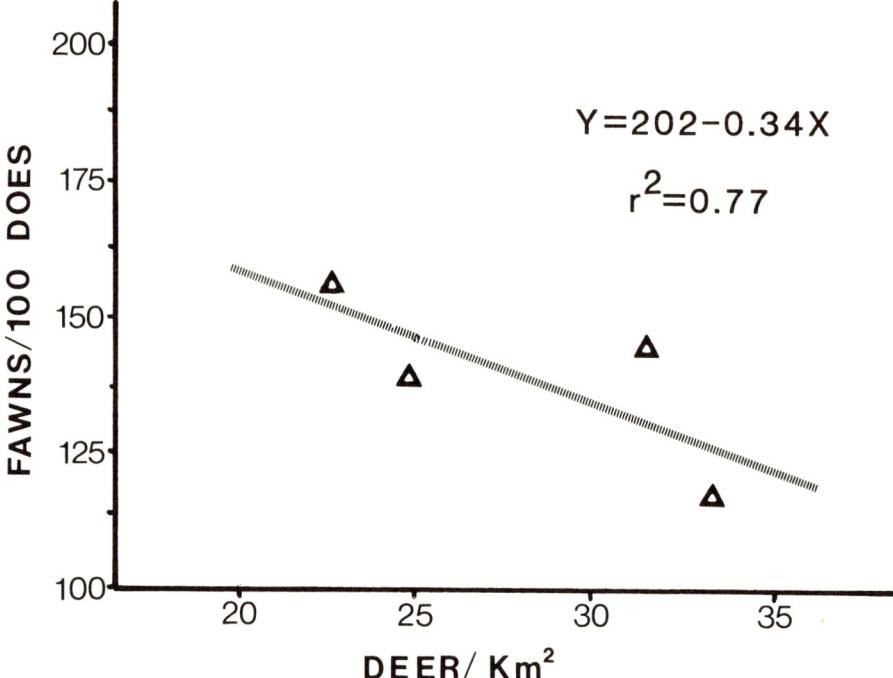

Fig. 3. The relationship between deer densities on the winter range areas of the Kapowsin Tree Farm in fall, and reproductive rates of adult deer harvested during the special permit hunts, 1979-83.

2. A series of deer density estimates made on a representative sample of 0-10-year-old clearcuts on the winter range through late fall and early winter will show level of winter density and time of arrival of migratory deer.
3. Systematic surveys of snow conditions on the summer range will correlate with the evidence obtained under (1) and (2) above.

Assuming that the antlerless harvest can be made at the proper season each year, it remains to fix the proper numbers to be harvested. As herd density is reduced, deer condition and productivity have increased. This means that a proportionally higher percentage of the population must be taken with each downward step in post-hunt deer winter density. The result will be an annual increase in the desired antlerless deer harvest until the target winter density is attained.

Public understanding and support of this system of management will be strengthened to the extent that there is reliable evidence that it has resulted in an amelioration of seedling damage and a substantial increase in the number and quality of harvestable deer.

LITERATURE CITED

AMARAL, M. 1978. Black-tailed deer (*Odocoileus hemionus columbianus*) and forest reproduction: Blake Island Marine State Park, Washington. Northwest Sci. 52:233-235.

BROWN, E. R. 1961. The black-tailed deer of western Washington. Wash. State Game Dep. Biol. Bull. 13. 124pp.

BURNHAM, K. P., D. R. ANDERSON, AND J. L. LAAKE. 1980. Estimation of density from line transect sampling of biological populations. Wildl. Monogr. 72. 202pp.

COWAN, I. McT., AND A. J. WOOD. 1955. The growth rate of the black-tailed deer (*Odocoileus hemionus columbianus*). J. Wildl. Manage. 19:331-36.

CROUCH, G. L. 1981. Food habits and nutrition. Pages 99-128 *in* O. Wallmo, ed. Mule and black-tailed deer of North America. Univ. Nebraska Press, Lincoln.

GATES, C., W. MARSHALL, AND D. OLSON. 1968. Line transect method of estimating grouse densities. Biometrics 24:135-145.

HARESTAD, A. S., AND G. W. JONES. 1980. Use of nightcounts for censusing black-tailed deer on Vancouver Island. Pages 83-96 *in* F. L. Miller and A. Gunn, eds. Symposium on census and inventory methods for population and habitats. Univ. Idaho Forest, Wildl. and Range Exp. Sta., Contrib. 217.

HINES, W. W. 1963. Relationships of black-tailed deer density to conifer survival. Proc. Western Assoc. State Game and Fish Comm. 43:189-192.

KISTNER, T. P., C. R. TRAINER, AND N. A. HARTMAN. 1980. A field technique for evaluating physical condition of deer. Wildl. Soc. Bull. 8:11-17.

KLEIN, D. R. 1969. Food selection by North American deer and their response to overutilization of preferred forage species. Pages 25-44 *in* A. Watson, ed. Animal populations in relation to their food resources. Blackwell Scientific Publications, Oxford, U.K.

PROGULSKE, D. R., AND D. C. DUERRE. 1964. Factors influencing spotlight counts of deer. J. Wildl. Manage. 28:27-34.

SHORT, H. L. 1981. Nutrition and metabolism. Pages 99-128 *in* O. Wallmo, ed. Mule and black-tailed deer of North America. Univ. Nebraska Press, Lincoln.

BUCK PERMITS AS A MANAGEMENT TOOL IN SOUTH TEXAS

HORACE G. GORE, Texas Parks and Wildlife Department, Austin, TX 78744
WILLIAM F. HARWELL, Texas Parks and Wildlife Department, Kerrville, TX 78028
MICHAEL D. HOBSON, Texas Parks and Wildlife Department, Laredo, TX 78041
WILLBERN J. WILLIAMS, Texas Parks and Wildlife Department, San Antonio, TX 78216

Abstract: Buck permits for the harvest of fork-antlered white-tailed deer (*Odocoileus virginianus*) were issued to landowners in Webb County, Texas from 1974 to 1982 as a means of controlling buck harvest. This regulation was imposed as a management tool for maintaining the high quality (body weight and antler development) for which that county is noted. Permit issuance rates were established to harvest 25% of the estimated annual buck population. Restrictive hunting pressure using buck permits decreased the average harvest by 10% but did not significantly change the downward trend in buck quality. Buck harvest was reduced by 59% on landownerships of less than 405 ha, but these tracts comprise only 6% of the deer range and 11% of the buck harvest. Buck permits failed to achieve widespread implementation as a method of conserving bucks and promoting an adequate antlerless deer harvest. The hypothesis that buck permits function as a better method of quality deer management was not proven, based on issuance rates acceptable to the public and a deer herd that was of relatively high quality when the program was started.

KEY WORDS: Permit system, Quality deer, Hunting pressure, Restricted harvest.

The South Texas Plains of Texas (Fig. 1) is known for producing heavy-bodied white-tailed deer with desirable trophy antler characteristics. In recent years, the quality of bucks harvested from south Texas has declined to a point of concern to landowners and hunters.

In 1974, the Texas Parks and Wildlife Department (TPWD) initiated a 5-year experimental buck permit regulation to determine what effect restricting the buck harvest would have on the quality (body weight and antler development) of bucks harvested in Webb County, which is best-known of all south Texas counties for producing trophy quality bucks.

The study was started at the request of several landowners who controlled the majority of the county's land area. They alleged that the harvest of bucks on small tracts was so excessive that bucks were being harvested before they achieved their potential body size and antler development. A cursory examination of limited available data supported this allegation by indicating a decline in the average age of bucks, a widening sex ratio, a decline in average field-dressed weight and antler development, and an indirect ratio of buck harvest:ranch size.

In 1978, the experimental buck permit regulation was ended, and all data were evaluated. Although there were some doubts whether buck permits would alter the general decline in deer quality that had beset the Webb County deer herd, recommendations were made to continue with buck permits so that landowners could take advantage of regulations and

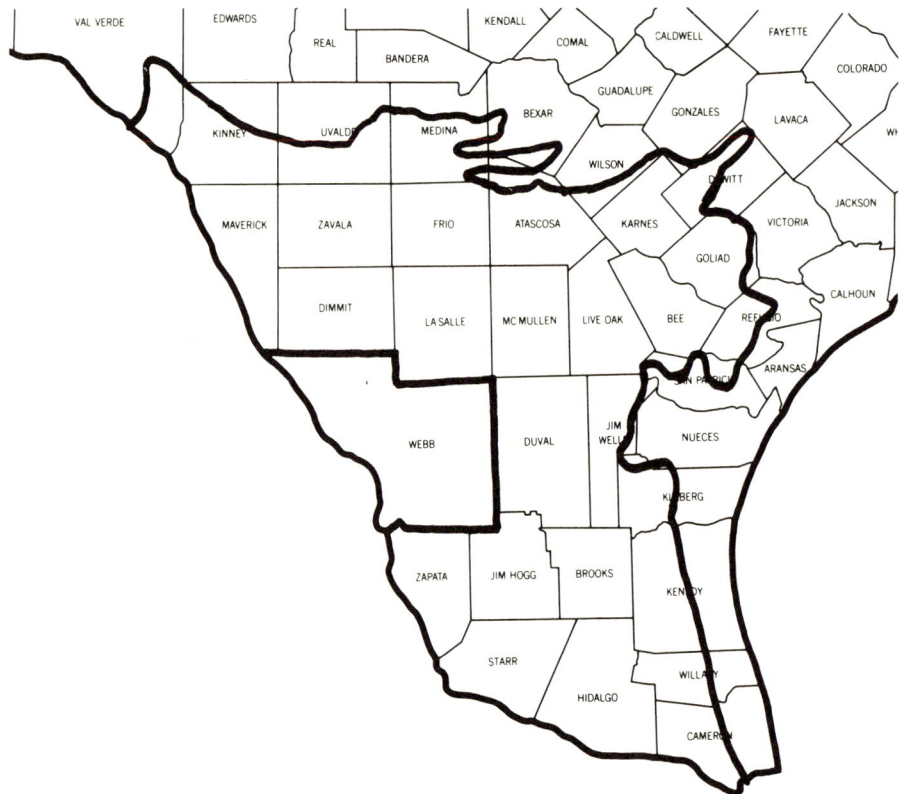

Fig. 1. Geographic location of Webb County within the South Texas Plains Ecological Area.

implement programs that sought to improve buck quality and to control the total deer population through acceleration of antlerless deer harvest.

The objectives for issuing buck permits on a restricted basis in Webb County were as follows:

1. To determine if hunting pressure on buck deer would be reduced in areas where small landownership tracts occur.
2. To determine if the issuance of buck permits on an acreage basis would result in a more balanced buck:doe ratio in the deer herd.
3. To determine if the age class and quality of the buck deer in Webb County would increase with the restricted issuance of buck permits.
4. To determine if the harvest of buck deer by permit would be a better method of managing the deer population in Webb County.
5. To determine if the harvest of buck deer by permit would provide a means for control and/or more equitable distribution of buck hunting pressure.
6. To determine if buck permits on a restricted basis would promote an adequate harvest of antlerless deer in Webb County.

We wish to acknowledge the contributions of B. C. Booth, J. L. Cooke, J. R. Fugate, J. G. Herrera, J. D. Hillje, R. E. Hutchison, S. C. Kierce, and C. R. Wilkins in collecting data for this study. Special acknowledgement is given to C. K. Winkler, D. B. Frels, and R. L. Cook for supervision of the study.

METHODS

During the initial 2 years of the experiment, buck permits were issued to landowners without limits or restrictions. Hunters, however, were required to check all harvested deer at 1 of 4 TPWD check stations (situated at strategic locations in the county) within 72 hours after a kill was made. At the check station, department personnel collected various biological data to include: date of kill, sex of deer, weight (field-dressed) of deer, age of deer as determined by tooth wear and replacement, name and location of ranch where the deer was killed, antler spread (inside), antler beam circumference (1 antler), number of points on each antler, and length of main beam (1978 only).

Beginning in 1976, the issuance of buck permits was restricted according to acreage using the formula:

$$P = \frac{A - B + C - D}{U}$$

where

A = standing buck crop (previous year),
B = buck harvest (previous year),
C = buck fawn replacement (current year),
D = desired buck carryover (75%),
U = anticipated permit use rate,
P = permits/405 ha.

An issuance rate of 1 permit/93 ha was calculated to restrict the buck harvest to 25% of the projected pre-hunting-season population. Although the issuance rate could have been liberalized in the final 2 years of the 5-year experiment, it was retained throughout the experiment to facilitate interpretation of the results. An original policy, which remains in effect, was that every *bona fide* landowner qualified for at least 1 buck permit, regardless of acreage.

During the first 2 years of restricted permit issuance (1976-77), biological data were collected from cold storage facilities in Laredo, Freer, Zapata, and other south Texas cities. A pilot study in 1975 had revealed no significant difference ($P > 0.05$) between check station data and that obtained from cold-storage facilities if collections were stratified by week. However, check stations were again operated in 1978 to collect a sample of biological data comparable to the samples obtained before restricted permit issuance.

Even before initiation of the permits, we recognized that any restriction of the buck harvest would be controversial. In the case of buck permits, which would be allocated to land operators according to the acreage they controlled for hunting, population levels and herd composition had to be estimated as accurately as possible. All population inventories were conducted by observations from fixed-wing aircraft flown on established transects at a height of 46 m above ground level at as slow a speed as possible. During the experiment, approximately 1,855 km of aerial census were flown annually in Webb County.

Since the conclusion of the 5-year experimental period, an operational system of permit issuance has been in effect in Webb County and has been implemented in 3 adjacent counties: Duval, Maverick, and Zapata. The annual issuance rates were formulated (when practical) on population levels and characteristics. Where accurate deer census was difficult because of visibility restrictions, permit issuance rates followed previous harvest trends as a control against unregulated increases in harvest.

RESULTS AND DISCUSSION

Census and Population Data

The estimated deer population in Webb County during the fall of 1982 was 61,396 deer (Table 1). The deer population increased from 20.8 deer/405 ha in 1970 to a high of 39.5 deer/405 ha in 1977. Statistical analysis of the population indicated a significant long-term increase in the deer herd until a severe drought in 1980 caused the population to plummet to an 8-year low (Table 2). However, in response to improved range conditions, the population is recovering.

Buck Harvest

Restricted buck permits did not significantly ($P > 0.05$) reduce the overall buck kill in Webb County (Table 3). Harvest estimates for 1982, based on

Table 1. Deer census data from aerial surveys for Webb County, Texas 1982.

1. Amount of deer range - 830,709 ha
2. Total ha sampled in county - 30,804
3. Total km aerial transects - 654
4. Total N bucks observed - 343
5. Total N does observed - 1,063
6. Total N fawns observed - 369
7. Total N undetermined deer observed - 502
8. Total deer observed in survey - 2,227
9. Buck:doe ratio - 1:3.1
10. Fawn:doe ratio - 1:0.4
11. Estimated deer density - 1/13.5 ha
12. Estimated deer/405 ha - 29.9
13. Estimated deer in Webb County - 61,396

Table 2. Deer density (*N*/405ha) from aerial surveys, as determined in Webb County, Texas, 1970-82.

	1970	1971	1972	1973	1974	1975	1976	1977	1978	1979	1980[a]	1981	1982
Bucks	5.0	4.5	5.0	6.3	6.7	6.3	5.4	7.5	8.7	6.5	6.0	5.6	5.8
Does	12.0	12.6	11.9	17.3	18.2	15.0	19.1	22.1	23.2	20.8	15.3	14.7	17.9
Fawns	3.8	6.0	6.8	5.2	2.8	7.4	7.9	9.9	5.8	8.0	3.3	10.4	6.2
Total	20.8	23.1	23.7	28.8	27.7	28.7	32.4	39.5	37.7	35.3	24.6	30.7	29.92
Estimated deer population	44,754	49,715	51,011	62,037	59,631	61,859	64,403	81,165	77,428	77,820	50,451	62,960	61,396

[a] Severe drought caused population decline.

Table 3. Comparison of buck harvest by ranch size during years of unrestricted and restricted permits in Webb County, Texas, 1974-82.

	Unrestricted permit issuance				1 permit/93 ha					
	1974		1975		1976		1977		1978	
Ranch size (ha)	Estimated kill	Kill/ 405 ha	Estimated kill	Kill/ 405 ha	Estimated kill	Kill/ 405 ha	Estimated kill	Kill/ 405 ha	Estimated kill	Kill/ 405 ha
1-40	94	21.4	122	24.6	46	7.6	87	11.2	39	4.4
41-101	160	11.7	100	9.7	39	2.5	42	2.8	20	1.2
102-202	184	9.3	168	8.3	30	2.0	25	1.5	27	1.3
203-405	237	5.7	317	6.4	104	2.2	102	2.1	140	2.7
406-1,012	458	3.4	522	3.9	250	1.7	282	2.0	257	1.7
1,013-2,024	741	2.8	762	2.9	526	2.1	557	2.1	569	2.2
2,025-4,048	421	1.5	512	1.7	328	1.2	433	1.5	423	1.4
4,049+	1,110	1.2	1,446	1.1	1,550	1.1	1,651	1.3	1,614	1.3
Totals	3,405	1.6	3,949	1.8	2,873	1.4	3,179	1.6	3,089	1.5

	1 permit/61 ha and 1 permit/91 ha				1 permit/73 ha and 1 permit/202 ha		1 permit/61 ha and 1 permit/101 ha	
	1979		1980		1981		1982	
Ranch size (ha)	Estimated kill	Kill/ 405 ha	Estimated kill	Kill/ 405 ha	Estimated kill	Kill/ 405 ha	Estimated kill	Kill/ 405 ha
1-40	141	6.0[a]	151	13.9	218	17.2	35	2.4
41-101	141	6.0[a]	81	4.6	82	4.8	186	9.8
102-202	44	2.5	45	2.0	47	2.4	98	3.7
203-405	187	3.2	174	3.1	196	3.6	220	3.3
406-1,012	429	2.6	449	2.7	461	2.8	788	4.1
1,013-2,204	524	2.1	536	2.3	535	2.4	904	3.2
2,025-4,048	587	1.8	624	1.7	571	1.6	612	1.5
4,049+	1,702	1.3	1,390	1.2	1,574	1.5	1,987	2.0
Totals	3,614	1.7	3,450	1.7	3,684	2.0	4,830	2.6

[a] Ranch size 1-40 ha and 41-101 ha combined in 1979.

deer permit receipts, were 2.6 bucks/405 ha. Harvest data summarized by ranch size indicated a significant ($P < 0.05$) change in the buck harvest rate on landownerships with less than 405 ha. Buck-permit return data showed that 4.2 bucks/405 ha were harvested on ranches of 405 ha or less in 1982, a 59% decrease from 1974. Ranches in this category comprised 73% of the landowners who drew permits, but they controlled only 6% of the county's deer range.

The 6-year average harvest before restricted permits was 3,945 bucks. During 7 years of restricted permits, the average harvest was 3,531 bucks, a decrease of approximately 10%. This decrease is not significant at the 90% confidence level (Table 3). The reason for this insignificant change in the long-term harvest is that 71% of the hunted deer range in Webb County is comprised of ranches larger than 2,024 ha (Table 4). These large ownerships receive more than an adequate number of permits to achieve their desired deer harvest. Accordingly, restricted permits apparently have little effect on the overall county buck kill.

Table 4. A comparison of buck permit issuance by ranch size in Webb County, Texas, 1974-82.

Ranch size (Ac)	N landowners		Acreage involved		Distribution of landowners		Distribution of acreage	
	1974	1982	1974	1982	1974	1982	1974	1982
1-40	104	510	4,416	14,371	18.6%	47.0%	0.3%	0.7%
41-101	84	120	13,603	19,006	15.8%	11.1%	0.8%	0.9%
102-202	55	72	19,813	26,873	9.8%	6.6%	1.1%	1.3%
203-405	61	88	41,985	66,703	10.9%	8.1%	2.4%	3.3%
406-1,012	92	116	133,690	190,207	16.4%	10.7%	7.7%	9.4%
1,013-2,024	74	78	266,858	278,949	13.2%	7.2%	15.5%	13.8%
2,025-4,048	42	60	288,495	420,456	7.5%	5.5%	16.7%	20.7%
4,049 +	48	41	956,368	1,010,967	8.6%	3.8%	55.4%	49.9%
Total	560	1,085	1,725,288	2,027,536	100.0%	100.0%	100.0%	100.0%

Table 5. Percentage of buck deer harvest by age class compared for 3 regulatory periods in Webb County, Texas, 1970-82.

	Buck permit regulatory periods												
	None				Unrestricted					Restricted			
Age class	1970	1971	1972	1973	1974	1975	1976	1977	1978	1979	1980	1981	1982
0.5-1.5	10	14	14	22	16	10	10	9	7	8	15	11	12
2.5-3.5	48	50	23	43	55	56	40	42	50	39	24	25	32
4.5+	42	36	62	35	29	34	50	49	43	53	61	64	56
Sample size	146	126	70	250	3,951[a]	3,867[a]	348	353	2,294[a]	100	100	136	119

[a] County-wide check stations.

Buck Age, Weight, and Antler Measurements

The age structure of the buck harvest in 1982 indicated 56% of the bucks harvested were 4.5 years old or older as opposed to 42% in 1970 (Table 5). We do not know whether this reflects a change in the population characteristics not associated with harvest or in buck selectivity by hunters. The age structure can furnish a large number of mature bucks harvestable at the existing harvest rate. In fact, Webb County may have an inordinate surplus of mature age-class bucks, which creates a potential for waste.

Table 6 shows field-dressed weight and antler data for 1982. Table 7 presents a 13-year trend in average field-dressed weights of bucks by age class. Data from 1970-82 show that field-dressed buck weights within age classes are still declining in Webb County ($P < 0.05$).

Bucks harvested between 1970 and 1978 also exhibited a long-term decline in antler beam circumference, antler spread, and number of points (Table 7). Increased competition for food by higher deer numbers may have caused the decline in antler quality and field-dressed weights (Table 2).

Antlerless Deer Harvest

From 1974 to 1979, the antlerless deer harvest increased (Table 8). A severe drought in 1980 reduced deer numbers and, subsequently, the number of antlerless permits issued to landowners. Although there appeared to be a gradual acceptance of antlerless harvest, the number of permits used annually was less than 50% of the number needed to control the increasing deer population. Regulation of population numbers through the harvest of antlerless deer is fundamental to a quality white-tailed deer management program. Failure to harvest them has resulted in increased competition for forage, resulting in reduced body weights/age class, poorer antler development, and reduced reproductive efficiency. The issuance of buck permits on an acreage basis alone did not improve the quality of bucks harvested in Webb County.

Table 6. Average field-dressed weights and antler measurements of bucks harvested in Webb County, Texas, 1982.

Age	N aged and measured	% in age class	Mean weight (kg)	Mean points	Mean spread (cm)	Mean circumference (cm)	Mean length main beam (cm)
1.5	14	11.8	29.1	2.5	12.4	4.6	13.2
2.5	12	10.1	36.3	5.8	22.1	6.4	27.7
3.5	26	21.8	45.9	8.0	33.3	8.4	41.4
4.5	13	10.9	49.5	9.2	38.4	9.4	47.8
5.5	23	19.3	55.8	9.5	43.2	10.4	51.8
6.5	27	22.7	55.4	10.0	45.2	10.4	51.8
7.5	3	2.5	53.6	10.0	37.3	10.4	47.0
8.5+	1	0.8	43.1	8.0	38.1	9.7	40.4

Table 7. Trend in physical characteristics, by age class, of bucks harvested in Webb County, Texas, 1970-82.

	1.5				2.5				3.5			
Year	Dressed weight (kg)	Beam circumference (cm)	Antler spread (cm)	Antler points	Dressed weight (kg)	Beam circumference (cm)	Antler spread (cm)	Antler points	Dressed weight (kg)	Beam circumference (cm)	Antler spread (cm)	Antler points
1970	41.9	6.6	22.4	5.5	50.2	8.1	33.5	8.0	56.2	9.4	37.6	8.6
1971	37.0	5.8	21.8	4.1	48.8	7.9	32.0	7.5	55.4	9.4	38.3	9.3
1972	34.0	6.6	22.4	5.4	40.6	7.9	30.1	7.6	47.7	9.1	33.0	7.6
1973	36.8	5.6	16.5	3.7	46.0	7.9	31.8	7.2	49.8	8.9	34.3	8.3
1974	34.5	5.8	17.5	4.0	42.5	7.9	29.0	7.0	47.4	8.6	33.0	7.9
1975	34.7	5.8	19.1	4.5	42.9	7.6	30.5	7.3	48.4	8.6	35.1	8.3
1976	34.4	4.8	14.5	3.4	43.6	9.9	30.2	7.4	51.3	8.9	35.8	8.3
1977	32.6	5.3	15.7	3.7	41.1	7.4	30.0	7.5	46.2	8.6	34.3	8.4
1978	32.3	4.8	15.0	3.1	41.9	7.1	28.4	6.8	46.8	8.1	33.0	7.8
1979	28.6	4.6	12.7	3.3	32.2	6.4	23.6	4.4	45.4	8.4	33.0	8.2
1980	31.8	4.8	12.1	2.7	36.3	5.6	21.8	4.4	45.4	7.4	30.1	7.0
1981	33.1	5.0	13.0	2.9	43.1	7.1	32.5	6.9	49.5	8.9	34.5	8.9
1982	29.1	4.6	12.4	2.5	36.3	6.4	22.1	5.8	45.9	8.4	33.3	8.0

	4.5				5.5				6.5			
Year	Dressed weight (kg)	Beam circumference (cm)	Antler spread (cm)	Antler points	Dressed weight (kg)	Beam circumference (cm)	Antler spread (cm)	Antler points	Dressed weight (kg)	Beam circumference (cm)	Antler spread (cm)	Antler points
1970	64.7	10.9	47.2	9.2	64.3	10.7	47.2	11.2	66.1	12.2	45.2	10.5
1971	64.2	11.2	46.5	9.8	67.1	11.2	47.8	9.2	71.6	11.7	48.0	11.0
1972	57.7	10.2	42.2	9.4	57.6	10.9	42.2	9.5	61.1	11.2	43.9	10.0
1973	59.7	10.4	40.4	9.4	61.6	11.2	43.7	9.7	60.2	11.9	46.2	10.4
1974	52.9	9.1	37.8	8.7	56.9	10.7	42.2	9.4	58.3	11.2	45.0	9.6
1975	53.9	9.1	38.9	8.9	60.6	10.2	41.1	9.1	62.6	10.9	43.7	9.7
1976	55.8	9.9	40.1	9.4	61.1	10.7	42.9	10.1	61.4	10.9	45.2	10.0
1977	55.8	9.9	41.1	9.6	58.0	10.7	43.2	9.8	59.5	10.9	46.5	10.1
1978	53.0	9.1	40.9	8.7	57.1	10.2	40.9	9.3	58.8	10.4	41.7	9.3
1979	50.8	9.4	45.2	9.5	59.5	10.9	45.2	10.1	54.5	11.2	47.2	10.5
1980	52.7	9.1	39.9	8.9	55.8	9.9	39.9	9.5	54.5	10.4	43.2	9.1
1981	55.8	10.4	40.9	9.4	58.6	9.9	40.9	9.5	60.4	10.9	45.7	9.8
1982	49.5	9.4	43.2	9.2	55.8	10.4	43.2	9.5	55.4	10.4	45.2	10.0

Table 8. Deer permit issuance in Webb County, Texas, 1974-82.

Antlerless permit	1974	1975	1976	1977	1978	1979	1980	1981	1982
Permits issued	1,333	2,966	4,504	5,286	6,347	7,714	2,802	3,225	7,644
Landowners involved	146	188	254	300	349	462	339	337	540
Area involved (ha)	217,754	494,211	605,983	636,327	752,608	729,743	586,871	678,397	760,510
Antlerless harvest	215	475	1,067	1,764	1,059	2,893	1,190	2,185	2,188
% utilization of permits	16.1	16.0	23.7	33.3	16.7	37.5	42.5	67.8	28.6

Buck permit	1974	1975	1976[a]	1977	1978	1979	1980	1981	1982
Permits issued	11,302	11,207	7,510	7,932	7,981	9,664	8,404	7,631	10,108
Landowners involved	560	551	590	661	785	756	858	886	1,085
Acre involved (ha)	698,717	839,522	867,355	851,766	845,745	857,707	834,967	763,503	821,152
Buck harvest	3,405	3,949	2,873	3,179	3,089	3,614	3,450	3,684	4,830
% utilization of permits	30.1	35.2	38.3	40.1	38.7	37.4	41.1	48.3	47.8

[a] Permits restricted on acreage basis beginning in 1976.

Evaluation of the Buck Permit Objectives

The following evaluation of the Webb County Buck Permit System includes an objective look at program results. Buck permits have definitely made the hunting public aware of problems associated with deer herd management in south Texas and in Webb County. Since proper deer herd management is largely people management, public acceptance is essential when program implementation depends upon public cooperation.

First, buck harvest data show that the issuance of restricted buck permits (1976-82) did reduce the buck kill in Webb County. The buck harvest on landownerships of less than 405 ha was reduced 59%. Public awareness of the deer herd problems in Webb County and the fact that restricted permits will eliminate buck overharvest on smaller landownership make the buck permit system a potential management tool for landowners who wish to maintain mature age-class bucks. Permit control of buck overharvest on smaller acreages provided an incentive for surrounding landowners to properly manage deer. The restricted issuance rates assured each landowner that his neighbors could not legally harvest more bucks than their land would sustain.

Second, the buck permit system did not affect the buck:doe ratio in Webb County. The doe segment of the population increased at approximately the same rate as the buck segment; consequently, the sex ratio was not altered.

Third, the number and percentage of adult buck deer (4.5 years old and older) in the harvest have increased since the buck permit system was started. We believe that since the initiation of buck permits some hunters are more selective in harvesting bucks. The system itself did not improve nor maintain the quality (antler size and body weight) of bucks harvested in Webb County. The continued decline in quality may be closely associated with an increasing deer population perpetuated by a low utilization of antlerless deer permits. Issuance of buck permits will not improve deer quality in Webb County or in other counties unless an adequate doe harvest also is applied, because improvement in antler development and body size depends upon adequate quantities of high quality deer food, not upon harvest regulations.

Fourth, the buck permit system to date is not a better method of managing deer. As a group, landowners and sportsmen have not responded favorably to the opportunities that the buck permit system has made available. Although there may be an increasing awareness for the need to reduce deer numbers and improve habitat conditions, progress is slow. Proper deer herd and/or trophy buck management depends upon an abundance of high quality, nutritious forage and population control to prevent competition for preferred deer food and overpopulation. Although an important facet of deer herd management, especially trophy deer management, the buck harvest rate is definitely second in importance to high quality nutrition in the production of quality buck deer of any age.

Fifth, buck permits are conducive to more efficient game law enforcement because they must be attached to each legally harvested buck deer. Illegal harvesting of bucks is discouraged since only landowners can supply buck permits. These permits reduced the legal buck harvest in Webb County on ranches less than 405 ha (Table 4). However, issuance of restricted buck permits diminished hunting's aesthetic and economic benefits on ranches less than 405 ha.

The state-wide white-tailed deer harvest survey showed that the number of deer hunters in Webb County dropped from a 3-year average of 10,366 hunters before buck permit issuance was restricted (1973-75) to an average of 9,314 hunters during the 7 years (1976-82) of restricted permits (Boydston and Harwell 1982, 1983); the number of hunters decreased 10%. During this period, the number of hunter days in Webb County dropped from a 3-year average of 66,395 during unrestricted buck harvest to a 7-year average of 51,435 hunter days during restricted permit issuance. The number of hunter days in Webb County decreased 23%. The reduction in the number of hunters and hunter days is probably a direct result of the buck permit. The reduction in hunter activity recorded in Webb County did not occur in LaSalle County, which has a similar season and bag limit. In fact, during the same 10 years, the number of hunters in LaSalle County (immediately north of Webb County) increased 10%. In Jim Hogg County, buck kill and hunter numbers remained constant. In 1976, Dimmit County officials requested that the hunting season be experimentally reduced to 30 days ending in mid-December; the number of hunters in that county decreased approximately 17% and the buck harvest 51% (Harwell and Cook 1979).

These data clearly showed that the buck harvest in south Texas can be regulated on small tracts by buck permits and area-wide by a shortened season that prevents hunting during the last 2 weeks of December when bucks are most active. Harvest chronology data from south Texas have previously indicated that almost 50% of the bucks are harvested during the last 2 weeks of December, which coincides with the peak of the area's rutting activity (Harwell and Barron 1975).

Last, antlerless deer permits have been issued for 11 consecutive years in Webb County. In 1972, only 10 antlerless deer were harvested. Since that meager beginning, the program has grown slowly and steadily. In 1982, 7,644 permits were issued and 2,188 were used. However, we cannot determine if the growth in antlerless deer harvest is a result of buck permits or simply an increased acceptance of the antlerless deer program. The interest and awareness in deer herd management created by buck permits has helped speed up the acceptance of the antlerless deer harvest. As a result, more antlerless deer have been harvested in Webb County since 1976 than would have otherwise been harvested.

These data also pointed out a potential problem resulting from restricting buck harvest. South Texas needs large numbers of hunters to properly harvest antlerless deer. By restricting the buck harvest in this area, hunter numbers and hunter days have been reduced. It is apparent that the present number of hunters are not adequately controlling deer numbers through antlerless deer harvest. For example, the 1982 kill of approximately 2,000 antlerless deer in Webb County was only 33% of the recommended harvest.

Advantages of Buck Permits (as issued).—

1. They provide the opportunity for landowners to manage deer by preventing the exploitation of bucks by neighboring landowners.
2. They enable more effective law enforcement because all bucks must be tagged with a permit obtainable only from a landowner.
3. They can make a long-range contribution to trophy deer management in south Texas and other areas of the state by limiting the buck kill to a desired level.
4. They serve as an annual reminder to landowners and hunters that buck harvest needs regulation.

Disadvantages of Buck Permits (as issued).—

1. The tracts can be divided among co-owners to increase the number of permits.
2. The format of the permit enables illegal re-use.
3. The utilization factor in the formula inflates issuance rate to the extent that large ownerships could overharvest bucks.
4. Buck permit issuance rates often exceed antlerless permit rates because of the utilization factor. Many landowners who are entitled to more buck than doe permits question this.
5. Deer population density may be so heterogeneous that an equitable issuance of buck permits is impractical.
6. Restricted issuance of buck permits has a severe effect on hunting economics and the aesthetic value and recreation associated with family hunting.
7. Buck permits often affect a high percentage of landowners who control a minute portion of the deer range.

CONCLUSIONS

During the 7 years of restricted buck permits in Webb County, the following observations were documented:

1. Restricted permits effectively reduced the buck kill on tracts of 405 ha or less.
2. Deer herd quality was not improved.
3. Antlerless deer harvest was not increased to adequately control the deer population.
4. The reduced hunting pressure on bucks was not shifted to the harvest of antlerless deer.

5. The age structure of harvested mature bucks was slightly increased.
6. In 1982, approximately 56% of the bucks harvested were at least 4.5 years old, indicating that the deer herd had an inordinately high percentage of mature bucks.
7. No improvement in the buck:doe ratio was documented.
8. Antler measurements and field-dressed weights (by age class) continued to decline.
9. Tracts of 405 ha or less accounted for 73% of the landowners, 6% of the deer range, and 11% of the buck harvest.
10. The hypothesis that buck permits function as a better method of managing deer in Webb County was not proven, based on issuance rates acceptable to the public and a deer herd that was of relatively high quality when the program was started.
11. Buck permits definitely made the hunting public more aware of the need for intensive deer management programs, but land managers did not fully take the initiative of implementing such programs.

LITERATURE CITED

BOYDSTON, G. A., AND F. H. HARWELL. 1982. Big game harvest regulations. Tex. Parks and Wildl. Dep. Prog. Report, P-R Proj. W-109-R-5. Job 5. 135pp.

———, AND ———. 1983. Big game harvest regulations. Tex. Parks and Wildl. Dep. Prog. Report, P-R Proj. W-109-R-6. Job 4. 139pp.

HARWELL, W. F., AND J. C. BARRON. 1975. The breeding season of the white-tailed deer in southern Texas. Tex. J. Sci. 25:417-420.

———, AND R. L. COOK. 1979. Evaluation of an experimental deer hunting season in Dimmit County. Tex. Parks and Wildl. Dep. Spec. Report, Big Game Invest. W-109-R-2. 14pp.

DEER HARVEST MANAGEMENT, WELDER AND McCAN RANCH, TEXAS

NOEL E. ADAMS, JR., Welder and McCan Ranch, P.O. Box T, Woodsboro, TX 78393

Abstract: The Welder and McCan Ranch was opened to lease hunting in 1974; by 1978, 21, 707 ha were under lease to 18 groups of hunters. Each group had exclusive and unrestricted hunting rights to their portion of the ranch. An overharvest of male white-tailed deer (*Odocoileus virginianus*) occurred under this arrangement. To reduce this disparity, a voluntary quota was set but was unsuccessful; post-season sex ratios widened to 1 buck:11.6 does. In 1980, a different harvest management strategy was initiated. Strict harvest quotas were set based on pre- and post-season helicopter censuses. The quotas represented 33% of the estimated standing crop of males, and does were to be harvested at a rate of at least 2 and preferably 3/buck. Control of the harvest was gained by use of a check station where hunters were required to sign in, report all game killed, and bring all deer killed for data collection. By January 1983, post-season sex ratios had improved to 1 buck:4.9 does with a corresponding increase in the quality of the bucks harvested. A September 1983 census showed a pre-season sex ratio of 1 buck:3.6 does. Hunters were initially skeptical and only grudgingly cooperative. The increase in the numbers and quality of the bucks on the ranch has changed their attitudes, and it is felt that their participation in the program has increased their hunting satisfaction.

KEY WORDS: White-tailed deer, Game management program, Hunter reactions, Harvest management, Controlled harvesting.

White-tailed deer have become increasingly important economically in Texas. Since the 1920's when the Texas lease hunting system began, the returns from leasing hunting rights have increased steadily. Teer and Forrest (1968) found that money derived from these leases comprised a major portion of the income on many ranches in central Texas. Because of this growth in importance of deer as a cash crop, many ranchers, when planning their operations, began to consider the needs of deer as well as the needs of livestock (Reardon et al. 1978). As landowners came to realize that unrestricted hunting by lease hunters could have deleterious effects on their deer herds (Adams and DeYoung 1979), they began to seek professional help in formulating deer management plans. This help came from state and federal agencies (Texas Parks and Wildlife, USDA Soil Conservation Service, etc.), private consultants, or individual biologists employed by the landowners. Much of this management activity has emphasized "trophy" animal production after Brothers and Ray (1975) published their popular book on the subject. Management specifically for trophy animals tends to be expensive, time consuming, and targeted for a relatively small number of hunters who are willing to pay high prices for the opportunity to hunt for a few deer of outstanding quality.

This paper presents the results of a game management program designed to establish and maintain a healthy, thrifty deer herd producing an optimum number of bucks for the enjoyment of the hunters leasing the ranch.

I wish to thank K. McCan and L. Welder for their support of this program.

STUDY AREA

The Welder and McCan Ranch, located in Refugio and Bee counties, Texas, contains about 22,986 ha of rangeland devoted to beef cattle and wildlife production. The Rob and Bessie Welder Wildlife Refuge lies about 8 km southeast of the ranch.

Gould (1975) described the Welder Refuge as lying on a transition zone between the Gulf Prairies and Marshes and the South Texas Plain. The same also is true for the ranch. Its eastern portions are more like the coastal prairies, and the western areas more closely resemble the south Texas plains. The predominant vegetative associations are similar to the mesquite-mixed grass community and the chaparral-mixed grass community described by Drawe et al. (1978) for the Welder Refuge. Both of these communities are similar in aspect, but the mesquite-mixed grass community tends to be associated with the heavier clay soils on the east. The chaparral-mixed grass community tends to be associated with the sandier, shallower soils on the west. Both plant associations contain honey mesquite (*Prosopis glandulosa*), black brush (*Acacia rigidula*), huisache (*A. farnesiana*), agarito (*Berberis trifoliolata*), granjeno (*Celtis pallida*), lotebush (*Ziziphus obtusifolia*), brazil (*Condalia hookeri*), Mexican persimmon (*Diospyros texana*), and lime prickly ash (*Zanthoxylum fagara*). Mesquite is more predominant in the mesquite-mixed grass community, and black brush is more abundant in the chaparral-mixed grass community. Huisache is the predominant shrub on the lakebed range sites. There are also several bands of upland oak "forest". These are made up predominantly of live oak (*Quercus virginiana*) and occur on poorly drained, sandier soils. The 2 major drainage features on the ranch are Aransas River and Sous Creek. Along these are riparian forests composed of hackberry (*Celtis laevigata*), elms (*Ulmus* sp.), ash (*Fraxinus berlandieriana*), anacua (*Ehretia anacua*), oaks (*Quercus* sp.), mustang grape (*Vitis mustangensis*), pecan (*Carya illinoinensis*), and mulberry (*Morus* sp.).

This area has a long history of cattle grazing. As early as 1768, the Spanish missions in the area had large herds of cattle grazing on the prairies around them. In the 1830's, Irish impresarios settled the area and brought with them large herds of cattle and horses (Drawe 1978). The ranch has been under the control of the present management since 1933. The ranch, as it is today, was formed by combining 2 estates under the administration of Welder and McCan. It was initially stocked with steers because of the infestation of the area by screw worm flies (*Cochiomia hominivorax*). The success of the USDA in eradicating the fly allowed the change to the present cow-calf operation in 1965. The ranch is now stocked with about 4,000 animal units of cross-bred cattle. The author could find no indication that the ranch had ever been farmed extensively. A program of brush control, primarily by chaining, is presently being practiced.

Early travelers through the area reported seeing game in abundance (Drawe 1978) on the prairies and marshes. John H. Adams (pers. commun.), who worked on some of the large ranches near Refugio and Goliad around the turn of the century, reported killing game to feed crews building windmills and fences. Deer and feral hogs (*Sus scrofa*) made up the bulk of his kill. Communication with ranch hands and other people who have had a long association with the Welder and McCan Ranch indicate that the bulk of the hunting on the ranch for many years was of the subsistence type to feed the cowhands and their families. Kerry McCan (pers. commun.), in recounting his experiences as a young man working on the ranch, has stated that venison, often used to feed the cow hands, was a welcome change from the normal fare of armadillo (*Dasypus novemcinctus*) and jackrabbit (*Lepus californicus*). The ranch also was subjected to sport hunting for deer by ranch managers, employees, and guests. Conversations with some of those involved indicate that the deer herd was not impacted to a great degree by sport or subsistence hunters during this period. Hunting pressure at this time was relatively light with only about 100 people hunting yearly. About 2,428 ha of the ranch was leased for sport hunting in 1974. By 1978, 21,707 ha of the ranch was under lease to 18 separate groups of hunters. Each group had exclusive and unrestricted hunting rights to a pasture or group of pastures. No restrictions were placed on them as to the number of hunters that could use a lease or the amount of game that could be taken from it. No reliable records were kept under this system, but an estimated 800-900 sportsmen used the ranch yearly. Observations made by the ranch staff caused the management to become concerned about the deteriorating quality of the deer herd. Not only were fewer bucks being seen, but also most of them were small. Prior to leased hunting rights, large bucks were commonly seen; they were rarely seen, and few were harvested after leasing.

Concern about the welfare of the deer herd prompted the management to monitor the harvest to determine the cause of the lessened quality of the deer and to devise a management plan to reverse the situation.

METHODS

Surveys of hunters (Peterle 1967, Berger 1974, Peterle and Scott 1977) have shown that participating in the array of activities associated with hunting was as important as the actual killing of game. Informal questionnaires and conversations with individuals who hunted on the ranch were conducted prior to formulating the management plan to determine their feelings about hunting and game management.

Data needed to set harvest quotas were gathered by counting deer from a helicopter. A Bell Jet Ranger has been used to conduct all counts since 1979. Surveys taken in October 1979 and January 1980 were made by M. D. Porter (unpubl. data). All subsequent counts were conducted by the author. Porter used a strip count technique similar to that described by Beasom (1979); the author preferred a total coverage technique similar to that outlined by Brothers and Ray (1975). Pastures were used as sampling units, and the pilot flew a series of parallel strips across the pasture. The distance between the flight paths averaged about 200 m but varied between 150 and 400 m according to the density of the vegetation and the actions of the deer. Strips were widened over areas of sparse vegetation or if the deer were flushing relatively far from the aircraft. Strips were narrowed over dense vegetation or if the deer were flushing close.

All deer seen during a flight were counted. The chance of counting the same deer twice was reduced by restricting strip lengths to about 1,000 m. If the pasture being counted was wider than 1,000 m, it was divided into parcels 1,000 m wide by making turns on easily recognizable linear landmarks such as roads or pipeline right-of-ways. On short strips, the location and group composition of previously sighted deer were more easily remembered and not added to the count if seen again on the next pass. The short strip length also reduced error in strip width caused by wind drift on the aircraft. The surveys were flown at an altitude of 9-15 m, depending on vegetation height, and at a ground speed of 45-85 km/hr. The slower speeds were preferable, but in certain wind conditions the aircraft would not operate safely at the slower speeds. Countability was improved by removing the doors for better visiability and by using 3 observers in addition to the pilot.

Each deer seen was classified as "doe", "fawn", or "buck" during the pre-season counts and as "buck" or "antlerless" during post-season counts. Bucks were further separated into "spike", "small", and "good" classes. Spikes had unforked antlers, small bucks had branched antlers with inside spreads estimated to be about 35 cm or less, and good bucks had branched antlers with inside spreads of about 35 cm or more. The number of deer seen during a count was corrected for visibility. Counts made in September-October were corrected for sightability by a factor of 1.5 because the woody vegetation was in full leaf. Post-season counts were made in January after most of the vegetation had lost its foliage, and a correction factor of 1.25 was used if conditions were ideal. If visibility was less than ideal, the 1.5 factor was used.

Initially, hunters failed to report or submitted questionable reports on the amount of game they killed. Since control of the amount of game harvested was essential to the game management program, stricter control was added. All gates to the ranch, except the main entrance, were locked, and hunters were monitored from a check station that was erected near the main entrance. All deer killed were field dressed and brought to the check station for data collection. Data recorded were: date and approximate time of the kill, pasture where it was harvested, and the name and license number of the hunter. The deer then was aged by tooth eruption and wear (Schemnitz 1980) and weighed. All bucks were photographed and their antlers measured, and lactation status of does was recorded.

Harvest quotas were based on an estimate of the standing crop of bucks. The January count provided both an estimate of the number of antlered bucks and of antlerless deer remaining after the hunting season. This value for antlerless deer was corrected for the number of does killed during the hunting season and then tabulated for the number of fawns based on their survival rate from the previous fall. Fifty percent of the estimated number of fawns then was added to the buck numbers to arrive at an estimate of the standing crop of bucks that should be present during the next hunting season. The buck harvest quota was 33% of this number. Doe quotas were set at 2-3 times buck quota levels. Harvest quotas were computed and distributed to the hunters by mid-February each year.

The ranch was divided into 5 management units of about 4,000 ha each. Each was administered separately, and harvest quotas were set unit-by-unit according to the census and harvest data gathered from them. The management units were set up using existing pasture fences as boundaries. Whenever possible, existing leases were not split by these units.

RESULTS

The response of the deer herd to the management program has been encouraging. Except for 1981, the number of bucks in the harvest quotas has increased, and the sex ratio of the herd has improved (Table 1). Harvest quotas for 1980 were set according to the guidelines previously discussed except that does were to be harvested at a rate of 2 for each buck killed. The hunters accomplished this, but the differences in pre- and post-season sex ratios indicated that the doe kill was not great enough to reduce sex ratios. The sex ratio had widened slightly to 1 buck:9 does. The buck quotas for the 1981 season were reduced in response to poor fawn survival in 1980 (13.2 fawns/100 does) caused by a drought. The doe quotas were raised to 3 for each buck killed to encourage hunters to take more does. That response did not occur. In fact, the lessees killed fewer does than in 1980. This caused the pre-season sex ratio of 1:4.3 to widen to 1:9 after the 1981 season. Harvest quotas for 1982 showed an overall increase, but not all leases were allowed the increase. To impress on the hunters that the proper number of does were required to be killed, those leases that did not kill does at a rate of at least 2 for each buck in 1981 were not allowed the increase. As a further incentive to kill more does, spike bucks were not to count against buck quotas after all does in the quotas had been removed. These changes had the desired effect, and the total doe kill increased to near 3 for each buck killed. The September 1983 census showed that the sex ratio of the herd had narrowed to 1:3.6. The increased doe kill also had caused a decrease in deer density, but the decrease was not serious.

An increase in the quality of bucks harvested (Table 2) accompanied the increase in buck numbers. Most measurements showed a yearly increase when spike bucks were excluded from the 1982 and 1983 data. If spikes were included, all measurements, except average age, remained the same or decreased slightly. However, spike bucks were not counted against lease quotas in 1982-83 and did count in previous years. Thus, spikes killed in

Table 1. Comparison of annual harvest quotas, harvest, and pre- and post-season sex ratios for the Welder and McCan Ranch, Texas.

Year	Quota		Pre-season F/M	Kill				Post season F/M
	Bucks	Does		Total bucks[a]	Total does	Quota bucks	Spike bucks	
1979	—	—	5.8	258	200	—	53[b]	11.6
1980	113	226	8.4	111	222	104	46	9.0
1981	100	300	4.3	94	133	82	15	9.0
1982	122	366	4.9	133	334	97	27[c]	4.9
1983	136	375	3.6	145	214	90	33[c]	4.0

[a] Total includes buck fawns.
[b] All deer killed in 1979 not reported.
[c] Spikes not counted against quotas.

1980-81 were taken, not as inferior animals to be culled from the herd, but as animals that hunters chose to take as their alloted buck. If spikes had been counted against quotas in 1982-83, most of those killed would have been passed because hunters would have been reasonably certain of harvesting a larger buck later.

The increase in buck quality was the result of improvement in the age structure in the male segment of the herd rather than in increases in size within age classes. In 1980, 55.8% of all bucks killed, excluding fawns, were 1.5-years old, and the average age was 2.36 years. The 1983 harvest had only 26.8% of the kill in the 1.5-year age class, and the kill was spread rather evenly among all age classes to 4.5 years. Average age that year was 3.69 years (Table 3).

DISCUSSION

The informal questionnaires and conversations with the hunters using the ranch showed that they considered the social activities and camaraderie in the hunting camp to be very important to their enjoyment of hunting. This was especially true since the groups that hunted the leases were made up of relatives, close friends, and business associates. For this reason, no limit was placed on the number of people allowed to use the ranch.

Table 2. A summary of the annual buck harvest on the Welder and McCan Ranch, Texas.

Year	Av age	Av weight (kg)	Av points	Av spread (cm)	Av beam (cm)
1980	2.36	34.22	5.00	24.82	25.45
1981	2.71	36.57	6.48	28.89	33.73
1982	2.82	35.14	6.48	27.10	33.33
1982[a]	3.20	38.85	7.81	31.95	39.45
1983[a]	3.69	41.76	8.53	36.24	43.65

[a] Averages without spike bucks.

Table 3. The number and percentage of bucks killed in each age class by year on the Welder and McCan Ranch, Texas.

Year	Age class													
	1.5		2.5		3.5		4.5		5.5		6.5		7.5	
	N	%	N	%	N	%	N	%	N	%	N	%	N	%
1980	58	55.8	13	12.5	16	15.4	13	12.5	2	1.9	1	1.0	1	1.0
1981	19	22.9	42	50.6	14	16.9	4	4.8	3	3.6	0	0.0	1	1.2
1982	51	40.5	20	15.9	34	27.0	12	9.5	3	2.4	5	4.0	1	0.8
1983	33	26.8	29	23.6	25	20.3	24	19.5	6	4.9	6	4.9	0	0.0

Many of the hunters using the ranch professed to be trophy hunters content with shooting only the very largest bucks. Actual experience with the size bucks that they considered to be trophy animals proved this to be not exactly true. Most of the hunters would have been very pleased with a buck having 8 antler points and an inside spread of 35 cm. The author considered 10 antler points and an inside spread of 45 cm to be the minimum standard for a trophy animal. They also indicated that they would prefer to kill several smaller bucks rather than 1 large one. The shooting of does was accepted as necessary for herd management but was not generally considered a part of the sport of deer hunting. It was considered a nuisance chore that took up time that could be better spent hunting bucks.

This and the fact that the hunters using the ranch had indicated that a large part of their enjoyment came from participating in the social activities associated with the hunting camp were the reasons for not using a trophy-oriented game management plan. Instead, the plan was designed to optimize the number of bucks produced on the ranch. Deer density in 1980 was 1 deer/9.1 ha, which the author felt was within the carrying capacity of the ranch. The problem was in the sex ratio and age structure of the bucks. The sex ratio after the 1979 season was 1:11.6. Prior to the 1980 season it had improved to only 1:8.4 with the addition of the 1979 buck fawns to the herd. Prior to the 1983 season, the sex ratio had narrowed to 1:3.6 and had widened to only 1:4.0 after the season (Table 1). Of the 104 antlered bucks killed in 1980, 58 (55.8%) were 1.5 years old. Only 33 (26.8%) of the 123 antlered bucks killed in 1983 were 1.5 years of age (Table 3). Harvest quotas were based on 33% of the estimated standing crop of bucks present prior to each hunting season in an attempt to increase the number of bucks present and, over a period of years, also increase their age structure while allowing the hunters to continue to harvest bucks at a reduced rate. Does were to be killed at a rate of 3/buck to reduce the sex ratio to 1:3 while maintaining the herd at approximately the same density. When the sex ratio reaches 1:3, harvest rates will be based on fawn survival which should theoretically maintain the deer herd at the same density and the pre- and post-season sex ratios also should remain the same.

A sex ratio of 1:3 was selected as a management goal because it was attainable. Brothers and Ray (1975) advocated a sex ratio of 1:1 for trophy management. However, this ratio was felt to be difficult if not impossible to reach and maintain without a deer-proof fence enclosing the deer herd. Also, trophy management requires a high degree of selectivity in the size of bucks harvested. The ranch did not have the deer-proof fence necessary for maintaining a 1:1 ratio, and the hunters did not possess the expertise or the desire to be selective in the size bucks they killed. The Welder Refuge had an unconfined deer herd that had not been sport hunted; the only animals removed from it were for scientific collections and through a small amount of poaching (L. Drawe, pers. commun.). The Welder herd has remained stable at a sex ratio of about 1:2 (J. Teer, pers. commun.), which should approximate the ratio to be expected in an unhunted, free ranging deer herd. This ratio should also be attainable in a hunted herd where the numbers and sex of the animals killed were closely regulated. However, the author felt that the amount of time necessary to reach this ratio while still harvesting bucks would be considered excessively long by the hunters. He believed that a sex ratio of 1:3 could be reached within 4-5 years. This would also be the time necessary to allow the age structure to improve. The average age of bucks in the harvest in 1980 was 2.36 years. An average age of 3.0-3.5 years was the target.

Another reason for a 1:3 ratio as a goal was that the production of bucks would be optimized at this level assuming that 30 fawns/100 does surviving to 6 months of age remains the ranch average. An over-simplified model (Table 4) was used to see what effect sex ratio had on recruitment. The model assumed that 30 fawns/100 does survived each year to reach 6 months of age, and after age 6 months the only mortality in the herd is from hunting. It also assumed that no change in herd composition occurred from ingress or egress and that the only recruitment was from the addition of fawns. The number of fawns added to the herd increased as the number of does in the herd increased. Further, assuming that half the fawns will be bucks, the number of bucks produced also increases as the number of females increase. To maintain this herd at 2,500 animals, which would be about the number of animals estimated on the ranch, the yearly harvest would have to equal the number of fawns, and to maintain the same sex ratio, bucks would have to make up half the harvest. At a sex ratio of 1:1, 375 animals would have to be removed yearly to maintain the population at 2,500. Of these, 188 would have to be bucks. When the ratio is 1:3, 282 bucks and 281 does would have to be removed yearly. This is an increase of 94 bucks from the 1:1 ratio. As the sex ratio widens, the rate of increase in the number of fawns produced lessens. A ratio of 1:3 seems to be about the point of diminishing returns. Widening the ratio from 1:3 to 1:7 only adds 48 additional bucks to the harvest, and 100% of them would have to be harvested yearly.

Table 4. Harvests required to maintain a deer herd of 2,500 animals at varying sex ratios assuming a fawn survival rate of 30 fawns/100 does.

Sex ratio (M:F)	Bucks	Does	Fawns[a]	Buck kill[b]	N bucks remaining	% bucks remaining
1:1	1,250	1,250	375	188	1,062	85%
1:2	833	1,667	500	250	583	70%
1:3	625	1,875	563	282	343	55%
1:4	500	2,000	600	300	200	40%
1:5	417	2,083	625	313	104	25%
1:6	357	2,143	643	322	35	10%
1:7	313	2,187	656	328	−15	0%

[a] N fawns equals the total harvest.
[b] The buck kill equals half the fawns.

Although Table 4 taken alone is unrealistic, it shows how widening sex ratios can affect production of deer in a population. The author felt that, in light if inaccuracies in the census method, it was reasonable when applied to the estimates of the ranch population. Sex ratios were not entirely accurate. Spike bucks, especially those with antlers less than 15 cm long, were difficult to recognize from the air. If antlers were not seen, the animal was classified as a doe, causing the estimated sex ratio to be wider than the true ratio. Observers also were more likely to count does twice, which also widened the ratio. Even with visibility corrections added, population size was underestimated. Those corrections were based on a preliminary study to evaluate the accuracy of helicopter censuses in which the author participated while at Texas A&I University, Kingsville, Texas. It showed that 55-75% of the deer in a population were seen. A study in progress at the Caesar Kleberg Wildlife Research Institute, Texas A&I University, Kingsville, Texas, has shown that as little as 30% of a population was seen dependent on the vegetation, weather conditions, and time of year (F. Leon, pers. commun.).

Prior to the restrictions on the number of deer allowed, the hunters were not very discriminating as to the size of bucks shot and tended to shoot at any buck seen. The use of harvest quotas actually reduced the buck kill to a greater extent than expected. The quotas on fork-antlered bucks have never been reached (Table 1), and the hunters began to pass shots at smaller bucks and wait for a larger one. As they began to harvest does, the does became more wary. Consequently, after the 1980 season, the doe quota has not been attained either.

The biggest problem encountered in initiating the program was gaining the confidence of the hunters and convincing them that they would benefit from it. A large majority of them expressed a concern for the well being of the deer herd. However, they also had little knowledge of deer ecology or game management principles. When they realized deer herd management was largely deer harvest management and that there would be restrictions on the number of buck deer they would be allowed to kill, their reaction was shocked disbelief. Porter (unpubl. data) found in 1979 that a voluntary system did not work. In 1980, quotas for the deer harvest were given by letter, and lessees were asked to stay within their quotas; 1 lessee dropped his lease rather than comply. There was no evidence that the remaining lessees overshot their quotas, but 1 lessee refused to bring his deer to the check station. A new lease agreement, renewed yearly, was written in 1981 that included clauses requiring the lessees to comply with the game management plan. All lessees agreed to the terms of the new lease. The lessee who refused to bring his deer to the check station in 1980 also refused in 1981 even though he had signed an agreement to do so. He was informed that he was no longer welcome on the ranch and that his lease would not be renewed. After this incident, there were no more problems with uncooperative hunters.

The attitude of the hunters using the ranch has changed since the start of the management program. Because of the noticeable improvements in the number and quality of bucks on the ranch, the program has been accepted by the hunters. They have related that participation in the program has increased their hunting satisfaction and given them a sense of pride in accomplishment that was not previously a part of their hunting experience.

LITERATURE CITED

ADAMS, N. E., Jr., AND C. A. DeYOUNG. 1979. Texas deer hunting: past, present, and future. Texas Hunting 1:46-47.

BEASOM, S. L. 1979. Precision in helicopter censusing of white-tailed deer. J. Wildl. Manage. 43:777-780.

BERGER, M. E. 1974. Texas hunters: characteristics, opinions, and facility preferences. Ph.D. Thesis. Texas A&M Univ., College Station. 142pp.

BROTHERS, A., AND M. W. RAY, JR. 1975. Producing quality whitetails. Wildlife Services, 1st Printing. Laredo, Tex. 245pp.

DRAWE, D. L., A. D. CHAMRAD, AND T. W. BOX. 1978. Plant communities of the Welder Wildlife Refuge. Welder Wildl. Found. Contr. 5, Ser. B. 37pp.

GOULD, F. W. 1975. Texas plants, a checklist and ecological summary. Texas A&M Univ. Agric. Exp. Sta. MP-585. 121pp.

PETERLE, T. J. 1967. Characteristics of some Ohio hunters. J. Wildl. Manage. 31:375-389.

———, AND J. E. SCOTT. 1977. Characteristics of some Ohio hunters and non-hunters. J. Wildl. Manage. 41:386-399.

REARDON, P. O., L. B. MERRILL, AND C. A. TAYLOR, Jr. 1978. White-tailed deer preferences and hunter success under various grazing systems. J. Range Manage. 31:40-42.

SCHEMNITZ, S. D., ed. 1980. Wildlife management techniques manual. 4th ed. The Wildlife Society, Washington, D.C. 686pp.

TEER, J. G., AND N. K. FORREST. 1968. Bionomics and ethical implications of commercial game harvest programs. Trans. North Am. Wildl. and Nat. Resour. Conf. 33:192-204.

SELECTIVE HARVESTING OF WHITE-TAILED BUCK DEER ON GROTON PLANTATION IN SOUTH CAROLINA

CARLYLE FRANKLIN, Small Woodlot Forestry Research and Development Program, North Carolina State University, Raleigh, NC 27607

GERALD MOORE, South Carolina Wildife and Marine Resources Department, Columbia, SC 29202

LEWIS ROGERS, Webb Wildlife Center, South Carolina Wildlife and Marine Resources Department, Garnett, SC 29922

Abstract: Results of 4 years of selective harvesting of buck white-tailed deer (*Odocoileus virginianus*) on a 8,500-ha plantation in Allendale and Hampton counties, South Carolina were compared to the previous 4 years of unrestricted buck harvests. Objectives of the harvest strategy were to maintain herd size in balance with the range (about 3 ha/deer), to reduce harvest of branch-antlered yearling bucks, to increase harvest of spike bucks, and to increase the proportion of branch-antlered bucks in the population that were at least 2.5 years old. To implement the strategy, guidelines for the first year of the program permitted each hunter to harvest unlimited numbers of spikes, as many does as there were quota tags (usually 2/hunter), and 1 or more branch-antlered bucks with antler spreads of 30.5 cm or more. During the second and third years the antler spread guideline was increased to 35.5 and 40.5 cm, respectively. The fourth year, a quota of 1 branch-antlered buck/hunter/season replaced the spread criterion. Data collected on all deer during the 8 years included live weight, age, sex, antler spread, and number of points 2.5 cm or longer. These harvesting guidelines altered the composition of the buck harvest as follows (percentages based on 4-year averages of total buck harvest without and with selective harvesting): branch-antlered yearling bucks declined from 38 to 15%, spike bucks increased from 24 to 39%, branch-antlered bucks 2.5+ years increased from 24 to 32%.

KEY WORDS: White-tailed deer, Selective harvesting, Antler development, Deer herd management.

White-tailed deer populations have literally exploded over vast areas of the southeastern United States during the last 20 years. For most herd and habitat managers the challenge to obtain more management knowledge is overshadowed by the debilitating lack of regulatory freedom to apply what is already known. South Carolina is exceptional in having a strong deer herd management research program, plus political support to apply what is learned. Effective, selective deer harvesting is supported in coastal South Carolina by a long (142-day) season, no daily or seasonal bag limits on bucks, and regulated harvests of antlerless deer through issuance of quota tags to landowners supervised by the South Carolina Wildlife and Marine Resources Department (SCWMRD).

This report is a case history of 8 years of harvest results, 4 years without and 4 years with selective buck harvesting. Groton Plantation owners and staff supported the project by implementing and administering harvesting guidelines and by collecting data. SCWMRD provided technical assistance and consultation throughout the project.

STUDY AREA

Groton Plantation in Allendale and Hampton counties, South Carolina, embraces 2 major land types. Approximately 35% (3,000 ha) is red-river swamp bordering the Savannah River. The remainder (5,500 ha) is gently rolling upper coastal plain. The dominant overstory vegetation in the swamp is hardwood, such as oaks (*Quercus* sp.), sycamore (*Platanus occidentalis*), and sweetgum (*Liquidambar styraciflua*) and on the upland is pine, such as loblolly (*Pinus taeda*) and longleaf (*P. palustris*). Approximately 600 ha of agricultural land are distributed throughout the upland, but in recent years the agricultural land base has been reduced, and intensive, irrigated agricultural operations have been concentrated in the center of the plantation on the best soils.

Groton Plantation is owned by a closely held family corporation, Groton Land Company of Athens, Georgia, and has been in continuous family ownership since 1906. The plantation has increased from the original 6,500 ha to the present 8,500 ha, all contiguous. Game production for hunting has always been the dominant management objective. Quail management started in the middle 1930's.

Deer have always been on Groton, but prior to 1950 most were concentrated in the swamp. Upland areas were extensively cultivated leaving only hedgerows and a few bays (wet thickets) for cover. Deer habitat improved as agricultural operations became more intensive and restricted to the better soils and as pine stands were planted or naturally reseeded. This improvement was enhanced by intensive quail management especially by prevalent use of prescribed burning to keep browse low, abundant, and nutritious.

From 1950 to 1970, the deer herd enlarged rapidly with no management-oriented harvesting. Deer hunting was not intensive until the mid-1970's when 2 clubs were formed, wherein each hunter paid an annual fee to hunt. In 1982, a second system of fee hunting was introduced, wherein each hunter paid a daily fee for hunting, lodging, and board. During the entire study period, plantation management provided close supervision of hunters.

METHODS

Individual deer records consisted of age, live weight, sex, antler width (outside at the widest point), and number of points 2.5 cm or longer. Objectives of the harvest strategy under quality herd management, 1975-78, prior to selective buck harvesting, were to maintain the herd in balance with the habitat, to reduce the proportion of does in the herd, and to reduce the harvest of fawns. In 1979, SCWMRD introduced selective buck harvesting guidelines which retained the previous objectives and added 2 more—to increase the number of bucks in the 2.5+ years and older age classes, thereby increasing the proportion of bucks with larger antlers, and to selectively harvest as many spike bucks as possible.

Implementation of harvesting guidelines was the responsibility of Groton corporate management through the manager and his staff. Harvesting guidelines for quality herd management were relatively simple to implement—harvest no antlerless deer without a quota tag (state law) and harvest no fawns (plantation rule). Selective buck harvesting guidelines were much more difficult to implement. During the first year, 1979, hunters were permitted to harvest unlimited numbers of spike bucks, as many does as allocated quota tags (usually 2/hunter), and unlimited numbers of branch-antlered bucks with spreads of 30.5 cm or greater. During the second and third years, the antler-width criterion was increased to 35.5 and 40.5 cm, respectively. In the fourth year, the spread criterion was replaced by a quota of 1 branch-antlered buck/hunter plus limited additional party quotas. Still-hunting was the only method used throughout the study period.

Groton management maintained a strong commitment to improved deer herd quality but recognized that special harvesting requirements should not be so restrictive as to jeopardize the pleasure of the hunt. Hunter education and peer pressure were seen as key elements in the implementation process, but modest fines and loss of deer were imposed to reinforce less direct methods. Uncooperative hunters were not invited to renew their memberships.

RESULTS AND DISCUSSION

Implementation of selective buck harvesting guidelines did not cause significant changes in total harvest, buck:doe ratios, or harvest intensities (Table 1). The area hunted increased only slightly in 1982, so the 2 study periods are similar with regard to these parameters.

Impact on the Buck Harvest

Implementation of selective buck harvesting had an immediate and lasting impact on the buck harvest. Comparing averages 4 years without and 4 years with the guidelines, the harvest of branch-antlered yearlings was reduced from 38 to 15% of the total buck harvest, the harvest of spike bucks increased from 24 to 39%, and the harvest of bucks 2.5+ years and older increased from 24 to 32%. Harvest of button bucks (15%) did not change (Fig. 1).

The immediate increase in the harvest of bucks 2.5+ years and older in 1979 was an unexpected result. Part of the explanation came from hunters. When they passed up smaller, branch-antlered bucks, they were often rewarded by the appearance of a larger, harvestable buck (Fleming 1983). In addition, the extra caution observed by hunters during that first year of selective harvesting, to avoid shooting small branch-antlered bucks, resulted in the lowest total buck harvest during the entire study period (Table 1). Therefore, in 1979 older bucks constituted an unusually high proportion of the total harvest (Fig. 1).

Table 1. Annual harvest statistics for the Groton Plantation deer herd by sex and age class, buck:doe ratios, harvest intensities, and a summary by 4-year management periods, 1975-82.

Age (years)	Without selective harvesting					With selective harvesting					Annual average by 4-year period	
	Year of harvest					Year of harvest					W/out	With
	75	76	77	78		79	80	81	82		75-78	79-82
Bucks 0.5	24	12	58	23		12	28	29	43		29	28
1.5 (Spikes)	55	41	53	29		45	68	68	103		44	71
1.5 (3+ points)	56	74	76	68		21	22	32	38		68	28
2.5+	45	44	38	41		51	56	61	55		42	56
Subtotals	180	171	225	161		129	173	190	239		184	183
Does 0.5	24	51	42	30		17	25	28	56		37	32
1.5	54	46	73	45		44	55	55	63		54	54
2.5+	79	130	157	152		149	147	169	176		130	160
Subtotals	157	227	272	227		210	227	252	295		221	246
Total harvest	337	398	497	388		339	400	442	534		405	429
Buck:doe ratio	0.9	1:1.3	1:1.2	1:1.4		1:1.6	1:1.3	1:1.3	1:1.2		1:1.2	1:1.4
Harvest/259 ha	12.6	14.9	18.7	14.6		12.7	15.0	16.6	18.0		15.2	15.6
N ha hunted	6,900	6,900	6,900	6,900		6,900	6,900	6,900	7,700		6,900	7,100

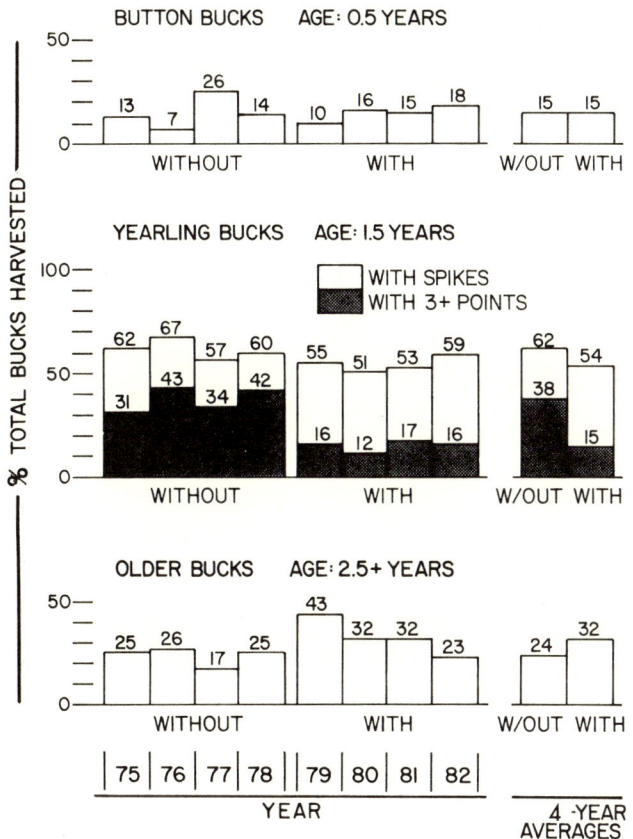

Fig. 1. Results of 4 years of selective harvesting of white-tailed buck deer on Groton Plantation, Luray, SC, compared to the previous 4 years without selective harvesting.

Numbers of older bucks (2.5+ years) in the harvest increased only slightly while the harvests of spike bucks increased steadily from 1980 through 1982 (Table 1). The result was a steady decline in the percentage of older bucks in the harvest because they were being passed up in preference for spikes and does (Fig. 1). This would seem to be a typical pattern in the first few years of selective buck harvesting.

Antler Development

Selective buck harvesting guidelines resulted in harvesting 2.5+-year-old bucks averaging 0.3 more points/deer even though live weights averaged 6.2 kg lower during the 4-year period (Fig. 2). Antler spread also averaged 2.1 cm wider despite the lower live weights (Table 2). In 1979, the first year of selective buck harvesting, the average live weights of older bucks was the same as the previous year, but antler spread increased from 29.5 to 36.6 cm. In the next 3 years, antler spread followed trends in live weight but maintained the wider average spread (Fig. 3).

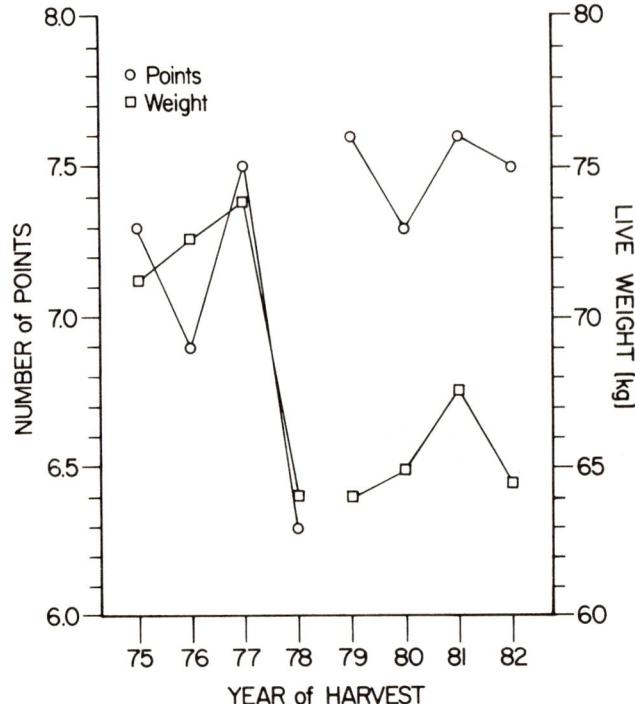

Fig. 2. Trends in number of points compared to live weights of bucks 2.5 years and older from 1975 through 1978 without and from 1979 through 1982 with selective harvesting on Groton Plantation, Luray, SC.

Number of points and antler spread of yearling bucks followed trends in live weight from 1975 to 1982. With the general drop in live weights of all deer harvested during that period (Fig. 4), it was impossible to attribute decreases in number of points or antler spread of yearling bucks entirely to selective harvesting. Average number of points was lower (3.7-2.8) as was average spread (18.0-17.3 cm) (Table 2). Without selective buck harvesting, the harvest of yearling bucks was 39% spikes; with, it was 72% spikes. Reduction in average antler size was caused in part by the change in composition of the yearling buck harvest. The increase in harvest of spike bucks may have also reflected an increase in their frequency because of poorer nutritional status of the herd in combination with higher selective hunting pressure (Brothers and Ray 1982, Goss 1983, Ullrey 1983).

Annual Trends in Live Weight

Results from selective buck harvesting might have been more impressive if animal weights had not been declining through the study period. Live weights of older bucks were significantly lower from 1977 to 1978. The same sharp drop appeared in 1978 in all other classes except buck fawns. Weights of buck fawns began a steady descent in 1979 (Fig. 4). The 4 years under

Table 2. Comparison of antler development for harvested yearling and older bucks based on averages of 4 years with and the preceeding 4 years without selective buck harvesting guidelines on Groton Plantation, Luray, SC..

Age (years)	N points		Antler spread	
	1.5	2.5+	1.5	2.5+
With selective buck harvesting	2.8	7.5	17.3	37.1
Without selective buck harvesting	3.7	7.2	18.0	35.0
Difference	−0.9[a]	+0.3[a]	−0.7[a]	+2.1[a]

[a] Differences significant at the 0.05 level based on Student's t test with a minimum of 384 df/comparison.

selective buck harvesting have coincided with generally declining live weights on Groton and neighboring plantations. In 1982, every class was near or, in most cases, below the lowest weights recorded since records were started on Groton in 1971. This was interpreted as a cyclical phenomenon that happened to coincide with initiation of the selective buck harvesting guidelines. Combinations of extreme drought, summer heat, and winter cold characterized portions of 1979-82. These were also years of decreasing and centralizing agricultural activities on the plantation. The combination

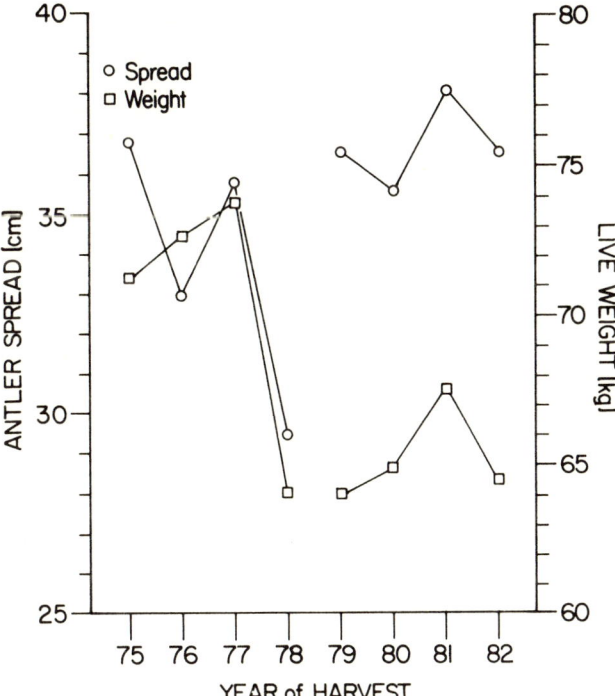

Fig. 3. Trends in antler spread compared to live weight of bucks 2.5 years and older from 1975 through 1978 without and from 1979 through 1982 with selective harvesting on Groton Plantation, Luray, SC.

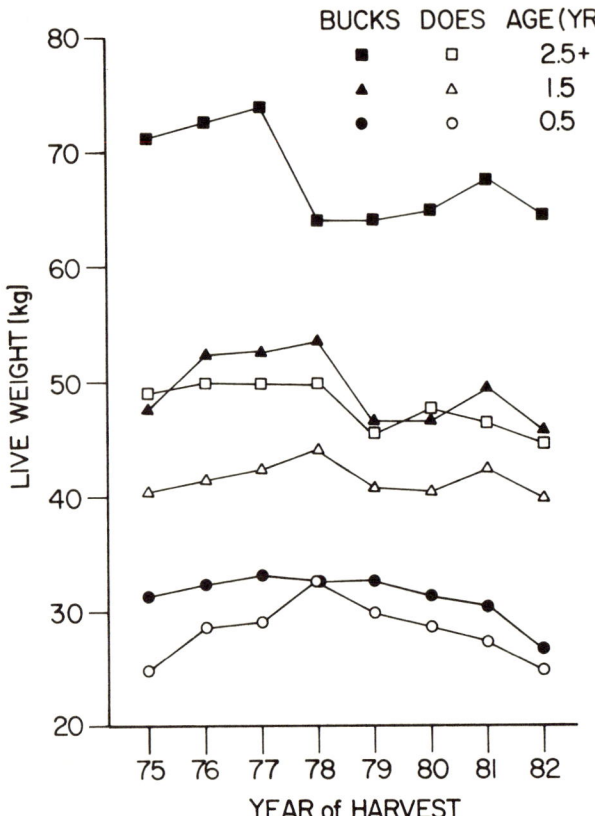

Fig. 4. Trends in live weight of harvested bucks and does in 3 age classes from 1975 through 1982 on Groton Plantation, Luray, SC.

of adverse weather and fewer, dispersed agricultural fields may have decreased the carrying capacity of the range below herd size.

CONCLUSIONS

Selective buck harvesting was effective in substantially reducing the proportion of branch-antlered yearlings harvested over a 4-year period compared to the previous 4 years with unrestricted buck harvesting. Results also reflect an 8% increase in harvest of 2.5+-year-old bucks and a similar decrease in total yearlings harvested. Antler development of 2.5+-year-old bucks showed small but real increases despite decreasing body weights during the 4 years with selective harvesting. As expected, antler development of harvested yearlings declined significantly as the proportion of spikes in the yearling harvest increased from 39 to 72%.

The quota system used in 1982 was the most effective in regulating the harvest of all branch-antlered bucks and received the highest level of hunter acceptance. The spread criterion was used for 3 years in this study and was effective but difficult in some respects to implement because of disagreements in defining a "trophy" rack.

Further evaluation of results of selective buck harvesting in terms of significant changes in the age structure of the buck population and the expected increase in numbers of trophy-class bucks should be possible in the near future.

LITERATURE CITED

BROTHERS, A., AND M. E. RAY, JR. 1982. Producing quality whitetails. Caesar Kleberg Wildlife Research Inst., Kingsville, Tex., 2nd printing. 247pp.

FLEMING, K. M. 1983. Quality white-tailed deer management on an east Texas hunting club. Proc. Annu. Conf. Southeast. Assoc. Fish and Wildl. Comm. 37: In Press.

GOSS, R. J. 1983. Deer antlers: regeneration, function, and evolution. Academic Press, New York, N.Y. 316pp.

ULLREY, D. E. 1983. Nutrition and antler development in white-tailed deer. Pages 49-60 in R. D. Brown, ed. Antler development in cervidae. Caesar Kleberg Wildlife Research Inst., Kingsville, Tex.

DEER POPULATION MANAGEMENT IN NEW YORK: USING PUBLIC INPUT TO MEET PUBLIC NEEDS[a]

DANIEL J. DECKER, Department of Natural Resources, Cornell University, Ithaca, NY 14853
TOMMY L. BROWN, Department of Natural Resources, Cornell University, Ithaca, NY 14853
GEORGE F. MATTFELD, New York State Department of Environmental Conservation, 50 Wolf Road, Albany, NY 12233

Abstract: Management of white-tailed deer (*Odocoileus virginianus*) populations in extensive areas having a variety of human land uses requires consideration of both biological and sociological factors. Often deer numbers and occurrence in a region must be managed below biological carrying capacity to keep them compatible with human activities. People do not always support needed management actions and may take actions that severely hinder sound management. These may range from resistance to professional deer management via political actions, whereby management agencies are not authorized to pursue the best management strategies for the existing environmental situation, to widespread disregard of laws designed to facilitate management. Managing deer in these situations requires a sophisticated approach to assess relevant human attitudes, values, beliefs, and preferences. Managers must know how key publics in each situation feel about and are affected by deer so management programs can be designed to best meet their needs and interests. Only in this way can deer managers provide acceptable deer management programs. This paper draws on research in New York for examples of the types and applications of public input information in deer management.

KEY WORDS: Attitudes, Deer management, Human dimensions, Surveys, Perceptions, Public input.

Management of white-tailed deer populations requires consideration of both biological and sociological factors. Sometimes deer in a region must be managed below biological carrying capacity to keep them compatible with human activities such as farming, grazing, and forest management (Stoll and Mountz 1983). In other instances, populations may be at or exceeding carrying capacity, causing extensive damage to their range. Experience has shown that failure to seek, consider, and be responsive to public preferences when making deer management decisions in such varied situations can lead to serious and sometimes debilitating management problems (Moncrief 1970, Evans 1979). These may range from resistance via political actions, whereby management agencies are not authorized to pursue appropriate management strategies (Cobb 1982), to widespread disregard of laws designed to facilitate management (Severinghaus and Free 1963, Heberlein and Laybourne 1978). Managing deer in these diverse situations requires a sophisticated approach to assessing relevant human attitudes, values, beliefs, and preferences (Langenau 1979), as well as other characteristics of key constituencies (Bevins et al. 1968, Klessig and Hale 1972, Applegate 1973, 1975, Hendee and Potter 1976, Lowe 1978, USDI 1982). Managers must know how constituencies in each situation feel about

---

[a]Research supported by New York Federal Aid in Wildlife Restoration Project W-146-R.

deer so management programs can be designed to meet their needs and interests (Weinrich, unpubl. data). Only in this way can deer managers provide effective, lasting deer management programs.

The New York State Department of Environmental Conservation (DEC) has long recognized the need for managing deer populations to be compatible with human land uses while meeting recreational needs. Achievement of this goal is difficult in a state as diverse as New York, which has one of the largest urban populations, one of the largest state parks, one of the largest dairy farming industries, and one of the largest deer herds in the U.S.

DEC wildlife managers have increasingly realized that public input should be sought and used to guide modern deer management. The purpose of this paper is to illustrate how 3 types of public information were applied for deer management in New York. The types of information needed and the kinds of decisions they served were: broad—for long-range planning; comprehensive—for short-range planning, commitment of resources, and establishment of goals and objectives; and focused—for action decisions and implementation of activities.

Of the various deer management problems that we could focus on to show how public input was sought and used to guide programs so that they better met public needs, we will concentrate on 2 perennial problems that have rather specific geographic associations, and then we will turn to a more general use of public input for program planning. Each example illustrates 1 of the 3 levels of sociological information needs identified above. We hope New York's experience with the human dimensions studies presented herein provides evidence of the usefulness of public input research for deer management.

METHODS

This paper is a summary of several studies conducted in New York. The specific methods and results of these can be found in the publications cited. Consequently, in the interest of brevity, we will not present sample sizes, response rates, etc., for each study cited in this paper. These details are not essential to the purpose of the paper, which is to show how the results of the various studies have been used by DEC since their completion (and publication). In essence, the procedure we used was to analyze New York's experience as a case study.

RESULTS AND DISCUSSION

Deer Management to Meet Agricultural Needs

Based on an overriding concern for agricultural interests in the region, the DEC has cautiously approached deer management in the fruit and intensive cash-crop producing Lake Plains Region of western New York. Before the mid-1970's, managers' decisions on antlerless deer harvest quotas were based largely on the level of unsolicited deer damage complaints from farmers. Indicators of deer health and range conditions showed that deer populations were well within biological carrying capacity and that a considerably larger deer population could exist. Managers recognized that if they were too conservative in their deer population management they would be unnecessarily limiting benefits for many deer enthusiasts. Deer hunters and other deer enthusiasts generally wanted more deer. The determining preferences, however, would be those of farmers. Consequently, "focused" (third level) data were needed to guide deer harvest quota decisions.

To accurately assess the perceptions of deer damage and the preferences for future deer population levels of the region's farmers, we conducted a mail survey (Brown et al. 1977, 1978, 1980). The results showed that farmers enjoyed deer, were willing to tolerate considerable economic losses, and overall wanted the deer population to increase. In some townships, populations were considered high enough; some farmers had excessive damage, but such situations were uncommon. Based on data from farmers surveyed, managers decided to allow a controlled increase in the deer populations of many deer management units (DMU's) in the region.

This initial investigation stimulated interest in extending the study into other areas of central and western New York that were characterized by field crop and dairy production. Even in these areas where deer populations were managed at higher levels, conditions indicated the potential for the range to carry a larger deer population. Managers also wanted to know if deer were being held at artificially low levels in this large area. Surveys of the region's farmers in 1978-79 determined that they would indeed tolerate more deer than their counterparts in the Lake Plain, but in some townships this level had already been reached (Brown and Decker 1979, Decker et al. 1981a). Deer population objectives for DMU's containing townships where more deer seemed acceptable were altered to account for this public input. These management modifications have resulted in increased opportunities for observing and hunting deer.

To improve management of population levels, farmers were recently resurveyed (Decker et al. 1983a). As we expected, damage reported in the region increased; in most DMU's a "sociological" carrying capacity seems to have been reached. Farmers in most units wanted the population to remain at current levels; few wanted another increase. In addition, in some DMU's slight population reductions may be appropriate to meet the needs of many farmers. A farmer-preference-monitoring effort is planned to assist DEC in program planning. Furthermore, the identification of deer damage severity zones is being considered to help adjust DMU boundaries which might enable DEC to manage deer to meet public needs even more effectively.

Following the initial studies in central and western New York, a similar survey was conducted in the fruit and dairy producing area of the mid-Hudson Valley (Decker and Brown 1982). This area has presented a management dilemma because of the close proximity of orchards to wooded hillsides and the woodlot-cropland habitat mosaic characteristics of the dairy farms. This study highlighted the differences in preferences that can exist among different types of farmers living in close proximity to one another; fruit farmers were much less tolerant of deer and deer damage than other farmers. The insights gained from farmers' input pointed out the potential for coupling mitigation measures with population management. This enabled managers to increase deer populations to levels desired by most people in a region, while keeping crop damage within tolerable limits. The appropriate population control and mitigation combinations are now being determined.

Deer Management in Northern New York

Northern New York has been a longstanding problem area for deer managers. Unlike the previous example, we cannot present the northern New York situation as one where public input has been used effectively to meet public needs via a demonstrably successful management program. But it is an example of how public input can be used to better define a problem and to devise an innovative, long-term plan to overcome it, paving the way for eventually achieving effective deer management.

The deer resource of the Northern Zone of New York (NZ), containing about 33% of the state's deer habitat, is not being managed effectively. Harvest is limited by law to bucks only, a policy that may be appropriate only in portions of the NZ as described below. The NZ consists of 3 major deer ranges: Central, Transitional, and Agricultural. The Central Deer Range includes central Adirondacks' high peaks and the Tug Hill Plateau. Much of this range is under stringent land use regulations that preclude or limit most forest management practices that could enhance deer habitat. Deer populations within this range cannot be controlled by hunting because of a sparse human population, limited road access, and overriding high winter mortality; however, the area is well suited for recreational hunting. Harvest of antlerless deer would increase use of this deer resource.

The Transitional Range surrounds the central Adirondacks and consists of fairly accessible, heavily forested, and predominately private lands where deer could be controlled by hunting. In this range, deer management could include approaches, such as antlerless deer harvest, that would serve to meet recreational needs of people and prevent undue damage to forest regeneration by deer.

The Agricultural Range surrounds the first 2 and consists of rolling farmland where deer populations are already being controlled by means other than legal hunting, such as poaching, motor vehicles, dogs, lack of winter range, and climate. Management strategies in some localities could foster deer population growth, whereas in others stabilizing populations is appropriate.

A persistent problem in the NZ has been illegal deer kill in the Agricultural Range. Addressing this problem seemed to call for an effective educational communications effort. Wildlife managers generally believed that illegal deer kill was a socially acceptable practice in the area, but basing a communications campaign on this unproven assumption seemed tenuous. Consequently, before embarking on such an effort, DEC wanted a situation analysis to determine if illegal activities were indeed socially acceptable. Input was sought from several publics that might be potential target audiences: opinion leaders on deer management, Environmental Conservation Officers (ECO's), Town and Village Justices (TJ's), and landowners.

ECO's and TJ's in the NZ were found to be no more lenient in their treatment of illegal deer kill offenses than their counterparts elsewhere in the state (Decker et al. 1980). In fact, more ECO's and TJ's from this region than from downstate believed the arrest and prosecution of deer hunting law violators to be extremely important to protect deer in their area. Opinion leaders on deer management believed that illegal deer kill was widespread, and over 50% of them felt this practice was socially acceptable (Decker et al. 1981b). This contention was not substantiated, however, by a survey of area landowners. They recognized that illegal deer kill occurred, but they clearly indicated that such activity was not generally acceptable (Decker et al. 1981b). Thus, the key audiences originally identified as potential targets for a communications campaign to raise awareness of the effects of illegal deer kill were largely already aware of, and disapproved of, these violations. An awareness-building campaign directed at them, as originally contemplated, would do little more than reinforce their existing beliefs. Furthermore, messages produced under the erroneous assumption that key audiences condoned illegal deer kill could possibly have had a negative backlash effect causing the DEC a public relations set back. By systematically soliciting public input, this potential pitfall was avoided, and the situation was much better understood. NZ residents needed programs that facilitated their taking actions to curb illegal deer kill, not "sermons" against poaching.

Concurrent with earlier investigations regarding the social acceptability of illegal deer kill in the NZ was an effort to determine the causes of communications barriers that DEC perceived to exist between it and the public regarding deer management. DEC administrators wanted to evaluate whether, and the extent to which, the agency suffered from an image problem with area residents, believing such a problem would contribute to lack of acceptance of deer management proposals. Again, the solicitation of public input supplied valuable information (Brown and Decker 1976). First, most area residents were unaware of the DEC's deer management program in their area. Second, the subgroup that did have an image of the agency (hunters) was more negative about DEC than nonhunters. An important communications outcome from this image study was the partitioning of overall agency image into 3 parts: personnel, management function, and communications behavior. The agency personnel component was viewed most favorably, while agency communications behavior was most criticized. Typically, perceived lack of "responsiveness" to people's concerns was high on the list of problems in the communications behavior arena.

The Northern New York Strategic Plan for Deer Management.—Based on these public surveys and other information, DEC took a new approach to the NZ problem. A team of deer managers developed the Northern New York Strategic Plan for Deer Management to establish the long-term direction DEC will take to manage deer. The plan specified 3 major short-term goals; the highest priority initially is to generate sustained public and governmental support for sound deer management programs in each of the 3 ranges of the NZ. This objective calls for a communications campaign that seeks and uses input from key publics and, in turn, provides them with information, rationales, and answers. This is to be a 2-way communications process, an attempt to establish a dialogue between the agency and its constituencies. The agency's job is to explain the biological situation and solicit public input to identify alternatives that will be both biologically sound and potentially acceptable socially. These alternatives will then be presented to the public for reaction as to acceptability. Based on this input, management actions will be implemented. The underlying premise of the approach is that by demonstrating genuine responsiveness to public input the agency's credibility will be enhanced and the course of action chosen will have a greater probability of success.

One of the first activities planned under this communications development objective was a study to identify the degree of support existing among NZ deer hunters for legislating greater deer management authority to DEC. This information was to be placed in the context of a situation analysis for a communications effort and is an example of the second (comprehensive) type of public input. Various data about NZ deer hunters needed for communication planning were obtained (Decker et al. 1983*b*). Hunters were placed into management support/opposition types based upon responses to several questions involving opinions of NZ deer management and antlerless deer harvests. These types were descriptively labelled: full support, conditional support, qualified opposition, and full opposition. Hunters of each type then were described and compared on standard socio-demographic characteristics; hunting experience, motivations, and satisfaction; opinions about deer management and DEC; organizational affiliation; and wildlife-related communications characteristics. This profiling analysis indicated potential management acceptability and identified characteristics of the opposition element. Furthermore, ways to reach and possibly influence those not in full support of management were identified. The following abbreviated results from the hunter survey illustrate data obtained from the "conditional support" and "qualified opposition" types (58% of the hunters). These were identified as the "target" audiences for an initial communications effort (details of this study can be found in Smolka et al. 1983):

1. Primarily blue collar workers with high school education.
2. Considerable deer hunting experience and hunt in the NZ for a variety of reasons.
3. Low success in NZ, but this may be an accepted norm.
4. Most had hunted antlerless deer in areas of New York where such harvests are instrumental to the management program.
5. Recognize that deer overpopulations are detrimental to range but not convinced that this is now the situation in NZ.
6. General acceptance of antlerless deer harvest will be possible only after considerable groundwork occurs to develop confidence in the agency's management intentions and ability.
7. Members of organized sportman's groups more predominant in opposition groups than in support groups.
8. Vast majority of hunters prefer receiving information at the time they received a hunting license, and most also would like to receive a wildlife newsletter from DEC and to see more newspaper coverage.

Another set of hunter characteristics that bear on communications is their image of the DEC. Our findings in this area reinforce the need for better communication. Of the 3 components of the DEC's image, that relating to communications behavior was consistently rated the most negative, as it did in the landowner study conducted several years earlier. An indication that the potential exists to influence many hunters regarding NZ deer management was the finding that nearly 40% of the conditional support and qualified opposition types had no opinion of the management component of the DEC's image, and as many or more of these hunters were already holding a positive image of the DEC's management programs. The image component toward which opinions currently were least formed was that regarding the competency of DEC personnel. Here lies an opportunity for building hunter's recognition of the DEC staff's management ability, which could logically lead to acceptance of management proposals. The process of building recognition of staff competency, which would necessitate increased interaction between hunters and DEC staff, should simultaneously improve hunters' perception of the DEC's communications behavior.

Achieving effective communications will require the establishment of feedback mechanisms to ensure a 2-way flow of information and ideas between the DEC and deer hunters. The foregoing has concentrated on the DEC-to-hunter portion, but problems were apparent in the complement. Few hunters take any actions to make their opinions on hunting and wildlife management known to policymakers. Those who do seem to be indirect in their communications; they are more likely to take some "political" action than to communicate their interests or concerns directly to a DEC representative. This behavior is consistent with hunters' belief that

DEC is not responsive to their needs; it is logical that they would not go to the DEC with their concerns if they believe they will not be considered. Furthermore, since 50% of the hunters were unfamiliar with DEC staff, they may be reluctant or not know to whom to express their views.

Although specific channels of communication related to personal, face-to-face contact were not sought in the survey, responses to the DEC image components indicated the utility of such contact. If the source of management direction is considered by hunters to be the impersonal, amorphous entity called the DEC, rather than individual, personally known, competent professionals, a barrier to persuasive communications and program approval will exist. Respect for staff will result in and is prerequisite to improved acceptance of staff-generated program ideas.

One of the major general findings of the NZ deer hunter study was that many hunters who are not now in full support of expanding the DEC's authority to manage the NZ deer resource seem to hold considerable potential to become supporters. For example, hunters in the conditional support type expressed an array of conditions under which they would support deer management. The conditions mentioned by many already exist, but currently are not recognized, indicating a communication gap. Messages should address the 1 condition of pervasive concern to hunters—the need to take antlerless deer when overpopulation is decimating habitat. Evidence of this condition will have to be indisputable and powerfully presented if it is to be convincing.

Examining the variables that were combined for the Hunter Acceptance Typology provides further insight into strategies to ameliorate the concerns of the qualified opposition type. For example, these hunters were more willing to support expanded management authority when reference to types of management actions were not limited to various forms of antlerless deer harvests. Most of the qualified opposition type indicated support for DEC assumption of complete or limited authority; however, few were supportive when antlerless deer harvest was considered specifically. Thus, if antlerless deer harvests are perceived by these hunters as the primary management approach being advocated by the DEC, chances of their acceptance of the new NZ deer management initiative would be remote. But, if other management aspects addressed in the plan were pursued first because they might meet with less resistance, and if successes in these were accomplished, communicated, and recognized, the atmosphere for greater acceptance of DEC management might improve to the point where a trial of antlerless deer harvest would be viewed more positively.

The foregoing illustrations show how public input has been used to guide both communications and deer management program planning in the NZ. Other audiences scheduled to be surveyed regarding NZ deer management planning include: leadership of key organizations relative to deer management, nonconsumptive wildlife recreationists, and educators in the NZ. Input from these groups is planned to provide DEC with a full picture of the interests in deer and to help focus communications efforts.

Public Input for General Program Planning

The previous examples of uses of public input were of 2 types, focused and comprehensive, with applications being made for particular problems in specific geographic areas. To a great extent these uses have been reactive; they were in response to problems already encountered by the agency. Uses of public input need not and should not be limited to such situations. When wildlife management issues are foreseen, preferably before they "go public," agencies should assess the likely reactions to management alternatives of affected citizens, especially the organizations representing them. Given agencies' broad responsibilities today for nongame as well as game species and given the multitude of organizations from the local to the national level that have interest in wildlife, it is difficult to identify all of the organizations that may become involved in a particular issue. An initial attempt has been made in New York to identify and classify key constituent organizations according to their interest in the management of wildlife and to understand how these organizations perceive and communicate with the DEC (Brown and Decker 1982). The general purpose of this study was to develop information that would enhance wildlife managers' understanding of organizations' values, concerns, and attitudes regarding wildlife and its management. This is an example of data needs and applications on the "broad" or first level presented in the introduction. The primary products of the study were wildlife value typologies; a cluster analysis technique placed 38 key wildlife interest groups in the state into types sharing similar values relative to 4 kinds of wildlife, 1 of which was deer.

An important general finding of this analysis was that the organizations who clustered together were different for the different kinds of wildlife considered. This finding indicates that the common practice of stereotyping organizations based solely on their attitudes toward either game or nongame species may be erroneous. Some organizations holding generally opposing attitudes toward the values of 1 or more species groups may hold similar attitudes toward the values of others.

This technique for identifying wildlife value typologies was not proposed as a definitive tool or as a substitute for specific research. If a new program is being considered that has a strong relationship to the interests of 1 or more wildlife-related organizations, the DEC may wish to elicit reactions from the organizations' leaders and perhaps from members. The typologies are most useful as a planning tool, permitting the agency to project the array of organizations most likely to support or express concern about a proposed program. The process for applying the information first requires definition and analysis of the management goal in terms of the values of wildlife affected and the feasible alternative management practices to reach the goal. The next steps involve determining value types who favor, oppose, or are neutral toward the proposal, thereby suggesting overall support or opposition, and the attitude types who support, oppose, or are neutral toward various management alternatives to reach the goal. These are then evaluated to choose the most acceptable alternative.

This information also is useful as a reference when a DEC staff member is preparing to address a wildlife-related organization on a deer management topic or when the agency is responding to a concern expressed by an organization about a particular regulation or management practice. These study results provide a review of the broader orientation of the organization toward deer.

The input from key publics has yet another application—identification of potential sources of communications problems between DEC and the public. Knowledge of the similarities and differences between groups can aid efforts at systematic communications. DEC staff who professed to be most knowledgeable about a particular wildlife organization were asked how they believed leaders of each organization would respond regarding values associated with wildlife and attitudes about wildlife management held by specific organizations. DEC staff responses were compared to the actual responses of the leaders of each organization. When DEC analyzed these data it could ascertain how well it understood each wildlife-related organization. A disparity ranking of the 38 key organizations was assembled for the actual vs. agency-perceived values of each of the 4 representative species groups and for the actual vs. agency-perceived attitudes toward management of game/furbearers and nongame/nonfurbearers. Although the correlation was far from perfect, DEC staff had a better understanding of the attitudes and values of game-oriented rather than the nongame-oriented wildlife organizations. Similarly, for organizations whose interests span both game and nongame species, DEC staff more frequently understood an organization's values toward game species. Further research is seeking to identify the specific causes of the management agency's misunderstanding of an organization's purview. Such research is important to improve communications and management programs developed for various groups. This proactive approach to wildlife management planning requires extensive knowledge of the public's attitudes toward specific species. Studies, such as that just described, provide agencies with the breadth of information they need to achieve farsighted planning.

SUMMARY

As biologists learn more about the ecological relationships of particular wildlife species, attempts to refine management programs for those species are inevitable. Management of the white-tailed deer probably is the best example of this. Unfortunately, some portions of user publics resist new deer management initiatives (Gilbert 1977). Often, managers perceive such opposition as being insurmountable. This reaction is understandable because, usually when those interested in wildlife are asked their opinions in an unstructured solicitation, deer managers hear in disproportionate numbers from those who oppose changes. In reality, a spectrum of views may lie between full support and full opposition. If management agencies can identify the programs the public will support through an analysis of their viewpoints and then effectively address issues that surface, previously unacceptable deer management programs may become reality. Furthermore, knowledge of the needs and interests of the public can help make the original design of deer management programs more acceptable to various audiences at the outset, thereby allowing agencies to avoid problems rather than react to them (Fazio and Gilbert 1981). The key to better understanding of wildlife constituency needs, interests, and management preferences is acquiring public input for broad, comprehensive, and focused levels of application in a systematic, representative fashion.

LITERATURE CITED

APPLEGATE, J. E. 1973. Some factors associated with attitude toward deer hunting in New Jersey residents. Trans. North Am. Wildl. and Nat. Resour. Conf. 38:267-273.

———. 1975. Attitudes toward deer hunting in New Jersey: a second look. Wildl. Soc. Bull. 3:3-6.

BEVINS, M. I., R. S. BOND, T. J. CORCORAN, K. D. MCINTOSH, AND R. J. MCNEIL. 1968. Characteristics of hunters and fishermen in 6 northeastern states. Agric. Exp. Sta., Northeast Regional Res. Publ. Bull. 655, Univ. Vermont, Burlington. 76 pp.

BROWN, T. L., AND D. J. DECKER. 1976. Identification of the image of the Bureau of Wildlife (N.Y.S.D.E.C.) held by residents in the peripheral Adirondack area of New York. N.Y. State Dep. Environ. Conserv. Final Report, Fed. Aid Proj. W-145-R-1. 239pp.

———, AND ———. 1979. Incorporating farmers' attitudes into management of white-tailed deer in New York. J. Wildl. Manage. 43:236-239.

———, AND ———. 1982. Identifying and relating organized publics to wildlife management issues: a planning study. Trans. North Am. Wildl. and Nat. Resour. Conf. 47:686-692.

———, ———, AND C. P. DAWSON. 1977. Farmer willingness to tolerate deer damage in the Erie-Ontario Lake Plain. Cornell Univ. Dep. Nat. Resour. Res. and Ext. Ser. 8. 33pp.

———, ———, AND ———. 1978. Willingness of New York farmers to incur white-tailed deer damage. Wildl. Soc. Bull. 6:235-239.

———, ———, AND D. L. HUSTIN. 1980. Farmers' tolerance of white-tailed deer in central and western New York. Search: Agriculture. Cornell Univ. Agric. Exp. Stn. 7, Ithaca, N.Y. 16pp.

COBB, T. L. 1982. Deer Management Unit-53. The Conservationist 37(2):12-17.

DECKER, D. J., AND T. L. BROWN. 1982. Fruit growers' vs. other farmers' attitudes toward deer in New York. Wildl. Soc. Bull. 10:150-155.

———, ———, AND C. P. DAWSON. 1980. Deer hunting violations and law enforcement in New York. Trans. Northeast. Sect. Wildl. Soc. 37:113-128.

———, ———, AND D. L. HUSTIN. 1981a. Farmers' preferences for white-tailed deer densities in New York: a comparison of 2 regions with different agricultural and deer population characteristics. N. Y. Fish and Game J. 28:202-207.

———, ———, AND W. SARBELLO. 1981b. Attitudes of residents in the peripheral Adirondacks toward illegally killing deer. N. Y. Fish and Game J. 28:73-80.

———, N. SANYAL, T. L. BROWN, R. A. SMOLKA, JR., AND N. A. CONNELLY. 1983a. Reanalysis of farmer willingness to tolerate deer damage in western New York. Proc. First East. Wildl. Damage Control Conf. 1:37-45.

———, R. A. SMOLKA, JR., N. SANYAL, AND T. L. BROWN. 1983b. Hunter reaction to a proposed deer management initiative in northern New York: antecedents to support or opposition. Trans. Northeast. Sect. Wildl. Soc. 40:76-93.

EVANS, R. A. 1979. Changes in landowner attitudes toward deer and deer hunters in southern Michigan, 1960 to 1978. M.S. Thesis. Univ. Michigan, Ann Arbor. 45pp.

FAZIO, J. R., AND D. L. GILBERT. 1981. Public relations and communications for natural resource managers. Kendall/Hunt Pub. Co., Dubuque, Iowa. 375pp.

GILBERT, A. H. 1977. Influence of hunter attitudes and characteristics on wildlife management. Trans. North Am. Wildl. and Nat. Resour. Conf. 42:226-236.

HEBERLEIN, T. A., AND B. LAYBOURNE. 1978. The Wisconsin deer hunter: social characteristics, attitudes, and preferences for proposed hunting season changes. Univ. Wisconsin working paper No. 10. School Nat. Resour., Madison. 96pp.

HENDEE, J. C., AND D. R. POTTER. 1976. Hunters and hunting: management implications of research. U.S.D.A. For. Serv. Gen. Tech. Report SE-9. 25pp.

KLESSIG, L. L., AND J. B. HALE. 1972. A profile of Wisconsin hunters. Wisc. Dep. Nat. Resour. Tech. Bull. 60. Madison. 24pp.

LANGENAU, E. E., JR. 1979. Human dimensions in the management of white-tailed deer: a review of concepts and literature. Mich. Dep. Nat. Resour. Wildl. Div. Report 2845. 68pp.

LOWE, T. M. 1978. Characteristics and attitudes of Mississippi deer hunters. M.S. Thesis. Mississippi State Univ., Mississippi State. 91pp.

MONCRIEF, L. W. 1970. An analysis of hunter attitudes toward the state of Michigan's antlerless deer hunting policy. Mich. Dep. Nat. Resour. Res. and Dev. Report 209. 7pp.

SEVERINGHAUS, C. W., AND S. FREE. 1963. Management implications of the trend and distribution of the legal deer kill in the Adirondack region. N. Y. Fish and Game J. 10:201-214.

SMOLKA, R. A., JR., D. J. DECKER, N. SANYAL, AND T. L. BROWN. 1983. Northern New York deer management: hunters' opinions and preferences. N. Y. State Dep. Environ. Conserv. Final Report, Fed. Aid Proj. W-145-R-8. 278pp.

STOLL, R. J., JR., AND G. L. MOUNTZ. 1983. Rural landowner attitudes toward deer and deer populations in Ohio. Ohio Fish and Wildlife Report 10. 18pp.

USDI, FISH AND WILDLIFE SERVICE and USDC, BUREAU OF THE CENSUS. 1982. 1980 national survey of fishing, hunting, and wildlife-associated recreation. U.S. Government Printing Office, Washington, D.C. 156pp.

DEMOGRAPHIC AND GENETIC CHARACTERISTICS OF WHITE-TAILED DEER POPULATIONS SUBJECTED TO STILL OR DOG HUNTING

KIM T. SCRIBNER, The University of Georgia's Savannah River Ecology Laboratory, Drawer E, Aiken, S.C. 29801

MICHAEL C. WOOTEN[a], The University of Georgia's Savannah River Ecology Laboratory, Drawer E, Aiken, S.C. 29801

MICHAEL H. SMITH, The University of Georgia's Savannah River Ecology Laboratory, Drawer E, Aiken, S.C. 29801

PAUL E. JOHNS, The University of Georgia's Savannah River Ecology Laboratory, Drawer E, Aiken, S.C. 29801

Abstract: White-tailed deer (*Odocoileus virginianus*) have been harvested from the U.S. Department of Energy's Savannah River Plant (SRP) in South Carolina since 1965. Data have been collected from 6,876 animals harvested from yearly Dog- and Still-Hunted Areas in adjacent upland hardwood units. The dynamics of different portions of the SRP herd were followed from 1977 to 1982 to document changes in herd age structure, sex ratios, and genetic characteristics relative to the different harvest methods. Age structure, sex ratios, and mortality rates of populations in the Still-Hunted Area were similar to those of populations collected from the Dog-Hunted Area. The greatest level of genetic variability in terms of year and year-age effects on allele frequencies were observed in dog-hunted populations and in populations in the Still-Hunted Area after initiation of dog hunting. Deer populations subjected to different harvest methodology exhibit strong genetic differences in population characteristics. Thus, biological resources are likely to respond genetically in varying ways to different harvest methods.

KEY WORDS: Harvest strategies, Harvesting deer, Controlled harvests, Deer dogs, Deer drives, Genetic variability, Demographic characteristics.

The use of dogs to hunt deer in the southeastern United States has a long tradition but has also been controversial. Arguments for and against the use of dogs in wildlife management programs involve socio-political issues (Marchinton et al. 1970), changing land use practices, and conflicts with the objectives of multiple species management programs for a particular area. Decisions as to the desirability of still or dog hunting for white-tailed deer should be partly based on the effects of these harvest strategies on population characteristics. Comparative studies on these effects are lacking, and their documentation will be difficult because of the mosaic of differences normally found in natural populations. Demographic and genetic differences are observed for populations of white-tailed deer separated by only a few kilometers (Manlove et al. 1976, Dapson et al. 1979, Ramsey et al. 1979, Chesser et al. 1982). Populations also show significant differences from 1 year to the next (Dapson et al. 1979, Smith et al. 1983).

Population differentiation over short distances and studies of deer movements suggest some degree of site tenacity and spatial organization in

[a]Present address: Department of Ecology and Evolution, SUNY, Stoney Brook, N.Y. 11794.

deer herds. This subdivision occurs even though deer are capable of long-range dispersal that normally would result in genetic homogeneity over large areas in the absence of selective pressures (Crow and Kimura 1970). The structure must have important effects on the genetic and demographic composition of a herd, and these are not independent sets of characters (Charlesworth and Giesal 1972). The effects of different harvest strategies may be mediated primarily by changes in the spatial structuring of a herd.

Our study was designed to document the effects of still and dog hunting on the genetic and demographic structure of a herd of white-tailed deer on the Savannah River Plant (SRP). Specifically, the objectives were to document whether the 2 harvest methods result in a different sex-age composition of the yearly kill, to determine if there is a difference in harvest intensity or kill/unit time that could affect herd structure, and to describe changes in the genetic structure of the herd through space and time as affected by the harvest method. The SRP herd is ideal for such a study because it produces large numbers of deer annually and is hunted in a highly controlled manner.

We would like to thank the many state and university researchers and biologists in the Southeast Region who provided valuable background information pertaining to dog hunting. We are indebted to Gus Cothran and the staff of the U.S. Forest Service Station on the SRP and those of the Savannah River Laboratory who assisted in the various aspects of the field work. We are especially grateful to H. O. Hillestad for his comments and discussion throughout the study. Mary Dibiell assisted in preparation of the manuscript. The work was supported by contract DE-AC09-76SR00819 between the U.S. Department of Energy and the University of Georgia's Institute of Ecology.

STUDY AREA

This study was conducted on the U.S. Department of Energy's SRP. This site (80,972 ha) lies within Aiken, Allendale, and Barnwell counties in west-central South Carolina, bordering the Savannah River. Vegetation patterns on the SRP corresponded to an environmental gradient based on soil moisture (Whipple et al. 1981). Forest vegetation on it ranges from predominantly planted longleaf pine (*Pinus palustris*) and slash pine (*P. elliottii*) on former row-cropped areas on the uplands to slope and bottomland hardwoods and swamp forest.

The present SRP white-tailed deer herd originated from small remnant groups in isolated swamp and bottomland areas (Jenkins and Provost 1964). With the acquisition of the site by the U.S. Atomic Energy Commission in 1951 and with the elimination of hunting, the herd rapidly expanded into all areas of the plant site. Controlled hunting began in 1965 to reduce car-deer and train-deer collisions (Urbston 1967).

The SRP is divided into 50 hunt compartments of varying sizes (Fig. 1). Yearly fall hunts traditionally used both still and dog hunting. Peripheral

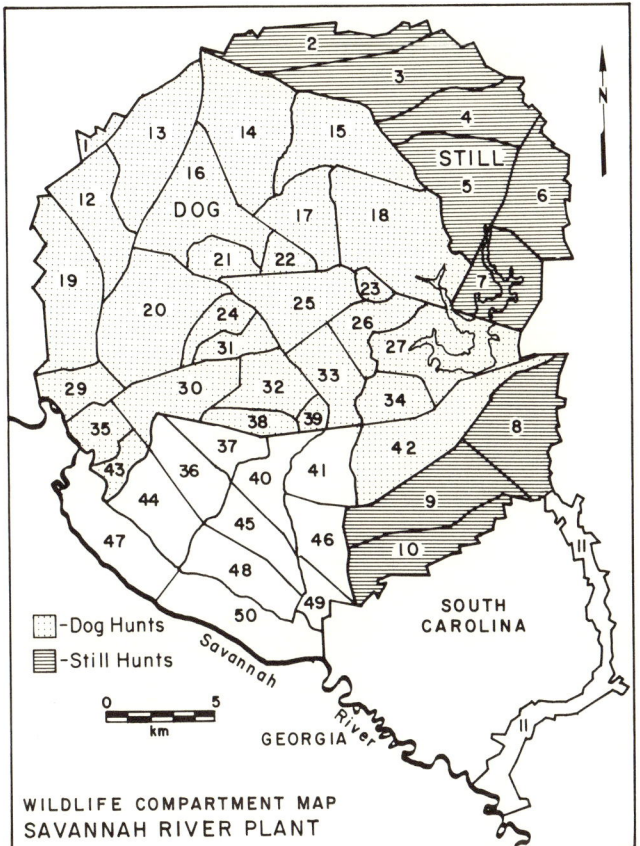

Fig. 1. Map of hunt compartments on the SRP and location of Still- and Dog-Hunted areas. Clear areas of the figure represent swamp- and bottomland-hardwood areas previously described as differing in demographic and genetic characters (Dapson et al. 1979, Ramsey et al. 1979).

compartments of the site (191.4 km^2) were consistently hunted solely by still hunting until 1981 when dog hunting became the only method used. Compartments consistently dog hunted (343.9 km^2) were designated as the Dog-Hunted Area. These 2 hunting areas (still and dog) were in adjacent upland habitats. Deer from the swamp or lowland areas have previously been documented as differing from animals in upland areas for a number of demographic, reproductive, and genetic characteristics (Urbston 1967, 1976, Johns et al. 1977, Dapson et al. 1979, Ramsey et al. 1979). Most of the differences were documented for the expanding herd. Because of these differences, the lowland areas were excluded from our analyses.

METHODS

Data were taken from deer on the SRP during still and dog hunts conducted twice weekly from 1 October through 31 December during 1977-82. Two to 4 compartments were traditionally hunted in each area the same day. Hunt compartments were not hunted concurrently or in the same order each year; however, all compartments were hunted at least once yearly. Comparisons between areas and years are justified in that mean dog-hunt day and mean still-hunt day did not differ between groups within a given year or between years ($P > 0.45$).

Techniques employed during still and dog hunts differed greatly. On the Still-Hunted Area 200-400 still hunters were usually allowed on the site hunt day. Hunters were allowed to hunt anywhere within the designated areas between 0600 and 1800 hours. Hunters were allowed to harvest as many deer of either sex and any age as possible.

Hunts in the Dog-Hunted Area consisted of an average of 90 hunters assigned to permanent stands located approximately 100 m apart along paved roads, power lines, or logging roads. Forty dog packs, each having 2 handlers and a minimum of 6 dogs, would drive deer through an area toward the standers. Several drives were made throughout the 2-4 hunt compartments designated for a particular day. The same areas were often driven repeatedly. Hunters and handlers were allowed to harvest as many deer of any sex or age as possible. Ages were determined by pattern of tooth eruption and wear (Severinghaus 1949), and age classes were designated as 0.5, 1.5, 2.5, and ≥ 3.5 years for statistical analysis. Liver and blood samples were collected from each animal for electrophoretic analysis. Tissue preparation, storage, and electrophoretic techniques were as described by Manlove et al. (1975).

Sex ratios and age structure from each area were obtained from annual and cumulative harvest records. Cumulative harvest and known-mortality data from 1977 through 1982 were used, with an adjustment for non-hunting mortality (Urbston 1976, Dapson 1979), to compute minimum population sizes for the dog and still groups for 1977-78 as described by Hesselton et al. (1965).

Nine electrophoretic loci—transferrin (Trf), β hemoglobin (βHb), esterase-2 (Es-2), lactate dehydrogenase-2 (Ldh-2), malate dehydrogenase-1 (Mdh-1), glutamate oxalate transaminase-1 and 2 (Got-1,2), phosphoglucomutase-2 (Pgm-2), and sorbitol dehydrogenase (Sdh)—had sufficient variability and were used in the genetic analysis. Genetic heterozygosity was calculated as the mean number of heterozygous loci of 9 possible loci/individual. A locus was heterozygous if an individual received a different allele from each parent.

Statistical analyses of demographic data were performed using the Statistical Analysis System (Barr et al. 1976). Analyses of electrophoretic data were performed using the BIOSYS program (Swofford and Selander 1981). Statistical significance was designated $P \leq 0.05$. Degrees of freedom are designated as subscripts to the test statistic.

Statistical analysis was based on comparisons of differences between groups (still vs. dog), year of collection, and age of the animal. To test for differences in the still-hunted group following the initiation of dog hunting in 1981, each group was divided into 2 sets, 1977-80 and 1981-82 (Fig. 2). Comparisons were made between still only and dog only (set 1 vs. set 3) and between set 1 and set 2 relative to the control of constant dog hunting (set 3 and set 4). Initial differences potentially associated with dog hunting would not be expected until 1982, the second year of intensive harvest in the previously Still-Hunted Area.

RESULTS

The number of hunters and the annual harvest of white-tailed deer on the SRP varied from year to year (Table 1). A significantly greater number of deer were removed from the Dog-Hunted Area from 1977 to 1980 than from the Still-Hunted Area ($t_3=7.99$). Hunter success (no./hunter day) was also much higher in the Dog-Hunted Area than in the Still-Hunted Area during this time. With the initiation of dog hunting in the previously Still-Hunted Area, harvest increased to a level approximating that of the Dog-Hunted Area, and hunter success also increased.

A total of 6,876 animals was removed from both Still- and Dog-Hunted Study Areas from 1977 through 1982. The total SRP white-tailed deer herd has a young age structure. Only 2.6% of the animals harvested from the study area over 6 years were estimated to be older than 3.5 years of age. Figure 3 gives the proportions of the 4 age classes for both sexes harvested from the Still- and Dog-Hunted Areas. No significant differences in the relative proportions of each age class in the harvest were observed between the still- and dog-hunted groups except in 1982. However, the frequency distribution of ages in the Dog-Hunted Area was narrower or more leptokurtotic, and there was a trend toward a younger overall age structure for males and females (Fig. 3). In the Dog-Hunted Area, mean harvest age declined during 1977-82 from 1.71 ± 0.05 (SE) to 1.54 ± 0.06 and from 1.81 ± 0.04 to 1.63 ± 0.04 for males and females, respectively. Mean harvest age of males in the Still-Hunted Area increased from 1.52 ± 0.08 in 1977 to 1.70 ± 0.09 in 1980 and then declined to 1.50 ± 0.07 after 2 years of dog hunting. Mean age of females in the Still-Hunted Area declined during 1977-80 from 1.86 ± 0.09 to 1.62 ± 0.09; then it increased to 1.82 ± 0.06 following 2 years of dog hunting. Mean harvest age of females was significantly higher than that for males in the Still- ($t_5=2.80$) and in the Dog-Hunted areas ($t_5=3.69$).

Although few differences in age structure were observed between Still- and Dog-Hunted areas, considerable year-to-year variations in harvest age structure were noted in both the still- ($X^2_{15}=27.68$) and dog-hunted groups ($X^2_{15}=75.26$). Significant differences in harvest age structure between years were noted for males and females of the still-hunted group ($X^2_{15}=27.13$ and $X^2_{15}=33.17$, respectively) and for males and females in the dog-hunted group ($X^2_{15}=44.92$ and $X^2_{15}=65.43$, respectively).

The proportions of an age class harvested during a particular year was negatively related to the proportion of the same cohort taken the previous

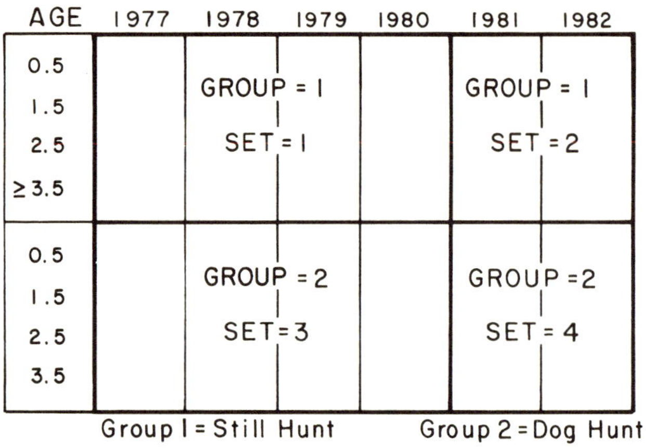

Fig. 2. Schematic representation of the comparisons used in the statistical analysis. Analysis involved year, age, and year-age comparisons within a hunt group and differences between the Still-Hunted and Dog-Hunted areas during 1977-80 (set 1 vs. set 3), and comparison of the solely Still-Hunted Area (set 1) to same area after initiation of dog hunting (set 2) relative to the control of constant dog hunting (set 3 + set 4).

year. Greater numbers harvested during a given year would result in diminished harvest of that cohort the following year.

The proportion of males in the annual harvest showed few differences between harvest groups (Table 2). More differences were noted within a harvest group between years ($X^2_5=20.9$) or age classes ($X^2_3=26.2$) than between harvest groups. Since organized hunting began on the SRP in 1965, males and females have been harvested in approximately equal numbers. In this study both sexes were harvested in approximately equal proportions from both groups for each year, except 1981-82 in the previously Still-Hunted Area (Table 3). A significantly greater proportion of females was

Table 1. White-tailed deer harvest data and hunter success ratios compiled from annual Still- and Dog-Hunted areas on the SRP from 1977 through 1982.

Year	Still area				Dog area			
	Animals harvested	Harvest N/km	Hunter days	Hunter[a] success (%)	Animals harvested	Harvest N/km	Hunter days	Hunter success (%)
1977	313	1.63	3,440	9.1	733	2.13	3,726	19.7
1978	333	1.74	3,932	8.5	717	2.08	3,667	19.6
1979	208	1.09	2,874	7.2	697	2.02	3,593	19.4
1980	244	1.27	2,554	9.6	541	1.57	3,033	17.8
[b]								
1981	573	2.99	1,288	44.5	856	2.49	2,951	29.0
1982	578	3.02	1,690	34.2	1,083	3.15	3,022	35.8
Mean[c]		1.43				1.95		

[a] Hunter success for each year was calculated by dividing the total number of deer harvested by the number of hunter days and multiplying by 100.
[b] Time at which dog-only hunting began in the formerly Still-only Hunted Area.
[c] Mean values for comparison of Still- and Dog-Hunted areas were calculated using data from Still Hunted Areas for 1977-80 inclusively. Significant differences were observed in harvest numbers/km^2 between 1977 and 1980, $t=7.99$, $P=0.005$.

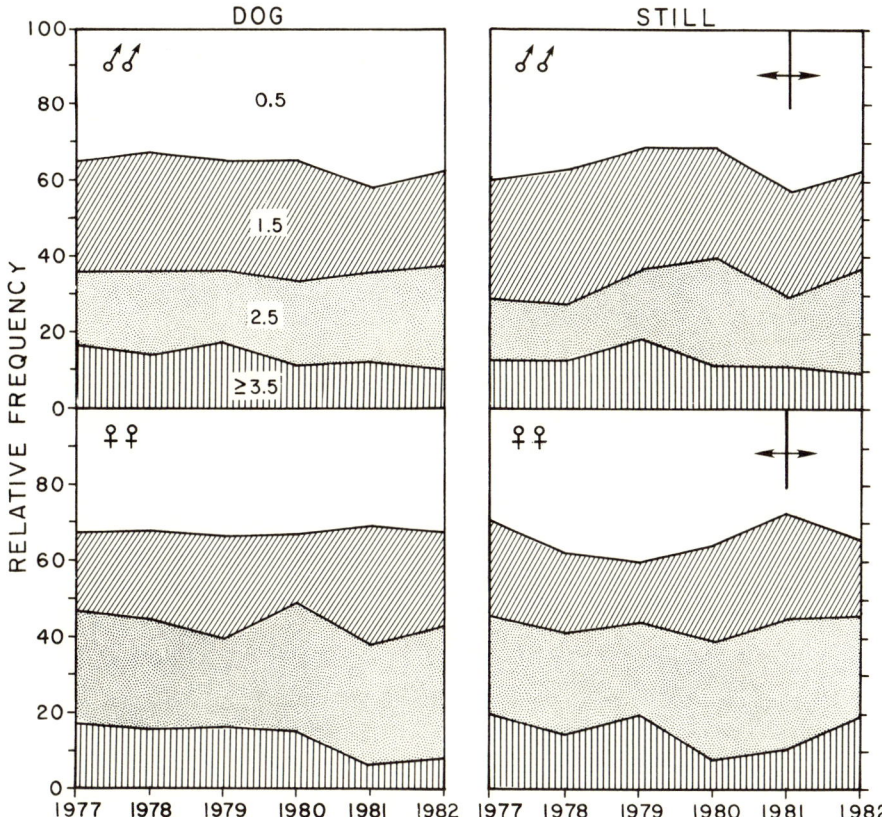

Fig. 3. Yearly variation in age structure of the harvest of male and female proportions of the dog- and still-hunted groups. The arrow designates the year in which dog hunting was initiated in the Still-Hunted Area.

harvested from the Still-Hunted Area in those years (Table 3). Both groups showed significant variations in male proportions between age classes in every year but 1979. Males accounted for a greater proportion of the harvest in the 0.5- and 1.5-age classes, whereas females were taken in greater proportions in the 2.5- and $\geq$ 3.5-age classes. The proportion of males harvested in the 1.5- and $\geq$ 3.5-age classes varied significantly between years in both areas.

Comparisons were made between age structure of the harvest from Still- and Dog-Hunted areas for 1977 and estimated numbers alive during that year. Estimates were made from age-kill data collected in subsequent years adjusted for yearly non-hunting mortality (Urbston 1976, Dapson et al. 1979). Bias in the 0.5-age-class population estimate used in this analysis and estimates of mortality rates may have arisen because of high fawn mortality before the initiation of fall hunts. In general, both harvest methods were biased in that animals in each age class were not harvested in proportion to that of the estimated population in the still (X^2_5=23.18) and dog groups (X^2_3=71.20). Animals in the 0.5- and 1.5-year classes were taken in lower

Table 2. Comparison of male percentages of white-tailed deer harvested from the SRP between 4 age classes from Still- and Dog-Hunted areas from 1977 through 1982.

	Age class (years)									
	0.5		1.5		2.5		≥3.5		Total	
Year[a]	Still	Dog	Still	Dog	Still	Dog	Still	Dog	Still	Dog
1977										
% males	59.6	46.9	59.1	53.1	39.4	36.6	42.0	44.3	52.4**[b]	45.5**
N	109	245	88	175	66	175	50	122	313	717
	4.84*[c]		NS		NS		NS		4.72	
1978										
% males	48.4	52.4	60.4	57.8	32.8	43.0	44.7	58.2	47.7**	50.7**
N	122	231	91	192	73	186	47	134	333	717
	NS		NS		NS		NS		NS	
1979										
% males	45.2	51.2	66.0	51.6	44.2	44.7	50.0	52.2	51.0	50.1
N	73	242	50	192	43	150	40	113	206	697
	9.89**		NS		NS		NS		NS	
1980										
% males	45.7	48.6	53.0	60.0	46.5	36.8	58.3	38.8	49.2***	46.8***
N	81	177	66	130	71	152	24	67	242	526
	NS		8.64**		NS		4.29*		NS	
1981										
% males	55.3	56.2	44.1	41.6	29.9	41.6	44.6	62.3	44.0***	48.8***
N	190	313	161	233	157	233	65	77	573	856
	NS		NS		5.51**		4.46*		NS	
1982										
% males	43.6	53.8	46.9	50.8	43.5	43.7	27.5	55.3	41.8**	49.7*
N	204	381	130	268	161	146	91	103	586	1086
	5.52**		NS		NS		15.36***		9.45**	

[a] Significant differences were noted between years for the 1.5 (X^2=13.6, P= 0.005) and ≥3.5-age class (X^2=11.84, P= 0.005) in the still-hunted group and for the 1.5-(X^2=16.06,, P= 0.005) and ≥3.5-age class (X^2=13.45, P= 0.005) in the dog-hunted group.
[b] Significance levels pertain to Chi-square test of differences in male % between age class within hunt group for a particular year.
[c] Chi-square test of difference in % males between group for an age class of a particular year.
[d] * $P < 0.05$, ** $P < 0.005$, *** $P < 0.001$.

numbers than they were present in the population in both Still- and Dog-Hunting areas during 1977 (Table 4). Animals in the 2.5 and ≥ 3.5 classes were taken in greater proportions than their estimated number in the population. Although a greater number of animals were taken/unit area in the Dog-Hunted Area (Table 1), there was no significant difference in number taken as a percentage of the total population in either harvest group (35.2 vs. 34.5% harvest for Still- and Dog-Hunted areas, respectively).

Age-specific mortality rates were calculated for 1977-78 for males and females from still and dog areas using life table analysis of animals known alive based on harvest data from subsequent years (Caughley 1977). Mortality rates increased with increasing age for animals from both areas (Table 4). Mortality rates were higher for males and females from Still-Hunted Areas than animals in the dog area in the 0.5 age class. Animals more than 1.5 years old showed a significant trend toward higher mortality rates in the Dog-than in the Still-Hunted Area (Sign test; X^2=13.2).

Table 3. Comparison of age-specific harvest numbers obtained from 1977 fall hunts in Still- and Dog-Hunted areas of the SRP and total estimated population levels.

Age (years)	Still area		Dog area	
	Number harvested	Population[a] estimate	Number harvested	Population[a] estimate
0.5	109	410	245	947
	(0.348)	(0.461)	(0.334)	(0.454)
1.5	88	265	175	607
	(0.281)	(0.298)	(0.239)	(0.291)
2.5	66	139	175	354
	(0.211)	(0.156)	(0.239)	(0.170)
≥3.5	50	76	122	177
	(0.160)	(0.085)	(0.188)	(0.085)
Total[b]	313	890	717	2,085

[a] Total population estimate and % total harvest in parentheses, based on sex-age-kill data collected from concurrent yearly hunt data adjusted for age-specific non-hunting mortality (Urbston 1967, Dapson et al. 1979).

[b] The relative proportions of animals harvested in each age class differed significantly from that of the estimated total population in the still group ($X^2_3 = 23.18$) and in the dog group ($X^2_3 = 71.20$).

Chi-square analysis of differences in allelic frequency, estimates of heterozygosity, and mean number of alleles/locus were based on animal groupings according to method of harvest, year of harvest, and age of the animal. In general, a significantly higher degree of genetic variability was observed in animals from Dog- than Still-Hunted areas related to year, age, and year-age effects (Table 5). Genotypic proportions of each year-age class for each group were analyzed for deviation from Hardy-Weinberg equilibrium at all 9 electrophoretic loci. One hundred-eighty tests were made for each group. Five of 180 age-year-locus tests showed significant deviations from expected Hardy-Weinberg proportions for deer from the still-hunted group, whereas 33 of 180 tests showed similar deviations for the dog group. Deviations from Hardy-Weinberg were usually the result of greater disequilibrium in the breeding structure; however, no trends were apparent.

Analysis of yearly differences at each age class revealed relatively small changes in allele frequency within each age class between years for the still-hunted group (Table 5). Highly significant year effects were observed for Mdh-1 ($X^2_5 = 14.87$) and Sdh ($X^2_5 = 27.61$) for the 0.5-age class. The 2.5-

Table 4. Mortality rates (q_x) of male and female white-tailed deer from 1977 to 1978 cohorts derived from harvest data of animals known alive each year in the Still- and Dog-Hunted areas.

Age (Years)	Males				Females			
	1977		1978		1977		1978	
	Still	Dog	Still	Dog	Still	Dog	Still	Dog
0.5	0.425	0.359	0.383	0.370	0.346	0.393	0.414	0.336
1.5	0.348	0.541	0.347	0.481	0.434	0.402	0.191	0.429
2.5	0.574	0.714	0.533	0.523	0.511	0.691	0.527	0.773
≥3.5	0.717	0.810	0.862	0.962	0.744	0.839	0.737	0.860

Table 5. Chi-square analyses of year effects on variability in allele frequency at 9 loci for 4 age classes of white-tailed deer collected from the SRP during still and dog hunts during 1977–80 and for the formerly Still-Hunted Area for the 0.5-age class in 1982.

Locus[a]	N alleles	Ages (still hunt)					Ages (dog hunt)				1982 Still/dog hunt
		0.5	1.5	2.5	≥3.5	Total	0.5	1.5	2.5	≥3.5	Total	0.5
Trf	2	3.50[b]	4.12	2.58	0.68	16.0	11.79*	17.00**	11.22*	7.68	58.7***	0.26
βHb	4	2.60	9.48	16.86	4.19	45.5	46.22***	33.61**	24.66	17.25*	143.4***	32.50***
Ldh-2	2	7.61	6.94	2.54	45.19***	45.2***	4.44	2.04	7.81	13.18**	57.4*	2.41
Mdh-1	2	14.87**	4.99	2.79	1.21	23.8	10.46*	27.65***	4.64	1.49	86.7***	4.92
Got-1	2	0.37	0.50	0.93	1.58	16.2	15.37**	5.86	3.71	6.32	30.5*	4.57
Got-2	2	6.20	6.99	4.53	3.29	24.8	11.06*	8.74	16.74*	1.53	59.0*	0.87
Pgm-2	3	0.74	16.54**	7.48	8.29	45.0	20.85**	8.14	14.47	9.39	87.1**	8.54
Sdh	4	27.61**	11.29	10.60	15.42**	68.9*	15.77	13.09	23.04*	14.78	101.8*	21.04**
Es-2	4	4.75	18.80**	3.39	6.20	36.7	29.37*	13.50	13.11	15.05*	74.3***	6.04
Total	25	68.25[c]	79.65***	51.71	86.03***	322.1***	121.20**	129.62***	119.37***	92.99***	732.2***	81.15***

[a] Abbreviations of each locus are described in the methods.
[b] Chi-square value for year-age effects of allele frequencies at each locus.
[c] Chi-square value for year effects of allele frequency summed over all loci for each age class.
* $P \leq 0.05$, ** $P \leq 0.01$, *** $P \leq 0.001$. Degrees of freedom were calculated as (N-1) (A-1) (Y-1) for number of alleles (N), number of age classes (A), and number of years (Y), respectively.

year class showed significant yearly variation at βHb ($X^2 = 45.19$). Greatest variability was noted for the 1.5- and 3.5-age classes. Significant overall Chi squares could be the result of greater year-to-year differences in the relative proportions harvested from these age classes (Table 5).

The dog-hunted group showed significantly higher variability in allele frequency in terms of number of significant age-year-locus effects than did the still-hunted group. Significant differences were observed between years for each age class (Table 5). The 0.5-age class in the dog-hunted group showed the most variability in terms of number of loci showing year effects in allele frequency. No significant overall difference was noted between 1977 and 1980 for the 0.5-age class in the Still-Hunted Area or for any age class in 1981. With initiation of dog hunting in the formerly Still-Hunted Area in 1981, a significant difference between years was noted in the 0.5-age class after the second year of dog hunting. Method of harvest had no effect on levels of heterozygosity (Table 6). Lower heterozygosities were noted for age classes in the Still-Hunted Area during 1978. A significantly higher number of alleles/locus was observed in the dog-hunted group than in the still-hunted group. These differences were eliminated in 1982 after the second year of dog hunting in the formerly Still-Hunted Area.

DISCUSSION

Differences in demography, body condition (Johns et al. 1977, 1984), and reproduction (Urbston 1976, Johns et al. 1977) between deer inhabiting different regions of the SRP have previously been attributed to density-dependent effects. Concern by SRP management regarding car-deer accidents has resulted in a policy of increased harvest intensity. Deer populations on the SRP have subsequently declined (W. Conley, pers. commun.); this has reduced most of the density-dependent differences in demographic characteristics (Urbston 1976, Smith et al. 1983). The present herd has good average body condition (Johns et al. 1984) and is thus assumed to be well below carrying capacity. SRP deer have a very low average age (Fig. 3) and higher fawn reproductive contribution (Urbston 1976) than has been described for other herds (Harlow and Jones 1965, Ransom 1967, Davis 1979). It is unlikely that habitat or density controls currently constrain SRP deer populations. Differences in observed demographic and genetic characteristics are probably due to the harvest method.

The demographic characteristics of deer harvested by the 2 methods were similar. Greater variability was noted within a harvest group between years or age classes than between harvest groups (Fig. 3). Hunters from Still- and Dog-Hunted areas harvested a greater number of fawn and 1.5-year-old males than females in these age classes, resulting in a significantly older female than male age structure in both areas. Data from other areas of the country have shown that populations have more males in the younger age classes than females (Severinghaus and Cheatum 1956, Harlow and Jones 1965). Males in younger age classes are more susceptible to hunting

Table 6. Comparison of mean number of heterozygous loci/individual (H) and mean number of alleles/locus (A) between white-tailed deer collected from Still- and Dog-Hunted areas on the Savannah River Plant for each of 4 age classes from 1977 through 1982.

Year		Age class (years)							Mean (still)	Mean[a] (dog)
	0.5		1.5		2.5		≥3.5			
	Still	Dog	Still	Dog	Still	Dog	Still	Dog		
1977 H	0.209	0.200	0.187	0.201	0.227	0.205	0.214	0.200	0.209	0.202
A	1.9	2.3	2.1	2.3	2.2	2.4	1.9	2.0	2.2	2.5
1978 H	0.170	0.183	0.197	0.200	0.131	0.209	0.157	0.209	0.179	0.197
A	1.6	2.5	1.9	2.1	1.6	2.4	1.5	2.0	2.0	2.5
1979 H	0.230	0.205	0.194	0.199	0.186	0.190	0.197	0.186	0.194	0.197
A	1.7	2.3	1.8	2.2	1.8	2.2	1.8	2.1	2.0	2.3
1981 H	0.205	0.194	0.205	0.197	0.197	0.185	0.181	0.210	0.200	0.194
A	2.2	2.5	2.3	2.5	2.4	2.4	2.2	2.1	2.5	2.7
1982 H	0.201	0.206	0.209	0.202	0.206	0.199	0.201	0.202	0.204	0.203
A	2.5	2.5	2.5	2.5	2.5	2.3	2.1	2.3	2.2	2.6

[a] Mean number of alleles/locus was significantly higher ($t=7.99$, $P< 0.001$) for deer from the Dog-Hunted Area than those collected from the Still-Hunted Area.

mortality (Dapson et al. 1979), whereas females in older age classes are more commonly taken. A sex ratio favoring males in the younger age classes could result from the very young age structure and large proportion of females breeding their first year. Verme (1983) has shown that females breeding for the first time will produce more males than females.

Mortality rates over the entire site were much higher than those reported for this herd in the 1960's and early 1970's (Dapson et al. 1979). Mortality rates generally increase proportionately with increased hunting pressure (Severinghaus and Cheatum 1956). Higher mortality rates among older animals (≥ 1.5 year) were more evident in the Dog-Hunted Area than in the Still-Hunted Area (Table 4). The trend for higher mortality in older age classes was consistent with the lower mean age of the animals in the Dog-Hunted Area, although there was no difference in the age structure between the 2 areas. The mortality rates may be somewhat high because of observed age-specific hunter selection (Table 3).

Population characterizations obtained from harvest data can be biased; however, population data can be compared between areas of the SRP because the bias is approximately equal relative to harvest method. Although there were some trends in the data, cumulative population data demonstrate that still- and dog-hunted populations on the SRP are demographically similar relative to harvest rate.

The genetic characteristics in contrast to the demographic data showed major effects from dog hunting. Greater variability is seen in yearly and age-specific allele frequencies because of dog hunting (Table 5). The summated X^2 values for every locus and age class are greater in the Dog-Hunted Area than in the Still-Hunted Area. There are also more significant effects seen for locus-age categories in the Dog- than Still-Hunted Area. The total X^2 for the 0.5-age class was not significant for the Still-Hunted Area, but it was for the Dog-Hunted Area and for the Still-Dog Area in 1982, the first year the effects of dog hunting were observed among the offspring (Table 5). In 1981, no significant differences in allele frequencies were noted for any age class in the Still-Dog Area. Thus, the effect of dog hunting on genetic characteristics is mediated through the altered breeding structure and is not an artifact of harvest intensity or shifting demography.

Another important effect of harvest method is the increased mean number of alleles/locus observed in deer from the Dog-Hunted Area (Table 6). In 1982, the increased number of alleles is also seen for deer in the Still-Dog Area. Deer do show significant genetic differences in allele frequencies over short distances on the SRP (Manlove et al. 1976, Ramsey et al. 1979, Chesser et al. 1982). Deer have a well-defined breeding structure and can be separated on a much finer scale based on social interactions during certain times of the year. In the fall, herds are composed of small matriarchal lines (Hirth 1977) with dominant bucks doing most of the breeding. Most dispersal is by young males (Hawkins et al. 1971, Downing and McGinnes 1975).

The use of dogs can result in greater movement and dispersion of deer than would naturally be the case (Jeter and Marchinton 1967, Sweeney et al. 1971). Mixing of genetically heterogeneous subgroups and subsequent increase in random mating result in more alleles observed/locus within the Dog-Hunted Areas of the SRP. This effect was observed among the offspring 1 year after the social structure of the populations in the Still-Hunt Area had been altered by dog hunting.

Breakdown of the social structure and/or greater uniformity in genotypic dispersion should, over a period of time, result in the population achieving genetic equilibrium at a larger effective population size than that characteristic of the Still-Hunted Area. Effective population size is primarily defined by the number of breeding animals and, as it increases, the population becomes more genetically stable over time because of the increased number of interactions between individuals. The year- and age-specific changes in allele frequency should, over a few generations, be minimized because of the effects of dog hunting on the SRP, which is obviously not the case (Table 5). In addition, significant deviations in expected genotypic proportions observed in Hardy-Weinberg tests are still observed, indicating that the populations in the Dog-Hunted Area have never come into equilibrium. Studies in the region have shown white-tailed deer to exhibit strong site tenacity (Byford 1969, Downing et al. 1969). Thus, the spatial structure seems to persist, even though dog hunting acts strongly in producing a homogenous population through space.

The large differences in genetic characteristics of deer in the Dog-Hunted Area could have been caused in a number of ways. Heavy hunting pressure and the use of dogs probably result in an increase in the year-age genetic differences through forced movement of animals, population mixing, and subsequent random mating. Specific mechanisms to explain this chain of events could be as follows: breaking up of female doe-fawn groups and subsequent mixing of subgroups with slight differences in allele frequency, movement of females out of their ranges to increase the probability of mating with males from previously non-overlapping ranges, and movement of dominant bucks away from their ranges to allow more younger bucks to breed before the social hierarchy is re-established. Alternatively, increases in random mating could result from a decreasing age structure and a less rigid social hierarchy. Almost half of the SRP buck population is composed of buck fawns that normally would not reproduce in any great numbers (Follmann and Klimstra 1969). With a greater proportion of doe fawns breeding, the average time of conception will be delayed (Johns et al. 1977), possibly allowing more male fawns to breed. Even if more fawns are breeding because of the younger age structure the genetic differences associated with the harvest method are not likely to be caused by this process because there is more fawn doe breeding in the Still-Hunted Area than in the Dog-Hunted Area (Scribner et al., unpub. data; up to 80% of doe fawns become pregnant in certain areas of the SRP). The genetic effects of dog hunting appear to be more directly mediated through the movement of individuals and subsequent indirect effects of the breeding structure than on the direct effects on the social hierarchy without movements considered.

Traditionally, wildlife management decisions have been based on habitat and demographic considerations. Genetic attributes are assumed to be constant; i.e., population genetic characteristics do not change in response to management practices. We have shown, in choosing just 2 of many possible harvest strategies available to managers, that this assumption is invalid. Harvest intensity on the SRP is high, and herd size and area involved are large. However, our results have general applicability to a wide variety of situations. Large herd size can have a buffering effect in dampening genetic differences because of harvest intensity over short periods. Smaller populations confined to more restricted areas could show the same or greater effects with far less hunting pressure. Harvest strategies can and should be thought of as resulting in genetic changes in the biological resource. For example, buck-only hunting can drastically alter sex ratios and breeding structure (Ryman et al. 1981). Trophy buck hunting or selective spike buck removal can potentially remove genetic material from the population (Harmel 1983). Relating these potential results to tangible phenotypic or physiological effects that would be of interest to game managers will require long-term studies directed at this problem. However, the importance of the genetic changes is already suggested by the large amount of correlative information for these genetic characters. Mean individual heterozygosity (H) and single-locus effects in white-tailed deer have been documented as being related to reproductive performance (Urbston 1976, Johns et al. 1977, Chesser and Smith, in press), fetal growth (Cothran et al. 1983), fat levels in females (Cothran et al. 1983), body size, and antler development (Smith et al. 1983). The awareness of the potential importance of genetics to wildlife management needs to be increased so that the relevant research questions will be addressed under natural conditions, which are of interest for both applied and theoretical reasons.

LITERATURE CITED

BARR, A., J. H. GOODNIGHT, J. P. SALL, AND J. T. HELWIG. 1976. A users guide to SAS-76. SAS Institute Inc., Raleigh, N.C. 329pp.

BYFORD, J. L. 1969. Movement responses of white-tailed deer to changing food supplies. Proc. Annu. Conf. Southeast. Assoc. Game and Fish Comm. 23:63-78.

CAUGHLEY, G. 1977. Analysis of vertebrate populations. John Wiley & Sons. New York, N.Y. 234pp.

CHARLESWORTH, B., AND J. T. GIESAL. 1972. Selection in populations with overlapping generations. II. Relation between gene frequency and demographic variables. Amer. Nat. 106:388-401.

CHESSER, R. K., M. H. SMITH, P. E. JOHNS, M. N. MANLOVE, D. O. STRANEY, AND R. BACCUS. 1982. Spatial, temporal and age-dependent heterozygosity of beta-hemoglobin in white-tailed deer. J. Wildl. Manage. 46:983-990.

―――, AND ―――. In Press. Growth and reproductive correlates of genetic variation in the white-tailed deer. C. Wemmer, ed. Biology of the cervidae symposium.

COTHRAN, E. G., R. K. CHESSER, M. H. SMITH, AND P. E. JOHNS. 1983. Influences of genetic variability and maternal factors on fetal growth rate in white-tailed deer. Evolution 37:282-291.

CROW, J. F., AND M. KIMURA. 1970. An introduction to population genetics theory. Harper and Row, New York, N.Y. 284pp.

DAPSON, R. W., P. R. RAMSEY, M. H. SMITH, AND D. F. URBSTON. 1979. Demographic differences in contiguous populations of white-tailed deer. J. Wildl. Manage. 43:889-898.

DAVIS, J. 1979. The white-tailed deer in Alabama. Ala. Dep. Cons. Spec. Report 8. 60pp.

DOWNING, R. L., B. S. MCGINNES, R. L. PETCHER, AND J. L. SANDT. 1969. Seasonal changes in movements of white-tailed deer. Pages 19-24 in L. K. Halls, ed. White-tailed deer in the southern forest habitat. South. Forest Exp. Sta., Nacogdoches, Tex.

―――, AND ―――. 1975. Movement patterns of white-tailed deer in a Virginia enclosure. Proc. Annu. Conf. Southeast. Assoc. Game and Fish Comm. 29:454-459.

FOLLMANN, E. H., AND W. D. KLIMSTRA. 1969. Fertility in male white-tailed deer fawns. J. Wildl. Manage. 33:708-711.

HARLOW, R. F., AND F. K. JONES, JR. 1965. The white-tailed deer in Florida. Fla. Game and Fresh Water Fish Comm. Tech. Bull. 9. 240pp.

HARMEL, D. E. 1983. Effects of genetics on antler quality and body size in white-tailed deer. Pages 339-348 in R. D. Brown, ed. Antler development in cervidae. Caesar Kleberg Wildlife Research Inst., Kingsville, Tex.

HAWKINS, R. E., W. D. KLIMSTRA, AND D. C. AUTRY. 1971. Dispersal of deer from Crab Orchard National Wildlife Refuge. J. Wildl. Manage. 35:216-220.

HESSELTON, W. T., C. W. SEVERINGHAUS, AND J. E. TANEK. 1965. Population dynamics of deer at the Seneca Army Depot. N.Y. Fish and Game J. 12:17-30.

HIRTH, D. H. 1977. Social behavior of white-tailed deer in relation to habitat. Wildl. Monogr. 53. 50pp.

JENKINS, J. H., AND E. E. PROVOST. 1964. The population status of the large vertebrates of the Atomic Energy Commission Savannah River Plant site. USAEC, Div. Biol. and Med., TID-19562. 45pp.

JETER, L. K., AND R. L. MARCHINTON. 1967. Preliminary report of telemetric study of deer movements and behavior on the Eglin Field Reservation in northwestern Florida. Proc. Annu. Conf. Southeast. Assoc. Game and Fish Comm. 18:140-152.

JOHNS, P. E., R. BACCUS, M. N. MANLOVE, J. E. PINDER, III, AND M. H. SMITH. 1977. Reproductive patterns, productivity and genetic variability in adjacent white-tailed deer populations. Proc. Annu. Conf. Southeast. Assoc. Game and Fish Comm. 30:487-492.

———, M. H. SMITH, AND R. K. CHESSER. 1984. Sex and age effects on the seasonal kidney fat indices in a southern white-tailed deer herd. J. Wildl. Manage. 48:969-973.

MANLOVE, M. N., J. C. AVISE, H. O. HILLESTAD, P. R. RAMSEY, M. H. SMITH, AND D. O. STRANEY. 1975. Starch gel electrophoresis for the study of population genetics of white-tailed deer. Proc. Annu. Conf. Southeast. Assoc. Game and Fish Comm. 29:392-403.

———, M. H. SMITH. H. O. HILLESTAD. S. E. FULLER, P. E. JOHNS, AND D. O. Straney. 1976. Genetic subdivision in a herd of white-tailed deer as demonstrated by spatial shifts in gene frequencies. Proc. Annu. Conf. Southeast. Assoc. Game and Fish Comm. 30:487-492.

MARCHINTON, R. L., A. S. JOHNSON, J. R. SWEENEY, AND J. M. SWEENEY. 1970. Legal hunting of white-tailed deer with dogs: biology, sociology and management. Proc. Annu. Conf. Southeast. Assoc. Game and Fish Comm. 24:74-89.

RAMSEY, P. R., J. C. AVISE, M. H. SMITH, AND D. F. URBSTON. 1979. Biochemical variation and genetic heterogeneity in South Carolina deer populations. J. Wildl. Manage. 43:136-142.

RANSOM, A. B. 1967. Reproductive biology of white-tailed deer in Manitoba. J. Wildl. Manage. 31:114-123.

RYMAN, N., R. BACCUS, C. REUTERWALL, AND M. H. SMITH. 1981. Effective population size, generation interval, and potential loss of genetic variability in game species under different hunting regimes. Oikos 36:257-266.

SEVERINGHAUS, C. W. 1949. Tooth development and wear as criteria of age in white-tailed deer. J. Wildl. Manage. 13:195-216.

———, AND E. L. CHEATUM. 1956. The life and times of the white-tailed deer. Pages 57-186 in W. P. Taylor, ed. The deer of North America. Stackpole Co., Harrisburg, Pa.

SMITH, M. H., R. K. CHESSER, E. G. COTHRAN, AND P. E. JOHNS. 1983. Genetic variability and antler growth in a natural population of white-tailed deer. Pages 365-387 in R. D. Brown, ed. Antler development in cervidae. Caesar Kleberg Wildlife Research Inst., Kingsville, Tex.

SWEENEY, J. R., R. L. MARCHINTON, AND J. M. SWEENEY. 1971. Responses of radio-monitored white-tailed deer chased by hunting dogs. J. Wildl. Manage. 35:707-716.

SWOFFORD, D. L., AND R. B. SELANDER. 1981. BIOSYS-1: a computer program for the analysis of allelic variations in genetics. Univ. Illinois Press. Urbana-Champaign. 65pp.

URBSTON, D. F. 1967. Herd dynamics of a pioneer-like deer population. Proc. Annu. Conf. Southeast. Assoc. Game and Fish Comm. 21:42-50.

———. 1976. Descriptive aspects of 2 fawn populations as delineated by reproductive differences. Ph.D. Thesis. Virginia Polytechnic Inst. and State Univ., Blacksburg. 102pp.

VERME, L. J. 1983. Sex ratio variation in *Odocoileus*: a critical review. J. Wildl. Manage. 47:573-582.

WHIPPLE, S. A., L. H. WELLMAN, and B. J. GOOD. 1981. A classification of hardwood and swamp forests of the Savannah River Plant, South Carolina. SRO-NERP-6 Savannah River National Environ. Res. Park, Aiken, S.C. 36pp.

MANAGEMENT OF EXOTIC DEER IN CONJUNCTION WITH WHITE-TAILED DEER

JOHN T. BACCUS, Department of Biology, Southwest Texas State University, San Marcos, TX 78666

DONNIE E. HARMEL, Texas Parks and Wildlife Department, Kerr Wildlife Management Area, Hunt, TX 78024

WILLIAM E. ARMSTRONG, Texas Parks and Wildlife Department, Kerr Wildlife Management Area, Hunt, TX 78024

Abstract: The populations of introduced or exotic species in Texas have increased dramatically in recent years. The increase of exotics, especially on white-tailed deer (*Odocoileus virginianus*) range, has the potential to become a major concern in the management of white-tailed deer. Three deer species—axis (*Axis axis*), fallow (*Dama dama*), sika (*Cervus nippon*)—have been identified as major forage competitors of white-tailed deer. Census data for these exotics indicate population increases of axis deer (254%), fallow deer (1,680%), and sika deer (611%) between 1966 and 1979. Studies on the Kerr Wildlife Management Area demonstrated that extensive competition (competition coefficient = 0.99) between sika and white-tailed deer occurred when sika deer populations were uncontrolled. The interaction between the 2 species resulted in the demise of the population of whitetails. The introduction of exotic deer in the Edwards Plateau and south Texas has occurred in many areas where the rangeland was already heavily stocked with domestic livestock. Today, the landowner with high exotic deer populations is faced with a multispecies management decision; if white-tailed deer are to survive, exotic deer populations must be reduced. With the emphasis on buck-only harvest for exotic deer, the populations continue to escalate. We recommend a program of heavy harvesting of both bucks and does. For the rancher interested in maintaining a quality white-tailed deer population, we do not encourage the introduction of axis, fallow, or sika deer; however, if they are introduced, we recommend an immediate population control management plan.

KEY WORDS: *Axis axis*, *Cervus nippon*, *Dama dama*, Edwards Plateau, Exotic deer, Harvest, Management, *Odocoileus virginianus*, White-tailed deer.

The introduction of exotic wildlife is a controversial issue. There is evidence of ecological upheaval—the rabbit (*Oryctolagus cuniculus*) in Australia and the red deer (*Cervus elaphus*) in New Zealand—and success—the ring-necked pheasant (*Phasianus colchicus*) and the chukar partridge (*Alectoris graeca*)—through such introductions.

The proponents of exotic game argue that their introduction can provide new game animals to occupy vacant niches in the ecosystem, provide an additional source of income to landowners from recreational hunting or nonconsumptive use, enhance the North American fauna, and provide a breeding stock and gene pool for threatened or endangered species. In Texas the additional revenues derived from exotic game is a strong incentive for stocking them, especially when we consider the instability of livestock market values.

Craighead and Dasmann (1966) outlined the major problems involving the introduction of exotic species. They opposed their introduction because (1) exotics entering an already species-packed range can cause an intensification of habitat destruction, (2) exotic game may compete with and thus displace native wildlife species, (3) management efforts are better directed toward the preservation of the North American faunal diversity, (4) funds spent on introductions are more cost effective when channeled to the improvement of habitat for native species, (5) the interaction of exotic species within natural communities may disturb the community's aesthetic value, (6) some exotics have the potential to breed with native species and to dilute or destroy their gene pool, and (7) exotic populations may be difficult or impossible to control.

Since the first-known introduction of exotic artiodactyls on the King Ranch in south Texas in 1930 (Jackson 1964), the number of species and their populations have proliferated. Landowner and hunter interests in stocking exotic game have grown rapidly in recent years despite little historical documentation. A state-wide census by the Texas Parks and Wildlife Department (TPWD) was an initial attempt to document the status of exotic populations. This survey indicated a state population of approximately 13,000 animals of 13 species (Jackson 1964). Additional surveys in 1966, 1971, 1974, and 1979 updated the original base-line information. The 1979 survey showed a population of over 72,000 exotic artiodactyls in the state (Armstrong and Wardroup 1980). Six species had populations in excess of 5,000 individuals. Three of the 6 species were axis, fallow, and sika deer. Table 1 presents their population estimates and percentage of change for 13 years. Trend data for the 3 species indicate a very high, if not astronomical, rate of population increase.

In the Edwards Plateau Region of Texas, most rangelands are grazed by 2 or more classes of livestock plus wildlife species. This area has the state's largest white-tailed deer population and also supports the greatest number of exotic species (Ramsey 1969). Originally, exotic species were confined to ranches with deer-proof fences; however, biologists have since observed ever-increasing numbers of free-ranging exotics. Of the 3 exotic deer species under discussion, 33% of the 1979 population were free-ranging in 17 of 35 counties of the Edwards Plateau Ecological Region. This influx of free-ranging animals on rangelands has resulted in species packing of the herbivore trophic level and increased the potential for interspecific competition.

Specialization is the most obvious source of species diversity among related forms or within groups of animals at 1 trophic level (Klopfer 1962). Since any natural community is composed of specialists and widely adapted generalists, some competition for food and space will occur. If the exotic species are dietary generalists vs. white-tailed deer, a specialist, the degree of interaction may become so intense that survival of 1 species is threatened when the population density of the other increases.

The niche concept explains competitive interactions (Elton and Miller 1954, Hutchinson 1957). This approach allows discussion of relationships within the ecological niches of potential competitors. Hutchinson (1957) used conventional set theory notations to describe these relationships. This method

Table 1. Population trends of 3 exotic deer in Texas from 1966 to 1979.

Species	Estimated population						
	1966	5-year % change	1971	3-year % change	1974	3-year % change	1979	13-year % change
Axis deer	6,450	73.2	11,171	75.3	19,581	16.4	22,799	253.5
Fallow deer	445	488.1	2,617	71.3	4,483	76.7	7,922	1,680.2
Sika deer	875	132.7	2,036	49.4	3,042	104.4	6,217	610.5
All deer	7,770	103.7	15,824	71.3	27,106	36.3	36,938	375.4

applies to all the variables relative to a species, regardless of their exact nature or quality, in defining a niche. Her formalization also included the fundamental niche that is expressed in the absence of competitive interactions and the realized niche that is occupied under competitive restrictions (Fig. 1).

If we consider the total array of variables that limit the survival of a species S_1, then it is possible to define the n-dimensional hypervolume N_1 or fundamental niche. This niche is the set of points in an abstract N space that completely defines the ecological properties of S_1. Secondly, if B is a limited volume of physical space comprising the biotope of species S_1, S_2, ... S_n, the biotope is complete relative to S_1 if B represents all points in N_1. If N_1 and N_2 are 2 fundamental niches, they may have no points in common and are therefore separate, or they may have points in common and intersect. $N_1 \cdot N_2$ is the subset of points common to N_1 and N_2 and their intersection subset.

Hutchinson (1957) distinguished 2 cases of intersection between fundamental niches: (1) N_2 is a proper subset of N_1 (N_2 of S_2 is inside N_1 and is a smaller niche), and (2) $N_1 \cdot N_2$ is a proper subset of both N_1 and N_2. A Euler diagram (Fig. 2) illustrates these relationships. Two independent variables, x and y that are measurable along ordinary rectangular coordinates, are associated with the habitat requirements of S_1 and S_2. In the first case, N_2 coincides with the intersection of subset $N_1 \cdot N_2$ and is included within N_1; whereas in the second, the intersection of subset $N_1 \cdot N_2$ results from the overlap of the 2 niches.

In the simplified, 2-dimensional relationship (Fig. 2) (Case 1), the coordinates $x_2 - x_3$ and $y_1 - y_3$ describe niche N_2, which is included within the total niche N_1. In Case 1, (a) competition proceeds in favor of S_1 in all elements of B corresponding to $N_1 \cdot N_2$ and, given adequate time, only S_1 will survive, or (b) S_2 survives in all elements of B corresponding to some part of the intersection subset and both species survive. The first alternative (a) implies S_1 is a superior competitor with a greater ecological amplitude and will eliminate S_2 from all parts of the fundamental niche N_1. Coexistence of S_1 and S_2 is impossible in the niche where S_1 is the superior competitor. The second alternative (b) requires that S_2 be a superior competitor, even though it has a narrow ecological amplitude. Under these conditions, S_1 will be excluded from N_2 but will survive in parts of N_1 that are outside the intersection subset.

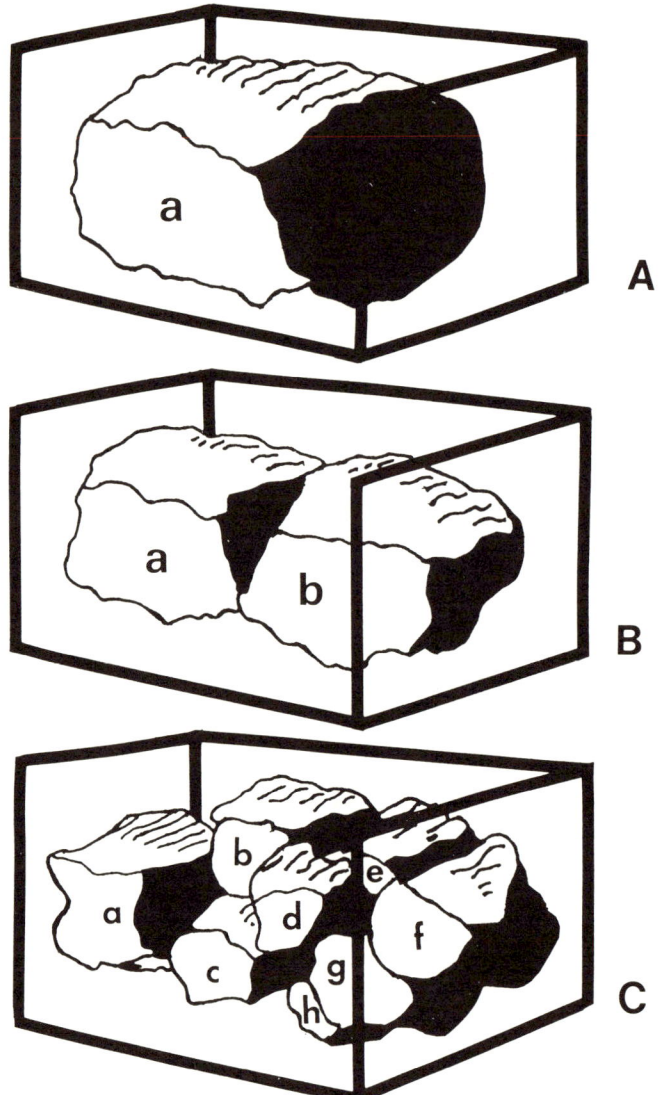

Fig. 1. An abstraction of the hypervolume of the niche. The open box represents the hypervolume. In A the hypervolume represents the fundamental niche of a species. Under the pressures of competitive interactions, the species is compelled to retreat to the portion of the hypervolume in which it is most highly adapted, thus leaving a vacated space of the niche to its competitor (B). The 2 species now occupy realized niches. With more species present (C) capable of exploiting the environment, the realized niches become even narrower (adapted from Hutchinson 1957, 1965).

Niche competition has elicited much interest among ecologists (Volterra 1926, Gause 1934, Slobodkin 1961, Hutchinson 1965, Miller 1967, Vandermeer 1972). Slobodkin (1961) summarized the formulas expressing the simultaneous growth rates of 2 competing species in the following notation:

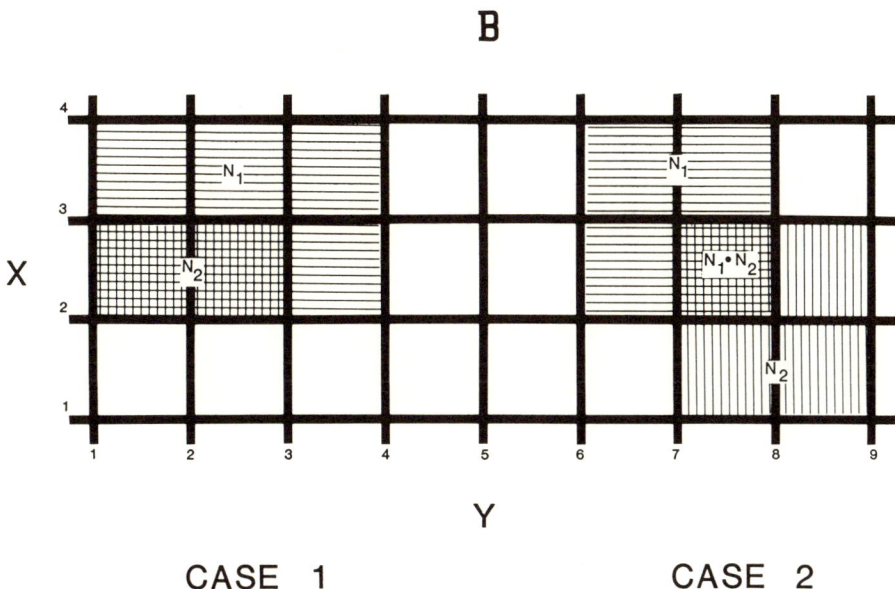

Fig. 2. Euler diagram showing the relationships between fundamental niches (N_1 and N_2) defined by 2 variables (x and y) in a biotope (B).

$$\frac{dN_1}{dt} = \frac{r_1 N_1 (K_1 - N_1 - \beta N_2)}{K_1}$$

$$\frac{dN_2}{dt} = \frac{r_2 N_2 (K_2 - N_2 - \alpha N_1)}{K_2}$$

N_1, r_1, and K_1 are the same values as in the logistic formula for S_1; N_2, r_2, and K_2 are the logistic values for S_2; β is the inhibitory influence of S_2 on S_1, and α is the inhibitory influence of S_1 on S_2.

These predictions seem to be verified by recent case histories. On Maryland's eastern shore, the number of white-tailed deer harvested has declined 39.3%, whereas sika deer populations have increased 39.3% from 1973 to 1977 (Feldhamer and Chapman 1978). Kean (1959) and Kiddie (1962) documented sika deer competition with red deer in New Zealand. In these cases involving sika deer, management must limit population densities to effect an equilibrium on rangelands.

This paper reviews research findings on the interspecific competition of white-tailed deer and 3 exotic deer species, presents a simplified model of white-tailed and sika deer interaction, and outlines management strategies and recommendations for dealing with the problem of competitive interactions between these species of deer.

The investigations leading to this publication were carried out by the Wildlife Division of the Texas Parks and Wildlife Department and the Biology Department of Southwest Texas State University under Pittman-Robertson

Projects (Federal Aid) W-56-D, Kerr Wildlife Management Area Development; W-62-R, Edwards Plateau Game Management Survey; W-76-R, Kerr Wildlife Management Area Research; and W-109-R, Big Game Investigations.

METHODS

Studies were conducted on the Kerr Wildlife Management Area, a 2,591-ha research facility located in the Edwards Plateau Ecological Region and owned by TPWD. Topography of the region is gently rolling to hilly with occasional draws and small canyons. Soils are generally rocky and shallow, covering a substrate of limestone. Mean annual rainfall is 62.5 cm.

Dominant overstory vegetation of the study area is composed of scrub live oak (*Quercus fusiformis*), white shin oak (*Q. sinuata* var. *breviloba*), and Texas oak (*Q. shumardii* var. *texana*) with regrowth ash juniper (*Juniperus ashei*) in abundance. These species are typical of the oak-juniper savannah community that dominates the area. Common grasses include 3-awns (*Aristida* spp.), Texas wintergrass (*Stipa leucotricha*), curly mesquite (*Hilaria belangeri*), sideoats grama (*Bouteloua curtipendula*), and little bluestem (*Schizachyrium scoparium*). Most forbs are annuals that are influenced by rainfall. McMahan (1964) and Ramsey and Anderegg (1972) have published other reports and descriptions of this area.

The study sites were 39-ha, high-fenced pastures. McMahan (1964) and Butts et al. (1982) present vegetative information and stocking rates. The study of white-tailed deer-sika deer competition involved a food habits study using the animal bite technique and a population study. Tame deer were allowed to graze, with an observer within 3 m, once a week for a 45-minute observation period. Total bites by species were recorded. Brood herds consisting of 2 males and 4 females of each species were placed in Pasture 7. The 2 deer populations increased without artificial control. The sika deer population was eliminated by hunting in February 1981.

Simulation modeling can be a useful tool for analyzing competition, testing hypotheses, and predicting causal pathways. However, the tool has limitations. For example, any model is limited to the applicable variables and cannot simulate interactions involving unforseen factors and relationships (Patten 1971).

An interspecific competition model (CONDUIT), written for the Apple IIe microcomputer by W. A. Reiners, W. E. Glanz, and S. F. Cornish and modified by D. G. Huffman, was used to simulate the white-tailed and sika deer populations in Pasture 7. Variables addressed by the program were growth rate, carrying capacity, and species overlap. The mathematical equation for the white-tailed deer population was:

$$S_1 = \frac{I\, r_1\, N_1\, (K_1 - N_1 - \beta\, N_2)}{K_1}$$

I is the number of generations; r_1, N_1, and K_1 are the same values as in the logistic formula for S_1; and β is the coefficient of overlap with its effect dependent upon the sika deer's degree of niche overlap with the white-tailed deer. Thus, the larger the value of β, the greater the competition.

The equation for the sika deer population was:

$$S_2 = \frac{I\,r_2\,N_2\,(K_2 - N_2 - \alpha\,N_1)}{K_2}$$

I, r_2, N_2, and K_2 relate as mentioned above, and α is the coefficient of overlap with its effect dependent upon the white-tailed deer's degree of niche overlap with the sika deer.

Two populations are related by connecting the output of 1 to the input of the other. In modeling parlance we are coupling 2 systems; α and β, the interacting coefficients (Patten 1971), express the rules of coupling. This coupled system has 4 possible outcomes; however, only 1 applies to the white-tailed deer-sika deer study. This is Case 4 (Slobodkin 1961:54), where S_2 is the sole survivor when:

$$\alpha > \frac{K_1}{K_2} \text{ and } \beta < \frac{K_2}{K_1}$$

In developing concepts concerning food resource use by native and exotic species, we draw from the naturalists' definitions of specialized vs. generalized: a specialized species is a narrow-niched animal, and a generalized species is a broad-niched animal. Levins (1968) and Colwell (1969) suggested the term "niche breadth" to explain this concept. We apply the concept to feeding diversity of the deer species under discussion. A species is broad-niched that has several forage classes in the diet and a wide array of species in each class. Niche breadth measures food items that define the niche. Food selectivity experiments are a way to learn about niche breadth (Levins 1968).

RESULTS AND DISCUSSION

Food Habits

White-tailed Deer.—The stocking rate of livestock and deer materially reduces the availability of preferred and some staple foods (McMahan 1964). Figure 3 shows the influence of grazing pressure. Their annual diet is characterized by a high preference for browse, which comprises over 50% of the yearly diet (regardless of grazing intensity), heavy seasonal use of forbs (grazing intensity determining forb availability), and small amounts of grass (McMahan 1964).

Axis Deer.—Forage availability, subject to grazing intensity, affects their food habits (Butts et al. 1982). In a pasture without grazing impact, axis deer use all 3 forage classes in nearly equal amounts. However, in moderate to heavily grazed pastures, they consume large amounts of grass. Forb consumption is insignificant in moderate to heavily grazed pastures (Fig. 3).

Axis and white-tailed deer compete for preferred browse, forbs, and succulent grass. Only grass is consumed in greater amounts by axis deer. As browse and forbs become less abundant, axis deer shift their diet to a mainstay

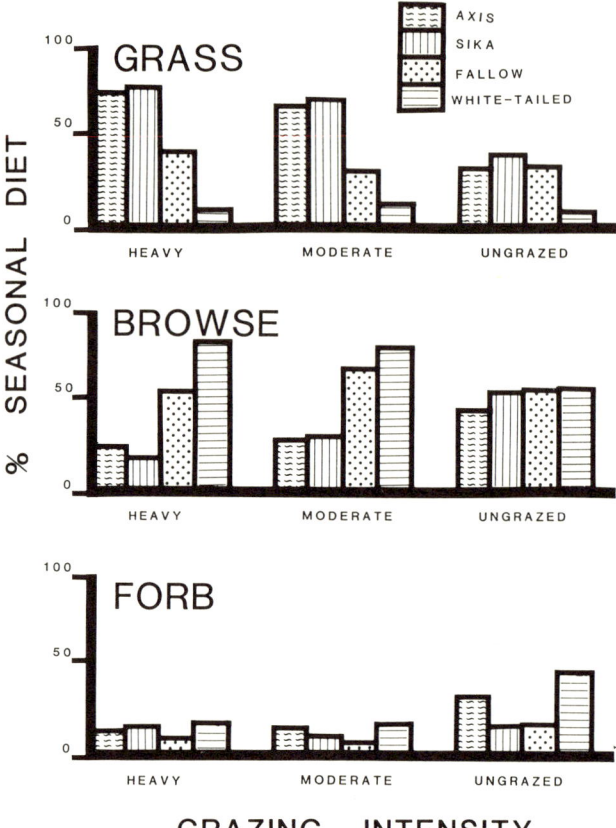

Fig. 3. Histogram of the feeding habits of axis, sika, fallow, and white-tailed deer. The influence of grazing intensity on food selection of 3 forage classes is presented, Kerr Wildlife Management Area, Texas.

of grasses (Butts et al. 1982). They have greater forage diversity than white-tailed deer and a competitive advantage over them in an unstable environment with species packing.

Sika Deer.—When forage composition contains readily available browse, sika deer are browsers (Butts et al. 1982). Otherwise, they primarily consume grass in pastures with moderate to heavy grazing pressures and reduced amounts of browse and forbs. Since white-tailed deer prefer browse (McMahan 1964), sika deer compete directly with them for browse (Butts et al. 1982). Because of greater intensity of browse use, the sika deer is a severe competitor of the white-tailed deer (Butts et al. 1982).

Fallow Deer.—Fallow deer consume more browse than sika deer (Butts et al. 1982). They forage on all 3 forage classes, adjusting their diet to the availability of forbs and grasses and rank as a major competitor of the white-tailed deer.

The ability of exotic deer to use the 3 forage classes makes them potential competitors with white-tailed deer for food. When the many herbivores on the rangelands of the Edwards Plateau forage heavily, the exotic deer species have a selective advantage over the white-tailed deer. In primeval times white-tailed deer evolved adaptations that enabled them to function in a fundamental niche (Fig. 1a). The introduction of livestock and, later, exotic deer has resulted in an ecological traverse for the native deer from the first partial niche to the mth partial niche (realized niche), where several species interact with native species (Fig. 1c). In other words, the species has moved from an environment without any density-dependent competitive effects to one with density-dependent competitive effects from several community members. When food resources are limited, interspecific competition and potential displacement of the white-tailed deer occur. Exotics and white-tailed deer consume similar browse species, but the depletion of browse has different results for each competitor. Exotics shift their diet to grass, whereas white-tailed deer are physiologically stressed by nutritional deficiencies that eventually result in population declines.

Population Interactions

The result of the interaction experiment involving white-tailed and sika deer was the demise of the white-tailed deer population (Fig. 4). Through modeling of the 2 populations, we had a better understanding of their competitive interaction and quantified several parameters of interest (Table 2). In the simulation, growth rates (r) were 1.06 and 0.366 for the white-tailed and sika deer, respectively. These numbers appear valid because twinning is common in white-tailed deer; as stress increases, a reduction in the twinning rate occurs (McCullough 1978). In sika, twinning is rare (Kiddie 1962).

The second parameter in the simulation, environmental capacity, addressed the number of animals that the habitat would support. During the study, the white-tailed population peaked at 16 deer; whereas, the sika population showed a steady increase. In the simulation (Table 2), the environmental capacities for white-tailed and sika deer were higher than the actual populations.

The degree of overlap is a factor that expresses competitive interactions. A species with a high overlap value directly competes with the other species. The implication of the model is that the 2 species are using the same environmental resources. An ecological axiom underlying Gause's model is that no 2 species can indefinitely continue to occupy the same ecological niche (Slobodkin 1961). According to Armstrong and Harmel (1980), sika and white-tailed deer competitively interact. The coefficient of competition (Table 2) of sika deer (0.99) coincides with Slobodkin's Case 4, and the model shows the demise of the white-tailed deer population (Fig. 4).

The model does have several problems; however, these shortcomings can be explained. The major problem was the lack of a parameter to express

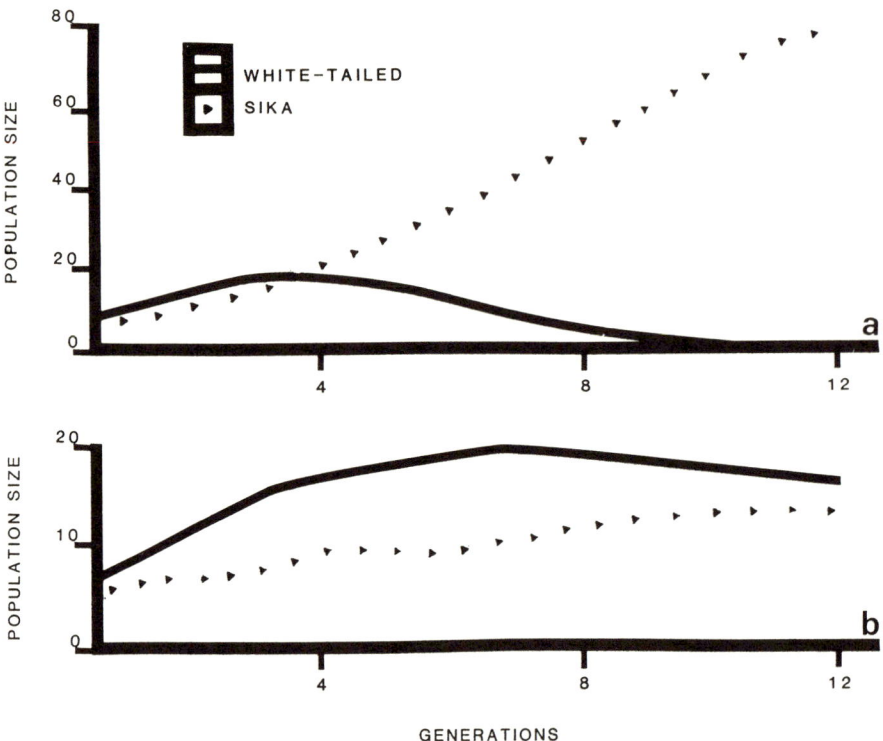

Fig. 4. Population curves for an uncontrolled competitive interaction between white-tailed deer and sika deer (a), and an interaction in which the sika deer population was controlled (b), Kerr Wildlife Management Area, Texas.

the habitat decline associated with the increase in sika and white-tailed deer. The model assumed a constant habitat quality. Second, no parameter addressed climatic conditions that vary from year to year. Climatic fluctuations influence habitat and food quality and reproductive success. The important dry years were not accounted for. Third, the model had no parameter to account for differential mortality in the populations. Although the model lacked these real-world situations, the computer produced basic information concerning competition. The model is useful in projecting trends and could be made stochastic to deal with these factors, but the changes would probably not appreciably improve upon the projected trends.

Finally, the model addressed the question whether white-tailed and sika deer could coexist. In the simulation we assumed that the density of the sika deer population must be artificially regulated. The simulation model was used to predict the degree of control (Fig. 4). The growth rate for the controlled population was 0.10 and was lower than that for the population that competed with the white-tailed deer (Table 2).

Table 2. Population statistics for simulated white-tailed deer and sika deer populations under the conditions of competitive interaction and intense control of the sika deer population.

Parameter	Population			
	Competition simulated		Control simulated	
	White-tailed	Sika	White-tailed	Sika
r	1.06	0.366	0.75	0.10
k	32	94	29	75
α	0.099		0.099	
β		0.99		0.9925

MANAGEMENT IMPLICATIONS

Instability in community structure contributes to uncertainty or "chance" in wildlife management. The species structure of rangeland communities, especially those strongly modified by human uses, changes in a time frame of years and decades rather than centuries and eons. The wildlife manager does not control many changes in community structure; the changes initially come as surprises and later as inevitable but unwelcome events. This certainly has occurred on the Edwards Plateau where monitoring of introductions has been minimal, and the increase in free-ranging exotics is a problem that can have long-term significance.

In many areas of Texas, exotic ungulates are released on private lands occupied by dense populations of white-tailed deer. The resultant stress on native deer caused by species packing with exotics on an already-crowded range is unclear. Because of our limited information, quantitative predictions on the outcome of a particular introduction are difficult. There is an urgent need for research on the interaction between animals, native and exotic, and the vegetative resource. We need to determine the degree of competition that exotic game offers for food, cover, or space and the effect that they have on white-tailed deer production. Certain exotic ungulates may fit an empty niche in an ecosystem without harm to native deer, whereas other species may be incompatible. Since Texas has few native ungulates in proportion to the total number of possible introductions, the potential for community disruption is immense. Because species interactions are partly dependent on the order in which species are introduced, the possible results are even further proliferated. The wildlife manager can thwart the proliferation of exotic species by advising landowners whether to stock exotic game.

Wilson and Willis (1975) wrote optimistically about "planned biotic enrichment" and future ability to design communities from our growing knowledge of species packing and the mechanisms that structure communities. However, our knowledge regarding biotic enrichment is not yet adequate for a wildlife manager to practice with confidence. We believe caution and restraint rather than optimism should prevade our present policies.

The Edwards Plateau has been described as the most important deer range in Texas from the standpoint of land area, deer numbers, hunting pressure, deer harvested, and economic return to landowners (Thomas et al. 1964). Presently, the plateau is overpopulated with white-tailed deer because of an inadequate antlerless deer harvest. Overgrazing by livestock and deer has generally caused poor habitat conditions as evidenced by browse lines on woody vegetation and depleted ground cover in many range areas.

The increasing free-ranging exotic population compounds management problems and community wellbeing of white-tailed deer. On some ranches exotics have displaced white-tailed deer (Butts 1979). The potential exists for a more widespread displacement where deer-proof fences do not confine exotics. Free-ranging populations of axis, fallow, and sika deer currently exist in several Edwards Plateau counties. These escaped animals are nearly impossible to control. Even on ranches with deer-proof fencing, the control of axis and sika deer is very difficult.

With the establishment of free-ranging populations, the management of exotic deer species presents TPWD with a unique challenge. The 1979 statewide exotic game survey indicated a population of approximately 10,000 free-ranging exotic deer in 17 of the 35 counties in the Edwards Plateau. Approximately 33% of the axis and fallow deer populations were free-ranging. The Maryland case with sika and white-tailed deer illustrated the need for a state policy regarding the harvest of exotic species. Although Article 978 gave TPWD limited regulatory authority for axis deer and aoudad sheep (*Ammotragus lervia*), the state game department's policy urgently needs reexamination regarding the increasing populations of free-ranging exotics. Although the situation is complex, we would not now suggest a specific course of action; however, management's option to do nothing and let nature take its course appears imprudent.

The results of food habit studies of axis, fallow, sika, and white-tailed deer (Butts et al. 1982) determined that the 3 exotic deer species severely competed with white-tailed deer in the Edwards Plateau. These species were a real threat to the management, well-being, and survival of the native species and should not occupy (unregulated) the habitats already ranged by white-tailed deer. Anyone introducing exotic deer into a habitat with a good white-tailed deer population should expect an adverse impact on the native species. We recommend that the landowners concentrate on enhancing white-tailed deer and forego the introduction of exotic deer.

For many ranchers of the Edwards Plateau, the question of introduction is a moot issue. Exotic deer species are already present and, in most instances, in large numbers. In some cases white-tailed deer population density has declined and is in serious trouble. Habitat has also been degraded. What can the rancher do to improve on this situation? A management plan should involve a census of the different deer species populations and the establishment of quotas to maintain each species at desirable densities. Results of the sika deer-white-tailed deer study indicated the need for intensive cropping of exotics. To effect an 81% decrease in the sika deer population, an annual harvest rate of 0.729 (Caughley 1977) would be necessary. The landowner with high densities of exotics and a degraded habitat should begin a radical herd reduction. Once the density is reduced, a yearly harvest quota should be established and faithfully followed.

Our knowledge of the patterns and processes of ecological systems, although still in the developmental stage, is beginning to disclose some underlying principles by which systems operate. The resources of any ecosystem are limited, and the fauna's reproductive and growth tendencies constantly exert pressure, especially in communities with species packing. In such instances we can expect competitive interactions between organisms. Since ecosystems tend to evolve toward stability and equilibrium of their components, disturbances of the system should elicit ecological problems such as interspecific competition. Murphy (1967) advocated the application of judicious cropping of all ecologically similar species within a trophic level. He concluded "the intelligent use of living resources by man must be based on a thorough understanding of the total ecology of the community involved."

LITERATURE CITED

ARMSTRONG, W. E., AND D. E. HARMEL. 1980. Exotic mammals competing with natives. Tex. Parks and Wildl. 38:6-7.

——, AND S. WARDROUP. 1980. Statewide census of exotic big game animals. Tex. Parks and Wildl. Dep. Prog. Report, Fed. Aid Proj. W-109-R-3. 33pp.

BUTTS, G. L. 1979. The status of exotic big game in Texas. Rangelands. 1:152-153.

——, M. J. ANDEREGG, W. E. ARMSTRONG, D. E. HARMEL, C. W. RAMSEY, AND S. H. SOROLA. 1982. Food habits of 5 exotic ungulates on Kerr Wildlife Management Area, Texas. Tex. Parks and Wildl. Dep. Tech. Ser. 30. 47pp.

CAUGHLEY, G. 1977. Analysis of vertebrate populations. John Wiley & Sons, New York, N.Y. 234pp.

COLWELL, R. K. 1969. Ecological specialization and species diversity of tropical and temperate arthropods. Ph.D. Thesis. Univ. Michigan, Ann Arbor. 79pp.

CRAIGHEAD, F. C., AND R. J. DASMANN. 1966. Exotic big game on public lands. U.S. Dep. Inter., Bur. Land Manage., Washington, D.C. 26pp.

ELTON, C., AND R. S. MILLER. 1954. The ecological survey of animal communities: with a practical system of classifying habitats by structural characters. J. Ecol. 42:460-496.

FELDHAMER, G. A., AND J. A. CHAPMAN. 1978. Sika deer and white-tailed deer on Maryland's eastern shore. Wildl. Soc. Bull. 6:155-157.

GAUSE, G. F. 1934. The struggle for existence. Williams and Wilkins, Baltimore, Md. 163pp.

HUTCHINSON, G. E. 1957. Concluding remarks. Cold Spring Harbor Symp. Quant. Biol. 22:415-427.

——. 1965. The ecological theater and the evoluntionary play. Yale Univ. Press, New Haven, Conn. 139pp.

JACKSON, A. W. 1964. Texotics. Tex. Game and Fish 23(4):7-11.

KEAN, R. I. 1959. Ecology of the larger wildlife mammals of New Zealand. N.Z. Sci. Rev. 17:35-37.

KIDDIE, D. G. 1962. The sika deer in New Zealand. N.Z. For. Serv. Inf. Ser. 44. 35pp.

KLOPFER, P. M. 1962. Behavioral aspects of ecology. Prentice-Hall, Englewood Cliffs, N.J. 161pp.

LEVINS, R. 1968. Evolution in changing environments: some theoretical explorations. Princeton Univ. Press, Princeton, N.J. 120pp.

McCULLOUGH, D. R. 1978. Essential data required on population structure and dynamics in field studies of threatened herbivores. Pages 302-317 *in* P. Scott, chairman. Threatened deer. Int. Union Conserv. Nat. & Nat. Resour., Morges, Switzerland.

McMahan, C. A. 1964. Comparative food habits of deer and 3 classes of livestock. J. Wildl. Manage. 28:798-808.

Miller, R. S. 1967. Pattern and process in competition. Pages 1-74 *in* J. B. Cragg, ed. Advances in ecological research. Academic Press, New York, N.Y.

Murphy, O. 1967. Vital statistics of the Pacific sardine (*Sardinops caerulea*) and the population consequences. Ecology 48:731-736.

Patten, B. C. 1971. Systems analysis and simulation in ecology. Academic Press, New York, N.Y. 607pp.

Ramsey, C. W. 1969. Texotics. Tex. Parks and Wildl. Dep. Bull. 49. 46pp.

―――, and M. J. Anderegg. 1972. Food habits of an aoudad sheep (*Ammotragus lervia*) (Bovidae) in the Edwards Plateau of Texas. Southwest. Nat. 15:267-280.

Slobodkin, L. B. 1961. Growth and regulation of animal populations. Holt, Rinehart & Winston, New York, N.Y. 184pp.

Thomas, J. W., J. G. Teer, and E. A. Walker. 1964. Mobility and home range of white-tailed deer on the Edwards Plateau in Texas. J. Wildl. Manage. 29:463-472.

Wilson, E. O., and E. O. Willis. 1975. Applied biogeography. Pages 522-534 *in* M. L. Cody and J. M. Diamond, eds. Ecology and evolution of communities. The Balknap Press, Cambridge, Mass.

Vandermeer, J. H. 1972. Niche theory. Pages 107-132 *in* R. F. Johnston, P. W. Frank, and C. D. Michener, eds. Annual review of ecology and systematics. Annual Reviews, Inc., Palo Alto, Calif.

Volterra, V. 1926. Vartatzioni e fluttuazioni del numero d' individui in specie animali conviventi. Mem. R. Acad. Lincei Ser. 6:1-36.

HARVEST STRATEGIES FOR OTHER MAMMALS

A SEX- AND AGE-SELECTIVE HARVEST STRATEGY FOR MOOSE MANAGEMENT IN SASKATCHEWAN

R. R. STEWART, Department of Parks and Renewable Resources, Regina, Saskatchewan S4S 5W6, Canada

Abstract: A sex- and age-selective moose (*Alces alces andersoni*) harvest strategy was implemented in Saskatchewan in the fall of 1977. The objectives of the program were to protect and increase the existing moose populations and to provide high quality recreation to the sportsmen of Saskatchewan. A 2-license system was devised to ensure control over harvest size and structure. A "special" moose license, valid for any sex or age class, was restricted by a predetermined quota for each game management area and was obtained through a lottery-type draw. A "regular" moose license, which was available to any legal hunter, restricted harvest to either a bull or calf (young-of-the-year) moose. The average 1977-82 moose hunting season kill consisted of 25% calves, 21% yearlings, 14% cows, and 40% bulls; this compares to 15% calves, 24% yearlings, 27% cows, and 34% bulls for the non-sex or age-selective 1965-76 period. The moose population, number of hunters, harvest, and recreation-days increased during the program's initial 2 years. However, population estimates have steadily declined since that time. The 1983 population estimate of 0.32 moose/km^2 was 32% below the 1979 level. Hunting seasons in 1981 and 1982 were charaterized by low harvests and record high hunter-days/moose killed. The number of hunters and hunter-days recreation have remained stable throughout the selective harvest program.

KEY WORDS: Moose, *Alces alces*, Saskatchewan, Harvest strategies, Selective harvesting, Game management.

Sex- and age-selective moose sport hunting was introduced in Saskatchewan in 1977. This harvest program, based on a Swedish model, was implemented because reduced moose populations had not increased adequately under an area-specific hunting license quota allocation system started in 1972. The restrictive license-quota system regulated the magnitude of the harvest, but not its composition, and allowed only 50% of the province's moose hunters to hunt moose each year.

Many studies have shown that young moose are most susceptible to natural mortality caused by severe winters, predation, and parasitism (Blood 1973, Coady 1974, Peterson and Allen 1974, Berg 1975, Stewart et al. 1977, Ballard et al. 1981). Stringham (1974) and Markgren (1969, 1974), working in Alaska and Sweden, respectively, have documented the benefits of the calf-dam association during the calf's first winter and suggested orphaned calf mortality may be high. Blood (1973) reported relatively constant annual pregnancy rates for moose in Elk Island National Park in Alberta with yearling pregnancy and adult twinning rates the flexible components of moose reproductive performance. In a study of ovulation rates, Markgren (1969) and Sylven et al. (1980) concluded that Swedish moose cows reach maximum reproductive capacity when 4-7 years of age.

Theoretically, maintaining winter moose populations comprised of high proportions of mature, breeding females should encourage optimal calf production.

This management concept was initiated in Sweden in 1967 by directing harvest pressure to calves and bulls while protecting females with calves. The annual harvest of moose increased from 35,000 to 132,000 animals by 1980 (Lavsund 1981). In light of the Swedish experience, a selective moose harvest strategy was designed for Saskatchewan to exert high pressure on calves, moderate pressure on bulls, and light pressure on females. The anticipated increase in the proportion and age of breeding females in the population was to provide the nucleus for higher sustained yields that would both protect the moose population and allow greater recreation opportunity for the sportsmen of Saskatchewan.

METHODS

Moose population trends were obtained from transect aerial surveys flown annually in January-February in small, fixed-wing aircraft. Two observers, seated on opposite sides of the aircraft, recorded all moose sighted within 195 m on each side of the plane flown at 120 m altitude and at 150-160 km/hr. Flight paths were oriented from systematic transect lines drawn on 1:250,000 scale topographic maps. The provincial annual population estimate was calculated by averaging moose observed in 12 survey blocks encompassing 3,200 km^2 from 1959 to 1983. The limitations and biases of transect aerial surveys are well known and amply reported in the literature. Trend survey information was used for the current analysis as it was the best available long-term population index information. Hunter harvest statistics were obtained from a combination of big-game hunter checking stations and a big-game hunter mail questionnaire. At checking stations, operated annually since 1963, sex and age data (incisors for age determination) were collected. The hunter questionnaire, sent to about 20% of the moose hunters, provided estimates of harvest, hunter days of recreation, success, effort, and harvest composition.

RESULTS AND DISCUSSION

Recent Changes in Moose Populations and Management

Moose populations have fluctuated considerably in Saskatchewan since 1930. Prior to 1946, moose hunting was regulated by a bulls-only license valid from mid-November to mid-December. However, in 1946, low moose populations, believed to be caused by a series of severe winters, resulted in closed hunting seasons until 1953. Populations had apparently recovered somewhat by 1953, and Saskatchewan residents were subsequently permitted to shoot 1 moose of any sex or age class during a 1-week, late November season. Transect aerial surveys for moose were initiated in 1954-55, and the moose population was considered sufficient to warrant a 2-week early

(September) and a 3-week late (November-December) either-sex moose season beginning in 1955. Treaty Indians have unrestrictive year-round hunting privileges in Saskatchewan. The impact of their activity on moose is believed to be extremely important, but attempts to quantify the size and structure of the kill have been unsuccessful.

Liberal, Either-Sex Seasons (1955-1972).—During the first 15 years of this management program, moose transect density estimates steadily increased. This phenomenon was reported for moose throughout western North America, Scandinavia, European Russia, and eastern Siberia (Lykke and Cowan 1968). From 1958 to 1969, the estimated Saskatchewan moose density rose 3-fold from 0.17 to 0.54 moose/km^2 but by 1971 had declined sharply to 0.38 moose/km^2 (Fig. 1). Several other statistics substantiated the growth of the moose population (Fig. 2). Between 1959 and 1969, the number of moose hunters more than doubled from 6,000 to over 13,000, and the estimated harvest increased from 3,200 to 6,800 animals. In both 1970 and 1971, approximately 18,000 hunters harvested in excess of 9,500 moose despite the fact that trend survey estimates were declining. The hunter effort or days hunted/moose declined to less than 8 days in each of these 2 years (Fig. 2). The reported harvest structure was relatively stable annually between 1961 and 1971 with calves, cows, and bulls averaging 15, 27, and 58% of the kill, respectively.

The average age of mature ($\geq$2.5-year-old) adult males and females harvested increased from 1967 to 1971. Females increased from 5.8 to 6.2 years and adult males from 4.1 to 5.0 years (Fig. 3). Mature adults averaged 60% of the 1965-71 kill with yearlings and calves comprising 26 and 14%, respectively. The yearling harvest varied greatly; in 1970, an estimated 3,000 yearling moose comprised 31% of the kill, but in the large 1971 harvest only 19% were yearlings.

Following a modest decline in the density estimate in 1972, the combination of declining populations and increasing hunting pressure generated considerable public concern. Consequently, license quotas were established for selected hunting zones in east-central Saskatchewan that year. A short 1971 summer growing season was followed by an extended, heavy-snowfall winter, subsequently judged by both MacLennan (1975) and Stewart et al. (1977) to be severe for moose in Saskatchewan. The 1972 harvest, although reduced by 60%, was still dominated by mature animals; adult females with an average age of 6.3 years comprised 36% of the kill. MacLennan (1975) concluded that the maximum sustained yield (MSY) was likely exceeded in much of the province in 1972.

License-Quota-Allocation Seasons (1972-76).—When the 1973 aerial survey showed a third successive decline in the population estimate, the license-quota-allocation system was expanded to encompass all northern wildlife management zones.

Restriction of license numbers had an immediate impact on harvest and recreation days (Fig. 2). In 1973, fewer than 5,500 sportsmen were allowed

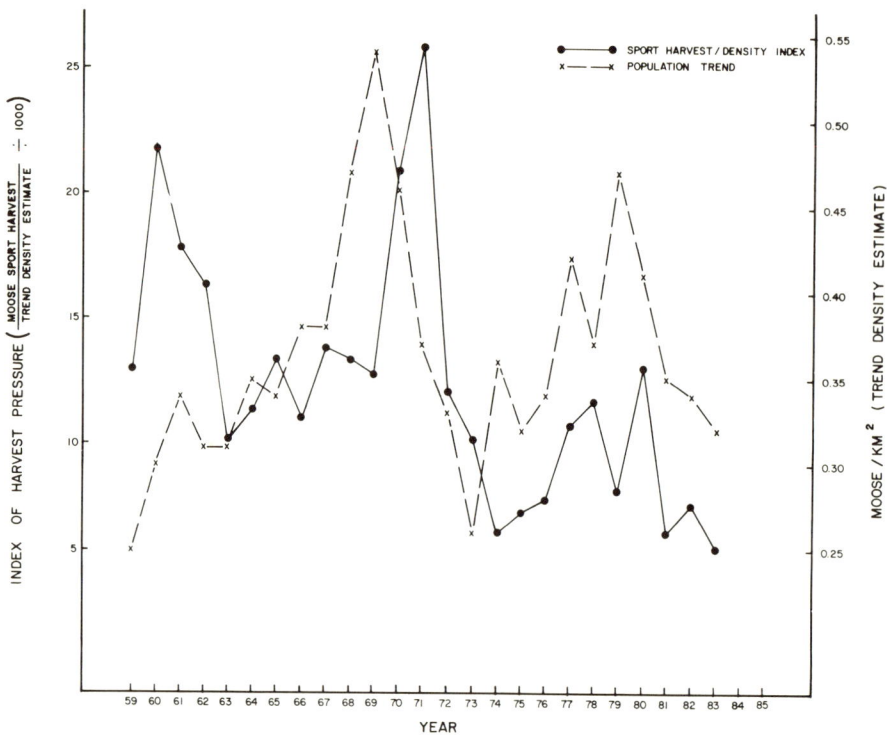

Fig. 1. Population density trend estimate and sport harvest-density index for moose in Saskatchewan, 1959-83.

to hunt providing less than 34,000 recreation days; only 2,800 moose were killed. Calves and yearlings comprised less than 30% of the harvest, and the average age of females was high at 6.8 years. The 1974 quotas were increased moderately in response to a 30% increase in the winter density estimate. However, the combination of a short 1973 growing season, a severe 1973-74 winter, and an unusually late spring leaf-flush in 1974 may have led to a serious negative energy balance for moose resulting in reduced productivity or recruitment (Stewart et al. 1977). Hunters spent more effort and harvested fewer moose in 1974 than in any other reported year. Again, the harvest heavily favored adults. The final 2 years (1975-76) of the quota allocation program were characterized by low stable densities and harvests. However, the adult moose harvest was lower so that by 1976 yearlings and calves accounted for 30 and 18% of the kill, respectively (Fig. 3).

The license-quota-allocation system was criticized from both administrative and biological perspectives:

1. Moose hunters were not satisfied with an allocation system that restricted an individual to hunting only once every 2 or 3 years.
2. The quota system did not guarantee a fair allocation of licenses because many hunters encouraged non-hunting family members or friends to

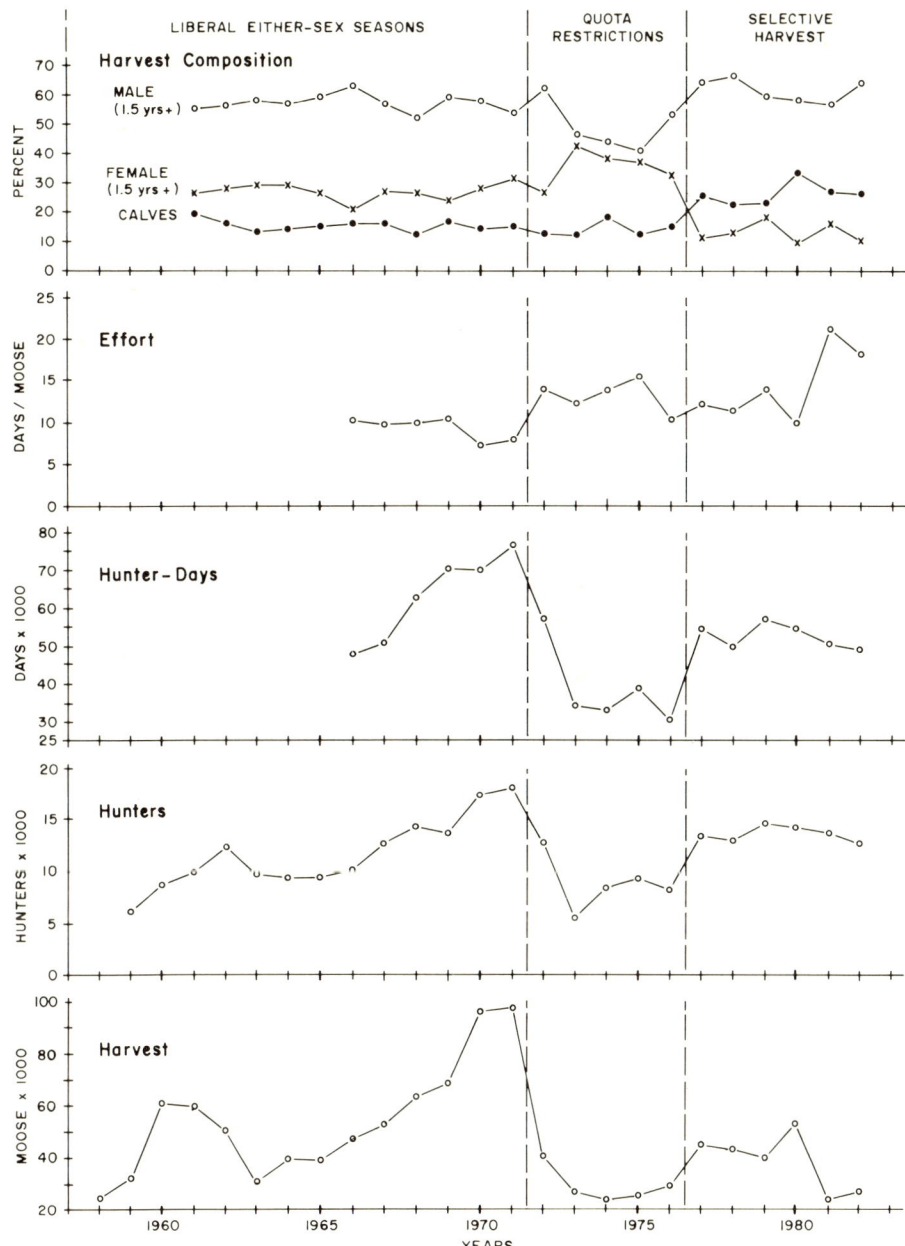

Fig. 2. Saskatchewan hunter questionnaire-moose harvest statistics, 1958-82.

apply in the lottery-type draw. The hunters, if unsuccessful in the draw themselves, would purchase a black bear (*Ursus americanus*), white-tailed deer (*Odocoileus virginianus*) or woodland caribou (*Rangifer tarandus caribou*) license and actually hunt for the family member or friend.

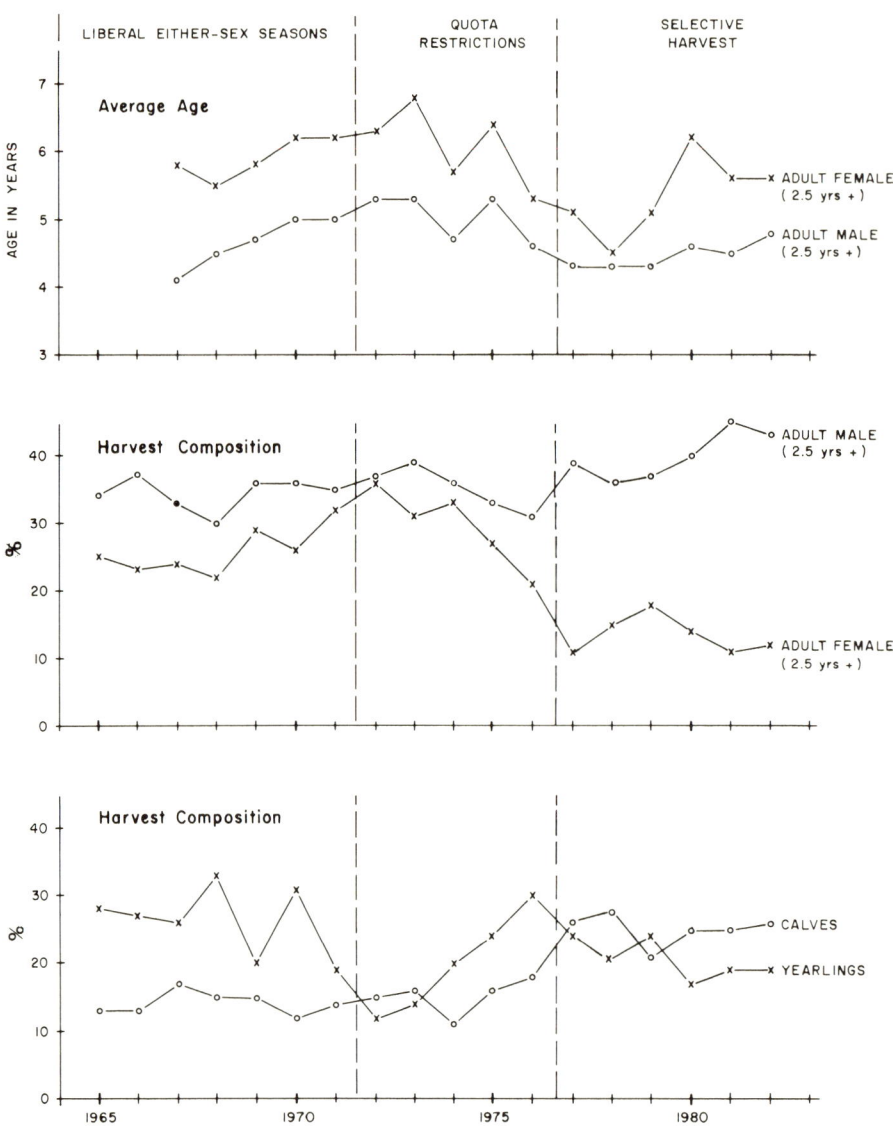

Fig. 3. Saskatchewan big-game checking station moose harvest statistics, 1965-82.

Caribou license sales alone jumped from 200 to 1,400 licenses/year during this period.
3. Moose populations had not recovered throughout the province, resulting in low annual quotas.
4. The disproportionately high harvest of breeding adults and low harvest of non-breeding young from 1972 to 1975 were considered counterproductive for optimum population recruitment.

Sex- and Age-Selective Harvest (1977-82).—Under the selective harvest management strategy, introduced in September 1977, each Saskatchewan resident had access to 1 of 3 types of licenses:

1. Special Moose License. This license was allotted to applicants on the basis of a non-priority computer draw until 1980, after which a 3-tiered priority pool system was introduced. Harvest is regulated by the number of licenses allotted to specific game management zones each year. Successful applicants are restricted to hunting in only 1 management zone but are entitled to harvest an animal of any sex or age class. The license is valid for both a 1-week early pre-rut (mid-September) and 2-week late (early November) season.

2. Regular Moose License. This license, which is not restricted to a particular zone, is valid for either a bull or calf moose only and is available to any legal-aged resident not holding a special moose license. Holders of regular licenses can hunt in an early post-rut (mid-October) and late (late November-early December) season. The early season is of 1-week duration, and late season extends from 1-2 weeks, depending on the management zone.

3. Guided Moose License. In addition to the resident licenses, a limited number of guided moose licenses are available to both residents and non-residents. License holders are required to use the services of a registered guide and may harvest a bull or calf moose only. The season dates generally coincide with those of the regular and special licenses.

During the first 3 years of this management program, changes became evident in trend survey and harvest data. By 1979, the survey estimate had increased to 0.47 moose/km^2, 38% above the 1976 level, and the number of hunters and hunter days recreation rose 56% and 89%, respectively. The 1977 harvest of 4,510 moose was 56% higher than in 1976 but was accompanied by an increase in effort from 10.4 to 12.1 days/moose harvested (Fig 2). Harvest declined somewhat in 1978 and 1979, but by 1980 the estimated kill was more than 5,300 animals, the highest since 1971. The hunter questionnaire and check-station data indicated the new management policy had influenced harvest structure with an increased proportion of young non-breeding moose and a large decline in the proportion of adult cows in the kill (Figs. 2,3). The estimate of the number of cows harvested increased from 500 in 1977 to more than 900 by 1980. The higher level compares to average harvests in the 1973-77 period but is far below the more than 3,000 cows taken during the high 1971-72 harvests. The unknown Treaty Indian moose harvest occurs largely in late winter, and adult females are believed to comprise a large percentage of their kill.

An initial decline in the average age of mature adult cows harvested in 1977-78 was reversed in 1979-80. The average age of adult males, which had declined to 4.6 years in 1976, remained stable throughout the 6 years of the selective harvesting program (Fig. 3). However, as Caughley (1977) explains, changes in age distributions are largely influenced by changes in survival and/or fecundity rates and are difficult to interpret. He also stated that the mean age of males will decline in sex-selective harvesting strategies that shift the sex ratios in favor of females, because males are loaded into the younger age classes.

Since 1979, the population estimate has declined over most of the range and today is 32% below the 1979 level. A large reduction in harvest has occurred, with the 1981-82 harvests 55 and 49% less than 1980. In addition, hunting effort has increased dramatically from 9.9 days/moose harvested in 1980 to 21.1 and 18.1 in 1981 and 1982, respectively (Fig. 2). The average harvest of 25% calves, 21% yearlings, 14% cows, and 40% bulls is similar to that reported by Lykke (1982) for the highly successful Norwegian Moose Management Program.

For the Saskatchewan moose population, it appears that mortality from all sources, including hunting, has exceeded the biological rate of increase and forced the population into decline. The broad application of the sex- and age-selective harvest strategy for sport hunters alone was not sufficient to guarantee realization of program objectives. It is interesting to note the relationship between the trend-survey density estimate and sport harvest as a function of the density estimate (Fig. 1). The population density estimate improved steadily during 1959-69, despite relatively heavy sport harvest pressure from 1961 to 1963. The sharp trend-density decline of 1970-73 was accompanied by 2 years (1970-71) of high harvest pressure. However, since 1973 the sport harvest index has been low in relation to trend density, and yet the population has declined steadily since 1979. In addition, the period 1977-82, except for 1979, was characterized by long summer growing seasons and generally short, low-snowfall winters.

Population models to be used for the projection of sustained yields require quality data on herd size and structure and reproductive and mortality rates. Efforts are now being directed to collect such information on local populations. Stratified-random-block and herd-segregation aerial surveys are being conducted to improve the population size and structure data base. Management studies to define the nature and extent of mortality are in progress. From 1 area documented to have low autumn calf/cow ratios, a 94% pregnancy and 27% twinning rate was determined by rectal palpation of 16 cows in March 1978. Subsequent early summer and autumn ratios were high and low, respectively, leading to the conclusion that calf mortality was an important limiting factor in this area (Haigh et al. 1981). In 1982, 12 neonatal calves were equipped with mortality-sensitive radio transmitters, and their activity was monitored until they were 6 weeks of age; of 7 calves found dead, black bears were implicated in the mortality of 6. In 1983, 14 black bears were removed from a 90-km^2 study area prior to and during the calving season; by September, 77 calves/100 cows were reported within the control area compared to only 37 calves/100 cows for similar, adjacent habitats. The process of elimination of the causes of moose mortality led Crichton (1981) to conclude that the moose resource in several areas of Manitoba was being jeopardized by unregulated hunting by Treaty Indians. Eason et al. (1981) reported overharvesting of moose to be a problem in recently logged areas in Ontario where extensive road networks and forest cover reduction increased moose vulnerability to hunters. Saskatchewan has the largest proportion of Treaty Indians in Canada and a recent (late 1960's) and expanding forest-harvesting industry. Hunting by Treaty Indians is believed to have intensified in conjunction with road access. In addition, severe winters and infestations of the moose tick (*Dermacentor albipictus*) periodically may add additional mortality pressure on the resource.

CONCLUSIONS

The sex- and age-selective moose management program was implemented in 1977 with the belief it would serve to protect and increase the moose population while offering Saskatchewan sportsmen maximum recreational opportunity. This was to be achieved by placing heavy hunting pressure on calves, moderate pressure on bulls, and light pressure on cows. Harvest structure has been altered by the management design, and recreational-days associated with moose hunting has increased. However, a declining provincial population-trend estimate since 1979 is incongruous with the stated objective to increase the moose population, and recreational opportunity must also decline. Moose mortality from all sources, including sport and unregulated hunting, appears to be overwhelming the anticipated benefits of the selective harvest program.

Wildlife managers in Saskatchewan must allocate more effort to modeling moose population dynamics and base harvest on sustained yield estimates that comply with long-term management objectives.

LITERATURE CITED

Ballard, W. B., T. H. Spraker, and K. P. Taylor. 1981. Causes of neonatal moose calf mortality in south central Alaska. J. Wildl. Manage. 45:335-342.

Berg, W. D. 1975. Management implications of natural mortality of moose in northwestern Minnesota. Alces 11:332-343.

Blood, D. A. 1973. Variation in reproduction and productivity of an enclosed herd of moose (*Alces alces*). Pages 59-66 *in* I. Kjerner, and P. Bjurholm, eds. Proc. XI Int. Congr. of Game Biologists, National Swedish Environment Protection Board, Stockholm, Sweden.

Caughley, G. 1977. Analysis of vertebrate populations. J. Wiley & Sons, New York, N.Y. 234pp.

Coady, J. W. 1974. Influence of snow on the behavior of moose. Nat. Can. 101:417-436.

Crichton, V. F. J. 1981. The impact of Treaty Indian harvest on the Manitoba moose herd. Alces 17:56-63.

Eason, G., E. Thomas, R. Jerrand, and K. Oswald. 1981. Moose hunting closure in a recently logged area. Alces 17:111-125.

Haigh, J. C., E. H. Kowal, W. Runge, and G. Wobeser. 1981. Pregnancy diagnosis as a management tool for moose. Alces 18:45-53.

Lavsund, S. 1981. Moose as a problem in Swedish forestry. Alces 17:165-178.

LYKKE, J., AND I. McT. COWAN. 1968. Moose management and population dynamics on the Scandinavian Peninsula with special reference to Norway. Alces 5:1-22.

———. 1982. Harvest strategy. Proc. Workshop Session North Am. Moose Conf. and Workshop. Whitehorse, Yukon Territory, Can. 64pp.

MACLENNAN, R. R. 1975. An analysis of fluctuating moose populations in Saskatchewan. Sask. Dep. of Parks and Renew. Resour. Tech. Bull 2. 14pp.

MARKGREN, G. 1969. Reproduction of moose in Sweden. Viltrevy 6:129-285.

———. 1974. The moose in Fennoscandia. Nat. Can. 101:174-185.

PETERSON, R. O., AND D. L. ALLEN. 1974. Snow conditions as a parameter in moose-wolf relationships. Nat. Can. 101:481-492.

STEWART, R. R., R. R. MACLENNAN, AND J. D. KINNEAR. 1977. The relationship of plant phenology to moose. Sask. Dep. of Parks and Renew. Resour. Tech. Bull. 3. 20pp.

STRINGHAM, S. R. 1974. Mother-infant relations in moose. Nat. Can. 101:325-369.

SYLVEN, S., A. W. HAWLEY, AND M. WILHELMSON. 1980. Study of the reproductive organs of female moose in Sweden. Alces 16:124-134.

SOCIAL DETERMINANTS OF BLACK BEAR MANAGEMENT FOR THE NORTHERN CATSKILL MOUNTAINS[a]

DANIEL J. DECKER, Department of Natural Resources, Cornell University, Ithaca, NY 14853
ROBERT A. SMOLKA, JR., Department of Natural Resources, Cornell University, Ithaca, NY 14853
JOHN O'PEZIO, New York State Department of Environmental Conservation, Wildlife Resources Center, Delmar, NY 12054
TOMMY L. BROWN, Department of Natural Resources, Cornell University, Ithaca, NY 14853

Abstract: Based on black bear (*Ursus americanus*) population studies prompted by declining hunter take of bears in New York's Catskill Mountains, the state's Department of Environmental Conservation determined that the range was below biological carrying capacity and initiated efforts to expand the population incrementally. A study conducted in 1978 prior to the first population increase found that landowners in the region had generally positive attitudes toward bears. A second study of the same landowners was conducted in 1983 to determine whether landowner attitudes had changed as a result of the first population increase and to determine the reasons behind opposition to a proposed further increase in the population. Results indicated that little attitude change occurred between 1978 and 1983 and that landowners who opposed vs. favored a further population increase were less familiar with bears and the Catskill Bear Management Program. It was recommended that the DEC implement an I&E program to familiarize landowners with bears and bear management in the Catskills. This study indicates how public input can be used to guide wildlife management.

KEY WORDS: Bear management, Black bear, Human surveys, Landowner attitudes, Landowner perceptions, Public input.

Black bears have been an important part of the history and ecology of the northern Catskill Region of New York (Decker et al. 1981). The northern Catskill bear range is an area of some 2,250 km^2 (McCaffrey et al. 1976) characterized largely by the Catskill Mountain Landform (Stout 1958). Bear habitat is provided by continuous forest, located predominantly on the publicly owned Catskill Forest Preserve.

Between 1954 and 1969, a general decline occurred in the number of bears that hunters took annually in the northern Catskills (McCaffrey et al. 1976) despite an increase in the number of big-game hunters in the region. Concern about the reasons for this decline prompted the New York State Department of Environmental Conservation (DEC) to begin a research program in 1970 to determine the status of the bear population, its ecology, and its interrelationship with the human population. McCaffrey et al. (1976) reported that hunting is the major limiting factor in the bear population, accounting for about 90% of bear mortality. Since 1970, data have been collected concerning property damage and other conflicts between bears and

---

[a]This research was supported by New York Federal Aid in Fish and Wildlife Restoration Projects W-89-R and W-146-R.

humans, as well as public attitudes toward bears. Findings showed that during 1970-75, when a low but stable population of about 150 bears inhabited the region, hunter use and hunting values of bears were high; conflicts with humans were relatively few (NYS DEC, unpubl. data).

In 1976, an experimental program of population increase was undertaken (O'Pezio and Clarke 1976). The strategy called for an immediate return to population levels comparable to those of the early 1960's (about 300 bears). Following this, incremental growth would be allowed, with a period of population stability planned to assess public acceptance of the greater number of bears as each population objective was reached. To achieve the first population increase, the bear hunting season in the Catskill region was closed for 2 years (1976-77) in an attempt to increase the population. As a result, the bear population increased by 80% (from 150 to about 270 bears) in the northern range (Clarke and O'Pezio 1978). This population has been maintained through the use of carefully timed hunting seasons.

METHODS

To provide adequate base-line data representing public attitudes before the increase cited above could be perceived by landowners, a questionnaire survey was undertaken in 1977 (Brown et al. 1979). The results of this earlier study provide the basis for the analysis of change in landowner perceptions between then and the most recent study reported herein. In developing the initial survey, little information was available regarding public attitudes toward bears. Previous studies (Stokes 1970, Burghardt et al. 1972, Bacon 1974, Cole 1974, 1976, Rowell 1976, Baptiste 1977, Baptiste et al. 1979) had concentrated on visitors' attitudes in various national parks and bear management at specific locations rather than on the attitudes of people owning land or living in a large geographic region inhabited by bears.

The primary audience for the initial study was private (noncorporate) landowners because, as a group, they control the greatest amount of nonpublic land and because, collectively, they should have a great deal of influence on management of the bear population. Lists of private landowners in the northern bear range (Fig. 1) who owned at least 0.4 ha of land were taken systematically from the tax rolls of towns in all or parts of Albany, Delaware, Greene, Orange, Otsego, Schoharie, Sullivan, and Ulster counties and approximated a geographical distribution by town. During the spring of 1978, landowners were surveyed using a mail questionnaire; 870 codable questionnaires were returned, producing a 73% return rate. Information sought included general attitudes toward bears, sightings and tolerance of bears, and nuisance or damage incidents involving bears.

The survey results indicated that landowners generally would accept a bear population larger than that which existed prior to the DEC's effort to increase the population and that they had a moderate to high degree of tolerance for bears. However, although many would accept the nuisance and

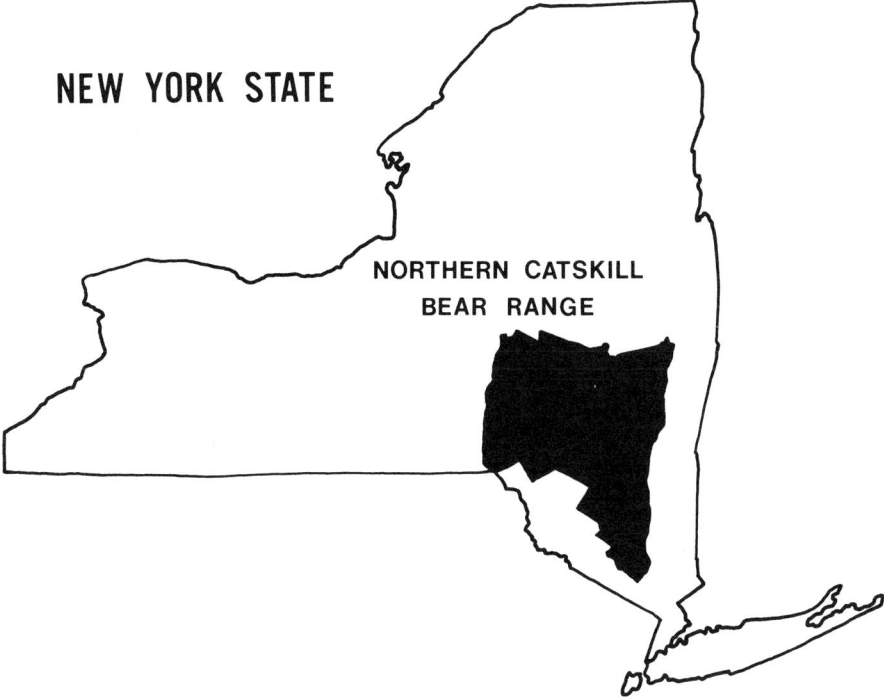

Fig. 1 Northern Catskill Bear Range Study Area.

some economic damage caused by bears, less than 2% had actually experienced such problems. Therefore, it was impossible to predict if their attitudes would change after experience with nuisance or damage situations created by bears.

Ecological studies by the DEC indicate the carrying capacity to be such that the northern range population could probably experience another incremental increase of 50% (100-150 bears) (NYS DEC, unpubl. data). However, before taking actions that would result in another increase in the bear population, the DEC wanted to update the 1978 landowner study. To gain these insights, samples of respondents to the 1978 survey were resurveyed. The objectives of the most recent study were to detect changes in public tolerance of bears resulting from the population increase in the late 1970's and to determine the informational and attitudinal barriers to public acceptance of a 50% increase in the bear population. Several questions in the 1983 questionnaire were identical or similar in format to those in the 1978 questionnaire; thus, change in experience and attitude could be analyzed. During the spring of 1983, landowners were mailed a questionnaire and cover letter with up to 3 follow-ups sent to nonrespondents. A 69% return rate was obtained.

RESULTS

1983 Situation

Recognizing that 1 major objective of this study was to identify the barriers to public acceptance of an increased bear population, we will first present the distribution of landowners' responses regarding their preferences for future bear population levels and will then compare and contrast pertinent landowner characteristics based on whether they wanted the bear population to increase. Most landowners (71%) favored management allowing the bear population to increase; these landowners will be referred to as the Increase Group. Nearly all others (26%) wanted it to remain the same; few (3%) wanted a population reduction. These latter groups will be referred to as the Nonincrease Group.

The Increase Group vs. the Nonincrease Group was younger and twice as likely to be hunters (Table 1). The Nonincrease Group had more years of familiarity with the Catskills than the Increase Group, although both groups had considerable experience in the area (Table 1); both groups were similar in the number of years they have lived in the Catskills (Table 1). The Nonincrease Group was more likely than the Increase Group to be resident vs. absentee landowners and had fewer years of education (Table 1). Landowners in both groups used many different sources of information about bears and their management; newspapers were cited by nearly 50% of them, and a substantial proportion found information in New York State or national magazines. The greatest percentage of landowners chose New York State magazines and newspapers as the sources of black bear information they would most prefer to use in the future. However, these sources may not now be providing adequate information on bears or their management because the majority of both landowner groups (Increase Group, 59%; Nonincrease Group, 71%) did not express a definite opinion regarding whether or not bears were being managed properly.

Landowners also were asked for their opinions of several statements concerning DEC bear management. These statements were organized into 3 groups reflecting 3 components of the overall image of the DEC: the image of the DEC's management programs, its personnel, and degree to which it communicates with the public. The majority of both groups had no opinion concerning any of these components (Table 2). The Nonincrease Group was more likely than the Increase Group to have no opinion about the DEC, perhaps indicating that they were less familiar with the management agency and its programs. Regardless of their preference for the future bear population, those with an opinion about management and personnel were likely to be positive. The communication behavior component had the smallest segment of no-opinion responses and the largest one of negative responses, indicative of communication problems.

Table 1. Landowners' background characteristics, 1983, northern Catskill Mountains, New York.

Landowner characteristics	Landowner groups	
	Increase (N=189)	Nonincrease (N=78)
Age ($\bar{X}$)	54.5	62.7
	(t = 5.39; $P \leq 0.05$)	
	(N=188)	(N=78)
Hunters(%)	58.0	24.0
Nonhunters(%)	42.0	76.0
	($X^2 = 25.66$, 1 df; $P \leq 0.05$)	
	(N=186)	(N=74)
N years familiar with Catskills ($\bar{X}$)	34.5	39.9
	(t = 1.98; $P \leq 0.05$)	
	(N=178)	(N=72)
N years lived in Catskills ($\bar{X}$)	28.7	34.1
	(t = 1.64; $P > 0.05$)	
	(N=189)	(N=78)
Year-round residents(%)	50.0	64.4
Absentees(%)	50.0	35.6
	($X^2 = 4.26$, 1 df; $P \leq 0.05$)	
	(N=187)	(N=76)
Years of education ($\bar{X}$)	13.4	12.5
	(t = 2.03; $P \leq 0.05$)	

Change Analysis

Most landowners (Increase Group, 93%; Nonincrease Group, 84%) were aware in 1978 that black bears were present in the Catskills. However, when asked in 1983 to select the species of bear present (i.e., black bear only vs. black, grizzly [*U. horribilis*], and brown [*U. arctos*] bears), 52% of the Nonincrease Group did not know that the black bear was the only bear species present in the Catskills; 82% of the Increase Group believed that the black bear was the only one present.

The majority of both groups of landowners did not know whether the size of the bear population had changed during the periods 1970-77 (Increase Group, 67%; Nonincrease Group, 78%) or 1978-83 (Increase group, 57%; Nonincrease Group, 73%). Few landowners perceived that the population remained the same from 1970 to 1977 (about 11% in each group) or that an increase occurred from 1978 to 1983 (about 12% in each group).

The Increase Group was more likely to have seen a bear in the Catskills at some time before 1978 (42 vs. 26%, respectively) or during the 5 years from 1978 to 1983 (24 vs. 12%, respectively). Only about 14% of landowners in either group had seen a bear on their property before 1978; fewer had seen one since then. Very few landowners (Increase Group, 0.5%; Nonincrease Group, 1.6%) reported experiencing problems with bears anytime before

Table 2. Landowners' opinions of 3 components of the DEC's public image concerning bear management, 1983, northern Catskill Mountains, New York.

Landowner groups	Opinion of management (%)			N
	Positive	Negative	No opinion	
Increase	40.7	4.7	54.6	181
Nonincrease	21.2	2.4	76.4	75
	($X^2 = 10.81$, 2 df; $P \leq 0.05$)			
	Opinion of personnel			
	Positive	Negative	No opinion	
Increase	42.8	5.0	52.2	181
Nonincrease	23.1	2.5	74.4	77
	($X^2 = 10.63$, 2 df; $P \leq 0.05$)			
	Opinion of communications behavior			
	Positive	Negative	No opinion	
Increase	21.8	27.9	50.3	185
Nonincrease	11.1	25.3	63.6	77
	($X^2 = 4.72$, 2 df; $P > 0.05$)			

1978; slightly more landowners (Increase Group, 5.0%; Nonincrease Group, 4.5%) reported problems for the period 1978-83. This change was significant for Increase landowners ($X^2 = 6.58$, 1 df, $P \leq 0.05$).

In 1978, 65% of the Increase Group compared to 32% of the Nonincrease Group believed that bears were timid, stayed away from or only occasionally approached residences, and seldom caused damage. The majority of the Nonincrease Group (57%) did not believe that they were familiar enough with bears to give an opinion. Attitudes in 1983 about bear behavior were essentially unchanged.

In 1978, when given the opportunity to describe the desired setting for bear sightings, the Nonincrease Group was 3 times less likely than the Increase Group (17 vs. 59%) to have stated that they would occasionally like to observe bears on or near their property. The former was more likely to want to see bears only in undeveloped or remote areas (60 vs. 37%); a portion of the Nonincrease Group (23%) preferred not to observe bears anywhere in the Catskills (although this does not infer that they opposed the presence of bears in the Catskills). Attitudes of both groups had changed little by 1983.

Landowners were given the opportunity to predict what effect an increase in the bear population would have on various human activities. In both 1978 and 1983, the responses of both groups can be summarized by the consistently greater percentage of the Nonincrease Group foreseeing that the negative aspects of bears' presence (i.e., nuisance, vehicle-bear highway accidents, and safety hazards) would escalate (Table 3). The majority of both groups believed that the opportunities for bear sightings and hunting would increase. In 1983, fewer landowners in both groups thought that a larger bear population would lead to an increase in any particular activity; the

Table 3. Landowners' 1978 and 1983 predictions that an increase in the bear population in 1978 and 1983, respectively, would increase the likelihood of various bear-human interactions, northern Catskill Mountains, New York.

Survey year/ landowner groups	Observing bears[a]	Hunting	Damage/ nuisances[a]	Vehicle-bear accidents[a]	Safety hazards[a]
			%		
1978					
Increase	89.0[b]	86.2[b]	34.9[b]	28.0	19.4[b]
Nonincrease	69.6	84.3	70.8	44.5	53.4
1983					
Increase	77.9	65.9	22.9	21.6	4.5
Nonincrease	58.4	74.0	62.1	55.8	34.9

[a] Significant difference between responses of Increase and Nonincrease Groups in both 1978 and 1983 ($P \leq 0.05$).
[b] Significant difference between 1978 and 1983 responses of Increase landowners ($P \leq 0.05$).

only exception was that the Nonincrease Group was more likely in 1983 to envision an increase in vehicle-bear highway accidents.

Perhaps most importantly, the percentage of landowners wanting a bear population increase rose from 60% in 1978 to 71% in 1983 ($X^2 = 6.78$, 1 df, $P \leq 0.05$); nevertheless, a noticeable minority were still opposed to such an increase. Ninety percent of the landowners who favored a population increase in 1978 and 42% of those who opposed an increase favored an increase in 1983, indicating that the population preference of previous supporters remained unchanged, whereas the preference of a large minority of previous nonsupporters did change.

SUMMARY

An analysis and comparison of both surveys (1978 and 1983) reveals 2 important findings. First, few statistically significant changes in beliefs and attitudes about bears were detected between 1978 and 1983; when significant change did occur, it was generally of low magnitude. If accurate information had been reaching landowners, we would have expected a change, as well as a higher proportion of landowners expressing opinions about bear management. We can only conclude that there were no pervasive influences on beliefs and attitudes and that the moderate change in bear population preferences may not have been due to a change in beliefs or attitudes.

Second, whereas landowners' bear population preferences do not seem to be based upon their knowledge of the size of the bear population or upon the incidence of bear nuisance or damage problems, there was a tendency for landowners who had seen a bear in the Catskills or who were otherwise familiar with bears to have favored an increase in the bear population. The Nonincrease Group was less familiar (in terms of both contact and opinions) with bears and bear management. These landowners were also less desirous of observing bears on or near their property and were more likely to believe that an increase in the bear population would result in landowners having more negative experiences with bears.

MANAGEMENT PROGRAM IMPLICATIONS

Based only on public input, we see no apparent reason why the DEC should not increase the Catskill bear population. A majority of landowners wanted an increase, and those who opposed one were unfamiliar with the Catskill bear population. Furthermore, it is likely that most landowners would not notice a 50% increase in the bear population.

Nevertheless, it is imperative that while the population is increasing the DEC should implement an information and education program to familiarize landowners with bears and the bear management program. Direct interaction between managers and landowners, or at least more information coming from managers, should accomplish this goal, as well as improve the landowners' image of the DEC and, ultimately, their attitude toward a bear population increase.

However, 1 caveat must be considered. It is possible that the planned expansion of the bear population could exceed a bear population threshold above which bear-human interactions increase disproportionately. An indication of such a phenomenon is suggested by the increase in bear problems reported between 1978 and 1983 disproportionate to the increase in the bear population. The possibility that this threshold has already been reached is only speculation at this time due to the small number of landowners reporting damage. However, the existence of a threshold is quite conceivable. It is essential, then, that the DEC continue its careful bear damage monitoring program and be prepared to mitigate potential increases in this area and in bear-vehicle highway accidents.

If increases in negative bear-human interactions do not occur, this fact should be communicated to the public, especially to alleviate the concerns of those landowners who opposed a bear population increase. Fortunately, if such a threshold exists and was exceeded, landowners have demonstrated a degree of tolerance for damage, barring substantial monetary losses. Also, it should be communicated that managers have a proven, effective tool for quickly reducing the population to acceptable levels—controlled hunting.

This study of public attitudes toward black bears and their management in the northern Catskills indicates how systematically collected public input can be used to guide wildlife management. In this case, the limits of people's tolerance of bears may be reached before biological carrying capacity is attained. Often reluctance on the part of portions of the public to endorse population management is the result of a combination of misperceptions about actual management situations, beliefs, and attitudes based on inaccurate or no information and inadequate 2-way communications between the agency and the public. Managers can use public input to identify these misperceptions and information voids and to point to specific channels through which education programs can be directed.

LITERATURE CITED

BACON, E. S. 1974. Use of a survey of park visitor attitudes and knowledge to help formulate education programs. Pages 207-213 in M. R. Pelton and R. H. Conley, eds. Eastern workshop on black bear management and research, Great Smoky Mountains National Park. Tenn. Wildl. Resour. Agency, Nashville.

BAPTISTE, M. E. 1977. A survey of visitor knowledge, attitude, and judgment concerning black bears at Shenandoah National Park. M.S. Thesis, Virginia Polytechnic Inst. and State Univ., Blacksburg. 90pp.

──, J. B. WHELAN, AND R. B. FRARY. 1979. Visitor perception of black bear problems at Shenandoah National Park. Wildl. Soc. Bull. 7:25-29.

BROWN, T. L., D. J. DECKER, AND D. L. HUSTIN. 1979. Public attitudes toward black bear in the Catskills. N.Y. State Dep. Environ. Conserv. Final Report, Fed. Aid Proj. W-89-R. 204pp.

BURGHARDT, G. M., R. O. HIETALA, AND M. R. PELTON. 1972. Knowledge and attitudes concerning black bear by users of the Great Smoky Mountains National Park. Pages 255-273 in S. Herrero, ed. Bears—their biology and management. Int. Union Conserv. Nature and Nat. Resour. IUCN Publ. New Ser. 23.

CLARKE, S. H., AND J. O'PEZIO. 1978. Recommendations for bear hunting seasons: 1978. N.Y. State Dep. Environ. Conserv. Fed. Aid Proj. W-89-R-22. Job X-6. 5pp.

COLE, G. F. 1974. Management involving grizzly bears and humans in Yellowstone National Park, 1970-1973. BioScience 24:335-338.

──. 1976. Management involving grizzly and black bears in Yellowstone National Park, 1970-1975. U.S. Dep. Inter., Natl. Park Serv. Nat. Resour. Report 9. 26pp.

DECKER, D. J., T. L. BROWN, D. L. HUSTIN, S. H. CLARKE, AND J. O'PEZIO. 1981. Public attitudes toward bears. N.Y. Fish and Game J. 28:1-20.

MCCAFFREY, E. R., G. B. WILL, AND A. S. BERGSTROM. 1976. Preliminary management implications for black bears, Ursus americanus, in the Catskill region of New York State as a result of an ecological study. Pages 235-245 in H. R. Pelton, J. W. Lentfer, and G. E. Folk, Jr., eds. Bears—their biology and management. Int. Union Conserv. Nature and Nat. Resour. IUCN Publ. New Ser. 40.

O'PEZIO, J., AND S. H. CLARKE. 1976. Recommendations for the Catskill bear hunting season: 1976-78. N.Y. State Dep. Environ. Conserv. Fed. Aid Proj. W-89-R-20. Job X-6. 6pp.

ROWELL, G. 1976. How Yosemite is solving the bear problem. Natl. Wildl. 14:24-28.

STOKES, A. W. 1970. An ethologist's view on managing grizzly bears. BioScience 20:1154-1157.

STOUT, N. J. 1958. Atlas of forestry in New York. N.Y. State Univ. Coll. For., Syracuse. Bull. 41. 96pp.

CHARACTERISTICS OF HARVESTED COLLARED PECCARIES IN RELATION TO RAINFALL PATTERNS IN SOUTHEASTERN ARIZONA

LYLE K. SOWLS, Arizona Cooperative Wildlife Research Unit, University of Arizona, Tucson, AZ 85721

BRIAN A. MAURER, Department of Ecology and Evolutionary Biology, University of Arizona, Tucson, AZ 85721

Abstract: A check station was operated for 16 years by the Arizona Cooperative Wildlife Research Unit to collect data on the harvest of collared peccaries (*Tayassu tajacu*, L.) in southeastern Arizona. Data on age class, sex, and weights were obtained from approximately 2,500 animals. We hypothesized that rainfall should be positively correlated with productivity of collared peccary populations. Summer rainfall was positively associated with weights of harvested animals, but winter rainfall was negatively associated with female weights and survival and with the proportion of the population represented by young born in the harvest year. This implies that winter rainfall is associated with stress in southeastern Arizona peccary populations. The mechanism of this stress may be a physiological response to cold, wet conditions by an organism poorly adapted to undergo thermal stress.

KEY WORDS: Arizona, Collared peccaries, Harvest strategies, Population regulation, Stress, Winter rainfall.

The collared peccary has one of the largest ranges of any ungulate, surpassed only by the white-tailed deer (*Odocoileus virginianus*) in the length of its distribution. Until recent years very little research had been done on this species, and few publications had appeared. Since 1950, however, a large number of projects have been completed and results published. Most of these studies have been in Arizona and Texas, which represent only the northern 10% (latitudinally) of the range. Although it is primarily a tropical and subtropical animal, most studies on the collared peccary have been carried out in colder and drier locations. In southeastern Arizona many people tend to think of it as a true desert animal. In this drier climate we hypothesized that productivity and general condition would be directly related to patterns of precipitation. In years of greater rainfall, within a given age class and sex, larger than normal weights should be expected. Not only should weights of harvested animals reflect rainfall patterns, but also the relative contribution of young animals in the harvest should reflect changing patterns in habitat productivity. Our objectives were to determine whether the amount and timing of rainfall affected the weights, age classification, and productivity of collared peccary populations in southeastern Arizona.

We want to thank the dozens of wildlife students who put in long hours helping us gather data at the check stations. We would like to also thank P. R. Krausman, R. William Mannan, and 2 anonymous reviewers for reading the manuscript and making suggestions.

METHODS

To collect a sample of the yearly kill of the collared peccaries, a hunter check station was established in 1957 at a convenient location for hunters. To entice them to bring their animals to the station, prizes, on a drawing basis, were offered. The stations and the drawings were publicized through the newspapers, television, and radio. The check station was located at the periphery of Tucson at the Rabies Control Center. It continued, with the exception of 1964 when no data were collected, until 1969. It was then moved to the Cash Box Pawn Shop and Gun Store where similar incentives were arranged. This arrangement lasted through 1973. By this time data on over 3,000 hunter-killed animals were obtained. Information received on each animal included sex, tooth wear or replacement pattern, weight of field-dressed carcass, kill location, and hunter's name and address. Animals were divided by age into 6 categories: 0-1 year, 1-2 years, and 4 adult age classes. These categories were based on the tooth replacement pattern determined by Kirkpatrick and Sowls (1962) and 4 classes of tooth wear as described by Sowls (1961). The weights obtained at the check station were from typically field-dressed animals as brought in by the hunter; head and hide were included, and all internal organs were removed. Rainfall data were obtained from Sellers and Hill (1974).

Statistical methods used to analyze the 16 years of collared peccary harvest data included several approaches. First, we examined the number of harvested animals of each sex falling into each age class in each of the 16 years. Second, we correlated the ratio of male to female survival rates with average monthly rainfall for southeastern Arizona for the 12 months prior to the February harvest. Finally, we used weights of harvested animals as an index of the condition of animals in each sex and age class for all southeastern Arizona and for each sex within 6 different mountain ranges in Arizona for which we had adequate sample sizes during the 16 years of the study.

A 3-dimensional contingency table was constructed in order to assess dependencies among age class, sex, and year categories of the harvested animals. Log-linear model analysis (Bishop et al. 1975) was used to test for independence among the 3 factors. We transformed the proportion of each harvested age class for each of the 16 study years, using an arcsin square root transformation; then we computed simple correlations and multiple linear regressions using the transformed proportions as dependent variables and average monthly rainfall for all southeastern Arizona for the 12 months before the harvest as independent variables. A stepwise procedure was used in the multiple regressions so that a subset was obtained of the months most closely associated with the transformed proportion in each age class.

We used the method of Paulik and Robson (1969:9-11) to calculate the number of males surviving/females surviving between each harvested pair. To calculate this, we used the proportion of males in a given year for all age classes and compared that to the proportion of males in only nonyearling age classes in the next year using the following formula:

$$S = \left(\frac{1 - P_1}{P_1}\right)\left(\frac{P_2}{1 - P_2}\right)$$

where S is the ratio of surviving males to females, P_1 is the proportion of males in the first year, and P_2 is the proportion of males in only nonyearling age classes in the second year (see Paulik and Robson 1969 for more details). As this ratio increases, more males survive than females between any 2 years. These survival ratios were correlated with the average rainfall for the 12 months between the 2 harvests used to calculate the ratio. Multiple linear regression using a stepwise selection technique was used to obtain a subset of months most closely associated with the survival ratio.

Log-transformed weights were used to perform 2 3-way ANOVAs. The first used age class, sex, and year as classification variables. For the second ANOVA, we ranked years by total rainfall and used sex, age class, and rank of year's rainfall as classification variables. To further understand the 3-way interactions of these analyses, we used correlation and multiple linear regression to relate monthly rainfall to log weight in each sex and age-class combination in the same manner as we did to relate age-class proportions and survival ratios to rainfall. For 6 geographic regions in southeastern Arizona—the Huachuca Mountains, the Santa Ritas, the Catalinas and Rincons, the Whetstones, the Tortolitas, and Arivaca—we had large enough samples to correlate local rainfall with the weights of harvested males and females from that region. Again, we used simple correlations and stepwise multiple regression to obtain a subset of months with the strongest relationship to weights of harvested animals.

RESULTS

Age-Class Structure

The changes in age-class structure over the 16 years of our study of harvested collared peccaries were the same for each sex as indicated by a nonsignificant interaction between sex, age class, and year in the log-linear model analysis (Table 1). Distribution of animals among sexes was the same across years and age classes (nonsignificant 2-way interactions of sex and year, and sex and age class, Table 1); however, there were significant differences among the age classes in the different years (Table 1). The changes in age-class distribution appeared to involve fairly large fluctuations in the relative frequencies of juveniles in the harvest for both juvenile age classes (Fig. 1).

We can partially understand the changes in age-class structure by considering rainfall from the 12 months prior to the late February/early March harvest. Proportional changes of juveniles in age-class 1 (young of the year) in the harvest were negatively correlated with rainfall in December and January, the strongest correlation being with January rainfall (Table 2).

Table 1. Chi-square partitioning for log-linear model analysis of a 3-way contingency table of the distribution of harvested collared peccaries among sex, age class, and year in Arizona, 1957-1973.

Factor	df	Test for partial association	
		X^2	P
Sex	1	5.91	0.015
Age class	5	312.97	<0.01
Year	15	268.39	<0.01
Sex by age class	5	8.26	0.14
Sex by year	15	11.47	0.72
Age class by year	75	328.21	<0.01
Sex by age class by year	75	72.46	0.56

April rainfall was positively associated with proportions of juveniles in age-class 2 (Table 2). Proportional relationships of the first 2 adult age classes with rainfall were very weak; only 1 variable entered the multiple regressions (nonsignificant in both cases), and R^2 values were very low. The relative frequencies of the 2 oldest age classes were positively correlated with summer rainfall and may be negatively associated with winter rainfall (Table 2).

These results suggest a significant amount of variation in age-class structure in harvested peccaries from year to year. The correlations with rainfall suggest that winter rainfall has a negative impact on young of the year, possibly on older animals as well, and that summer rainfall is

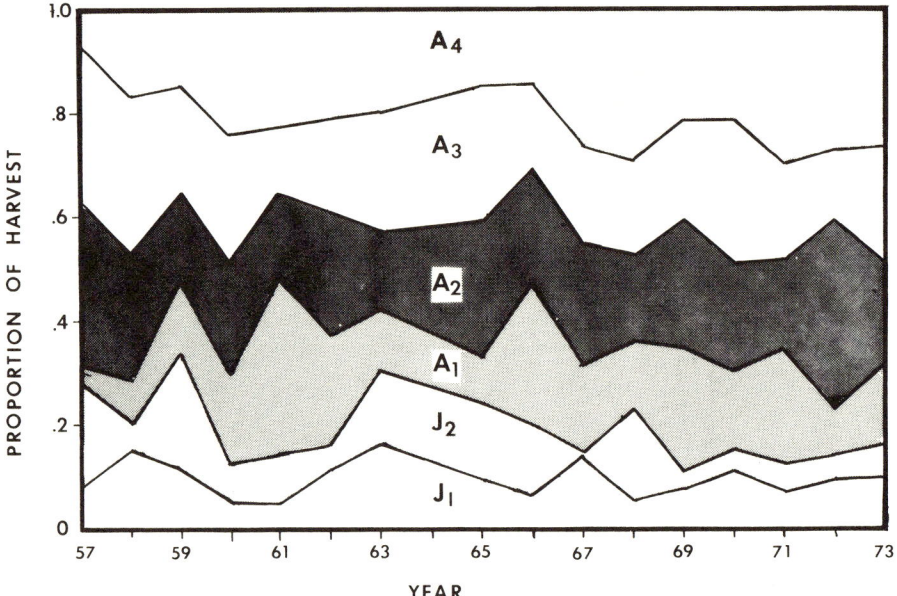

Fig. 1. Proportion of harvested collared peccaries in 6 age classes from check station data obtained from 1957 to 1973 in Arizona. Data were not collected in 1964.

Table 2. Correlations and multiple regressions of transformed proportions of each of 6 age classes in the collared peccary harvest with monthly rainfall in the 12 months preceding the harvest in Arizona, 1957-1973. Harvests were in late February-early March. Only significant correlations shown ($P<0.15$).

Month	Age class					
	J1	J2	A1	A2	A3	A4
Mar		0.288		−0.360		
Apr		0.505				
May						
Jun						
Jul	0.283	0.426	−0.345		0.331	
Aug		−0.422		0.316	−0.293	0.387
Sept				−0.424		0.386
Oct						
Nov						
Dec	−0.415				−0.362	
Jan	−0.456[a]					−0.349
Feb				−0.323		
Stepwise regressions:						
Months entered (in order, with sign of coefficient)	Jan (−)[a]	Apr (+)[a] Aug (−)[a] Oct (+)	Jul (−)	Sep (−)	Jul (+)[a] Dec (−)[a] Feb (+)[a] Mar (−)[a]	Aug (+)[a]
r²	0.278	0.624	0.175	0.189	0.782	0.286
F	4.61[a]	5.52[a]	2.54	2.80	8.08[a]	4.81[a]

[a] = $P<0.05$.

positively associated with increases in the number of older adult animals harvested.

Male and Female Weights Within Age Classes

Weights of harvested animals was used as an index of an animal's condition at harvest. We sought to determine if the condition of males and females varied in different years and age classes. When the year factor was ordered both sequentially and by total rainfall, a significant 3-way interaction (Table 3) suggested that male and female weights (and hence condition) differed in different years and age classes. We then correlated weights of males and females within each age class with monthly rainfall in the 12 months preceding the harvest (March-February).

The correlations and regressions suggested that female weights were correlated positively or associated with summer rainfall and sometimes negatively associated with winter rainfall, whereas the relationships between male weights and rainfall differed among age classes (Tables 4 and 5).

Geographical Differences in Male and Female Weights

Another approach to analyzing the different condition of harvested males and females is to examine the relationships between weights of the sexes

Table 3. Analyses of variance for log-transformed weights of harvested collared peccaries in Arizona using years as a factor (A) and ranking years by total rainfall (B), 1957-73.

Source	df	SS	MS	F	P
A. Years					
Year	15	168.31	11.22	5.59	<0.001
Age class	5	3,731.14	746.23	372.05	<0.001
Sex	1	6.11	6.11	3.05	0.081
Year by age class	75	215.95	2.88	1.43	0.011
Year by sex	15	56.52	3.77	1.88	0.022
Age class by sex	5	79.87	15.97	7.96	<0.001
Year by age class by sex	73	193.32	2.62	1.31	0.048
Error	2,236	4,484.80	2.01		
B. Years ranked by rainfall					
Rainfall	15	49.94	3.33	5.84	<0.001
Age class	5	226.82	45.36	79.58	<0.001
Sex	1	3.59	3.59	6.30	0.012
Rainfall by age class	75	81.91	1.09	1.92	<0.001
Rainfall by sex	15	19.26	1.28	2.25	0.004
Age class by sex	5	16.09	3.22	5.64	<0.001
Rainfall by age class by sex	73	66.51	0.91	1.60	0.001
Error	2,236	1,274.61	0.57		

Table 4. Correlation and multiple regressions of log transformed male weights in 6 age classes of harvested collared peccaries with monthly rainfall in the months preceding the harvest in Arizona, 1957-73. Harvests in late February-early March. Only significant correlations shown ($P<0.15$).

| Month | Age class | | | | | |
	J1	J2	A1	A2	A3	A4
Mar						
Apr						
May		−0.391				
Jun						−0.495
Jul						
Aug				0.428	0.407	0.438
Sep						
Oct						
Nov			0.530[a]		0.772[a]	
Dec	0.503					0.406
Jan		0.444				
Feb	0.501					−0.402
Stepwise regressions: Months entered (in order with sign of coefficient)	Dec (+)[a] Jan (−)[a] Aug (−)	Jan (+)	Nov (+)[a]	Aug (+) Sep (−)	Nov (+)[a] Feb (−)[a] Jul (−)[a] Jun (−)[a] Jan (+)	Jun (−)[a] Nov (+)
r^2	0.773	0.197	0.281	0.347	0.880	0.418
F	12.48[a]	3.19	5.47	3.46	14.6[a]	4.67[a]

[a] = $P<0.05$.

Table 5. Correlations and multiple regressions of log transformed female weights in 6 age classes of harvested collared peccaries with monthly rainfall in the months preceding the harvest in Arizona, 1957-73. Harvests in late February-early March. Only significant correlations shown ($P < 0.15$).

Month	Age class					
	J1	J2	A1	A2	A3	A4
Mar					−0.401	
Apr						
May						
Jun						
Jul		0.665^a	0.554^a			
Aug	0.506^a		−0.475	0.483	0.574^a	
Sep					0.524^a	
Oct						0.417
Nov	0.571^a	0.414				
Dec						
Jan						
Feb						
Stepwise regressions: Months entered (in order, with sign of coefficient)	Nov (+)^a Aug (−)^a	Jul (+)	Jul (+)^a Aug (−)^a Oct (+)^a Feb (−)^a	Aug (+) Mar (−)^a	Aug (+)^a Sep (+)^a Mar (−)^a Jan (+)	Oct (−)^a Sep (+) Jun (−)
r^2	0.468	0.442	0.735	0.421	0.705	0.491
F	5.720^a	11.080^a	7.640^a	4.720^a	9.560^a	3.860^a

$^a = P<0.05$.

and rainfall in the 6 different geographic regions for which we had adequate sample sizes. Generally, male weights were associated positively with rainfall during summer, as expected (Table 6). For some areas male weights were negatively correlated with winter rainfall, although this relationship was not strong. Female weights also tended to have positive relationships with rainfall in summer months but often had strong negative relationships with rainfall in winter months (Table 7). The amount of summer rainfall apparently has a positive effect on the condition of harvested males and females, whereas winter rainfall appears to stress females to a much greater degree than males.

Male:Female Survival Ratios

The ratio, male:female survival, is an index of relative mortality rates. As the ratio increases, either male survival increases, or female survival decreases, or both. Ratio increases were associated positively with winter rainfall and negatively with summer rainfall (Table 8). Since high winter rainfall is more closely associated with lower weights of females than males (Tables 4 and 6), winter rainfall may be more stressful to females. The implication is that female mortality increases when high amounts of

Table 6. Correlations and multiple regressions of log transformed male weights of harvested peccaries in 6 geographic regions in southeastern Arizona with monthly rainfall in the 12 months preceding the harvest, 1957-73. Harvest in late February-early March. Only significant correlations shown ($P < 0.15$).

Month	Geographic region					
	Huachuca	Santa Rita	Catalina	Whetstone	Tortolita	Arivaca
Mar	0.445[a]					−0.361
Apr	0.506[a]	0.429[a]			0.322	
May	−0.428[a]		0.291	−0.424		
Jun						
Jul					0.357	
Aug		0.650[a]	0.347	0.345		
Sep	0.416[a]		−0.487[a]			
Oct						
Nov						
Dec				−0.455[a]		0.419
Jan						
Feb				−0.439[a]		
Stepwise regressions: Months entered (in order, with sign of coefficient)	Apr (+)[a] Sep (+)[a] Jul (−)[a]	Aug (+)[a] Apr (+)	Sep (−)[a] Jun (−)	Dec (−)	Jul (+)	Dec (+)
r^2	0.596	0.562	0.399	0.198	0.109	0.176
F	6.400[a]	8.330[a]	4.320[a]	3.500	1.580	2.990

[a] = $P < 0.05$.

rainfall occur during winter. Also, the fact that winter rainfall may be stressful to females and may lead to higher female mortality may help explain why the proportion of first-year juveniles in the harvest decreases with winter rainfall.

DISCUSSION

High summer rainfall undoubtedly improves food availability for the collared peccary in Arizona and may explain the increased weights of both sexes during years of high summer rainfall. The apparent effect of winter rainfall on the collared peccary, however, may be more complex. Our data suggest lower female weights during years of high winter rainfall, thus winter rainfall may stress females more than males. One reason for this, which needs further study, is that winter rainfall in much of the collared peccary range at the higher elevations has very little effect on winter vegetation growth. In the collared peccary's range above 760 m, winter vegetation does not immediately respond to winter rainfall and does not increase the food for wildlife until warmer weather. In Arizona's low desert country (below 760 m elevation), however, heavy winter rains bring an abundance of winter annuals, which not only bring late winter flowers but excellent winter and spring food for wildlife. Hungerford (1964)

Table 7. Correlations and multiple regressions of log transformed female weights of harvested peccaries in 6 geographic regions in southeastern Arizona with monthly rainfall in the 12 months preceding the harvest, 1957-73. Harvests were conducted in February. Only significant correlations shown ($P < 0.15$).

Month	Geographic region					
	Huachuca	Santa Rita	Catalina	Whetstone	Tortolita	Arivaca
Mar			−0.282	−0.417		
Apr			−0.302	−0.325		
May			0.353			
Jun				0.282		
Jul					−0.363	0.529[a]
Aug			−0.329	0.319		0.350
Sep		0.481	0.327	0.285		0.301
Oct				0.425		
Nov	0.527[a]	−0.336				0.389
Dec					0.376	
Jan		−0.608[a]				
Feb				−0.408		
Stepwise regressions:						
Months entered (in order, with sign of coefficient)	Nov (+)[a]	Jan (−)[a] Nov (−)[a] Mar (−)[a]	Feb (+)[a] Nov (−)[a] Jan (−)[a] Mar (−)[a]	Oct (+)[a] Nov (−)[a] Mar (−)[a] Sep (+)[a] Aug (+)[a]	Dec (+)[a] Jul (−)[a] Aug (+)[a] Mar (+)[a]	Jul (+)[a]
r^2	0.277	0.646	0.667	0.763	0.650	0.281
F	5.760[a]	7.310[a]	5.500[a]	6.440	4.110[a]	5.460[a]

[a] = $P < 0.05$.

demonstrated a direct relationshp between the percentage of ground cover in spring and the percentage of young quail in the fall population. He associated the increased production of young quail with the presence of Vitamin A in plants during years of high winter rainfall. The particular elevation where winter rainfall does not affect the winter growth has not been determined. It probably depends on aspect, slope, soils, vegetation, and other factors.

Our data suggest that the percentage of males in older population classes may increase during winters of high winter rainfall due to higher female mortality. A shift in sex ratio to increase the percentage of males in the poulation has been described by Sowls (1966) and Low (1970) who both found a higher percentage of females at birth than in adult populations in Arizona and Texas. Their data revealed a differential survival that favored males. The data from our check station suggest that these changes may occur by loss of females during wet winters.

When we consider that the collared peccary is generally a tropical or subtropical animal, we begin to look for anatomical and physiological reasons for the stress that might affect the females during wet winters in Arizona. One of the first things to consider is the insulating value of the

Table 8. Correlations and multiple regression of ratio of male survival:female survival and rainfall in the 12 months prior to late February-early March. Only significant ($P<0.15$) correlations shown.

Month	r	Step entered	Regression coefficient	r^2 change
Mar		4	0.114[a]	0.131
Apr				
May				
Jun		3	−0.533[a]	0.103
Jul				
Aug				
Sep	−0.348			
Oct				
Nov	0.436	2	0.365[a]	0.235
Dec	0.325			
Jan	0.606[a]	1	0.284[a]	0.367
Feb	0.336	5	0.110[a]	0.075
$r^2 = 0.912$ $F = 16.65$[a]				

[a] = $P<0.05$.

collared peccary's pelt. Scholander et al. (1950), in studying the body insulation of some arctic and tropical birds and mammals, found that the insulating value of the fur of the collared peccary was near zero. Zervanos' (1975) study of collared peccary metabolism concluded that in winter collared peccaries exhibited an increased basal metabolic rate in order to compensate for poor insulation.

In Arizona and Texas, collared peccary bear young in most months, including autumn and winter. The colder months place another stress on females. Lactating females in captivity, even on good diets, lose weight during these periods. In years of higher winter rainfall, animals may be subject to illnesses that would not be as severe in drier weather. More data are needed on the relationship of moisture and temperatures and their effects on survival.

For a wildlife manager setting seasons and harvest figure quotas, a knowledge of the factors affecting population changes is essential. We believe that the collared peccary at the higher elevations in southeastern Arizona is a marginal animal, vulnerable to winter stresses. These winter stresses, especially when accumulated over several seasons, may result in population declines that would necessitate altering hunting quotas. On the other hand, unusually mild winters accompanied by moderate rainfall may allow populations to increase, allowing higher harvest rates. However, we advocate caution in applying such suggestions without further detailed work on the relationship between demographic parameters, such as birth and death rates and environmental stress. It is likely that rainfall interacts with temperature in leading to stress, and we suggest further data collection on temperature and winter stress.

As the complex interactions among rainfall, temperature, food production, and collared peccary demography are elucidated, management and harvest strategies for collared peccaries in southeastern Arizona can be designed to protect and perpetuate this unique animal.

LITERATURE CITED

BISHOP, Y. M. M., S. E. FIENBERG, AND P. W. HOLLAND. 1975. Discrete multivariate analysis. Massachusetts Inst. of Tech. Press, Cambridge. 557pp.

HUNGERFORD, C. R. 1964. Vitamin A and productivity in Gambel's quail. J. Wildl. Manage. 28:141-147.

KIRKPATRICK, R. D., AND L. K. SOWLS. 1962. Age determination of the collared peccary by the tooth-replacement pattern. J. Wildl. Manage. 26:214-217.

LOW, W. A. 1970. The influence of aridity on reproduction of the collared peccary (*Dicotyles tajacu* (Linn)) in Texas. Ph.D. Thesis, Univ. British Columbia, Vancouver. 170pp.

PAULIK, G. J., AND D. S. ROBSON. 1969. Statistical calculations for change-in-ratio estimators of population parameters. J. Wildl. Manage. 33:1-27.

SCHOLANDER, P. F., V. WALTERS, R. HOCK, AND L. IRVING. 1950. Body insulation of some arctic and tropical mammals and birds. Biol. Bull. Mar. Biol. Lab. Woods Hole 99:225-236.

SELLERS, W. D., AND R. H. HILL. 1974. Arizona climate. Univ. Arizona Press, Tucson. 616pp.

SOWLS, L. K. 1961. Hunter check stations for collecting data on the collared peccary (*Pecari tajacu*). Trans. North Am. Wildl. Conf. 26:497-505.

———. 1966. Reproduction in the collared peccary (*Tayassu tajacu*). Pages 155-172 *in* I. W. Rowlands, ed. Comparative biology of reproduction in mammals. Zool. Soc. London, U. K.

ZERVANOS, S. M. 1975. Seasonal effects of temperature on the respiratory metabolism of the collared peccary (*Tayassu tajacu*). Comp. Biochem. Physiol. 50A:365-371.

HARVEST STRATEGIES TO CONTROL EXOTIC UNGULATE POPULATIONS IN NEW MEXICO

BRUCE L. MORRISON, New Mexico Department of Game and Fish, Villagra Building, Santa Fe, New Mexico 87503

Abstract: New Mexico is inhabited by 4 species of exotic ungulates: aoudad (*Ammotragus lervia*), gemsbok (*Oryx gazella gazella*), Persian wild goat (*Capra aegagrus*), and Siberian ibex (*C. ibex siberica*). These animals were released into the wild and/or escaped from game-proof pastures between 1950 and 1977. Aoudad and Persian wild goat populations have increased so much that their numbers must be controlled. Until 1979, the aoudad were hunted under a permit system with hunters restricted to a limited area. As a means of controlling aoudad, in 1979, a hunt was begun in the Guadalupe Mountains of southeastern New Mexico and the Mount Taylor area of west-central New Mexico. An unlimited number of permits was issued for this hunt with a legal harvest of 1 aoudad of either sex. In 1980, this system of hunting aoudad was adopted statewide, except for 2 trophy areas still under a limited permit system. The Persian wild goat was first introduced into an isolated desert mountain range in southwestern New Mexico in 1970. From 7 releases of 73 animals, this species has increased to over 600 animals. Trophy hunts have been conducted from 1975 to the present with a legal bag limit of 1 mature male. In 1980, the Department of Game and Fish began a nontrophy hunt with 1 beardless wild goat as the legal bag. Since 1975, the number of trophy permits has increased to 100 and beardless permits to 200. In 1983, the bag limit changed to include 1 beardless goat in the trophy hunt and 2 beardless goats in the nontrophy hunts. Gemsbok and Siberian ibex have not grown in population size so that an increased harvest is unnecessary for population control.

KEY WORDS: Exotic ungulates, Population control, Harvest strategies, New Mexico, Aoudad, Persian wild goat, Gemsbok, Siberian ibex.

Four species of exotic ungulates have been released into the wild in New Mexico. They are the aoudad, gemsbok, Persian wild goat, and Siberian ibex. The New Mexico Department of Game and Fish (NMDGF) has made all intentional releases except 1 aoudad release. The San Juan County Wildlife Federation made an unauthorized aoudad release during 1956 in Canyon Largo in northwestern New Mexico. Unintentional escapes have also occurred from private game parks in southeast and west-central New Mexico.

Joe McKnight, a private landowner of Picacho, New Mexico, first brought aoudad, a native of northern Africa, to the state (Ogren 1965). In 1950, State Game Warden Elliott S. Barker purchased 12 from McKnight and released them into the Canadian River Gorge in northern New Mexico (Morrison 1981). The Canyon Largo release was made with animals purchased from Louis Gobels, a wild-animal dealer from California (Morrison 1980). Between 1955 and 1970, numerous aoudads escaped from McKnight's Class "A" Park in the Hondo Valley of southeast New Mexico (J. McKnight, pers. commun.) and in 1975 from a Class "A" Park in the Mount Taylor area of west-central New Mexico (R. Isler, pers. commun.). As a result, aoudad populations have become established in the eastern half and the northwestern quarter of the state. They do not inhabit the higher mountain regions of northern New Mexico and its southwestern quarter. Unofficial aoudad population estimates are as high as 3,000 animals.

The gemsbok, a native of the Kalahari Desert of southern Africa, was first released into the wild in 1969 (Saiz 1975) at White Sands Missile Range in south-central New Mexico. Between 1969 and 1977, 93 more animals were released (Morrison 1983a). Since then, they have increased to more than 600 animals.

The Persian wild goat, native to rugged mountain areas of Iran, Saudi Arabia, Pakistan, and Afghanistan (Spillett and Bunch 1979), was first introduced into the Florida Mountains of southwestern New Mexico in 1970 (Sutcliffe 1972, Bavin 1975). Seventy-three goats were released between 1970 and 1976 (Woodruff 1979). Their range has recently expanded to include the Little Florida, Tres Hermanas, and Cook's mountain ranges that are in proximity to the original release site. Now over 600 wild goats range free in New Mexico (Morrison 1983b).

The last exotic ungulate released in New Mexico was the Siberian ibex, a native of Afghanistan, Pakistan, India, southern China, and southern Russia (Spillett and Bunch 1979). In 1975 and 1977, 53 animals were released in the Canadian River Gorge in northeastern New Mexico (Morrison 1981), and they now number between 100 and 125 animals.

METHODS

The aoudad was first hunted in New Mexico in 1955 when 24 permits were issued from the Canadian River Gorge area. Because of a special agreement with the landowners on whose property the aoudad were released, these and all subsequent permits in Game Management Unit 47 are divided equally between landowner and public license holders. Public licenses are issued by a computer drawing at the Santa Fe office. Landowner licenses are issued to hunters who have obtained permission from the landowner.

The aoudad inhabiting the Canyon Largo were first hunted in 1972 when 10 permits were issued through a drawing system. Since the Bureau of Land Management administers all land in this unit, there are no landowner permits.

When the aoudads escaped from McKnight's Park, they became established on land administered by the U.S. Forest Service in the Guadalupe Mountains (Dickinson and Simpson 1980). This population was hunted on a limited permit basis from 1975 to 1979. In 1979, an unlimited permit hunt was inaugurated to control the population. The unlimited permit system was also started on the Mount Taylor region in 1979 to control aoudad that had escaped from a Class "A" Park in that area.

By 1980, the aoudad population expanded and inhabited eastern New Mexico and all but the higher elevations of northern New Mexico. After considerable debate, the NMDGF established 2 aoudad management units—Game Management Unit 2, the Canyon Largo area, and Game Management Unit 47, the Canadian River Gorge. These aoudad populations will provide quality hunting on a limited permit basis. Currently, the department's policy is to manage the population outside these units so that they will be reduced or eliminated. The permits for both aoudad management units are now issued on a limited basis by a lottery system with 50% of those allocated for the Canadian River Gorge reserved for landowners. All permits for the Canyon Largo area will continue to be public permits. For the remainder of the state, an unlimited number of licenses are available for aoudad hunting, and they may be purchased at any of 5 NMDGF offices throughout the state. The state-wide hunting season is held in conjunction with open deer seasons. To legally hunt aoudad, the hunter must have both an aoudad license and a valid deer license. For 9 days in January, the aoudad season is also open and runs concurrently with the established seasons in the limited permit management units.

The legal bag limit for the state-wide hunt is any 1 aoudad. Accordingly, aoudad season is open for approximately 65 days; some areas open only to deer bow-hunting are open to aoudad hunting for as many as 90 days.

The Persian wild goat was first hunted in New Mexico with the issuance of 4 permits for trophy males. All these permits are issued to the public by lottery. Trophy permits have now increased to 100. In 1980, a nontrophy hunt was initiated to control the population (a nontrophy goat is a wild goat without a beard). Fifty permits were available for this hunt. In 1981, the strategy was changed from 1 50-permit nontrophy hunt to 2 75-permit nontrophy hunts. In the following year, permits for each nontrophy hunt were increased to 100; and since 1982, 100 permits for the trophy hunt have been issued. The release site in southeastern New Mexico, in Game Management Unit 25, is a Persian wild goat management unit, and we will attempt to restrict the goat populations to the isolated Florida Mountains in that unit.

The first gemsbok hunt was held in 1974 when 5 permits were issued. This population occupies lands administered by the U.S. Army on White Sands Missile Range. The Santa Fe office issues all gemsbok permits by lottery. Forty permits a year are now issued for trophy gemsbok hunting. By 1981, a large segment of the gemsbok population had developed nontypical or broken horns. That year a nontrophy hunt was started to remove those animals. Ten permits are now allocated annually for this hunt. Game Management Unit 19 is the Gemsbok Management Unit, and population expansion will be restricted to that unit.

Siberian ibex were released in the area of the Canadian River Gorge that aoudad occupy and have been hunted for the last 2 years. There is the same 50:50 split of permits for ibex as there is for aoudad in this area. Since 1981, 4 permits, 2 landowner and 2 public, have been allocated. The Siberian Ibex Management Unit has the same boundaries as Aoudad Management Unit 47.

RESULTS

In 1955, 24 aoudad hunters harvested 11 animals. Since then, 5,221 hunters have harvested 2,165 aoudads, for a 41.5% success rate (Dziadulewicz 1983). Since unlimited permit hunts began (1979), 53.4% (1,157 animals) of the above figure has been harvested. A harvest of 1,157 animals represents over 33% of the population. These figures indicate that population control is being achieved through harvest. However, the following basic facts of aoudad biology tend to dispute the population decrease: (1) in New Mexican aoudad populations, twinning is the rule rather than the exception, with the birth of triplets being common (Habibi 1983); (2) aoudad populations tend to concentrate in initial release areas until the range is overcrowded and then disperse by establishing small population pockets in the adjacent countryside (Dickinson and Simpson 1980); and (3) aoudads have peak lambing seasons, but offspring are born throughout the year with 3 age classes of young accompanying many ewes (Habibi 1983). These facts present special problems in controlling the population through hunting. Since a lamb may replace any harvested aoudad, harvesting 33% of the population may not reduce total numbers in areas with high populations. Hunting does not lead to the removal of aoudads established in small, isolated population pockets because sportsmen prefer to hunt where aoudads occur in large concentrations. Thus, small populations remain undisturbed until their numbers increase the chances for a successful hunt. At this time, the population has reached the point where the birth rate matches or exceeds the hunter-induced death rate.

The aoudad's ability to breed throughout the year prevents adjusting the hunting season to coincide with the rut when chances of success increases. Some biologists (K. Habibi, pers. commun; D. Simpson, pers. commun.) have maintained that aoudad hunting may cause a shift in their peak rutting season and that season dates should not be set until this shift is determined. Despite negative factors, in some cases sport harvest can successfully control aoudad numbers, such as in the Guadalupe Mountains. Escaped aoudads were first sighted in these mountains in 1951 (Dickinson and Simpson 1980); this represents a direct-line movement of approximately 120 km. The first hunt held in the Guadalupes was in 1975 when 15 hunters harvested 7 aoudads. From 1975 to 1978, it was a limited-permit, ram-only hunt, with 105 hunters harvesting 29 aoudads. In 1980, sport harvest was used for population control, and it became an unlimited permit, either-sex hunt. In 1979, the population was estimated at 200-225 animals; since then, 638 hunters have harvested 111 aoudads (Dziadulewicz 1983). In such a small population, the removal of 50% of the herd may have had the intended effect.

Because of budgetary limitations, no surveys are conducted for aoudad population numbers. Without this source of data, we cannot determine if the harvest strategies have had the desired results. To determine if aoudads were decreasing in the Guadalupe Mountains, I conducted interviews with ranchers and U.S. Forest Service personnel knowledgeable about these mountains and its environs. The major portion of the aoudad range in the Guadalupes is in 4 Forest Service allotments. Three of these are active sheep ranches, whereas the third is an active cattle ranch. All 4 landowners or their hired help are in the area daily. Each rancher reports a dramatic decrease in aoudads observed since the start of the unlimited permit, either-sex hunt. The major concentrations of aoudad occurred on the Prude Allotment. Prude reported seeing 20-25 aoudad/week until 1981; since then he has only observed 5-6 aoudad/week if "looking hard" (N. Prude, pers. commun.). Forest Service staff have also reported a drastic decrease in the number observed. During the summer of 1981, the NMDGF had a crew of 6 summer students conducting browse surveys in the mountains. This team observed 21 aoudads, whereas another crew, 6 years earlier on the same transects, reported 87 aoudads. Although statistical data are unavailable from population surveys, the NMDGF is confident that the harvest strategy used in the Guadalupes has significantly reduced aoudad populations. The same success has been noted in other isolated populations where aoudad numbers are high enough to induce hunters into the area. In areas of small populations, we have not received the hunter pressure needed to reduce aoudads. The major dispersion center of aoudads in southeastern New Mexico is on private land. Because landowners view the animals as an income source, they only hunt the concentrations lightly. Until we can convince these landowners to harvest more aoudads, we must rely on hunters to control animals on adjacent public lands. The number of permits available in the aoudad management units will have to be constantly monitored to prevent these populations from colonizing areas outside the designated unit boundaries.

The Persian wild goat is also increasing faster than expected. By 1980, this exotic ungulate had grown from 73 to 450 animals. Before 1980, 52 hunters harvested 34 goats on a limited permit, male-only hunt system. In 1980, a beardless hunt with 50 permits available was authorized, and 24 beardless goats were harvested. By 1981, the population had increased to about 500 animals, and 2 beardless hunts with 75 permits each were authorized; 54 beardless goats were harvested. When fall surveys indicated a population of over 600 animals in 1982, 2 nontrophy hunts with 100 permits each were authorized. The major problem of the 1982 nontrophy hunt was that only 67 hunters applied for the 200 permits available. The remaining 133 permits were issued from the Santa Fe office on a first-come basis. When hunting season opened for beardless goats, only 167 of the permittees were afield, with 62 beardless goats harvested. Obviously, the harvest strategy was ineffective in controlling the wild goat population. In order to have more hunters use the recreational opportunities available for the 1983 hunt, the bag limit was changed to 1 trophy male *and* 1 beardless goat. There will be 100 permits for the trophy goat hunt and 100 permits/hunt for 2 nontrophy hunts. The bag limit for the latter is 2 beardless wild goats/hunter. This strategy has the potential of removing 600 animals, close to the total estimated population. The overall success rate on the Persian wild goat hunts has been 57%. Therefore, potentially, we can remove 342 goats, reducing the population by 50% and achieving the desired population of 300 animals. The success rate for the trophy hunts has averaged 78% and for the nontrophy hunts 49%. Using these success rates, we could remove 323 animals and also reduce the goats to the desired numbers. Realistically, NMDGF does not expect to reach that potential and will be satisfied with removing 200 goats this year. If that removal can be achieved, 3-4 years of the double bag limit may reduce the goat population to the desired level.

Harvest strategies for gemsbok were changed for reasons other than population control. In 1981, it was noted that some gemsbok had nontypical horns, caused by a genetic deficiency or damage during early stages of formation, or broken horns caused by fighting or accidents. To enhance herd trophy quality, a nontrophy hunt was started in 1981 to remove the undesirable animals from the population. Ten nontypical permits/year are issued and, so far, 15 animals have been removed from the population. Ten permits/year will continue to be allocated until the goal is reached. Another 3-4 years of the strategy is needed to achieve success.

The Siberian ibex has yet to reach a population level where control is necessary. This exotic will be monitored and controls will be instituted, if necessary, to prevent the overpopulation seen in the aoudad and Pesian wild goat populations.

All of New Mexico's free-ranging exotic ungulates have been hunted. Except for the Siberian ibex, different harvest strategies have been used to control an aspect of their population dynamics. We have attempted to control the population numbers and range expansion of aoudad and Persian wild goat and the gemsbok's nontypical horn growth. These efforts have been successful to a limited degree in some areas. Different harvest strategies, however, may have to be employed to achieve the desired results in other areas.

The success or failure of these harvest strategies to control or alter any wildlife population is dependent upon an open-minded administration that will allow experimentation with bag limits and season dates despite opposition from uninformed public organizations and lay groups that oppose any change. A program is doomed to failure if it lacks the full support of the regulatory board or agency that controls wildlife policy. Public education and persistance can overcome public opposition for effective control programs. New Mexico has a progressive administration that allows experimentation and continues its support in spite of setbacks. We are confident that, in the future, we will be able to successfully control exotic ungulate populations. If manipulation of harvest strategies are unsuccessful, more direct action will have to be taken.

LITERATURE CITED

BAVIN, R. L. 1975. Ecology and behavior of the Persian ibex in the Florida Mountains, New Mexico. M.S. Thesis. Colorado State Univ., Fort Collins. 141pp.

DICKINSON, T. G., AND C. D. SIMPSON. 1980. Dispersal and establishment of Barbary sheep in southeastern New Mexico. Pages 33-45 *in* C. D. Simpson, ed. Proc. Barbary sheep ecology and management symp. Texas Tech Univ. Press, Lubbock.

DZIADULEWICZ, M. 1983. Barbary sheep harvest and population trend information. N.M. Dep. of Game and Fish Perf. Report, Fed. Aid Proj. W-93-R-25. WP5 J1. 5pp.

HABIBI, K. 1983. Social behavior of the aoudad (*Ammotragus lervia*) in Hondo Valley, New Mexico. Ph.D. Thesis. Michigan State Univ., East Lansing. 111pp.

MORRISON, B. L. 1980. History and status of Barbary sheep in New Mexico. Pages 15-16 *in* C. D. Simpson, ed. Proc. Barbary sheep ecology and management symp. Texas Tech Univ. Press, Lubbock.

———. 1981. New Mexico's exotic wildlife program: its past, present, and future. Proc. Western Assoc. State Game and Fish Comm. Conf. 61:88-91.

———. 1983*a*. Oryx population trends, distribution, and harvest information. N.M. Dep. of Game and Fish Perf. Report, Fed. Aid Proj. W-93-R-25. WP 17 J1. 7pp.

———. 1983*b*. Ibex population trends, distribution, and harvest information. N.M. Dep. of Game and Fish Perf. Report, Fed. Aid Proj. W-93-R-25. WP 16 J1. 6pp.

OGREN, H. A. 1965. Barbary sheep. N.M. Dep. of Game and Fish Tech. Bull. 13. 117pp.

SAIZ, R. B. 1975. Ecology and behavior of the gemsbok on the White Sands Missile Range, New Mexico. M.S. Thesis. Colorado State Univ., Fort Collins. 122pp.

SPILLETT, J. J., AND T. D. BUNCH. 1979. The evolution, systematics, and cytogenetics of *Ovis*. Trans. Desert Bighorn Counc. 23:2-18.

SUTCLIFFE, D. H. 1972. Post release investigations of Iranian ibex in New Mexico and evaluation of a proposed release site. M.S. Thesis. New Mexico State Univ., Las Cruces. 38pp.

WOODRUFF, W. O. 1979. Ecology and behavior of the Persian wild goat (*Capra aegagrus*) in New Mexico. M.S. Thesis. New Mexico State Univ., Las Cruces. 95pp.

CONSERVATION AND MANAGEMENT PLAN FOR THE MOUNTAIN GAZELLE IN ISRAEL

YORAM AYAL, Nature Reserves Authority, 78 Yirmeyahu, Jerusalem, Israel 94467
DAN BAHARAV, Society for the Protection of Nature, Hashfela St., Tel Aviv, Israel 66183

Abstract: The mountain gazelle (*Gazella gazella*) is a species engrossed in an ironic struggle for survival in the heavily human-populated Middle East and nearby regions. Overhunted and in threat of extirpation from most of its original range, the mountain gazelle was protected from hunting, which, in turn, resulted in a population increase in Israel to the point where severe crop depredations have become a serious problem. A scheme for the establishment of fenced "sanctuaries" to confine the species in subpopulations away from agriculture-cropped areas to prevent depredation, and the implementation of controlled harvests to regulate their populations therein is discussed.

KEY WORDS: Mountain gazelle, *Gazella gazella*, Crop depredation, Controlled harvesting, Species preservation.

The mountain gazelle is found in northwest Africa, the Middle East, Persia, Afghanistan, and northwest India. Several subspecies have been described from different areas within this range, of which *G. g. gazella* Pallas, 1766, is distributed in Syria, Lebanon, and Israel (Ellerman and Morrison-Scott 1966, Harrison 1966). The gazelle, together with other big game animals, was sought by the earliest hunters in this area. Mendelssohn (1974) reviewed the history and techniques of game hunting from the earliest times until now. Today, the gazelle is still widely hunted throughout its range and is on the verge of extinction. Only in Israel and very recently in Jordan and Oman is hunting prohibited and the gazelle abundant or recovering from overhunting.

In Israel the law prohibiting hunting of big game animals, the Wild Animal Preservation Law (WAPL) enacted in 1955, resulted in a rather rapid buildup of the mountain gazelle population from a few hundred during the early 1950's (Mendelssohn 1974) to the present population of 10,000 animals. Simultaneously, the growing demand for arable land has greatly reduced the available area of the gazelle's natural habitat. As a result, most mountain gazelles are presently concentrated in long and sometimes narrow hilly stretches along the Jordon Valley (Fig. 1). These natural areas are surrounded by irrigated, cultivated areas supporting highly nutritious and palatable crops that attract the gazelles, especially during summer and autumn when much of the natural food is dry and rather poor. Damage to crops has created pressure for the Nature Reserves Authority (NRA) to limit the gazelle population in order to reduce the damage that they cause.

Baharav (1974, 1975, 1981, 1983) has studied the biology, energy budget, and population structure of the mountain gazelle population in Israel and Grau (1974) and Grau and Walther (1976) its social behavior. This paper examines the available data to determine the dynamics and population trends

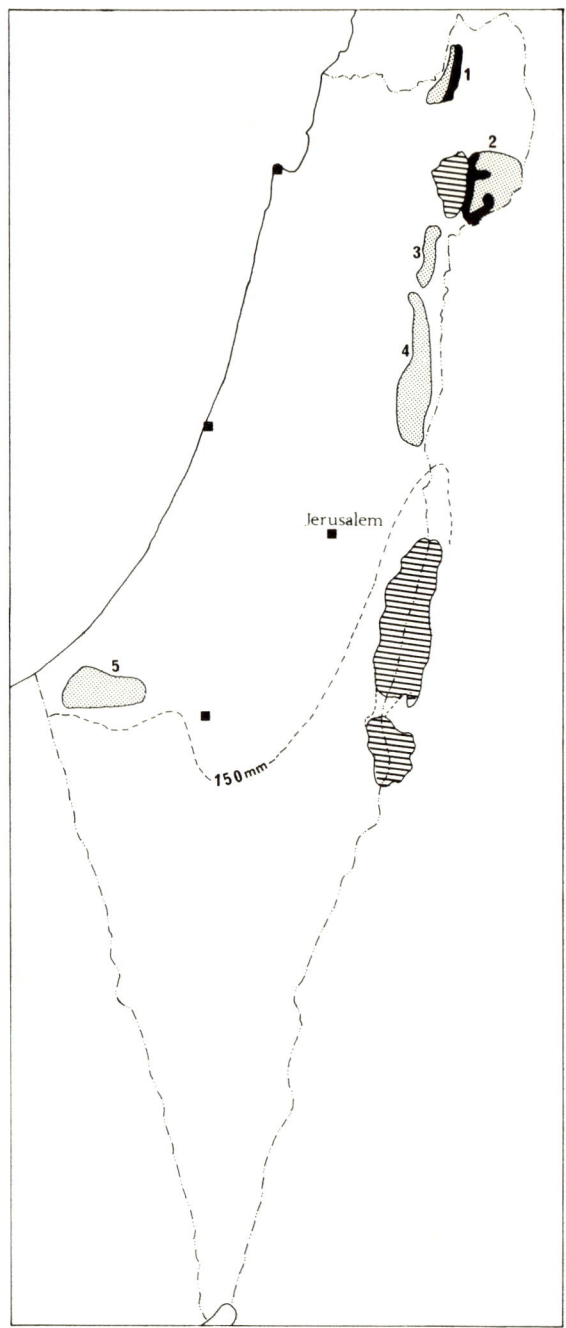

Fig. 1. The present distribution of the mountain gazelle in Israel. Dotted areas represent populations of high density, dark areas represent wintering areas of northern populations (1 = Qedesh Naftali, 2 = Golan Heights, 3 = Ramot Yissakhar, 4 = Eastern Sammaria, 5 = Western Negev, hatched line = mean annual precipitation isohyet).

of this species and considers alternative plans for conservation and management of the gazelle populations that will minimize their impact as agricultural pests.

The authors are indebted to many of the Nature Reserves Authority staff and other naturalists who contributed data used in this work. Y. Ayal particularly thanks G. Ilani and D. Kaplan for the census data and Z. Horesh, a naturalist who has contributed greatly to techniques in minimizing wildlife damage to agriculture while protecting wildlife. Dr. R. Schuster provided many ideas on gazelle behavior; Prof. H. Mendelssohn and Dr. N. M. Ben-Eliahu critically read the manuscript. The P. N. Foundation provided a travel grant to Y. Ayal to participate in the conference.

GAZELLE POPULATION DYNAMICS FOR THE PAST 35 YEARS

The mountain gazelle population has increased steadily since 1948 when hunting was first prohibited. Although the increase was not evaluated during the first 15 years, the population was figured at below 500 in the early 1950's. However, the true number may have been larger due to the inaccessibility of some populations (Z. Horesh, pers. commun.).

When the gazelle population was censused 20 years later, it numbered about 2,500 animals, a mean rate of increase of $r_s=0.0807$/year (Fig. 2) for a population that had already suffered heavy losses because of poaching and legal hunting by farmers in areas with damage to crops (Z. Horesh, pers. commun.) (For discussion of the different r parameters, see Ayal and Safriel 1982). The increased rate can be attributed mainly to more irrigation, making more crops and water available to gazelles; to some extent to the establishment of the NRA in 1964, which improved WAPL enforcement and reduced poaching; and to the increased availability of wild habitat because of the inclusion of the Golan Heights area in Israel.

The year-round availability of highly nutritious food has caused a marked demographic change in the gazelle population. We reach this conclusion because a female mountain gazelle in nature produces her first fawn when 2 years old and, thereafter, 1 litter/year. The mortality rate among the young is rather high (Mendelssohn 1974), as observed in the Ramat Qedesh Naftaly population (Baharav 1983). Table 1 presents a life and fecundity table, estimated for a population under natural conditions. From these estimates the population capacity for increase, $r_{c(s)}$ (Laughlin 1965) can be calculated using the following equation:

$$r_c = \frac{\ln R_o}{T_c}$$

where T_c is the cohort generation time given by $T_c = (1/R_o)\int_0^\infty x l_x m_x d_x$ (Leslie 1966). Thus, the population has a positive, though low, rate of increase only in good years when $l_1 = 0.680$, $r_{c(s)}>0$. Females in populations with access to cultivated fields, enjoying an enriched supply of food and water,

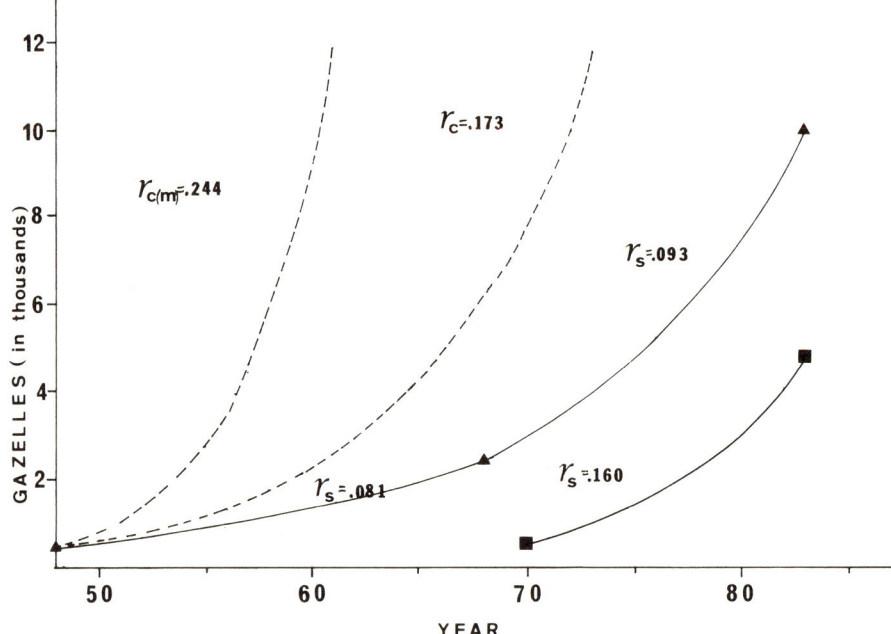

Fig. 2. Population increase of mountain gazelles in Israel in the last 35 years (1948-83) (triangles=total number, rhomboses=the Golan Heights population, hatched lines=expected increase from life table data. For explanations see text).

begin to give birth at the age of 1 year and seem to reproduce continuously, thus producing an average of more than 1 fawn/year (Baharav 1975). Also, the fawns survive better than in natural food restricted conditions. Table 2 presents a fecundity table estimated for a population living under enriched food conditions in Ramot Yissakhar area (Area 3, Fig. 1). Using the equations

Table 1. Life and fecundity table for a mountain gazelle population living on natural resources (estimated from Baharav 1983).

Age (yrs) (x)	Survivorship (l_x)	Fecundity (m_x)
1	0.530	
2	0.424	0.4
3	0.339	0.4
4	0.271	0.4
5	0.217	0.4
6	0.173	0.4
7	0.139	0.4
8	0.111	0.4
9	0.089	0.4
10	0.071	0.4
11	0.057	0.4
12	0.008	0.4

Table 2. Life and fecundity table for a mountain gazelle population with access to cultivated fields (estimated from Baharav 1975).

Age (yrs) (x)	Survivorship (l_x)	Fecundity (m_x)
1	0.680	0.7
2	0.544	0.7
3	0.435	0.7
4	0.362	0.7
5	0.290	0.7
6	0.231	0.7
7	0.186	0.7
8	0.148	0.7
9	0.119	0.7
10	0.095	0.7
11	0.076	0.7
12	0.061	0.7
13	0.049	0.7
14	0.039	0.7

above, a maximum rate of increase in this population is calculated as $r_{c(m)}=0.244$/year, an estimated rate of increase that is much higher than the one seen in the Golan Heights population, which increased markedly in the past 15 years (Fig. 2). In 1967, 176 gazelles were counted on the Golan, and, by 1970, the population had increased to 250, based on the assumed mean rate of increase $r_s=0.160$. At that time 350 gazelles were transplanted from Area 3 (Z. Horesh, pers. commun.). The Golan Heights is an area of intensified agricultural development; thus, the 600 gazelles enjoyed the most favorable conditions and could be expected to increase at a maximum rate. However, in the 1983 census, this population numbered only 4,840 gazelles (D. Kaplan, pers. commun.), a mean rate of increase $r_s=0.160$/year over the last 13 years and one much lower than that calculated from the life table data for enriched conditions. The discrepancy between these rates is probably not due to poaching because that would require about 800 gazelles/year to be hunted illegally.

The differences between the estimated rate of increase and the rate observed in the field may be due to overestimating the assumed birthrate of gazelles in enriched conditions; the estimate assumed continuous breeding. Yet, the ratio of fawns to adult females in the enriched population in Ramot Yissakhar showed 2 distinct breeding peaks over the year, May-June and September-October (Baharav 1975, 1981); if continuous breeding takes place, we would expect rather constant ratios throughout the year. The autumn breeding may be supplementary in females that did not become pregnant in winter or aborted their fetuses and bred again in spring and of first-year females that became pregnant at the age of 1 year and gave first birth at 1.5 years (G. Ilani, pers. commun.). Thus, the enriched agricultural-crop food enables female gazelles to have 1 breeding success/year, whereas under natural conditions success is much lower (as in the population of Qedesh Naftali, which does not give birth in the autumn [Baharav 1983]). Using an estimated birth rate of 1/year (or $m_x=0.5$, assuming a 1:1 sex ratio), the calculated maximal rate of increase is $r_{c(m)}=0.168$/year, which is more realistic and reduces the necessary estimate of poaching to about 75 gazelles/year in the Golan Heights and 45 gazelles/year in Ramot Yissakhar, one closer to the estimate given by the local NRA superintendent (A. Boldo, pers. commun.).

THE MOUNTAIN GAZELLE AS AN AGRICULTURAL PEST

Damage to crops by mountain gazelles was already reported in the early 1950's when the population was small and rather sparse. In some areas gazelle damage to newly planted orchards and vineyards was so severe that intensive hunting was carried out to reduce the population before affected areas were replanted. Some young plantations that were completely destroyed were abandoned (Z. Horesh, pers. commun.). The increased agricultural damage was probably due to gazelle behavioral changes following hunting prohibition rather than to a concomitant increase in their numbers (Mendelssohn 1974). Before the early 1940's, when gazelles were hunted intensively, their flight distance was so great that it was difficult to observe them in nature. Moreover, dogs roaming around communities prevented gazelles from venturing into cultivated areas. A reduction of gazelle flight distance closely followed the hunting prohibition. Concomitantly, changing agricultural methods led to an increase in the amount of irrigated land, and free-ranging dogs were destroyed to prevent outbreaks of rabies. Consequently, gazelles were more often found around human habitations with increased foraging on crops.

Two different aspects of gazelle crop damage are caused by male territorial activity and by grazing by the entire population. The territorial system enables males to monopolize mating with females that move in small herds over a large area in pursuit of food, water, and shade. The male establishes and defends a territory in a key area rich in one of these resources or located on a path between them (Baharav 1975, R. Schuster, pers. commun.). Cultivated areas are rich in all 3 resources and thus are preferred territorial sites. When young orchards are selected as territories, hornrubbing of males on tree trunks leads to destruction of trees or retards their development. The damage caused by only 1 male results in a delay in harvesting the first crops and may necessitate replacement of young trees. Considerable damage of this type is found in areas where small orchards are planted within natural habitats, such as is commonly done in the Mediterranean Mountains and in semi-arid areas.

The second type of damage is related to population size and depends on the crop type. A partial list of annual crops damaged includes cereals, corn, cotton, watermelon, and eggplant; orchard trees include citrus, banana, mango, avocado, and others. In old orchards, browsing does not damage trees severely, but it retards the growth of young orchards and, where severe, may kill young trees. Instances of complete leaf removal in newly planted orchards have been reported. Destruction of a high proportion of cotton fields by nibbling on seedlings or grown plants causes a decrease in their cotton yield. In cereals, nibbling of seedlings during early winter inhibits development and decreases yields. The damage level is related to timing and quantity of rain, which, in turn, determines development of natural wild pasture. Israeli farmers irrigate fields to ensure early sprouting if there is any delay in first rainfall. At such times the marked contrast between the high quality, rich-cultivated food and the poor natural one available in their habitat attracts gazelles to the fields, and damage increases with the delay of the rain. In fields located on the boundaries of natural habitats, gazelle grazing may be considerable even in years with high rainfall.

The NRA offers farmers a variety of means, other than hunting, to protect crops from damage by gazelles and other wild animals. Hunting the territorial male, after damage to orchards, is not useful since bachelors from nearby herds reoccupy vacant territories, and damage will recur within a short time. Dogs, living at an orchard, are effective in excluding gazelles and other mammals. Radio-transistors tuned to stations that broadcast through the night are another inexpensive and efficient means of keeping gazelles away (Z. Horesh, pers. commun.). In large, open areas, however, fencing alone efficiently reduces gazelle damage; the best and cheapest is electrical fencing, charged by regular 24-v batteries. Properly maintained fences are completely successful in preventing gazelles from entering the fields.

PROPOSED MANAGEMENT STRATEGY

The conflict between the increasing mountain gazelle population and agriculture has forced the NRA to look for a new policy that will reduce gazelle crop damage and maintain the population in its natural habitat. This policy must prevent access of the gazelles to cultivated areas either by fencing them in their natural habitat or by closing-off the cultivated areas. Unfortunately, this will divide the mountain gazelles into several small isolated subpopulations separated by cultivated areas and minimize migration between them.

Thus, gazelles face the consequences of insularity, reduction of genetic variability (Gorman et al. 1975), and increased probability of chance extinction. This outcome is inevitable. Moreover, fencing-off the cultivated areas also reduces the available resources and further decreases their numbers. Therefore, we must ascertain the population size necessary to prevent the above-mentioned danger attached to small populations. Concerning genetic variability, the present minimal estimate is 50 gazelles, but 500 is the recommended limit (Franklin 1980) in populations where breeding is random and open to all members. However, where social behavior leads to monopolization of mating by fewer males than are actually present, then the effective population size, N_e, is given by the equation:

$$N_e \ ^{1/}(\frac{1}{4N_f} + \frac{1}{4N_m})$$

where N_f and N_m are the effective numbers of females and males, respectively, which take part in mating.

Observations of gazelle populations showed the proportion of territorial males to be 20% with the remaining 80% bachelors (D. Baharav, pers. commun.). Assuming a 1:1 sex ratio and denoting $N_f=N_m=0.5$, where N_t is the total number of gazelles in the population, the effective size of the gazelle population is calculated as follows:

$$N_e \, ^{1/}(\frac{1}{4 \times 0.5 N_t} + \frac{1}{4 \times 0.2.2 \times 0.5 N_t}) = 0.33 \, N_t$$

In other words, the effective population size equals to 33% of its total number. This calculation assumes all females and males to be in a reproductive state. However, a considerable proportion is yearlings that do not reproduce. Consequently, the effective population size is much lower than calculated with the $0.25 N_t$ conservative estimate.

There is no reliable evaluation of optimal density for a gazelle population living on natural resources. Present density estimates are $10/km^2$ in Qedesh Naftali (Baharav 1983) and $30/km^2$ in the Golan (D. Kaplan, pers. commun.) and Ramot Yissakhar (Baharav 1975, 1981). The size of the natural habitat area for gazelles is approximately 80 km^2 in the Golan and 67 km^2 in Ramot Yissakhar; thus, the effective population size that can be maintained is 600 and 500, respectively. However, in both areas gazelles have access to cultivated fields and water; this access favors increased density. The carrying capacity of the natural resource in these areas is 20-25 gazelles/km^2, bringing these population levels to the lowest limit recommended from the genetic point of view.

Evaluation of chance extinction differs from those with genetic considerations. Every animal counts because bachelors and yearlings can replace reproductively active gazelles. Given the high capacity for increase, the possibility of stochastic extinction is lessened when total population size is above 500 (MacArthur and Wilson 1967). When long-term conservation plans are evaluated, the critical size should be that of the genetically effective population size rather than chance extinction population size.

Several different management methods can reduce most of the decreased genetic variability in small populations. The exchange of individuals, preferably females, between isolated populations can ease genetic exchange. As far as we know, all females mate and reproduce, whereas the possibility seems small that a newly introduced male can successfully replace an established territorial male in a foreign population. Genetic turnover in any population can also be hastened by culling a certain proportion of territorial males after each reproductive season ends.

Culling should be part of any long-term management plans to keep gazelles at their recommended density. To ensure a future for the mountain gazelles, there must be a total separation between them and cultivated areas; "gazelle sanctuaries" in natural habitats must be allocated for this purpose. In the sanctuaries their numbers should be as high as possible within the limits of the resources in order to keep them healthy and to minimize pressure by them on means (fences, etc.) used for keeping them out of the cultivated areas. Thus, their population should be kept somewhat below the sanctuary's carrying capacity by culling superabundant animals. The extent of culling should reflect differences in precipitation between years, with intensive culling in bad years with low precipitation to adjust the population level to poor resources and less culling, if any, in good years. Recommended population levels for given amounts of precipitation should be determined experimentally as data on this subject are unavailable.

The maintenance of gazelles in well-managed, special sanctuaries will absolve the expected increase of conflict between their needs and those of Israeli farmers. The small size of the natural habitat allocated for this purpose does not allow trial-and-error experiments to determine recommended management practices, and management policy should rely on hard data gathered through costly scientific research. Management of the gazelle sanctuaries will also be expensive. A possible way of funding this research and management is by permitting licensed hunting of gazelles in the sanctuaries. This measure will also carry out the culling of the excess numbers of gazelles. Licensed hunting will require a change in the present policy of the Israeli NRA which enforces total prohibition of gazelle hunting. If organized properly, upon predetermined plans, restricted hunting can help in direct management and in providing income for research and maintenance of the gazelle populations so that their conservation will be assured.

LITERATURE CITED

AYAL, Y., AND U. N. SAFRIEL. 1982. R-curves and the cost of the planktonic stage. Am. Nat. 119:391-401.

BAHARAV, D. 1974. Notes on the population structure and biomass of the mountain gazelle, Gazella gazella gazella, Pallas 1766. Isr. J. Zool. 23:39-44.

———. 1975. Energy flow and productivity in the mountain gazelle (Gazella gazella gazella, Pallas 1766). Ph.D. Thesis. Tel-Aviv Univ. (in Hebrew). 101pp.

———. 1981. Food habits of the mountain gazelle in semi-arid habitats of the Eastern Galilee, Israel. J. Arid Environ. 4:63-69.

———. 1983. Observations of the ecology of the mountain gazelle in the Upper Galilee, Israel. Mammalia 47:59-69.

ELLERMAN, J. R., AND T. C. S. MORRISON-SCOTT. 1966. Checklist of Palaeartic and Indian mammals 1758-1946. British Museum Natural History, London, U.K. 810pp.

FRANKLIN, I. R. 1980. Evolutionary changes in small populations. Pages 135-149 in M. E. Soule and B. A. Wilcox, eds. Conservation biology. Sinauer Assoc., Inc. Sunderland, Mass.

GORMAN, G. L., M. E. SOULE, D. Y. YONG, AND E. NEVO. 1975. Evolutionary genetics of insular Adriatic lizards. Evolution 29:52-71.

GRAU, G. A. 1974. Behavior of mountain gazelle in Israel. Ph.D. Thesis, Texas A&M Univ., College Station. 103pp.

———, AND F. WALTHER. 1976. Mountain gazelle agonistic behavior. Anim. Behav. 24:626-636.

HARRISON, D. L. 1966. The mammals of Arabia, II. Ernest Benn., London, U.K. 381pp.

LAUGHLIN, R. 1965. Capacity for increase: a useful population statistic. J. Anim. Ecol. 34:77-91.

LESLIE, P. H. 1966. The intrinsic rate of increase and the overlap of successive generations in a population of guillemonts (*Uria aalge*). J. Anim. Ecol. 35:291-301.

MENDELSSOHN, H. 1974. The development of the population of gazelles in Israel and their behavioral adaptations. Pages 722-743 *in* V. Geist, ed. The behavior of ungulates and its relation to management. Morges, Switzerland.

MACARTHUR, R. H., AND E. O. WILSON. 1967. The theory of island biogeography. Princeton Univ. Press, Princeton, N.J. 203pp.

COMMERCIAL HUNTING OF WILD RED DEER IN NEW ZEALAND

C. N. CHALLIES, Protection Forestry Division, Forest Research Institute, P.O. Box 31-001, Christchurch, New Zealand

Abstract: Red deer (*Cervus elaphus scoticus*), introduced into New Zealand during the late 1800's, thrived, increased rapidly, and spread into a wide range of forested and high country habitats. The greatest impact on their numbers has been made by the game-meats industry which, since about 1959, has processed over 1.5 million deer carcasses for export. Hunting was initially on foot, but in the mid-1960's helicopters were introduced in mountainous areas and became the mainstay of the industry. Over 60,000 deer have been captured live for farmstock since the mid-1970's. Hunting has been competitive and unrestricted. Its main effect has been a progressive and large-scale reduction in deer densities of 75-95% in predominantly forested, high-country areas. Hunter success has declined by a similar amount. If the industry is to survive, some form of harvest management for sustained yields should be implemented.

KEY WORDS: Capture, *Cervus elaphus*, Commercial hunting, Helicopters, New Zealand, Red deer, Venison, Game-meats industry.

Red deer of British stock were introduced into many parts of New Zealand during the late 1880's (Logan and Harris 1967). Most herds increased and spread rapidly so that by the mid 1900's red deer were present throughout most of the forested and high country parts of the main islands. They adapted well to a wide variety of habitats, particularly favoring areas with a mixture of forest and scrub or native grassland, but they also colonized expanses of unbroken forest and grassland (Wodzicki 1950). By the 1920's, it was apparent that red deer were becoming a significant problem on farmlands and in areas of indigenous vegetation where they were depleting palatable plant species (Perham 1922). In 1931, the Government commenced large-scale hunting operations in efforts to control deer numbers. This remains a primary management consideration.

The extensive deer herds in New Zealand also have been hunted commercially for a variety of products; these operations accounted for several times as many animals as were killed for control purposes. Initially only skins were taken, with over 1 million exported between 1945 and 1960. Since the early 1960's, commercial hunters have concentrated mainly on taking whole carcasses for venison for export and, more recently, live deer for farm stock. These enterprises have been lucrative and accordingly have attracted considerable investment in buildings and machinery and in the development of new, more efficient hunting methods. Commercial hunting has been encouraged by the Government to help control deer numbers, but no attempts have been made to sustain or maximize yields; rather, the hunting has been opportunistic and exploitive.

This paper describes the development and general character of commercial hunting for venison and live deer and its effects on wild red deer populations. It is based principally on overviews and field studies undertaken by staff of the Forest Research Institute, New Zealand Forest Service. The situations described are from the predominantly forested mountainlands of the South Island, unless otherwise stated.

COMMERCIAL HUNTING FOR VENISON

The commercial venison industry in New Zealand originated about 1958-59 with a series of trial shipments of wild red deer venison to Europe. These generally were well received and led to the development of substantial markets for New Zealand venison, especially in the Federal Republic of Germany and to a lesser extent several other west European countries. To date, over 1.5 million wild deer carcasses have been processed for export. Although taken primarily for venison, these deer also provided a variety of by-products including antlers in velvet, tails, testicles, and sinews for quasi-medicinal use in eastern Asia and maxillary canines for use in hunting jewelry in Europe.

Initially the industry was supplied with carcasses by hunters working in areas easily accessible from roads; the deer were either stalked on foot during the day or shot from vehicles equipped with spotlights at night. This type of hunting was steadily extended into more remote regions with the aid of off-road vehicles, pack horses, jet boats on rivers, and light, fixed-wing aircraft from improvised airstrips. By the mid-1960's, most areas of suitable valley flats and forest were being intensively hunted commercially for deer, either by full-time professional hunters or, where most accessible, by casual and "weekend" hunters. These hunters sold the deer they killed by carcass weight at roadside depots operated by processing companies.

The demand for venison soon exceeded the supply obtainable from ground hunters, and helicopters were introduced to recover carcasses from otherwise inaccessible deer range, especially in the extensive areas above timberline. They were used at first to service ground hunters, lifting them into suitable areas and returning later to ferry the kill to the nearest roadside staging point or depot. About 1964, attempts were made to shoot deer from airborne helicopters and to pick up the animals from where they fell. This method proved practical and economical and quickly came into regular use in west Otago and south Westland where red deer were then in high numbers (Osmers 1972). By the late 1960's, hunting from helicopters was a common practice throughout the high country of the South Island and provided about 80-90% of the carcasses processed locally; this also has become the case in the North Island. These operations have been serviced by road, by light, fixed-wing aircraft in some remote areas, and by a ship in the Fiordland Sounds.

During the first few years of aerial hunting, the general purpose light helicopters, Hiller 12E and Bell 47G, were commonly used. A "shooter" flew with the pilot to find, shoot, and pick up the deer, and a "gutter" was left at a central point on the hillside to eviscerate the deer and assemble them into helicopter loads. The helicopters flew mainly above timberline along the contour of hillsides; the deer were shot where found, and their bodies were taken to the gutter. Loads of carcasses later were ferried to the staging point (Challies 1974a). Under favorable conditions, this process continued all day.

During the 1970's, the mode of these operations changed as costs increased and the numbers of deer found in the open declined. More suitable helicopters were introduced, especially the turbine-powered Hughes 500, which is faster and has greater range and maneuverability than the models used earlier. These usually were crewed by the pilot and 1 man filling the roles of shooter and gutter. The crews now concentrated their efforts on finding deer along forest margins, on mid-slope clearings, and in areas of forest with an open canopy. At the same time hunting was confined mainly to the early morning and evening hours when deer were most likely to be found in the open.

Commercial hunting has been subject to few restrictions. There have been no statutory limits on the numbers, age, or sex of the deer that could be taken or on the seasons in which they could be hunted. Permission to hunt on state lands usually has been given on request, without charge, and often without regard to the number of permits already issued for that area. Local restrictions on the areas and seasons in which helicopters could be operated usually have proved difficult to enforce. As a result, venison hunting has tended to be competitive, especially where helicopters have been involved. On freehold and leased lands, hunting has been permitted by the occupiers under a variety of arrangements ranging from free access to agreements to share in the take.

Traditionally, deer killed for venison were eviscerated and had their heads and legs removed in the field, i.e. reduced to a "German-market carcass". Initially there were few controls on the handling of carcasses; minimum conditions were determined by what was accepted for processing at the factories. This changed in 1967 when the Department of Agriculture became responsible for periodic inspections of storage and processing facilities to ensure that approved standards were met. New regulations introduced in 1975 set stringent time limits for the delivery of carcasses to chillers and factories and for their processing. Hearts, lungs, livers, and kidneys had to remain attached to the carcasses for inspection by government-employed meat inspectors.

The numbers of deer killed by commercial hunters have not been recorded but can be inferred by dividing the weight of venison exported each year by 33 kg, the mean weight of venison/carcass (Challies 1973). Carcass production increased rapidly during the 1960's as the industry developed and expanded. It reached a peak in 1971-72 when about 133,000 deer were processed in 1 year and then declined steadily to an average kill of about 45,000 deer/year in the early 1980's. This drop in production resulted from a decrease in the productivity of hunting operations and an increasing interest in the live capture of deer rather than from an overall decrease in hunting effort.

The value of processed venison (in actual dollars/unit f.o.b.) increased at an average rate of 16%/annum between 1965 and the early 1980's (annual figures from N.Z. Dep. of Statistics). When inflation of the NZ dollar is taken into account, this represents a doubling in the real value of venison and, presumably, a doubling in the real value of deer carcasses. The current value (f.o.b.) of the exportable venison from an average wild red deer carcass is about $US115.

LIVE CAPTURE OF DEER FOR FARM STOCK

The farming of deer as domestic stock became legal in New Zealand in 1969, and the first deer-farm licenses were issued in 1970. Interest in deer farming increased rapidly during the late 1970's and early 1980's, caused initially by the lucrative Korean market for antler velvet and more recently by prospects for venison production. In 1983, there were about 240,000 deer on farms in New Zealand (predominantly red deer but including some fallow deer [*Dama dama*], sika deer [*Cervus nippon*], and wapiti [*C. e. nelsoni*]) of which at least 60,000 had originally been caught in the wild; the others were bred on farms.

Over 85% of the deer captured from the wild have been taken by helicopter crews (Wallis and Hunn 1982), initially as an adjunct to the recovery of carcasses but later mainly in specific live capture operations. This shift in emphasis occurred during the late 1970's in response to the high prices offered by farmers for live deer (up to $US2,000 was paid for captured animals that were farm trained [Yerex 1979]). The annual take of live deer increased from about 3,500 in 1977-78 to a peak of 25,000 in 1979-80 then declined sharply to less than 5,000 in 1982-83 as reduced tallies and lower prices for deer made live capture from helicopters marginally economic. During the late 1970's, all accessible wild deer were captured regardless of age or sex. Since then females have been increasingly preferred because they fetched much higher prices. Many of the males encountered were shot for their carcasses.

A wide variety of capture techniques have been used by helicopter crews at different times. Initially, deer were caught by "bull-dogging", which involved a crew man jumping from the helicopter onto the animal and physically constraining it. This method was incorporated into normal carcass recovery operations and was particularly suitable for catching fawns. From the outset, considerable efforts were made to develop more appropriate and efficient capture techniques. Early trials with tranquilizers met with limited success, but with the introduction of the versatile drug 'Fentaz' (Fentanyl citrate, 10mg/ml, and Azaperone, 80mg/ml) in the mid-1970's, the method subsequently came into wide use. Dart guns of the 'Paxarms' type were fired from airborne helicopters, which hovered in view until the deer became sedated. Miniature radio-transmitters first were fitted into separate darts fired alongside the tranquilizer darts from 2-barrelled guns; subsequently transmitters were fitted into the tranquilizer darts. These techniques enabled helicopter crews to relocate tranquilized animals later. Nets also were tried at an early stage with some success but did not come into common use until the late 1970's when net guns were developed; the charge from a rifle cartridge propels a large-mesh net over the deer. Net guns are either hand-held from the doorway of the helicopter or mounted on the helicopter skid (Wallis and Hunn 1982). They have proved effective, quick, and simple to operate in open country but of limited use in tall vegetation where the net can easily become snagged. Some crews now carry a net gun and a dart gun and use whichever is most suitable for capturing the animals found.

Once caught, the deer's legs are tied together, it is placed in a canvas carrying bag with only its head and neck protruding, and it is ferried to the staging point, either hanging in the bag from the cargo hook or lying on the floor of the helicopter. There the deer is untied and left standing in either a small, darkened pen or in an enclosed road trailer ready for transport to a deer farm.

Traps of various kinds also have been used extensively to catch deer but have supplied less than 15% of the wild deer captured. The most practical have been pen traps, typically comprising a fenced area with a swinging gate in 1 side fitted with a catch-and-release mechanism triggered by a trip wire within the pen. The gates are spring-loaded or weighted to close automatically when the release is tripped. Pen traps are commonly built around the edges of forest clearings and range in size between 0.025 and 0.25 ha. Some are cultivated, fertilized, and planted in pasture grasses and legumes or crops to attract deer, whereas others are left closed periodically to allow growth of the established vegetation. Trapped deer are either "bull-dogged", netted, or tranquilized from a dart gun.

EFFECTS ON RED DEER POPULATIONS

Before the development of the commercial venison industry, wild red deer populations in New Zealand varied greatly in density and general well-being. This was attributable mainly to the different lengths of time that deer had been present in different areas and the types, timing, and intensity of hunting they had sustained. As a rule, long-established, little-hunted populations were either at high density or declining naturally as they depleted their habitat, whereas those recently established or intensively hunted for control purposes were at lower density. The well-being of populations generally has declined with increasing density of deer and time since their introduction (Challies 1974b). This pattern has changed radically during the last 15-20 years.

The most obvious result of commercial hunting of deer has been a progressive, large-scale reduction in numbers over most of their range. The few areas of high country exempt from legitimate commercial hunting have mostly been hunted illictly with a similar effect; overall, reductions in density generally have been in the order of 75-95%.

The largest percentage reductions have occurred where deer were initially at high density and on range with a predominant cover of short vegetation where deer were particularly vulnerable to hunting from helicopters. This type of hunting has virtually eliminated the resident deer populations from the larger expanses of native grassland. In predominantly forested areas of high country, helicopter crews now encounter few deer in the open, above timberline, or on river flats where they previously had been common. Within the forests, deer numbers tend to be higher at greater distances from areas that have been hunted intensively from helicopters and are now highest in the larger, unbroken expanses of forest and locally in forested valley bottoms.

The following brief case histories demonstrate the extent to which commercial helicopter hunting has affected deer numbers and local distribution under different circumstances. The 3 areas described are mountainous and mainly forested below timberline with extensive subalpine scrub and grasslands. Each has been hunted intensively by helicopter crews.

Arawata Valley, South Westland

Red deer spread into the lower Arawata Valley about 1950. By the mid-1960's, they were reaching moderate to high densities throughout and were concentrated locally on the valley flats, subalpine grasslands, and adjacent forests. Since 1965, this herd has been hunted commercially from helicopters, continuously and without restriction; these operations remained competitive despite an 80% drop in their kill rate. A series of deer-pellet-count surveys made in the Arawata Valley between 1970 and 1980 showed a 75% reduction in deer numbers on all parts of their range. These surveys represent an approximately 90% decrease in deer density since 1965. Deer have made only minimal use of the subalpine grasslands since the mid-1970's. The residual population now is concentrated mainly on the forested mid and lower valley slopes where densities average 300% higher than in forests near timberline (Challies 1977, C. N. Challies, unpubl. data).

Wangapeka, Owen and Matiri Valleys, West Nelson

Red deer colonized this area between 1900 and 1910, reached high densities throughout around 1935-45, and then declined in numbers as they depleted their habitat (Clarke 1976). During this eruptive fluctuation, deer progressively utilized all available habitats, making extensive use of forested and subalpine areas. Since 1967, hunting was without restriction except for a period during the early and mid-1970's when hunting was limited to 5 months of the year and 1 crew at a time on each of several blocks. Despite these restrictions, kill rates dropped 75% from about 10-12 deer/helicopter hour in 1967 to 3 deer/hour in the mid-1970's; rates since have dropped further. An extensive pellet-count survey during the summer 1982-83 showed deer were confined to the forests in an average density of about 2.2 animals/ km^2. Within the forests, deer were concentrated on the lower valley slopes and valley flats; densities there were 5-10 times higher than those in the forests near timberline. The commercial take in 1982 was equivalent to about 0.9 deer/km^2 of forest. Current deer numbers reportedly are no more than 5% of those in the area during the early 1940's (Clarke 1984, Hickling 1984).

Murchison Mountains, Fiordland

Red deer colonized the Murchison Mountains between 1930 and 1950 and reached high densities locally within 20 years. They have been hunted since 1962 to control their numbers to limit the extent of deer browsing on plant species preferred by the takahe (*Notornis mantelli*), an endangered, native rail. This animal control has been undertaken by government employed hunters working on foot; since 1975, this effort has been supplemented with hunting from helicopters. With the introduction of helicopters, the foot hunters shifted their efforts from the open areas to concentrate mainly on deer in the forests. After a period with little change, deer pellet densities dropped an average of 60% between 1974 and 1976. This coincided with the start of helicopter hunting and an increase in the numbers of foot hunters employed. Between 1976 and 1984, the kill rate dropped by 80% for foot hunters to 0.1 deer/man day, and by 65% for helicopter crews to 1.2 deer/ machine hour, despite a halving in the hunting effort. The combined annual kill dropped 75% during this period and is now equivalent to 0.5 deer/km^2 of forest (Parkes et al. 1978, New Zealand Forest Service, unpubl. data).

As deer numbers have been reduced, the physical well-being of the surviving animals and their offspring has improved markedly, presumably as a result of the increased availability of food *per capita*. This has been pronounced in long-established populations which were near the carrying capacity of their range before the reduction in numbers. The most noticeable effect has been increased growth rates and, to a lesser degree, increased body fat and antler size of young animals. The lean body weights of young deer are now up to 35% higher than those of comparable animals taken in the same areas in the mid-1960's. There have been similar increases in the productivity of populations. In most populations, about 96% of adult females now calve annually. The greatest changes in productivity have occurred in the 2-year-old (first breeding) age group with calving rates increasing from 15 to 60% in some populations within 10-15 years of the commencement of hunting (Challies 1978).

DISCUSSION

Wild red deer in New Zealand have been exploited in a "boom and bust" fashion for the past 20 years. What started off as a few trial export shipments of venison quickly developed into a lucrative game-meats industry based on a plentiful, free, and unrestricted supply of deer and a ready market. The industry has been wholly privately owned and has subscribed to private enterprise. Considering the competitive nature of many of the hunting operations, it is surprising, however, that commercial hunting, especially from helicopters, remained viable for so long. This probably is attributable to the progressive outlook of the industry in continuously striving to improve and update its techniques and equipment. A good example of that was the rapid shift made from carcass recovery to the taking of live deer. That in effect gave the industry a "new life" by greatly increasing the value of individual deer at a time when some operators found that carcass hunting was not economical. Despite the current low deer numbers, about 60 helicopter crews still hunt on either a part- or full-time basis, mainly for live deer.

Commercial hunting has had some important secondary effects. It has virtually eliminated the need to artificially control deer numbers, which otherwise would have had to be done at public expense as in the past (1,133 deer were shot by government employed hunters in 1982 compared with 35,600 in 1962). Deer numbers have been reduced generally to lower levels than believed possible, even in the areas given highest priority for deer control. The few remaining non-commercial-control operations are being undertaken in special areas, such as the Murchison Mountains, where lower animal numbers are required than can be attained with commercial hunting alone. On the negative side, the opportunities for recreational hunting have been much reduced as a direct result of the lower deer numbers. The easily accessible animals, that in the past have provided abundant hunting for all who wanted it, no longer exist.

The future of commercial hunting from helicopters in New Zealand is open to speculation. Its viability at present deer population levels is dependent primarily on the prices obtained for female deer caught live and secondarily on the prices for deer carcasses. The demand for captured deer seems likely to decline as the deer-farming industry becomes more self-sufficient in stock and less speculative. If commercial hunters then have to rely primarily on deer carcasses for their income, it is unlikely that their industry can be maintained at its present scale without management (through regulated harvesting) for the sustained production of larger numbers of deer.

LITERATURE CITED

CHALLIES, C. N. 1973. The effects of the commercial venison industry on deer populations. Pages 164-177 *in* Assessment and management of introduced animals in New Zealand forests. N.Z. For. Serv., For. Res. Inst. Symp. 14.

———. 1974*a*. Use of helicopters in the New Zealand commercial venison industry. E. Afr. Agric. For. J. 39:376-380.

———. 1974*b*. Trends in red deer (*Cervus elaphus*) populations in Westland forests. Proc. N. Z. Ecol. Soc. 21:45-50.

———. 1977. Effects of commercial hunting on red deer densities in the Arawata Valley, South Westland, 1972-76. N. Z. J. For. Sci. 7:263-273.

———. 1978. Assessment of the physical well-being of red deer (*Cervus elaphus* L.) populations in South Westland, New Zealand. Ph.D. Thesis, Univ. Canterbury, Christchurch, N.Z. 153pp.

CLARKE, C. M. H. 1976. Eruption, deterioration, and decline of the Nelson red deer herd. N.Z. J. For. Sci. 5:235-249.

———. 1984. History of wild animals and domestic stock. *In* M. R. Davis and J. Orwin, eds. Report on a survey of the proposed wapiti area, West Nelson. N. Z. For. Serv., For. Res. Inst. Bull. In press.

HICKLING, G. 1984. Distribution and abundance of introduced mammals. *In* M. R. Davis and J. Orwin, eds. Report on a survey of the proposed wapiti area, West Nelson. N. Z. For. Serv. For. Res. Inst. Bull. In press.

LOGAN, P. C., AND L. H. HARRIS. 1967. Introduction and establishment of red deer in New Zealand. N. Z. For. Serv., Infor. Ser. 55. 36pp.

OSMERS, D. 1972. Venison recovery. T.G.M.L.I. Review 24:61-66.

PARKES, J., K. TUSTIN, AND L. STANLEY. 1978. The history and control of red deer in the Takahe Area, Murchison Mountains, Fiordland National Park. N. Z. J. Ecol. 1:145-152.

PERHAM, A. N. 1922. Deer in New Zealand: report on the damage done by deer in the forests and plantations in New Zealand. Appendix to Journals, House of Reps., N. Z., C.-3A. 6pp.

WALLIS, T., AND R. HUNN. 1982. Helicopter live capture. Pages 84-89 *in* D. Yerex, ed. The farming of deer—world trends and modern techniques. Agric. Promotion Associates, Wellington, N.Z.

WODZICKI, K. A. 1950. Introduced mammals of New Zealand: an ecological and economic survey. N. Z. Dep. Sci. Industr. Res. Bull. 98. 255pp.

YEREX, D. 1979. Deer farming in New Zealand. Agric. Promotion Associates, Wellington, N.Z. 120pp.

HARVESTING GAME AT NIGHT IN SOUTH WEST AFRICA

EUGENE JOUBERT, Directorate of Nature Conservation, Private Bag 13306, Windhoek, South West Africa 9000

Abstract: Harvesting game at night in South West Africa proved to be a method that is humane, economical, and in compliance with health and veterinary regulations. Hunting procedure, evisceration, and a mobile field abattoir are discussed in detail. Attention is also given to the economic viability of this method. The accepted price in 1979 for springbok (*Antidorcas marsupialis*) rose from $7.50/head to $35.00/head and from $25.00/head to $225.00/head for kudu (*Tragelaphus strepsiceros*). The number of springbok carcasses exported to Europe rose from 7,739 in 1976 to 43,663 in 1979. Landowners earned between $50,000 and $75,000/annum/ranch by allowing game harvesting on their land. Doubt, however, remains on whether the long-term influence of this harvesting at night succeeds in removing a random sample from populations of springbok, kudu, and oryx (*Oryx gazella*).

KEY WORDS: Springbok, Kudu, Oryx, Marketing game, Abattoir, Trophy hunting, Wild game harvesting.

Game populations in South West Africa appear to have generally increased since approximately 1955 (Table 1); higher-than-average rainfall in the 1970's led to a substantial increase during that period. At the same time the Department of Agriculture began to insist that the numbers of game on ranches be taken into account when assessing the carrying capacity of the ranches. This approach was enforced by refusing subsidies unless game numbers were included in ranch development schemes.

Ranches wanting to reduce the numbers of game on their property then began to inquire at the Directorate of Nature Conservation about methods to be used and markets for the meat produced. Evaluation of various methods showed that the best technique was night harvesting (Joubert 1974). This worked well with springbok but showed less success with kudu and oryx. Unfortunately, production costs are high, and only the fact that venison is marketed in Europe makes the game harvesting profitable.

Legislation was changed in 1975 to accommodate the private sector in night-harvesting operations. The market in Europe was expanded, and a profitable industry developed (Joubert et al. 1983). Nevertheless, several lingering doubts remained. The most important concerned the stability of the European venison market. Other questions that will be dealt with are centered around the influence of night harvesting on the male:female ratio, the influence of night harvesting on the age structure of the population, and finally the influence on the breeding success of the species discussed. No ready answers exist, and certain aspects are a cause of concern to the directorate. Several research projects are presently under way, the results of which will hopefully increase our knowledge base concerning this problem.

Table 1. Population trends for the 3 game species most commonly harvested at night in South West Africa.

Year	Kudu	Oryx	Springbok
1955[a]	72,500	26,900	45,700
1960[b]	60,800	24,500	37,300
1973[c]	111,900	40,600	141,900
1980[d]	200,000	45,000	250,000
1983[d]	83,700	20,600	91,700

[a] Bigalke (1958).
[b] Van Der Spuy (1962).
[c] Joubert and Mostert (1975).
[d] E. Joubert, unpubl. data.

I am indebted to P. A. J. Brand for making available unprocessed data and to Drs. A. J. Williams and H. H. Berry, and Mr. K. Panagis for critically reading through the manuscript. Janet Lautenbach is thanked for preparing the figures.

METHODS

Development of Harvesting Procedure

From 1976 to 1982, several harvesting procedures were evaluated, but the only method that proved to be of value was to harvest the animals at night with the aid of strong spotlights. This method was used during the dry, cold season and has the following advantages:

1. No flies are encountered.
2. Herd disturbance is minimal.
3. It is possible to follow up and kill wounded animals.
4. Low temperatures and the fact that the animals are hardly disturbed ensure high quality meat.
5. It is possible to harvest randomly.
6. Harvesting can be carried out economically.
7. With the high degree of shooting accuracy that is achieved, meat damage is limited.

Hunting Equipment and Tactics

A wide variety of vehicles on the market can be used in the culling operation; however, none can be used without mechanical and electrical modifications. The vehicle should be sturdy with 4-wheel drive and capable of carrying at least 1,000 kg.

Harvesting is a team effort between the handlers of the spotlights, the driver, and the marksman. When a herd is located, the spotlights are shined onto a selected animal, and it is killed with a shot to the brain or neck; misplaced shots are the most frequent cause of carcasses being condemned upon inspection. Several animals may be killed before the herd moves on, but not more than 5 animals should be killed in any particular spot. When a carcass is reached, the throat is cut at the angle of the lower jaw, and the animal is hung on the trellis or hoisted into the loading platform with its head down. Since the heart continues beating for several minutes after death, carcasses are thus properly bled.

The vehicle then moves again, and more animals are killed. Carcasses must be eviscerated within 20-30 minutes after death; otherwise, bacterial infection from the intestines may take place.

A requirement of the night-harvesting operation was that each night the leader of each vehicle had to complete a logsheet giving numbers of individuals shot, the age (assessed by lower jaw analysis), weight, sex, and the reproductive condition for females. This paper is based on the information contained in these logsheets (with the understanding that there is bound to be some variation in the meticulousness with which the logsheets were completed in the field).

Evisceration

The operator washes his hands with a disinfectant soap and uses a disinfected knife to make an incision in the abdominal wall posterior to the cartilage of the sternum. Using a belly ripper, he opens up the abdominal cavity to the *symphysis pubis*. The contents of the rectum are separated upwards and downwards, and a fencing stapler is used to seal off the rectum with 2 staples approximately 2 cm apart; the rectum then is severed. The esophagus similarly is severed where it enters the rumen. The mesenterium, which joins the intestines to the wall of the abdominal cavity, is cut, and all the intestines except the liver are removed. The abdominal cavity then is closed with the fencing stapler and the carcass is hoisted into the vehicle.

The Field Abattoir

The site of the abattoir has to be chosen carefully. It should be on reasonably level ground, close to a regular supply of water, and in the proximity of a main road and the culling area. The ground on which the abattoir is erected must be sprinkled with water to eliminate dust and then covered with wooden slats. Ideally, a concrete floor should be constructed. The abattoir itself is constructed of 50-mm pipes, which, when assembled, should form a firm framework 3x3x3 m with 3 sliding rails on which carcasses may be hung (Figs. 1 and 2). It also is essential to have hot and cold running water, 220-V power source to supply lighting, hot water geyser, etc. and a refrigeration truck with a 20-ton capacity.

A stock inspector must be present to carry out inspections. The abattoir is manned by a butcher and 5-10 laborers, depending on the number of animals and species to be culled.

The carcasses are loaded into a delivery rail (Fig. 2). The head, feet, and red offal are removed. The latter is given the same number as the carcass and hung on a separate rack to facilitate the work of the stock inspector.

292 GAME HARVEST MANAGEMENT

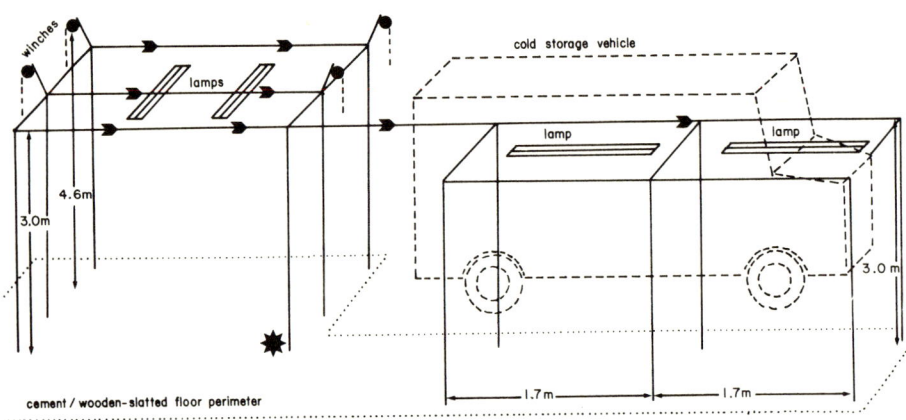

Fig. 1. Diagrammatic delivery vehicle and delivery rails used in field abattoir in South West Africa.

The kidneys are the only organs left in the carcass, which is inspected and approved or condemned. Approved carcasses are then moved into a refrigerator truck, which must reach the factory within 72 hours.

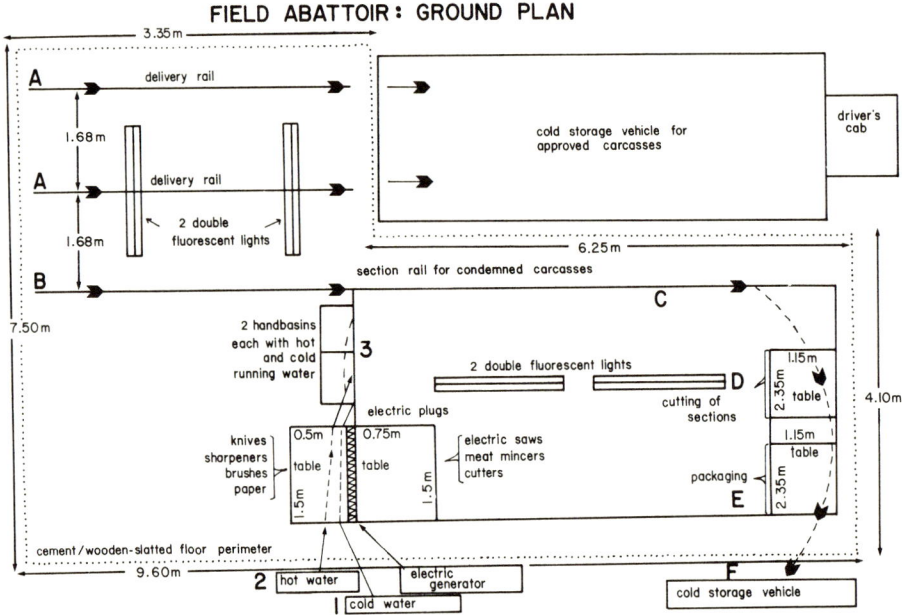

Fig 2. Ground plan of field abattior used in South West Africa.

RESULTS AND DISCUSSION

Before harvesting became established, the accepted price for springbok was $7.50/head and for kudu $25.00/head. During 1979, a rancher who allowed harvesting on his land earned $30.00-35.00/head for springbok and $190.00-225.00/head for kudu, and during 1980, many ranchers earned between $50,000-75,000 by harvesting game on their land.

The harvesting team earned $12.50/springbok and $62.50/kudu. Transport costs in the refrigeration truck (+10c/kg) have to be added, which means that a springbok costs in the region of $43.75-50.00 and a kudu to $250. The best markets had to be exploited; the venison had a very good reception in France and Germany. An interesting aspect was that in France springbok were more popular than either kudu or oryx. The easier handling of the smaller carcass caused the bias, not the quality of the meat.

Four commercial, private game-harvesting units consisting of 6-10 hunting teams are presently operating in the territory. They normally do their own financing, pay the rancher before they leave his land, rent the refrigeration truck, and assume responsibility until the meat reaches an overseas market. They have to pay $250/night "standing fees" for the refrigeration truck while harvesting, plus an additional 10c/kg freight. The truck reaches capacity when 500 head of springbok have been loaded. In accordance with the veterinary regulations (which are especially strict for export), the animal must be completely bled and gutted within 30 minutes of being shot. The carcass must be delivered at the point of export within 72 hours after being shot. This means that only 2 nights are available for harvesting before the truck has to leave for Cape Town.

A group of 6-10 hunting teams with well-equipped vehicles and experienced personnel may harvest as many as 500-600 head of springbok/night. Their expenditure is approximately $5/springbok. With a profit of approximately $7.50/animal, a team may earn between $300-450/night.

For the export of venison, the game harvesting season starts at the beginning of April and ends 18 September. Table 2 presents harvest statistics for springbok, kudu, and oryx taken during the 1980 harvesting season.

The harvesting method developed in South West Africa has proved to be practical. During 1976-79, there has been a gradual increase in the total numbers of game animals used (Table 3); this corresponds with the growth rate of game populations. However, there has been a definite shift in the utilization of these animals, particularly noticeable with springbok. In 1979, the number of carcasses exported considerably exceeded the carcasses used locally. The same trend is noticeable with kudu. Game carcasses used locally represent those animals shot by the ranchers as rations for their laborers, by the so-called "meat hunters", and by trophy hunters. The low percentage of kudu used, as compared to springbok, is probably due to their more secretive habits and the brush encroachment in their haunts, which makes it extremely difficult to carry out harvesting operations there.

Table 2. Analysis of the 1980 game harvesting season for export purposes for 4 commercial harvesting teams operating on 268 ranches in South West Africa.

Species	N offered	N harvested	Carcasses approved for export	Carcasses condemned
Springbok	45,748	40,232	39,035	1,197
Kudu	4,610	3,496	3,442	54
Gemsbok	4,082	3,294	3,248	46

The increase in gross income for the territory in the form of foreign exchange from $1 million during 1978 to $3 million in 1979 indicates that game harvesting on private land has become an important method of game utilization in South West Africa.

Characteristics of Species Harvested

Data from 3 harvested species are presented: kudu and oryx in 1977-78 and sprinkbok data from 1978 only. These species differ in habitat preference, social structure, and time of reproduction. Springbok, primarily grazers, prefer open range where they occur for most of the year in large herds containing both sexes and both old and young animals. Most springboks lamb in the rainy season, January-April, but there may be a secondary lambing season in August-September of females that did not lamb in the main season. Kudu are browsers that prefer densely vegetated habitat. For most of the year, males and females move in discrete units, the 2 sexes mingling only during the short rutting season. Calves may be born throughout the year, but there is a peak of calving during January-April. Oryx frequently graze in open rangeland but move to thick vegetation when disturbed. Their social structure is not yet understood. They may calve throughout the year.

These habitat, social, and seasonal differences influence the numbers of animals harvested and may bias harvesting towards animals of a particular sex or age.

Male:Female Ratio.—Many ranchers were concerned that night harvesting might affect the sex ratios of their animals and thus the rate of reproduction

Table 3. The numbers of game harvested at night by 4 commercial game harvesting teams operating in South West Africa.

Year	Springbok	Kudu	Oryx	Total
1976	7,739	110	249	8,089
1977	23,764	1,117	1,237	26,100
1978	34,487	1,389	1,359	37,235
1979	43,663	3,547	3,020	50,230
1980	40,232	3,496	3,294	47,022
1981	43,327	1,141[a]	4,325	48,793
1982[b]	19,182	54	1,641	20,877

[a] The decline in kudu corresponds to a die-off resulting from rabies.
[b] The decline in this year represents a die-off resulting from a severe drought.

Table 4. Sex ratios of harvested kudu, oryx, and springbok in South West Africa.

Year	Kudu				Oryx				Springbok			
	Male	%	Female	%	Male	%	Female	%	Male	%	Female	%
1977	379	43.3	496	57.7	414	51.9	383	48.1				
1978	502	46.7	573	55.3	344	49.4	352	50.6	4,497	44.2	5,667	55.8

on their ranch. Analysis of the logsheet data shows no overall substantial departure from a 1:1 male:female sex ratio in the harvested animals, although there was some annual variation in the sex ratio that was observed (Table 4).

Age Classes.—Some ranchers insist that old animals be selectively harvested. This presents practical difficulties and is discouraged since it removes a selected segment of the population rather than a random one, the latter approach having a smaller impact on the population dynamics of the species.

The proportion of young animals in the total harvest was 55% in springbok, 43% in kudu, and 40% in oryx, though populations of all 3 species were believed to be increasing during 1977-78. The higher proportion of young springbok harvested may be the result of 2 factors. First, in springbok young animals rapidly attain adult size, whereas in the kudu and oryx young animals remain noticeably smaller than adults throughout their first years. Since the marksmen (paid by mass) tend to shoot the larger, heavier animals available, this may lead to a higher proportion of adult kudu and oryx being shot. Second, springbok have distinct lambing seasons, whereas both kudu and oryx may calve throughout the year, resulting in a bias towards adult animals in kudu and oryx harvesting.

Trophy Animals.—Ranchers also are concerned that night harvesting may adversely affect the numbers of trophy animals on their ranch, especially in kudu. Kudu trophy animals are those over 190 kg in weight, and field observations indicate that about 10% of male kudu fall in this category. Of male kudu harvested, 9% were in this weight class (Table 5), suggesting that there was no bias towards selective harvesting of trophy animals. Since springbok and oryx are not sexually dimorphic in size, the trophy situation does not arise.

Pregnant and Lactating Females.—Ranchers have expressed concern over the number of pregnant and lactating females killed in night harvesting. Table

Table 5. Age classes and mass of male kudu harvested during the 1977 season in South West Africa.

%	Approximate age	Mass (kg)
50.3	Young (2 years)	<120
25.1	Subadult	121 - 160
15.6	Adult	161 - 190
7.2	Prime adult	191 - 220
1.8	Old	>220

Table 6. Reproductive state of harvested female springbok, kudu, and oryx in South West Africa during 1977.

Month	Reproductive state			Total
	Inactive	Lactating	Pregnant (%)	
Springbok				
Mar	138	183	60(16.7)	381
Apr	130	172	78(20.5)	380
May	321	122	35(7.3)	478
Jun	215	71	24(7.7)	310
Jul	335	105	31(6.6)	471
Aug	473	60	87(14.0)	620
Sep	54	4	71(55.0)	129
Total	1,666	717	386	2,769
Kudu				
Mar	21	4	0	25
Apr	0	0	0	0
May	27	6	1(2.9)	34
Jun	77	7	1(1.2)	85
Jul	62	12	15(16.9)	89
Aug	0	0	0	0
Sep	28	11	73(65.1)	112
Total	215	40	90	340
Oryx				
Mar	10	2	14(53.8)	26
Apr	0	0	0	0
May	63	6	10(12.7)	79
Jun	59	7	18(21.4)	84
Jul	23	9	23(41.8)	55
Aug	43	4	10(7.5)	57
Sep	5	0	1(16.6)	6
Total	203	28	76	307

6 shows the distribution of the percentage of pregnancies among harvested springbok, kudu, and oryx during the harvest season. The proportion of pregnant and lactating females harvested could be reduced in springbok and kudu by harvesting in restricted seasons in relation to known peaks in lambing or calving. This harvesting would not be possible with the oryx since calving occurs throughout the year.

CONCLUSION

Successful harvesting for meat and an increased interest in trophy hunting has resulted in game playing an increasingly important role as a source of revenue in South West Africa. Ranchers are paying increased attention to the habitat requirements of game on their property (including the placing of water points, fences, etc.). The research findings summarized in this paper—

particularly the absence of bias (selective harvesting) in terms of sex ratios, age ratios, trophy kudu, and pregnant or lactating females—confirm the suitability of night harvesting as a management tool.

LITERATURE CITED

BIGALKE, R. C. 1958. On the present status of ungulate mammals in South West Africa. Mammalia 22:478-480.

JOUBERT, E. 1974. The development of wildlife utilization in South West Africa. J. Afr. Wildl. Manage. Assoc. 4:35-42.

———, and P. K. N. MOSTERT. 1975. Distribution patterns and status of some mammals in South West Africa. Madaqua 9:5-44.

———, P. A. J. BRAND, AND G. P. VISAGIE. 1983. An appraisal of the utilization of game on private land in South West Africa. Madaqua 13:197-219.

VAN DER SPUY, J. S. 1962. A preliminary report on the distribution of population of some ungulate mammals in South West Africa. Ann. Cape Prov. Mus. 2:41-52.

RESPONSE OF GAME BIRD POPULATIONS TO HARVEST STRATEGIES

REGULATIONS AND RESTRICTIONS PERTAINING TO BOBWHITE QUAIL HARVESTS IN THE SOUTHEAST

GEORGE A. HURST, Department of Wildlife and Fisheries, Mississippi State University, Mississippi State, MS 39762
WALTER ROSENE, 127 Oak Circle, Gadsden, AL 35092

Abstract: This paper summarizes state regulations pertaining to bobwhite quail (*Colinus virginianus*) hunting in 12 southeastern states and restrictions imposed on 19 southern quail plantations. Opening of the hunting season varied from 15 November-Thanksgiving Day and closed on 15 February-4 March on a statewide basis. The latest closing date was 15 March in the Georgia Piedmont. Total number of hunting days averaged 101 (87-115), but 3 states did not allow hunting on Sundays. Daily bag limit averaged 10 (7-12); however, 5 of the 11 game zones in South Carolina allowed 15 quail/day. Possession limits were usually twice the daily bag limit; only North Carolina with 100 and Virginia with 125 had season limits. Two states do not permit hunting if snow covers the ground, and 6 states have regulations against the use of electronic callers. In addition to state regulations, plantations have self-imposed restrictions to manage the harvest. Some plantations have a harvest quota limited to 40% of the estimated population.

KEY WORDS: Bobwhite quail, *Colinus virginianus*, Southeastern U.S., Quail hunting, Harvest regulations, Restrictions, Quail plantations.

Game management began by controlling the harvest, and law enforcement remains a basic management tool (Morse 1971). One of the first-order objectives of wildlife law enforcement is to assure that desired, calculated harvests be achieved (Giles 1978).

Game harvest management includes promulgation and enforcement of regulations and collecting data on harvest effort and rate (Steffen 1982). Research has been conducted on the effect of regulations on bobwhite quail populations and harvest (Baumgartner 1944, Bennitt 1951, Parmalee 1953, Gale 1954, Vance and Ellis 1972). However, little attention has been given to the principles of quail harvesting (Roseberry 1982) or bobwhite population responses to different harvest strategies and long-term yields (Roseberry 1979, 1981, Anderson and Burnham 1981, Doster et al. 1982).

Wildlife agencies in the southeastern United States attempt to manage the quail harvest by various regulations pertaining to the hunting season, limits, and methods. A special type of hunting occurs on privately owned and intensively managed quail plantations (clubs) in the South. Plantations must adhere to state regulations, but they also impose their own restrictions (Scott and Klimstra 1954). The objective of this paper is to summarize state regulations and plantation restrictions pertaining to the quail harvest.

We thank D. Wilson, J. Lewis, J. Durell, T. Dotson, C. Betsill, B. McTeer, L. Marcum, M. Olinde, F. Stanberry, F. Ward, R. Simpson, D. Cotton, I. Kenyon, J. Gwynn, B. Coggins, and other state wildlife agency personnel for their assistance. We also acknowledge the assistance of the plantation managers and owners.

METHODS

A questionnaire concerning bobwhite quail harvest regulations was mailed to 12 southeastern state wildlife agencies—Virginia, West Virginia, Kentucky, Tennessee, North Carolina, South Carolina, Florida, Georgia, Alabama, Mississippi, Louisiana, and Arkansas—and to Missouri, Texas, and Oklahoma. Each state cooperator was also telephoned to discuss certain regulations or the harvest management schemes.

A questionnaire dealing with restrictions on quail harvest was mailed to managers of plantations in Florida, Georgia, and South Carolina. Harvest management was also discussed via telephone with managers and at the annual South Carolina Plantation Managers meeting. The junior author has been the consultant to plantations for many years.

Regulations and restrictions presented here pertain to wild bobwhite quail, not pen-raised or released quail. States have special regulations for shooting preserves.

RESULTS

State Regulations

Quail hunting begins from early November to Thanksgiving Day in southeastern states (Table 1). Opening day is based on tradition, consideration of hunting conditions (e.g., cool weather), and estimated percentage of the quail population that is of acceptable size or age. Earlier opening dates were instituted in North Carolina and Tennessee because studies showed most quail were sufficiently large (old) to warrant earlier harvest (Weber 1961, McConnell 1972). In 1972, Mississippi changed opening day from early December to Thanksgiving Day after the presumed conflict with white-tailed deer (*Odocoileus virginianus*) hunting was resolved. Missouri changed its opening from 10 November to 1 November in 1983. The earliest opening date, 29 October, was reported in Texas.

Virginia starts quail hunting on 7 November west of the Blue Ridge Mountains and 21 November east of the Blue Ridge. Information gathered over the past 6 years indicated that the peak hatch was later in eastern Virginia. Texas has 2 opening dates, with an earlier date in west Texas where the peak hatch is thought to be earlier. A study is underway to determine if the split season is warranted in Texas. Oklahoma also has 2 opening dates because of a conflict with deer hunting.

The earliest closing date is 12 February in Kentucky, but most southeastern states close their quail season on the last day of February (early March in South Carolina and Florida). The latest closing date is 15 March in the Georgia Piedmont. Hunting in the Georgia Coastal Plain terminates on 28 February.

Table 1. Regulations pertaining to quail harvests in 12 southeastern states.

Regulation	Description (N of states)
Hunting season	
Starting date	5 Nov(1), 2nd-3rd week Nov(9), Thanksgiving Day (2)
Closing date	12 Feb(1), last day Feb(10), 1-4 Mar(2)
Total hunting days	87-88(2), 91-105(7), 111-116(3)
Statewide season	Yes(10), split season(2)
Legal hunting hours	½ hour before sunrise to ½ hour after sunset(9), daylight hours(1), no reg.(1)
Hunting allowed on Sunday	Yes(9), no(3)
Limits	
Daily	7(1), 8(3), 10(3), 12(4), 10-12-15(1)
Season	No limit(10), 100(1), 125(1)
Possession	2× daily limit(9), 3× daily(1), no limit(1), equal to aggregate of daily limits(1)
Equipment	
Shotgun	Any gauge up to 10 gauge(12)
Shot size	Any or not larger than No. 4 shot
N shells/gun	No limit(8), maximum 3 shells/gun(4)
Electronic callers	No regulation(6), illegal(6)
General	
Bait or trap	Illegal(12)
Vehicles	Illegal to shoot from(12)
Roads, rights-of-way	Illegal to shoot from or across(12)
Weather	Illegal to hunt quail if snow covers the ground(2), severe flood(1)
Hunting access	Written or verbal permission required from private landowners(11), permission not required(1)
Use of dogs for hunting	Not required(12)

Total quail hunting days will average 101 in 1983-84 in the 12 southeastern states. The longest seasons occur in the Georgia Piedmont (115 days), Florida (114 days), and Tennessee (111 days). The shortest seasons occur in Virginia (87 days) and North Carolina (88 days) because these states, and West Virginia, do not allow hunting on Sundays. Missouri increased its season from 52 to 76 days in 1983. Texas has a 92-day season and Oklahoma either a 74- or 84-day season, but the latter state does not permit hunting on Wednesdays or Sundays on private land. Hunting is allowed on all days on open, public land.

Opening and closing dates vary within states on wildlife management areas and on some federally owned properties. On those areas hunting is confined to certain days of the week, and special permits or fees may be required.

Daily bag limit averaged 10 for the 1982-83 season in southeastern states and varied from 7 in West Virginia to 15 in 5 of the 11 game zones in South Carolina, which have a bag limit of 10, 12, or 15 depending on what game zone is hunted. Mississippi increased its bag limit from 8 (1967) to 10 (1968) and to 12 in 1971. Missouri decreased the bag limit from 10 to 8 in 1972 and reduced it to 6 in 1977, following a severe winter, but increased the limit to 8 in 1981. Texas is the only state that adjusts the bag limit (12, 16, or 20) according to an estimate of annual production.

A season limit is present in North Carolina (100) and Virginia (125). Possession limits are generally twice the daily bag limit. Virginia does not have a possession limit.

In addition to setting regulations, 10 southeastern states conduct annual or less frequent (i.e. every 2-3 years) surveys to assess quail hunting effort and harvest during the previous year. Georgia and Virginia gather more data from quail hunter report cards or cooperators. Texas, Oklahoma, and Missouri conduct annual small game surveys, with Missouri obtaining the most detailed information.

Plantation Restrictions

Information was obtained from 19 plantations. Hunting on these plantations is restricted to club members and guests. Members are restricted to 2-5 weeks of hunting/season, and all hunts are scheduled. Hunting hours are from 0930-1000 hours to about 1300 hours, then a 1.5-hour break is taken, and hunting resumes at 1430 hours for about 2 hours (Table 2).

Small plantations (1,215 ha) restrict hunting to 1 party, 2 hunters/day, but larger plantations (2,228 ha) accommodate 2-3 parties/day. Plantations that frequently had 2 parties/day averaged 172 hunting days/year, and plantations that frequently had 2 or 3 parties/day averaged 210 and 231 hunting days/year, respectively. Because of a conservative attitude, most plantations hunt fewer days than state regulations permit. Also, if the allowable harvest is approached, hunting is restricted (e.g., shooting only 1 bird/covey). Hunting might be modified to allow management practices, such as controlled burning in February.

Plantations have well-defined hunting areas or shooting courses to allow hunting on a rotational basis. Hunting is restricted to once/week or even at longer intervals on a given course. Most plantations hunt mornings and afternoons but on different courses. Hunting on Sunday is disallowed on all plantations to give employees a day off, rest dogs and horses, and permit members to travel.

All plantations allow covey and single-bird shooting, but 15 restrict the number of birds removed from a covey on any 1 day to 3-4. If 3 quail are harvested on the initial covey rise, hunting "singles" is not allowed on 14 plantations. Seventeen plantations will not shoot a covey down below 8 birds.

Most hunters use double-barreled shotguns with number 8 shot, and 7 plantations will not allow pumps or semiautomatic guns. If the latter guns are permitted, the number of shells/gun is often restricted to 2 or 3. Eighteen plantations allow only 2 hunters/covey rise.

All plantations keep records of the hunts and harvest, and many collect wings from harvested quail to obtain data on sex and age ratios and hatch dates (Rosene 1969). Hunting and harvest records are maintained over many years.

Table 2. Questions and responses pertaining to quail harvest restrictions on 19 southern quail plantations.

Question	Response (N of plantations)
Is your hunting season as long as the state's	Yes(14), no(5)
What is the avg. N days hunted/season	48(16), with range of 20-95 for 1 party(2 hunters) days
What is the avg. hours hunted/day	5.13(16) for 1 party hunts
Do you hunt only in morning	Yes(1), no(18)
Do you hunt only in afternoon	Yes(5), no(14)
Do you hunt morning and afternoon	Yes(13), no(6)
Do you hunt on Sundays	Yes(0), no(19)
Do you hunt by	Horseback(17), shooting buggy(12), walk(5), mixed(15)
Do you restrict hunting because of rain/cold	Yes(2/1), no(17/18)
Do you restrict gun type	Yes(7), no(12); no pump or semi-auto
Do you restrict N shells/gun	Yes(9), no(11); 2(4) 3(5)
Do you restrict N guns/covey rise	Yes(18), no(1); 2(18) 3(1)
Do you hunt coveys and singles	Yes(19), no(0)
Do you restrict N quail harvested/covey/hunt	Yes(15), no(1); 3(13), 3-4(1), 4(1)
Do you reduce covey size to <8	Yes(2), no(17)
How often is an area (shooting course) hunted	1/7-10 days(15), 1/14-21 days(2), 1/month(2)
Do you keep hunt and harvest records	Yes(19), no(0)
Do you have a bag limit/party/day	Yes(15), no(4)
Do you have a total plantation bag limit for the year	Yes(9), no(9)
Do you set a plantation harvest quota	Yes(11), no(8)

Most plantations allow the same daily bag limit as the state regulation, but several restrict the daily limit to less than allowed by the state. A party bag limit (i.e., twice the daily limit) is in effect on 15 plantations. One plantation has a member limit, restricting the member and his guest to 100-300 quail/season, depending on the estimated quail population size.

The number of crippled quail is recorded by some plantations, but these quail are not included in any limit. Plantations generally use 2 pointing-retrieving dogs/hunt and might have a dog on the hunt that is used solely to find and retrieve dead and crippled quail.

Nine plantations reported a plantation bag limit, which is the total allowable harvest/season. This limit, an educated guess, is based on the general success of the reproductive effort (hatch) and past harvest records. Eleven plantations have a more sophisticated method of determining a plantation harvest quota. Number, size, and location of coveys is determined from September-December by field hands, dog trainers, guides, and the manager. Using this information, the manager and plantation consultant estimate the size of the quail population. The plantation harvest quota is then set at 40% of the estimated total population. Plantation managers and the consultant reported that the quota has never been attained.

DISCUSSION

Quail harvest regulations have developed from tradition, emotion, experience, biopolitics, sportsmen's perceptions, and research. Regulations dealing with season dates and total number of hunting days differ slightly in the southeastern states. No quail hunting on Sundays decreases total number of hunting days and greatly reduces hunting on weekends.

Daily bag limits are more liberal, 10-12, in the deep south than in the more northerly southeastern states that allow 7 or 8 birds/day. Do current quail regulations, allowing 7-15 quail/day for 87-100+ days, affect the quail harvest? Game harvest surveys in 3 deep-south states (Mississippi, Alabama, and Louisiana), reported that the average daily kill was 2.9-3.1 quail (Prickett 1981, Kelley 1982, Steffen 1982). The number of quail bagged/day by hunters considered average in Virginia was 1.2, and above-average hunters averaged 3.2 (I. L. Kenyon, unpubl. data). Hunters in the 3 deep-south states hunted 7-8 days/year and harvested an average of 17-25 quail/year. Avid quail hunters averaged 6.4 quail/day, 47 days-afield, and 298 quail/year in Mississippi (Hurst and Warren 1982).

Many variables enter into the quail harvest including quail density and behavior; cover; number of quality places to hunt; weather (especially on weekends and holidays); hunter effort, experiences, and skills; and bird dog quality. Hunting regulations do not consider any of these variables.

One function of regulations is to distribute the harvest on an equitable basis, or the fair-share approach. A season limit of quail seemingly applies only to avid hunters. Most southeastern states do not have a season limit. Regulations provide guidelines for quail hunter behavior. Undoubtedly, regulations involve public relations and agency credibility. Regulations also serve to protect the sport of quail hunting through public perceptions of a managed harvest.

Quail hunting has certain unwritten tenets or rules that govern hunter behavior or hunting methods. These rules are generally self-imposed traditions that may affect total harvest. For example, it is unethical to shoot quail on the ground, but only Oklahoma declares "ground shooting" illegal. No state requires quail hunters to use trained bird dogs (or retrievers), but hunting without dogs is not typical quail hunting.

Plantations exemplify traditional southern quail hunting, and most plantations abide by state regulations as well as self-imposed restrictions. A considerable financial and managerial investment is made annually to maximize quail production. Harvest management is obtained by restrictions on hunting methods and limits and by restricting the harvest to 40% of the estimated population. A target harvest rate of 40-45% seems appropriate for Illinois (Roseberry 1979).

Harvest effort and rate can be managed on plantations, relatively small areas compared to a whole state. State wildlife agencies must rely on a general framework of regulations to control the harvest. In the past, many southeastern states varied regulations with fluctuations in quail populations and public perceptions (Mosby and Overton 1950, Lay 1954, Allen and Waters 1963). Roseberry (1979) suggested that the quail hunting season in Illinois be shortened by about 2 weeks when populations were down. Current regulations in the southeast are liberal, and most agencies do not envision any major changes in the near future. The long-term decline in quail habitat and populations has state agencies concerned, but changes in regulations do not seem imminent, despite the realities of current demands on a shrinking resource (Roseberry 1979).

LITERATURE CITED

ALLEN, R. H., AND R. E. WATERS. 1963. Bobwhite quail management: facts and fiction. Ala. Dep. Conserv. and Nat. Resour. Bull. 5. 40pp.

ANDERSON, D. R., AND K. P. BURNHAM. 1981. Bobwhite population responses to exploitation: 2 problems. J. Wildl. Manage. 45:1052-1054.

BAUMGARTNER, F. M. 1944. Bobwhite quail populations on hunted vs. protected areas. J. Wildl. Manage. 8:259-260.

BENNITT, R. 1951. Some aspects of Missouri quail and quail hunting (1938-1948). Mo. Conserv. Comm. Tech. Bull. 2. 51pp.

DOSTER, G. L., F. E. KELLOGG, W. R. DAVIDSON, AND W. M. MARTIN. 1982. Hunter success and crippling losses for bobwhite quail. Pages 45-47 in F. Schitoskey, Jr., E. C. Schitoskey, and L. G. Talent, eds. Proc. 2nd Natl. Bobwhite Quail Symp., Oklahoma State Univ., Stillwater.

GALE, L. R. 1954. The effects of season changes on hunting effort and game kill. Proc. Annu. Conf. Southeast. Assoc. Game and Fish Comm. 8:117-120.

GILES, R. H., JR. 1978. Wildlife management. W. H. Freeman and Co., San Francisco, Calif. 416pp.

HURST, G. A., AND R. C. WARREN. 1982. Harvest rates and efforts of avid quail hunters in east central Mississippi. Pages 48-50 in F. Schitoskey, Jr., E. C. Schitoskey, and L. G. Talent, eds. Proc. 2nd Natl. Bobwhite Quail Symp., Oklahoma State Univ., Stillwater.

KELLEY, W. F. 1982. Annual report—game kill survey in Alabama. Ala. Dep. Conserv. Fed. Aid Proj. W-35-28. Study VI. 17pp.

LAY, D. W. 1954. Quail management handbook for east Texas. Tex. Parks and Wildl. Dep. Bull. 34. 46pp.

MCCONNELL, C. A. 1972. Early quail hunting season in Tennessee: reasons and results. Pages 100-115 in J. A. Morrison and J. C. Lewis, eds. Proc. 1st Natl. Bobwhite Quail Symp. Oklahoma State Univ., Stillwater.

MORSE, W. B. 1971. Law enforcement—a tool of management. Pages 120-123 in R. D. Teague, ed. A manual of wildlife conservation. The Wildlife Society, Washington, D.C.

MOSBY, H. S., AND W. S. OVERTON. 1950. Fluctuations in the quail population on the Virginia Polytechnic Institute farms. Trans. North Am. Wildl. Conf. 15:347-355.

PARMALEE, P. W. 1953. Hunting pressure and its effect on bobwhite quail populations in east central Texas. J. Wildl. Manage. 17:341-345.

PRICKETT, T. 1981. Quail hunters survey, 1975-79. La. Dep. Wildl. and Fish., Baton Rouge. 1pp.

ROSEBERRY, J. L. 1979. Bobwhite population responses to exploitation: real and simulated. J. Wildl. Manage. 43:285-305.

———. 1981. Bobwhite population responses: a reply. J. Wildl. Manage. 45:1054-1056.

———. 1982. Sustained harvest of bobwhite populations. Pages 51-56 in F. Schitoskey, Jr., E. C. Schitoskey, and L. G. Talent, eds. Proc. 2nd Natl. Bobwhite Quail Symp., Oklahoma State Univ., Stillwater.

ROSENE, W. 1969. The bobwhite quail: its life and management. Rutgers Univ. Press, New Brunswick, N.J. 418pp.

SCOTT, T. G., AND W. D. KLIMSTRA. 1954. Report on a visit to quail management areas in southeastern United States. Ill. Wildl. 9:5-9.

STEFFEN, D. E. 1982. Mississippi mail survey of game harvest and hunter effort for 1981-82. Miss. Dep. Wildl. Conserv. Annu. Report, Fed. Aid Proj. W-48-28. Study VI-1. 18pp.

VANCE, D. R., AND J. A. ELLIS. 1972. Bobwhite populations and hunting on Illinois public hunting areas. Pages 165-174 *in* J. A. Morrison and J. C. Lewis, eds. Proc. 1st Natl. Bobwhite Quail Symp. Oklahoma State Univ., Stillwater.

WEBER, A. J. 1961. Quail wings tell the story. Wildl. in N.C. 25:6-7.

FEBRUARY HUNTING OF AMERICAN WOODCOCK: BREEDING IMPLICATIONS

R. MONTAGUE WHITING, JR., School of Forestry, Stephen F. Austin State University[a], Nacogdoches, TX 75962

RONNIE R. GEORGE, Texas Parks and Wildlife Department, Austin, TX 78744

M. KEITH CAUSEY, Department of Zoology-Entomology and Alabama Agriculture Experiment Station, Auburn University, Auburn, AL 36849

THOMAS H. ROBERTS[b], Department of Wildlife and Fisheries, Mississippi State University, Mississippi State, MS 39762

Abstract: Wintering range of American woodcock (*Scolopax minor*) includes portions of 12 southern states. Several of these states allow woodcock hunting during February. Although these states are also within the species' breeding range, until recently there have been few investigations of breeding activity. Recent studies have shown that considerable breeding and nesting takes place in the South during late winter and early spring. From 1978 to 1983, 7 states permitted February hunting. Hunting season during that month lasted an average of 18.1 days, 27.8% of the 65 days federal regulations allow; 14.2% of the total season's bag was taken during that time period. Thus, woodcock were not harvested in greater proportions during February than during the entire season. Although most males bagged during February were probably sexually mature, we can draw no strong conclusions on the impacts of such harvest. We do suggest, however, that reducing the number of dominant males in the breeding population could result in a decrease in breeding potential. Slightly over 35% of February-shot adult females had ovarian follicles 5.0 mm or larger in diameter and were thus approaching egg laying. If we use state and U.S. Fish and Wildlife Service estimates, this indicates an average annual February kill of 1,840 gravid adult females/state. If woodcock hunting increases in popularity, February seasons could take an undesirable number of nesting hens. Presently 3 southern states have seasons that extend from late November to late January. We believe these dates to be biologically satisfactory; only 7 of 164 adult females taken in 7 southern states during January had enlarged follicles.

KEY WORDS: *Scolopax minor*, Woodcock, Woodcock nesting, Woodcock breeding, Woodcock harvest.

The known breeding range of American woodcock extends southward almost to the Gulf of Mexico, thus overlapping most of the species' wintering range (Owen 1977). Until recently, incidence of woodcock breeding in the South was considered low and of little consequence (Dwyer n.d., Causey 1981). Studies conducted since about 1970 have indicated otherwise.

Male breeding readiness as indicated by testicular recrudescence has been widely reported throughout the South (Stamps and Doerr 1977, Roberts and Dimmick 1978, Pace and Wood 1979, Whiting and Boggus 1982). Recrudescence begins in early December and is completed in mid-February (Stamps and Doerr 1977, Roberts and Dimmick 1978, Whiting and Boggus 1982). Initiation of courtship behavior appears to be somewhat weather

---

[a] In cooperation with USDA Forest Service, Southern Forest Experiment Station, Wildlife Habitat and Silviculture Laboratory, Nacogdoches, TX 75962.

[b] Present address: Waterways Experiment Station, Corps of Engineers, Vicksburg, MS 39180.

dependent and can occur as early as mid-November (Roboski and Causey 1981). However, regular courtship behavior generally starts about 1 January in the southern portions of the wintering range (Glasgow 1958, Whiting and Boggus 1982).

Causey et al. (1974) recorded nesting and fledging activity in Alabama comparable to that in more northern states. Their work indicated that hens and chicks disperse after brood breakup (Horton and Causey 1981), and at least 1 banded chick migrated north (Causey et al. 1979). From 1974 to 1980, nesting dates ranged from 25 January to 13 June, with nesting peaks ranging from 15 February to 28 March (Causey 1981, Roboski and Causey 1981). Stamps and Doerr (1977) speculated that when an ovarian follicle is 4.0 mm or larger in diameter it is approaching a rapid eruption stage whereby the follicle develops into a shelled egg within 4 days. In North Carolina, they noted that 9 of 13 woodcock hens collected during February were thus approaching egg laying.

In Tennessee, Roberts and Dimmick (1978) reported 44 and 52% of the females collected in February 1977 and 1978, respectively, had follicles 4.0 mm or larger. They suggested that 5.0 mm might better define the point of rapid eruption. Whiting and Boggus (1982) in East Texas found that 20% of the adult hens collected in February 1978 and 1979 had follicles 5.0 mm and larger and 38% were 4.0 mm or larger. No subadult hens ($N = 55$) had follicles exceeding 4.0 mm. They also noted that follicle diameter was significantly related to weight of the adult hens. They used these findings to suggest that only adult hens reach breeding readiness in East Texas. In Alabama, 6 and 28% of the adult hens collected in February 1979 and 1980, respectively, had spermatozoa in the uterovaginal glands. Yellow-yolked follicles were the best indicator of whether a bird had bred or would soon do so. When we used that criteria, 38% of the February 1980 birds were judged to be southern nesters (Walker and Causey 1982).

At least 2 studies have indicated that few woodcock nested in the South. Dwyer (n.d.) examined 174 females killed in Georgia, Louisiana, and Mississippi during January-February of 1977-78 and found only 4 with ova larger than 3.0 mm. However, only 20 birds were killed in February. Pace and Wood (1979) examined ova from 24 birds collected in coastal South Carolina during February 1979 and found that only 2 exceeded 4.0 mm. The objective of this paper is to examine February woodcock hunting and its potential effects on breeding.

We are indebted to J. Tautin, U.S. Fish and Wildlife Service (USFWS), for providing woodcock wing survey data and harvest estimates. W. Mozina compiled courtship flight data, J. Roese performed statistical tests, and R. N. Wilkins made editorial comments.

METHODS

Questionnaires were sent to Alabama, Arkansas, Florida, Georgia, Louisiana, Mississippi, North Carolina, Oklahoma, South Carolina,

Tennessee, Texas, and Virginia asking for information on season dates and estimated season and February kills for the 1977-78 through 1982-83 hunting seasons. Seven states returned the questionnaires; follow-up phone calls obtained data from the remainder. USFWS woodcock wing collection survey data were used to estimate, by state, the proportions of the following:

1. Total season's bag that was killed in February.
2. Total season's bag of adult hens that was killed in February.
3. Total season's bag that was adult hens.
4. February bag that was adult hens.

Students' t-tests were used to compare the proportions of the hunting seasons that occurred in February vs. 1 and 2 above and to compare between 3 and 4 above. Because of small sample sizes from the other states, we used Louisiana data only in these comparisons. We used a null hypothesis of no difference between groups being tested and a significance level of 0.10. Finally, numbers of woodcock killed by purchasers of federal duck stamps by year and by state were obtained from the USFWS, Office of Migratory Bird Management, Laurel, Maryland (J. Tautin, pers. commun.).

In Texas, male courtship was monitored on singing grounds during January, February, and early March during 1978-83. Data recorded included numbers of nuptial males and nuptial flights by date. These data were grouped by 5-day periods; then the average numbers of nuptial birds and flights/observer-day during the period were determined.

Woodcock were collected in 5 states during February 1977-83. Females were separated into adult or subadult age classes (Martin 1964); birds hatched the previous spring were classified as subadults, all others as adults. We measured diameter of the largest ovarian follicle to the nearest 0.5 mm for both age classes. If follicle diameter was 5.0 mm or larger, we considered it to be in the stage of rapid development, with the bird presumably approaching egg laying. Many females were taken during the legal hunting season; others, especially in Alabama and Texas, were collected under state and federal permits.

RESULTS AND DISCUSSION

During the 1977-78 through 1982-83 hunting seasons, 7 of 12 southern states allowed February woodcock hunting (Table 1). It was permitted in Florida, Louisiana, Mississippi, and Tennessee every year, in Arkansas 2 years, and in South Carolina and Texas for 1 year. Tennessee is the only state that had a split season, with 28 hunting days in February. Changes in season dates of several states indicate that game and fish agencies were not satisfied with previous year's dates. Lack of information concerning woodcock biology and management may be a reason for shifting season dates. For example, only Alabama and Georgia provided estimated annual kills for all years in question.

State estimates of kills are generally imprecise with wide confidence intervals (Table 2). Federal estimates of woodcock killed by duck stamp purchasers

Table 1. Dates of legal woodcock hunting seasons in states allowing February hunting during 1977-78 through 1982-83. Also included are states with estimated season kills.

State	Year					
	1977-78	1978-79	1979-80	1980-81	1981-82	1982-83
AL	11/28-1/31	11/28-1/31	11/28-1/31	11/28-1/31	11/28-1/31	11/28-1/31
AR	12/1-2/3	12/1-2/3	11/15-1/18	11/15-1/17	11/1-1/4	11/1-1/4
FL	12/17-2/19	12/16-2/18	12/18-2/20	12/6-2/8	12/5-2/7	12/4-2/6
GA	11/20-1/22	11/20-1/21	11/20-1/20	11/20-1/18	11/20-1/24	11/20-1/23
LA	12/3-2/5	12/9-2/11	12/8-2/20	12/13-2/15	12/12-2/14	12/10-2/13
MS	12/10-2/12	12/12-2/18	12/15-2/17	12/20-2/22	12/26-2/28	12/25-2/27
SC	11/24-1/27	11/23-1/26	11/22-1/25	12/12-2/14	11/27-1/30	11/25-1/28
TN	10/15-11/20, 2/1-2/28	10/21-11/26, 2/1-2/28	10/20-11/25, 2/2-2/29	10/18-11/23, 2/1-2/28	10/17-11/22, 2/1-2/28	10/16-11/21, 2/1-2/28
TX	11/19-1/22	11/18-1/21	11/17-1/20	11/15-1/18	12/12-2/14	11/27-1/30

are much lower, ranging from 11.4 to 62.5% and averaging 31.3% of state estimates. Federal estimates are used primarily as trend indicators (Martin 1979).

Using wing data from Louisiana, we found no significant differences in the average proportions of legal hunting days and of all birds ($P = 0.14$) or adult females ($P = 0.35$) killed during February (Table 3). These data suggest that in Louisiana, at least, woodcock are not being harvested in greater proportions during February than during the entire season. The percentage of adult females in the February bag did not differ significantly from the

Table 2. State and federal estimates of woodcock killed by state and year.

State	Source	Estimated harvest						
		Year						
		1977-78	1978-79	1979-80	1980-81	1981-82	1982-83	Average[a]
AL	State	40,000	23,000	25,000	33,000	21,000		28,400
	Federal	8,000	4,500	4,800	5,100	2,400	2,700	4,583
AR	State							
	Federal	20,600	6,100	7,600	6,400	5,400	4,800	8,483
FL	State	14,188		10,975	15,898	6,724		11,946
	Federal	6,600	5,700	4,000	5,300	4,200	4,000	4,967
GA	State	21,350	29,687	30,189	17,743	12,194		22,233
	Federal	9,900	6,700	6,000	6,700	4,400	4,300	6,500
LA	State							
	Federal	130,300	214,800	146,600	327,800	211,400	111,100	190,333
MS	State				59,707	56,520		58,114
	Federal	10,500	11,000	11,900	21,700	7,300	8,800	12,283
SC	State		22,830			20,310		21,570
	Federal	7,700	8,900	6,200	7,500	7,300	4,400	7,000
TN	State							
	Federal	3,700	9,400	6,300	2,800	4,400	4,700	5,217
TX	State							
	Federal	15,900	6,700	10,400	16,900	5,200	5,500	10,100

[a] Years with no harvest estimates are excluded.

Table 3. Characteristics of February woodcock hunting seasons by state with proportions of total birds bagged during February and of adult hens in the bag during the entire season and during February. Harvest data proportions are based on USFWS wing survey samples.

State	N years with Feb hunting seasons	Avg. length of Feb season		% birds bagged in Feb		% adult females in bag			
		N days	% total			Throughout season		Feb only	
AR	2	3.0	4.6	7.9	(3)[a]	18.4	(7)	16.1	(1)
FL	6	20.0	30.8	6.2	(10)	5.2	(16)	13.1	(3)
LA	6	11.3	17.4	12.4	(789)	21.8	(1,378)	25.5	(206)
MS	6	19.4	29.8	18.3	(77)	26.0	(91)	21.0	(18)
SC	1	14.0	21.5	27.3	(12)	27.2	(12)	25.0	(3)
TN	6	28.0	43.1	21.4	(51)	18.6	(41)	18.3	(13)
TX	1	14.0	21.5	47.6	(20)	14.9	(6)	10.0	(2)
Weighted average		18.1	27.8	14.2		21.8		24.5	

[a] = sample size of numerator.

percentage in the season-long bag ($P = 0.19$), indicating that adult females were not discriminated against by February hunting in Louisiana during the study years. These tests covered only 6 years, thus n = 6; a larger sample size might have changed the results (J. Roese, pers. commun.).

Males

Roberts (1980) reported that 76% of male testes 6.0 mm or longer contained spermatozoa in seminiferous tubes; thus they were from sexually mature birds. All 29 birds he collected in Louisiana, Mississippi, and Tennessee after 1 February had testes 6.0 mm or longer. Whiting and Boggus (1982) reported similar findings in East Texas. Obviously, many males are sexually mature by 1 February.

Peaks of courtship activity indicate that male reproductive maturation is complete (Whiting and Boggus 1982). In Texas, except for 1979, numbers of nuptial males peaked between 13 and 17 February (Table 4). The major peaks for numbers of flights occurred during the same period for 3 of the 6 study years. These data suggest that by 15 February virtually all male woodcock are sexually mature.

February hunting probably discriminates against dominant male woodcock. As courtship activity peaks, males concentrate near early-successional-stage singing grounds (T. G. Boggus and R. M. Whiting, unpubl. data). This makes them more accessible to hunters, especially quail hunters. Secondly, because of aerial and terrestrial courting activity, they are more visible. Finally, dominant males appear to be faithful to a particular site on a singing ground, and aerial performances last later in the morning as the season progresses. Therefore, it would not be especially difficult for a hunter to bag actively courting males.

As woodcock are polygamous, it is possible that there are no adverse biological impacts of harvesting courting males. Several studies have shown

Table 4. Dates of peaks of woodcock courtship activity in East Texas as indicated by average numbers of nuptial males and flights/observer-day. Data are grouped by 5-day periods; date shown is third day of the period.

Year	Nuptial birds	Nuptial flights	
		Minor	Major
1978	15 Feb	5 Feb	15 Feb
1979	25 Feb	26 Jan	25 Feb
1980	15 Feb	10 Feb	20 Feb
1981	15 Feb	31 Jan	15 Feb
1982	15 Feb	20 Feb	31 Jan
1983	15 Feb	31 Jan	15 Feb

that when a dominant male is removed from a singing ground, another soon takes its place (Sheldon 1967, Goudy et al. 1970). If, however, dominant (and presumably older) males are heavily harvested during late hunting seasons, there is some evidence that breeding success could be adversely impacted. In Michigan, Whitcomb (1974) found that prior to mid-May, 72% of the males occupying singing grounds were mature birds, whereas later in the breeding season only 36% were mature birds. This suggests that older males are more efficient at establishing and maintaining territories during the peak breeding period and are therefore needed for the species to maintain optimum reproductive efficiency. This relationship should be clarified if southern states continue with February hunting seasons.

Females

The effect of February hunting is more obvious on females. Ovarian follicles of 35.3% of the adult hens collected were 5.0 mm or larger in diameter (Table 5). Only 3.9% of the subadult hens had ova that size. This strongly suggests that a large proportion of the adult females harvested in February were approaching egg laying.

The proportions of gravid adult hens varied widely during the sample years, indicating that the percentages of adult hens that nest in the South do likewise. Causes of this variation are probably weather related. However, the weather factors involved and their timing are unclear. For example, Walker and Causey (1982) suggest that below normal January temperatures contributed to reduced nesting in Alabama during February 1979. Conversely, in East Texas there were more freezing days in January 1982 (16) than normal (14), yet woodcock nesting incidence was higher and earlier than in 1978 or 1979 (R. M. Whiting, unpubl. data). In 1982 only, the major peak for number of nuptial flights occurred in January, and it preceded the minor peak (Table 4). Unseasonably warm weather during December 1981 apparently stimulated some males to begin regular courtship flights by 16 December. This activity may have triggered the onset of breeding readiness in adult females. Research on the weather factors that cause the variation in incidence and dates of nesting of woodcock is needed.

Table 5. Follicle diameters of female woodcock collected during February in 5 southern states, 1977-83.

Year	State	Collection dates	Ovaries ≥ 5.0 mm					
			Adult females			Subadult females		
			Total	N	%	Total	N	%
1977	AL	1-24 Feb	9	1	11.1	26	0	0.0
	TN	24-28 Feb	8	5	62.5	16	3	18.7
1978	TN	16-28 Feb	14	3	21.4	5	1	20.0
	TX	1-28 Feb	26	6	23.1	9	0	0.0
1979	AL	1-27 Feb	35	7	20.0	11	0	0.0
	LA	1-26 Feb	4	0	0.0	6	0	0.0
	MS	1-26 Feb	5	0	0.0	1	0	0.0
	TN	1-26 Feb	1	1	100.0	0	0	0.0
	TX	1-28 Feb	9	2	22.2	10	0	0.0
1980	AL	1-29 Feb	26	16	61.5	13	1	7.7
	TX	1-2 Feb	1	1	100.0	0	0	0.0
1982	TX	1-14 Feb	27	15	55.5	33	0	0.0
1983	LA	12-13 Feb	5	3	60.0	4	0	0.0
	Summary		170	60	35.3	134	5	3.9

From the data presented, we derived an estimate of the average number of gravid adult females annually harvested during February portions of the 1977-78 through 1982-83 hunting season. An estimated 1,313,700 birds were killed by federal duck stamp purchasers during the 28 seasons that included a portion of February (Tables 1 and 2). If duck stamp purchasers bagged 31.3% of all woodcock harvested, then the total harvest was 4,190,700. The February portion of this was 14.2% (Table 3), equating to 595,080 birds; 24.5% (Table 3) or 145,790 birds were adult females, and 35.3% of these were gravid (Table 5); therefore, an estimated 51,470 gravid adult females were killed during the 28 hunting seasons or 1,840 such birds every season. Four states had February hunting seasons during 1982-83, so an estimated 7,350 potentially nesting females were bagged. Although this is only 1.8% of the total bag of those states, this number will certainly increase if woodcock hunting continues to gain popularity.

Although the impact of February harvesting of gravid females on the continental woodcock population is probably very slight, on a regional basis it could be much more significant. Late hunting seasons in southern states could be significantly impacting local breeding populations by reducing the number of woodcock that are genetically predisposed to breed in the South.

In our opinion, another major problem with February hunting involves aesthetics and management credibility. We have no data on hunter reaction to shooting a bird and then discovering that it was a hen that flushed from a nest. From personal experience and from talking with other hunters who have done it, however, it is unpleasant. Such an event reduces the quality of the hunt (Clarke 1971), causing both novice and experienced hunters to question management strategies regarding hunting season dates, and it certainly does little for the image of sport hunting.

CONCLUSIONS

Seven southern states allowed woodcock hunting in February from the 1977-78 through 1982-83 seasons; an average of 27.8% of the total season lengths occurred during that month. Most males killed in early February were probably sexually mature; virtually all were sexually mature by mid-February. There is no scientific information on the effects of harvesting sexually mature male woodcock. Dominant males are probably more susceptible to harvest than subdominants, which could result in reducing reproductive efficiency of the species. As 35.3% of the adult females collected during February were gravid, hunting during that month may have an adverse impact. The contribution of hens that nest in the South to the continental population is unknown, as is the distribution of hens and chicks after dispersal. Until these implied questions are answered with sound research, restriction of February woodcock hunting should be considered, especially in the Gulf Coast states. During the 1982-83 hunting season, Alabama, South Carolina, and Texas had season dates from late November through January. Based on biological and ethical considerations, these dates would seem to be satisfactory; only 7 of 164 (4.3%) adult females we collected in 7 southern states during January had enlarged ovaries.

LITERATURE CITED

CAUSEY, M. K. 1981. Alabama woodcock investigation. Ala. Dep. Conserv. and Nat. Resour. Final Report, Fed. Aid Proj. W-44-5. Study II. 23pp.

———, J. ROBOSKI, AND G. HORTON. 1974. Nesting activities of the American woodcock (*Philohela minor* Gmelin) in Alabama. Proc. Am. Woodcock Workshop 5:1-12.

———, G. HORTON, J. ROBOSKI, R. JOHNSON, AND P. MASON. 1979. American woodcock hatched in Alabama killed in Michigan. Wilson Bull. 91:463-464.

CLARKE, C. H. D. 1971. Hunting and fishing values and concepts. Pages 41-43 *in* R. D. Teague, ed. A manual of wildlife conservation. The Wildlife Society, Washington, D.C.

DWYER, T. J. No date. Evaluation of the incidence of nesting by woodcock in the southern United States and its importance in rangewide recruitment. U.S. Dep. Inter., Fish and Wildl. Serv., Migratory Bird and Habitat Research Lab., Patuxent Wildl. Res. Center, Laurel, Md. Final Report, Work Unit No. 903.08. 7pp.

GLASGOW, L. L. 1958. Contributions to the knowledge of the ecology of the American woodcock, *Philohela minor* (Gmelin), on the wintering range in Louisiana. Ph.D. Thesis. Texas A&M College, College Station. 153pp.

GOUDY, W. H., R. C. KLETZLY, AND J. C. RIEFFENBERGER. 1970. Characteristics of a heavily hunted woodcock population in West Virginia. Trans. North Am. Wildl. and Nat. Resour. Conf. 35:183-195.

HORTON, G. I., AND M. K. CAUSEY. 1981. Dispersal of American woodcock in central Alabama after brood breakup. J. Wildl. Manage. 45:1058-1061.

MARTIN, E. M. 1979. Hunting and harvest trends for migratory game birds other than waterfowl: 1964-76. U.S. Dep. Inter. Fish and Wildl. Serv. Spec. Sci. Report - Wildl. 218. 37pp.

MARTIN, F. W. 1964. Woodcock age and sex determination from wings. J. Wildl. Manage. 28:287-293.

OWEN, R. B., JR. 1977. American woodcock (*Philohela minor*). Pages 148-186 *in* G. C. Sanderson, ed. Management of migratory shore and upland game birds in North America. Int. Assoc. Fish and Wildl. Agencies, Washington, D.C.

PACE, R. M., III, AND G. W. WOOD. 1979. Observations of woodcock wintering in coastal South Carolina. Proc. Annu. Conf. Southeast. Assoc. Game and Fish Comm. 33:72-80.

ROBERTS, T. H. 1980. Sexual development during winter in male American woodcock. Auk 97:879-881.

———, AND R. W. DIMMICK. 1978. Distribution and breeding chronology of woodcock in Tennessee. Proc. Annu. Conf. Southeast. Assoc. Game and Fish Comm. 32:8-16.

ROBOSKI, J. C., AND M. K. CAUSEY. 1981. Incidence, habitat use, and chronology and woodcock nesting in Alabama. J. Wildl. Manage. 45:793-797.

SHELDON, W. G. 1967. The book of the American woodcock. Univ. Massachusetts Press, Amherst. 227pp.

STAMPS, R. T., AND P. D. DOERR. 1977. Reproductive maturation and breeding of woodcock in North Carolina. Proc. Woodcock Symp. 6:185-190.

WALKER, W. A., AND M. K. CAUSEY. 1982. Breeding activity of American woodcock in Alabama. J. Wildl. Manage. 46:1054-1057.

WHITCOMB, D. A. 1974. Characteristics of an insular woodcock population. Michigan Dep. Nat. Resour. Wildl. Div. Report 2720. Lansing. 78pp.

WHITING, R. M., JR., AND T. G. BOGGUS. 1982. Breeding biology of American woodcock in East Texas. Pages 132-138 *in* T. J. Dwyer and G. L. Storm, eds. Woodcock ecology and management. U.S. Dep. Inter. Fish and Wildl. Serv. Wildl. Res. Report 14.

HARVESTING RED GROUSE IN THE NORTH OF ENGLAND

PETER J. HUDSON, The Game Conservancy, North of England Grouse Research Project, Askrigg, Leyburn, N. Yorks DL8 3HG, England

Abstract: Driven red grouse (*Lagopus l. scoticus*) flew over the hunters in packs of up to 100 birds. Relatively few grouse were shot from large packs due to the effects of dilution and not confusion. Although it was not the intention of the hunters, they selectively shot old birds, particularly cocks. The proportion of grouse shot at low and medium densities was lower than a maximum-yield relationship derived from a simulation model. There was limited evidence that losses from harvesting were compensated for, and a possible mechanism for this is discussed.

KEY WORDS: Red grouse, *Lagopus l. scoticus*, Compensatory mortality, Maximum sustained yield, Game management, Simulation model.

The red grouse, a subspecies of the widely distributed willow ptarmigan (*Lagopus lagopus*), is restricted to the heather (*Calluna* spp.) moorlands of the British Isles. Large tracts of this habitat are managed to produce a harvestable surplus of grouse each autumn. In the past, the shooting of red grouse was principally a sport for country landowners, but with increased economic pressures and the general loss of game habitat (Potts 1980, Anderson and Yalden 1981) many upland landowners now lease their grouse shooting for commercial gain. As a consequence, there is a need to understand the factors influencing grouse production and to develop optimal harvesting strategies.

In a managed population, where there is no significant level of predation, a reduction in numbers through harvesting could result in reduced competitive pressure on a limited resource and a density dependent response among the surviving population. For instance, Nicholson (1954) demonstrated that exploitation of blowflies (*Lucilla cuprina*) in experimental conditions resulted in increased fecundity and adult survivorship. Research on natural populations also suggests that some harvesting mortality can be compensated for by a corresponding decline in natural mortality (Anderson and Burnham 1976, Rogers et al. 1979, Hill 1984). In other cases shooting mortality could be strictly additive to natural mortality (Geis et al. 1969, Bergerud 1985).

This paper investigates the harvesting of red grouse by describing the dynamics and selectivity of driving grouse to hunters, comparing harvest pressure with a maximum-yield relationship, and finally attempting to estimate whether there is any compensation after harvesting.

I would like to thank the landowners and keepers in the north of England who kindly allowed me to work on their estates. David Newborn provided energetic field assistance, David Jackson conducted some of the counts, and Dick Potts provided comments. Special thanks go to The Earl Peel for making this study possible and British Caledonian Airlines for sponsorship. Tom Bergerud provided helpful comments on the manuscript.

METHODS

Grouse Counts

Numbers of red grouse were regularly counted on managed estates in the north of England. Sample plots of 81 ha were systematically searched with trained dogs as outlined by Jenkins et al. (1963). Counts were made usually in early April to provide estimates of breeding-pair density and again in late July to measure the production of young. After the shooting season (12 August–10 December), records were obtained from each estate on the numbers of grouse shot and, when available, the ratio of young to old birds shot. Counts were conducted regularly on 20 estates and less frequently on 12 more. These counts provided 46 data sets on bird density before shooting, the number shot from that area, and the number of old birds present in the following season. These counts were then used to provide estimates of total annual mortality and shooting mortality.

This method of estimating losses from count data assumes that all adults counted were survivors from the previous year, and there is no egress or ingress into the population. Studies on the dispersal of grouse on well-managed estates find "red grouse are remarkably sedentary" (Jenkins et al. 1963:323; Hudson, unpubl. data). Grouse numbers on the main study areas remained stable during summer months, and over-winter losses were associated with birds dying on or near the study area. Thus, although the effects of ingress and egress cannot be ruled out, the estimates of over-winter mortality were considered reliable.

In 1981, 22 estates were visited on shooting days and grouse counts made to determine the proportion of driven grouse that flew over the hunters, the size of groups flying over the hunters, and the proportion shot from different-sized groups. Shot birds were inspected, sexed, and aged according to the techniques of Watson and Miller (1976).

Simulation Model

Field observations were compared with outputs from the simulation model of a grouse population, developed by Potts et al. (1984), to evaluate the harvesting strategies monitored. Two relationships in this model are relevant to the paper: the proportion of the population harvested with respect to density and over-winter survival.

In the model, a logistic curve describes the relationship, for grey partridge (*Perdix perdix*), between the proportion shot and density (Potts 1980). Using a microcomputer, I altered the shape of this logistic curve to discover the relationship that produced the maximum long-term yield and compared this with the harvesting rates monitored.

Over-winter survival in the model is based on data from counts conducted at Moorhouse National Nature Reserve (Taylor and Rawes 1974), an area of unshot moorland in the north of England. Annual variations in adult losses were inversely related to density on 1 August, indicating over-winter survival is density dependent. In the model this relationship is used to estimate adult survival after shooting and, consequently, compensates for a degree of shooting mortality. I have used the model to generate a relationship between annual mortality and shooting mortality to compare with the estimates from the count data.

RESULTS

Selectivity of Harvesting

An average day's driven grouse shooting on the 22 estates monitored consisted of 8.4 guns (range 6-12), 16 beaters (range 15-19), and usually 4 drives. The size of each drive was between 80 and 240 ha. During the 51 drives monitored, 24.5% (S.E. = ± 2.7) of the birds flew over the beaters instead of over the hunters; there was no correlation between the percentage of birds lost and the density of birds ($r=0.16$, $P > 0.01$).

Driven grouse frequently passed over the hunters in groups, and on occasion these groups consisted of more than 100 birds. The size distribution of these groups conformed to the negative binomial (Southwood 1966) described by k, a measure of the amount of clumping known as the dispersion parameter; k was not correlated with density ($r=0.294$, $P > 0.1$, 19 estates) but with the number of days the area had been driven for shooting ($r=0.453$, $P < 0.05$). Hence, after several days of shooting, grouse were more clumped.

The proportion of grouse shot was less from large groups than from small groups (Table 1). The number of shots fired at a group increased with group size ($r=0.74$, $P < 0.1$ but not proportional to the number of birds. There was no relationship between the number of shots/bird killed and the group size ($r=0.073$, $P > 0.1$; Table 1).

In all 22 cases, the ratio of young to old shot was lower than the ratio counted before shooting, indicating that hunters shoot proportionately more old birds. In 17 of 20 cases, more old cocks were shot than old hens. On 10 estates where both cocks and hens were counted before shooting, all killed a greater proportion of old cocks than were recorded in the population.

Shooting Mortality and Annual Mortality

Figure 1a shows the best-fit relationship for the proportion of grouse shot with respect to density ($r=0.90$, $P< 0.02$). The increase in the proportion shot with density was similar to Potts' (1980) description for grey partridge, although the shape and asymptote were different. The maximum long-term yield relationship derived from the model produced a greater harvesting pressure at low and medium densities but had a similar asymptote (Fig. 1b).

Table 1. Frequency of pack size and shooting statistics, in relation to pack size for red grouse in the north of England. With packs of more than 35 birds it was not possible to record accurately the number of birds killed.

Pack size	N packs observed	% birds shot	N shots/pack	N shots/bird killed
1	1,140	60	1.64	2.07
2	342	38	2.47	2.71
3	166	26	2.39	1.35
4-5	207	17	2.59	2.41
6-7	154	16	3.22	2.78
8-10	118	12	2.98	2.32
11-15	96	9	2.89	1.67
16-20	35	7	3.62	2.07
21-25	45	6	4.57	2.46
25-35	30	6	5.00	2.05
35-50	13	3	3.67	-
50-75	8	5	5.00	-
75-100	3	3	11.00	-
100 +	1	2	-	-

A secondary polynomial produced a better fit to the relationship between annual losses and shooting mortality than a straight line (Fig. 2a), although the fit was not significant at the 5% level ($r=0.26$, $P > 0.1$). The relationship suggests that annual mortality is constant when shooting mortality is low and compensates after harvesting. The same relationship derived from the simulation model produced a curve of similar shape but with an overall greater mortality rate (Fig. 2b).

DISCUSSION

Driven grouse flew in packs over hunters, and proportionately fewer birds were shot from large packs. Hamilton (1971) considered gregarious behavior as a form of cover-seeking in which individuals reduced the chances of being killed by positioning themselves close to conspecifics. Gregarious behavior can reduce the chances of being killed either by confusing a predator so it cannot concentrate on an individual to make an attack (Neill and Cullen 1974) or by simply diluting the probability of being a victim (Bertram 1979). In this study the success rate of hunters, measured as the number of birds killed/shot, did not vary with pack size, indicating that large packs did not confuse the hunters. Although the number of shots fired/group increased with group size, it was not proportional to the number of birds; thus few grouse are shot from packs because of the effects of dilution, not confusion. Jenkins et al. (1963, 1967) recorded that grouse begin territorial behavior during the shooting season and that the non-territorial birds are in packs. It is not clear whether the non-territorial birds form into packs because of territorial behavior, being driven, avoiding predation, or an alternative strategy to territorial defense (Davies 1976).

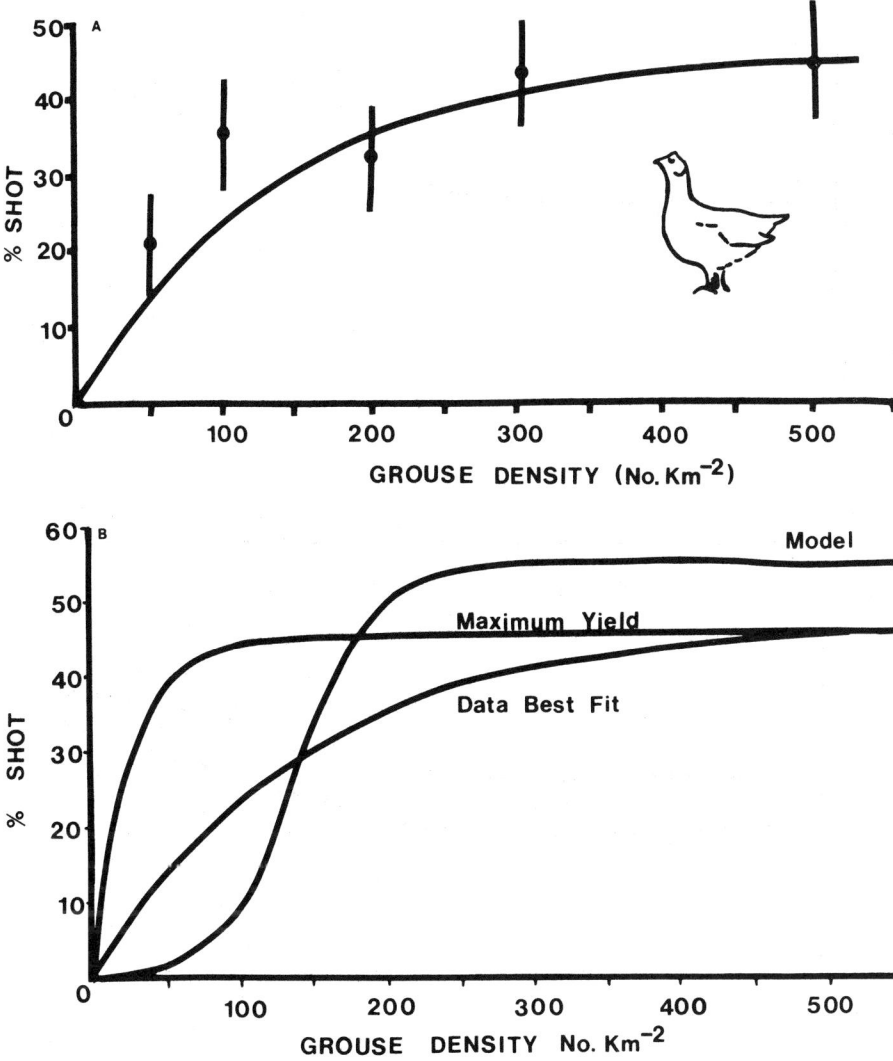

Fig. 1. Proportion of red grouse shot, with respect to density in the north of England (1a derived from data in this study—$r=0.90$, $P<0.02$, points show mean $\pm$ 1 S.E.; and 1b is a comparison with the relationships of maximum sustained yield and with the model of Potts et al. 1984).

The proportion of grouse shot at low and medium densities was lower than the maximum-yield relationship produced from the model. This suggests that grouse populations in the north of England are currently being underexploited. Although an increased harvesting rate would result in a greater yield/annum, the harvest/day would be lower, and sportsmen may wish to sacrifice consistent shooting for a few productive days.

The analyses from the count data indicated that when the harvesting rate was less than 10% there was complete compensation, and above this level

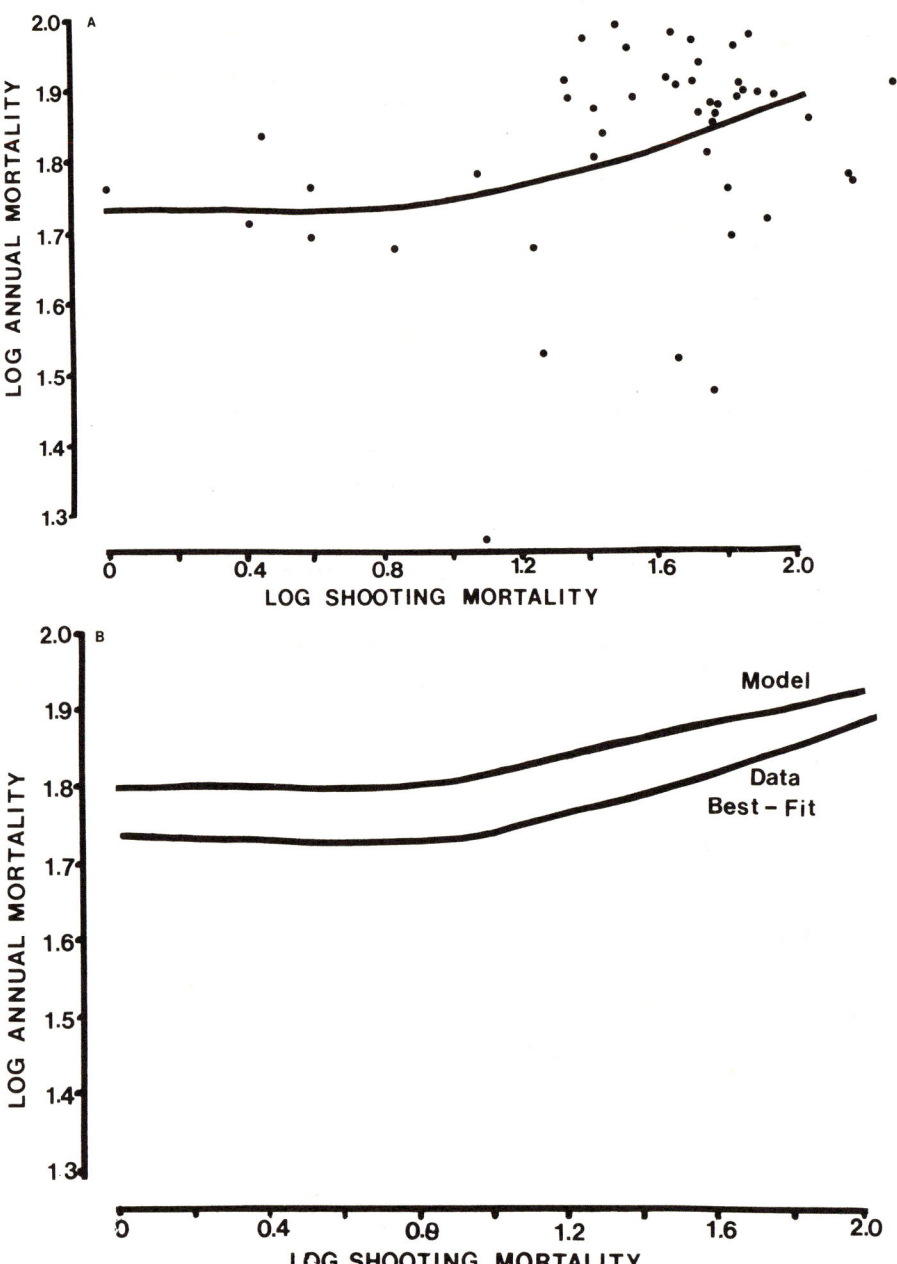

Fig. 2. The relationship between total annual mortality and shooting mortality (2a is derived from data in this study—$r=0.26$, $P<0.10$; and 2b is a comparison with the model of Potts et al. 1984) for red grouse in the north of England.

there was partial compensation. The data fit was poor and may reflect either the inaccuracies in obtaining estimates of population size or the effects of dispersal. It should be stressed that this study estimated mortality from count data, not band data, and the apparent compensation recorded could be due to movements of birds as opposed to a density dependent response. One explanation for the mechanism of compensation can be derived from the experiments conducted by Watson and Jenkins (1968). They found that when territorial cocks were removed they were rapidly replaced by non-territorial ones, and when birds obtained a territory their chances of survival increased. This compensation would presumably continue until all surplus, non-territorial birds obtained a territory. After such a point, any further harvesting would reduce future yields. Game management must discover such thresholds before good advice on optimal harvesting strategies can be given.

LITERATURE CITED

ANDERSON, D. R., AND K. P. BURNHAM. 1976. Population ecology of the mallard, VI: the effect of exploitation on survival. U.S. Fish and Wildl. Serv. Resour. Publ. 128. 66pp.

ANDERSON, P., AND D. W. YALDEN. 1981. Increased sheep numbers and the loss of heather moorland in the Peak District, England. Biol. Conserv. 20:195-213.

BERGERUD, A. T. 1985. The additive effect of hunting mortality on the natural mortality rates of grouse. Pages 345-366 *in* S. L. Beasom and S. F. Roberson, eds. Game harvest management. Caesar Kleberg Wildlife Research Inst., Kingsville, Tex.

BERTRAM, B. C. R. 1979. Living in groups: predators and prey. Pages 64-96 *in* J. R. Krebs and N. B. Davies, eds. Behavioral ecology. Blackwell Scientific Press, Oxford, U.K.

DAVIES, N. B. 1976. Food, flocking and territorial behavior of the pied wagtail (*Motacilla alba yarellii*) in winter. J. Anim. Ecol. 45:235-254.

GEIS, A. D., R. K. MARTINSON, AND D. R. ANDERSON. 1969. Establishing winter regulations and allowable harvest of mallards in the United States. J. Wildl. Manage. 33:848-859.

HAMILTON, W. D. 1971. Geometry of the selfish herd. J. Theor. Biol. 31:295-311.

HILL, D. A. 1984. Population regulation in the mallard (*Anas platyrhynchos*). J. Anim. Ecol. 53:191-202.

JENKINS, D., A. WATSON, AND G. R. MILLER. 1963. Population studies on red grouse (*Lagopus lagopus scoticus*) in north-east Scotland. J. Anim. Ecol. 32:317-376.

———, ———, AND ———. 1967. Population fluctuations in red grouse (*Lagopus lagopus scoticus*) J. Anim. Ecol. 36:97-122.

NEILL, S. R. ST. J., AND J. M. CULLEN. 1974. Experiments on whether schooling by their prey affects the hunting behavior of cephalopods and fish predators. J. Zool. Lond. 172:549-569.

NICHOLSON, A. 1954. Compensatory reactions of populations to stress, and their evolutionary significance. Austr. J. Zool. 2:1-8.

POTTS, G. R. 1980. The effects of modern agriculture, nest predation, and game management on the population ecology of partridges (*Perdix perdix* and *Alectoris rufa*). Adv. in Ecol. Res. 11:1-82.

———, S. C. TAPPER, AND P. J. HUDSON. 1984. Population fluctuations in red grouse: analysis of bag records and a simulation model. J. Anim. Ecol. 53:21-36.

ROGERS, J. P., J. D. NICHOLS, F. W. MARTIN, C. F. KIMBULL, AND R. S. POSPAHALA. 1979. Trans. North Am. Wildl. and Nat. Resour. Conf. 44:114-126.

SOUTHWOOD, T. R. E. 1966. Ecological methods. Methuen, London, U.K. 524pp.

TAYLOR, P., AND M. RAWES. 1974. Aspects of the ecology of the northern Pennines 6. The ecology of the red grouse. Occas. Pap. Moorhouse NNR, Nature Conservancy Council. 32pp.

WATSON, A., AND D. JENKINS. 1968. Experiments on population control by territorial behavior in red grouse. J. Anim. Ecol. 37:595-61.
———, AND G. R. MILLER. 1976. Grouse management. The Game Conservancy, Fordingbridge, U.K. 86pp.

EFFECTS OF CHANGES IN HUNTING REGULATIONS ON BLUE GROUSE POPULATIONS

RICHARD W. HOFFMAN, Colorado Division of Wildlife, Wildlife Research Center, 317 W. Prospect, Fort Collins, CO 80526

Abstract: From 1975 to 1983, blue grouse (*Dendragapus obscurus*) populations in Middle Park, Colorado were studied to document the stability of breeding populations and measure effects of hunting upon grouse densities. Spring densities remained stable at 22 birds/km^2 (range 20-24) as season length (23-67 days) and number of grouse harvested (2,545-4,117) increased. Liberalization of the season was accomplished by allowing blue grouse hunting during the big game season. Of 3,000 big game hunters surveyed, 52% were aware of the extended grouse season; only 11% of those aware participated. Harvest was not related ($r = 0.27$) to season length. Number of hunters and production combined accounted for 85% of the variation in harvest. Neither of these variables was related to season length. Spring densities were not affected ($r = 0.10$) by the harvest the preceding fall. Direct recovery rates indicated a small proportion (3.8%) of the fall population was removed by hunting compared to what could be safely harvested (25%) without affecting the spring population.

KEY WORDS: Blue grouse, Breeding density, Colorado, *Dendragapus obscurus*, Harvest, Hunter activity, Recovery rates, Season structure.

Blue grouse are the most widespread grouse in Colorado, occurring in varying densities over 51,000 km^2 of diverse habitats and terrain throughout the state (Rogers 1968). They rank first in population numbers and annual harvest among resident grouse species. Colorado has had a long history of conservative seasons on blue grouse despite its abundance and wide distribution. Bag limits were frequently in aggregate with other grouse species, and seasons were short and discontinuous (Rogers 1968).

This conservatism continued into the mid-1970's because early research efforts (Steinhoff 1956, Rogers 1968) were inadequate to justify more liberal seasons. Meanwhile, population studies in Montana (Mussehl 1960), Washington (Zwickel 1958, Zwickel et al. 1968, 1975), Wyoming (Harju 1974), British Columbia (Bendell and Elliott 1967), and Alberta (Boag 1966) were providing evidence that fall hunting of blue grouse had no detrimental impact on spring populations. In 1975, Colorado initiated a population study on blue grouse, the results of which enabled wildlife managers to set longer seasons (R. W. Hoffman, unpubl. data, Colo. Div. Wildl. Fed. Aid Proj. W-37-R-34, 1981). The objectives of this paper are to describe hunter response to the more liberal seasons; changes in harvest, grouse densities, and hunter activity associated with more liberal seasons; and the effects of hunting on blue grouse populations.

STUDY AREA AND METHODS

Hunter activity and harvest data were obtained from operation of check stations and volunteer wing collection stations (Hoffman 1981) in Middle

Park, Colorado and from the annual small game harvest survey (unpubl. data, Colo. Div. Wildl., 1975-82). Middle Park is in north-central Colorado approximately 161 km west of Denver. Vegetative and physiognomic features of the area have been described by Gilbert et al. (1970). Unlike other intermountain parks in Colorado, Middle Park is mountainous and locally heavily forested. Vegetation consists of coniferous and quaking aspen (*Populus tremuloides*) types above 2,700 m; sagebrush (*Artemisia* spp.) communities dominate open areas below this elevation.

Demographic data were collected from an intensively studied population of blue grouse on Green Mountain, 19 km south of Kremmling in the southwest corner of Middle Park. The study area encompassed 181 ha. Coniferous types—including Douglas-fir (*Pseudotsuga menziesii*), Douglas-fir/aspen, and Douglas-fir/Rocky Mountain juniper (*Juniperus scopulorum*) associations—cover 38% of the area, and stands of pure aspen constitute 2%. Intermixed with the coniferous types, unforested areas comprise the remaining 60%, of which 90% is dominated by sagebrush communities.

Breeding and production surveys were conducted on Green Mountain by systematic search with the aid of pointing dogs and by acoustic census (Sterling and Bendell 1966). These surveys were performed annually (1975-83) between April and August. Repeated searches resulted in the location of most (>90%) breeding birds. Attempts were made to capture (Zwickel and Bendell 1967, Schladweiler and Mussehl 1969) any unmarked birds. Captured grouse were weighed, measured, classified to age and sex (Caswell 1954, Zwickel and Lance 1966, Braun 1971, Redfield and Zwickel 1976, Hoffman 1983), and individually marked with color combinations of anodized aluminum leg bands (Gullion 1965). Birds less than 6 weeks of age were marked with serially numbered patagial tags. To determine their sex, breeding status, and band combinations, all grouse encountered were observed closely.

The blue grouse season in Middle Park varied from 23 to 67 days between 1975 and 1982 with constant daily bag and possession limits of 3 and 6 birds, respectively (Table 1). The traditional opening date was the second Saturday in September. An experimental blue grouse season was held in 1976 in conjunction with the elk (*Cervus elaphus*) season. Evaluation of the season was based on results of a questionnaire sent to all holders of cow validations (1,450) for big game units in Middle Park. The total population of elk hunters (6,719) was obtained from estimates based on the state-wide survey of elk hunters (unpubl. data, Colo. Div. Wildl., 1976). About 22% of the elk hunters received a questionnaire, which was sent immediately after the elk season. Responses were received from 1,017 hunters (70%). A follow-up letter was sent to all non-respondents (443), and 246 additional responses were received for a total return of 1,263 surveys (87%).

In 1977-78, after the blue grouse season was liberalized statewide, surveys were conducted at the Idaho Springs big game check station. A total of 1,500 big game hunters was contacted each year ($N = 3,000$) during the deer (*Odocoileus* spp.) (500), elk (500), and combined deer-elk seasons (500).

Table 1. Blue grouse hunting seasons, Middle Park, Colorado, 1975-82.

Year	Season dates	Season length(days)	Remarks
1975	13 Sep-05 Oct	23	State-wide—regular season
1976	11 Sep-10 Oct and	30	State-wide—regular season
	16 Oct-26 Oct	11	Middle Park only—blue grouse hunting permitted during the elk season
1977	10 Sep-09 Oct and	30	State-wide—regular season
	15 Oct-15 Nov	27	State-wide—blue grouse hunting permitted during the deer, elk, and combined deer elk seasons
1978	09 Sep-08 Oct and	30	Same as 1977
	14 Oct-14 Nov	27	Same as 1977
1979	08 Sep-07 Oct and	30	Same as 1977
	13 Oct-13 Nov	27	Same as 1977
1980	13 Sep-07 Oct and	25	Same as 1977
	11 Oct-11 Nov	27	Same as 1977
1981	12 Sep-10 Nov	60	State-wide—continuous season
1982	11 Sep-16 Nov	67	State-wide—continuous season

Sampling periods included days at the beginning, middle, and end of each season. One hunter was contacted from each party, and only residents were surveyed.

Simple correlation analyses were used to evaluate relationships between season length and number of hunters, season length and harvest, season length and hunter success, season length and subsequent spring densities, harvest and subsequent spring densities, number of hunters and harvest, and production and harvest. Production and number of hunters were compared to harvest using multiple regression analyses. The 95% confidence level was accepted as significant unless otherwise noted.

RESULTS AND DISCUSSION

Hunter Participation and Response

Few elk hunters (22%) were aware of the experimental season, and only 21% (5% of total sample) of those aware of the season participated. About 46% of the elk hunters who hunted grouse were successful; they harvested 49 birds for a success rate of 1.8 grouse/successful hunter (0.8 grouse/elk hunter hunting grouse). Applying these figures to the total number of elk hunters provided an estimate of 257 blue grouse harvested in Middle Park during the experimental season (total elk hunter population = 6,719; 22% aware of season = 1,478; 21% participation = 310; 46% successful = 143; 1.8 grouse/successful hunter = 257 total harvest).

These calculations do not consider crippling loss or those individuals that hunted grouse but were not elk hunters. Crippling loss, as measured at check stations, was minimal (5%), and no individuals who were hunting only grouse were contacted during the elk season.

Middle Park encompasses about 5,960 km^2 of which about 3,370 km^2 (forest, mountain shrub, sagebrush-aspen, and sagebrush-conifer communities) constitutes potential blue grouse habitat. Projecting the calculated harvest estimate, 1 bird was harvested for every 13 km^2 of habitat. Nearly 39% of the elk hunters observed grouse. However, most did not shoot grouse apparently for fear of spoiling their chances of harvesting a big game animal. Thus, even if more elk hunters had been aware of the experimental grouse season, participation and the resulting harvest would still have been low.

This argument was supported by surveys conducted in 1977 and 1978 at the Idaho Springs Big Game Check Station. Although hunter awareness increased (1977 = 48%, 1978 = 55%), participation by those aware of the season remained low (1977 = 13%, 1978 = 10%) (Table 2). General response of big game hunters to the extended blue grouse season was favorable (Table 2). The primary complaint of those hunters who opposed the season was their concern about the potential increase in the number of hunters (big game + grouse hunters) afield. However, less than 1% of all hunters ($N = 3,000$) contacted during the 1977 and 1978 big game seasons were strictly grouse hunters.

Effects of Season Length

No relationships existed between season length and number of hunters ($r = 0.22$), harvest ($r = 0.27$), hunter success ($r = 0.24$), or subsequent spring densities ($r = 0.41$) (Table 3). Season length also had no influence on the distribution of the harvest. Based on analysis of wing collections by time period (R. W. Hoffman, unpubl. data), hunters exhibited the "opening weekend syndrome" regardless of season length. Over 40% of the wings collected in most years were obtained on opening weekend (1975 = 44%, 1976 = 47%, 1977 = 51%, 1978 = 48%, 1979 = 56%, 1980 = 36%, 1981 = 45%, 1982 = 23%).

Factors Affecting Harvest

When harvest was compared with previous spring densities, no relationship ($r = 0.57$) was found; however, there was a slight relationship ($P < 0.10$) between harvest and number of hunters ($r = 0.63$), and harvest and production (juveniles/female in the harvest sample) ($r = 0.65$) (Table 3). Multiple linear regression analysis indicated both variables were significant and, combined, accounted for 85% of the variation in harvest. Other factors, such as weather, indirectly affected the harvest by directly affecting production or number of hunters afield. For instance, in 1982, adverse weather persisted through the opening weekend and deterred many hunters from going to the field. Although

Table 2. Response of big game hunters to longer blue grouse seasons, as determined from surveys conducted at the Idaho Springs Big Game Check Station, Colorado, 1977-78.

Parameter	1977	1978	1977-78
N surveyed	1,500	1,500	3,000
N big game hunters aware of season (%)	723 (48)	827 (55)	1,550 (52)
N big game hunters aware of season who hunted grouse (%)	94 (13)	83 (10)	177 (11)
N grouse observed	3,415	4,892	8,307
% big game hunters observing grouse	28	35	32
N grouse harvested	53	77	130
Grouse/big game hunter hunting grouse	0.6	0.9	0.7
% big game hunters favorable of extended grouse season	52	60	56
% negative	11	11	11
% indifferent	37	29	33

1982 was a good production year, the lack of hunters on opening weekend resulted in a moderate harvest compared to previous years.

Effects of Harvest on Blue Grouse Populations

Spring densities remained stable about a mean of 22 birds/km^2 and were unaffected ($r = 0.10$) by the harvest the preceding fall (Table 3). This is not surprising since direct recovery rates (Table 4) suggest hunters remove a negligible portion (3.8%) of the fall population. Bendell and Elliott (1967) reported that 5% of the hens and chicks and less than 1% of the males banded on their study areas on Vancouver Island, British Columbia were shot each year. Mussehl (1960) found that hunters removed 7 (1957) and 12% (1958) of the blue grouse banded in the Bridger Mountains, Montana, the majority

Table 3. Blue grouse population trends, production indices, and harvest statistics, Middle Park, Colorado, 1975-83.

Year	Grouse/km^2 (spring)[a]	Juveniles/ female (fall harvest)[b]	Hunters[c] N	Harvest[c] N	Birds/ hunter[c]
1975	20	1.4	1,312	2,552	1.9
1976	20	1.8	1,559	2,732	1.7
1977	23	1.9	1,467	2,640	1.8
1978	24	4.0	1,563	4,117	2.6
1979	22	2.4	1,851	4,105	2.2
1980	22	2.2	1,678	3,772	2.2
1981	22	1.4	1,650	2,545	1.5
1982	20	3.1	1,251	2,777	2.2
1983	23				

[a]Based on breeding and production surveys conducted on Green Mountain.

[b]Based on the analysis of wings from fall harvest samples.

[c]Taken from the Annual Colorado Small Game, Furbearer, and Varmint Harvest Report for Small Game Unit 28 (Middle Park) (unpubl. data, Colo. Div. Wildl., 1975-82).

Table 4. Direct returns of banded blue grouse harvested by hunters in Middle Park, Colorado, 1977-82.

Year	Males % harvested	Females % harvested	Juveniles % harvested	Total % harvested
1977	0.0 (16)[a]	0.0 (16)	14.3 (14)	4.3 (46)
1978	8.3 (12)	0.0 (28)	7.7 (26)	4.5 (66)
1979	5.9 (17)	8.8 (34)	0.0 (62)	3.5(113)
1980	5.9 (17)	4.0 (50)	1.4 (69)	2.9(136)
1981	2.7 (37)	7.9 (38)	8.0 (50)	6.4(125)
1982	3.8 (26)	0.0 (46)	2.4 (42)	1.7(114)
1977-82	4.0(125)	3.8(212)	3.8(263)	3.8(600)

[a] N banded.

of which were juveniles. Most chicks captured in Colorado were too young (< 6 weeks) to carry leg bands and, therefore, were marked with patagial tags. Patagial tags were less conspicuous than leg bands and may go unnoticed by hunters, a factor which undoubtedly contributed to the calculated low harvest rate of juveniles. In most years, juveniles comprised about 55% of the harvest, whereas equal numbers of adult (including yearlings) males (49%) and females (51%) comprised the remaining 45% (R. W. Hoffman, unpubl. data).

Hickey (1955) suggested that gallinaceous birds can withstand a harvest equivalent to 50% of their annual mortality rate. Based on a 7-year average for Green Mountain, production contributes to about a 49% increase in the population by autumn (Table 5). In a stable population there must be an annual loss from fall to fall of this amount. Thus, the population could absorb a harvest of about 25% with no measurable impact on the subsequent spring density. The allowable yield greatly surpasses the estimated harvest rate (3.8%) and supports the conclusion that hunting has had no detrimental impact on this population. Similar calculations by Bendell and Elliott (1967) produced a recommended harvest rate of 20% for blue grouse on Vancouver Island.

Another way to estimate allowable yield incorporates the mean annual death rate of adults and the number of juveniles alive in autumn (Bendell and Elliott 1967). Table 5 summarizes these data for Green Mountain. Zwickel (1965) and Bendell and Elliott (1967) reported a mean annual death rate of approximately 30% for breeding populations of blue grouse on Vancouver Island. An estimate of 39% was obtained from reobservation of marked birds in Middle Park (R. W. Hoffman, unpubl. data). Assuming a constant death rate (39%) among breeding birds, an estimate of total production necessary to maintain a stable breeding population can be determined. Production by mid-August, rather than total production, was used because mid-August data more closely approximate production and survival of juveniles until fall. The replacement requirement then becomes an estimate of the fall-spring juvenile mortality that should occur in a stable population (Table 5). It is apparent

Table 5. Spring populations, production, and mortality of blue grouse, Green Mountain, Middle Park, Colorado, 1976-82.

Year	Spring population	Males/ female	Annual mortality spring population[a]	Nesting success (%)	Total production	Juvenile mortality Jun-Aug (%)	Production by mid-Aug	Total population by mid-Aug[b]	Gain (%)	Juvenile mortality fall-spring[c] (%)
1976	36	1.1	14	76	57	43	32	64	50	56
1977	41	0.9	16	81	68	51	33	70	47	52
1978	43	1.1	17	75	81	40	49	88	56	65
1979	40	1.4	16	56	58	58	24	59	41	33
1980	40	1.2	16	67	60	42	35	71	49	54
1981	40	1.1	16	74	63	46	34	69	49	53
1982	36	1.1	14	76	58	47	31	63	49	55

[a] N birds expected to be lost from the spring population assuming a constant mortality rate of 39%.
[b] Assumes 10% loss of adults.
[c] Mortality necessary to maintain the spring population.

that production was more than adequate to replace natural losses in the spring population. The average annual fall-spring survival of juveniles required to maintain the population on Green Mountain was 45%. These data suggest that surplus birds were available in the fall population.

MANAGEMENT IMPLICATIONS

Liberalization of the blue grouse season provided additional recreational opportunity but did not influence the harvest rate of blue grouse. Although harvest can be predicted using production indices and number of hunters, from a management standpoint, this relationship has little practical importance. Hunter numbers are unknown prior to the season, and preseason production surveys are not feasible on a state-wide basis in Colorado (Rogers 1968, Hoffman 1981). Furthermore, because spring densities are not affected by the previous fall harvest, and because only a small portion of the fall population is removed each year, there is no reason for managers to collect breeding and production data to justify hunting seasons.

Grouse hunting regulations in Colorado are reviewed annually, a task that requires considerable time and manpower. Often the regulations vary from year to year, adding to the confusion of the hunter. Data collected in this study suggest the season-setting process could be simplified. A mid-September to mid-November season with daily bag and possession limits of 3 and 6 birds, respectively, could be held each year without concern of impacting the spring population.

Bendell and Elliott (1967) and Zwickel (1982) have documented the deficiency of adult males in harvest samples from Vancouver Island, British Columbia. This is caused by early migration of males from breeding areas, where hunting is concentrated, to higher-elevation wintering sites that are less accessible. This problem does not occur in Colorado. However, vast areas remain that receive little pressure during the regular season. The extended season has allowed for a better distribution of the harvest because big game hunters venture into areas seldom visited by those hunting only grouse.

LITERATURE CITED

BENDELL, J. F., AND P. W. ELLIOTT. 1967. Behavior and the regulation of numbers of blue grouse. Can. Wildl. Serv. Rep. Ser. 4. 76pp.

BOAG, D. A. 1966. Population attributes of blue grouse in southwestern Alberta. Can. J. Zool. 44:799-814.

BRAUN, C. E. 1971. Determination of blue grouse sex and age from wing characteristics. Colo. Div. Game, Fish and Parks. Game Infor. Leafl. 86. 4pp.

CASWELL, E. B. 1954. A method for sexing blue grouse. J. Wildl. Manage. 18:139.

GILBERT, P. F., O. C. WALLMO, AND R. B. GILL. 1970. Effects of snow depth on mule deer in Middle Park, Colorado. J. Wildl. Manage. 34:15-23.

GULLION, G. W. 1965. Improvements in methods for trapping and marking ruffed grouse. J. Wildl. Manage. 29:109-116.

HARJU, H. J. 1974. An analysis of some aspects of the ecology of dusky grouse. Ph.D. Thesis, Univ. Wyoming, Laramie. 142pp.

HICKEY, J. J. 1955. Some American population research on gallinaceous birds. Pages 326-396 *in* A. Wolfson, ed. Recent studies in avian biology. Univ. Illinois Press, Urbana.

HOFFMAN, R. W. 1981. Volunteer wing collection station use for obtaining grouse wing samples. Wildl. Soc. Bull. 9:180-184

———. 1983. Sex classification of juvenile blue grouse from wing characteristics. J. Wildl. Manage. 47:1143-1147.

MUSSEHL, T. W. 1960. Blue grouse production, movements, and populations in the Bridger Mountains, Montana. J. Wildl. Manage. 24:60-68.

REDFIELD, J. A., AND F. C. ZWICKEL. 1976. Determining the age of young blue grouse: a correction for bias. J. Wildl. Manage. 40:349-351.

ROGERS, G. E. 1968. The blue grouse in Colorado. Colo. Div. Game, Fish and Parks Tech. Publ. 21. 63pp.

SCHLADWEILER, P., AND T. W. MUSSEHL. 1969. Use of mist nets for recapturing radio-equipped blue grouse. J. Wildl. Manage. 33:443-444.

STEINHOFF, H. W. 1956. The dusky grouse and its ecology in Colorado. Ph.D. Thesis, Syracuse Univ., Syracuse, N.Y. 173pp.

STERLING, I., AND J. F. BENDELL. 1966. Census of blue grouse with recorded calls of a female. J. Wildl. Manage. 30:184-187.

ZWICKEL, F. C. 1958. North-central Washington grouse studies. Wash. State Game Bull. 10(4):3-4.

———. 1965. Early mortality and numbers of blue grouse. Ph.D. Thesis. Univ. British Columbia, Vancouver. 153pp.

———. 1982. Demographic composition of hunter-harvested blue grouse in east-central Vancouver Island, British Columbia. J. Wildl. Manage. 46:1057-1061.

———, AND J. F. BENDELL. 1967. A snare for capturing blue grouse. J. Wildl. Manage. 31:202-204.

———, AND A. N. LANCE. 1966. Determining the age of young blue grouse. J. Wildl. Manage. 30:712-717.

———, I. O. BUSS, AND J. H. BRIGHAM. 1968. Autumn movements of blue grouse and their relevance to populations and management. J. Wildl. Manage. 32:456-468.

———, ———, AND ———. 1975. Autumn structure of blue grouse populations in north-central Washington. J. Wildl. Manage. 39:461-467.

EFFECTS OF CHANGES IN HUNTING REGULATIONS ON SAGE GROUSE HARVEST AND POPULATIONS

CLAIT E. BRAUN, Colorado Division of Wildlife, Wildlife Research Center, 317 West Prospect, Fort Collins, CO 80526
THOMAS D. I. BECK, Colorado Division of Wildlife, P. O. Box 83, Crawford, CO 81415

Abstract: Effects of changes in hunting regulations on harvest levels of sage grouse (*Centrocercus urophasianus*) were investigated in North Park, Jackson County, Colorado from 1974 through 1982. All hunters were required to obtain a free permit before hunting from 1974 through 1977, and all participants were contacted through questionnaire surveys. Season length varied from 3 to 30 days between 1974 and 1982 with bag and possession limits of 2 and 4 (1974-75) or 3 and 6 (1976-82). Hunter numbers increased from 1974 to 1975, declined in 1976-77, and remained constant from 1978 to 1982. Total harvest estimated from questionnaire surveys and hunter check stations remained stable through 1977, increased from 1978 through 1981, and decreased in 1982. Harvest was a function of total birds available in the fall as band recovery data indicated that hunters harvested 7-11% of the fall population regardless of season length and bag and possession limits. During 1974-82, number of male sage grouse counted increased from 28-33 (N = 17-26 leks) to 39-43 cocks/lek (N = 29-35 leks) within the study area. Liberalizing season length and bag limits did not result in more hunters or more sage grouse harvested. Hunting had no measurable impact on spring densities of sage grouse.

KEY WORDS: Sage grouse, *Centrocercus urophasianus*, Colorado, Hunting regulations, Harvest rate.

Sage grouse were historically widespread in sagebrush-dominated rangelands in western North America and occurred in 3 Canadian provinces and 13 states (Aldrich 1963). The present distribution is somewhat less, and the species has been extirpated in British Columbia, Nebraska, and New Mexico (West. States Sage Grouse Comm., unpubl. data). The reduction in overall distribution is widely attributed to habitat alteration (Patterson 1952). Despite lower numbers from presumed higher historic levels, the sage grouse is a major game species in Colorado, Idaho, Montana, Nevada, Utah, and Wyoming.

There has been considerable interest in sage grouse primarily because of its unique dependence on sagebrush (*Artemisia*), especially big sagebrush (*A. tridentata*). Consequently, most research efforts have investigated the relationships of sage grouse to their seasonal habitats (Braun et al. 1977, Call 1979, Autenrieth et al. 1982). Its general biology is adequately known (Patterson 1952) as is the behavior of males on leks (Wiley 1973*a*, *b*, 1974, 1978, Wittenberger 1978). However, published references on its population dynamics are scattered, and the sparse data sets are incompletely analyzed (Patterson 1952, Pyrah 1960, Dalke et al. 1963, June 1963*a*, *b*, Gray 1967, Jarvis 1973). Long-term studies of the population dynamics of sage grouse in Colorado were initiated in 1973. The objective of this paper is to describe the apparent impacts of changes in season lengths and bag limits on a discrete population of sage grouse.

This study would not have been possible without the assistance of many temporary assistants and graduate students. We thank all who helped. We especially acknowledge the assistance of F. G. Giese, S. H. Porter, and J. L. Wagner. H. D. Funk provided supervision in the 1970's and assisted in numerous ways. K. M. Giesen and R. W. Hoffman reviewed an early draft of the manuscript. This is a contribution from Colorado Divison of Wildlife Federal Aid to Wildlife Restoration Project W-37-R.

STUDY AREA AND METHODS

The study was conducted in North Park, Jackson County, Colorado, a large intermountain basin. Elevation of sagebrush areas there approximates 2,500 m with the surrounding mountains rising to about 3,850 m. Long, cold winters and a short growing season ($\approx$ 46 days) (U.S. Dep. Commerce 1979) characterize the area. The annual precipitation is low ($\approx$ 23 cm) with about 59% occurring from May through September (U.S. Dep. Commerce 1979).

Subspecies of big sagebrush (primarily *A. t. vaseyana* and *A. t. wyomingensis*), native bunchgrasses, and perennial forbs dominate the upland vegetation. Other shrubs—*Artemisia longiloba, A. cana, A. argilosa, Chrysothamnus* spp., *Sarcobatus vermiculatus,* and *Gutierrezia sarothrae*—are locally common. Uplands comprise about 1,252 km^2 of the total potential sage grouse range of about 1,870 km^2. Hay meadows, primarily of native sedges and grasses, dominate the remaining area of about 618 km^2 (Beck 1977). Predominant land uses are livestock grazing (mostly cattle) and hay production. No annual, cultivated crops are grown.

Data on sage grouse population dynamics were collected through counts of males on leks, trapping and banding, collection of harvest statistics, and band recoveries. Sage grouse present on known leks were counted from late March through late May each year following procedures described by Braun and Beck (unpubl. rep., Colo. Div. Wildl. Fed. Aid Proj. W-37-R-29, 1976) and Emmons and Braun (1984). Searches for new leks were made each spring from the ground and from fixed-wing aircraft or helicopter surveys every 2-4 years.

Sage grouse were located at night along roads or on leks, using night-lighting techniques, and captured with long-handled nets (Giesen et al. 1982). Most captures were in April-May, although in some years substantial numbers of females were captured in January-March. All birds captured were marked with serially numbered aluminum bands and either plastic or anodized aluminum bands color-coded by location or year of banding. Classification of age and sex followed Eng (1955) and Beck et al. (1975).

Harvest data were collected through questionnaires (100% sample of permittees), check stations, and volunteer wing-collection stations (Hoffman and Braun 1975). All hunters in North Park were required to obtain a free permit before hunting in 1974-77. Questionnaires were sent to all permittees immediately after the hunting season with 1 follow-up letter mailed in mid-October to non-respondents.

Two-4 check stations were operated each year on the opening weekend and the following Sunday of the season. These check stations were on major highways out of the park. During 1977-82, volunteer wing-collection stations were placed at 4-6 locations on the periphery of hunting areas. Band recoveries were obtained from check stations, field checks, and hunter reports.

RESULTS

Counts of Males

Number of known, active sage grouse leks in North Park increased from 17 in 1973 to 35 in 1979 and decreased to 31 in 1983 (Table 1). Before beginning intensive study in 1973, known active leks counted each year varied from 10 to 22. Average peak number of males counted/lek was 28-33 in 1973-77 and increased to 39-43 in 1978-83 (Table 1).

Trapping and Banding

The number of grouse banded varied by sex, age class, and year (Table 2). Females were consistently under-represented in the trap samples even though they comprised about 67% of the spring population (Beck 1977). Early in the trapping period, hens were in flocks and were difficult to locate and approach. Once winter flock breakup occurred, hens roosted singly or in small groups of 2-3 birds. Females roosted infrequently on leks, whereas males roosted on or near leks from late March into mid- to late May. Thus, males could be consistently located and captured. They were sampled by establishing quotas for each of 4 zones; efforts were made to capture all hens encountered. Trapping occurred on or near most known, active leks each year.

Hunting Regulations

Before 1975, sage grouse hunting season lengths in North Park varied from 1 to 3 days with bag and possession limits of 1 and 2, 2 and 2, or 2 and 4. Starting in 1974, the season was progressively lengthened from 3 to 30 days (Table 3). In 1976, bag and possession limits were increased to 3 and 6 where they have remained.

Table 1. Peak counts of male sage grouse on leks, North Park, Colorado, 1973-83.

Year	Leks counted	$\bar{x}$ males/lek	Year	Leks counted	$\bar{x}$ males/lek
1973	17	33.1	1979	35	43.5
1974	19	27.7	1980	30	40.1
1975	19	30.9	1981	31	40.9
1976	21	31.9	1982	31	41.2
1977	26	31.1	1983	31	39.4
1978	34	39.5			

Table 2. Sage grouse banded in North Park, Colorado, 1973-82.

Year	Females		Males		Totals
	Yrlg	Ad	Yrlg	Ad	
1973	41	68	80	99	288
1974	22	27	54	88	191
1975	62	68	138	153	421
1976	71	74	120	114	379
1977	101	133	183	123	540
1978	32	22	106	98	258
1979	48	52	111	146	357
1980	72	94	127	173	466
1981	31	38	110	190	369
1982	42	69	110	190	411

Hunter and Harvest Statistics

Check Stations.—Hunters checked decreased from 1974 to 1978 and then stabilized. Hunter success (birds/hunter) varied from 0.7 to 1.9 (Table 4). Liberalization of bag and possession limits in 1976 had no effect on hunter success.

Sage grouse hunters contacted at check stations were interviewed to learn if more liberal season lengths and bag limits in the study area (than elsewhere in Colorado in most years) had influenced their choice of hunting areas (Table 5). Before liberalization of hunting regulations in 1975, about 7% of the hunters contacted responded that they normally hunted sage grouse elsewhere. This percentage remained constant until 1977 when season length was increased to 16 days, decreased in 1978 to previous levels, increased markedly in 1979-80 even though there were no regulation changes in those years, and decreased again in 1981-82. There was no relationship between season length and where sage grouse hunters chose to hunt. About 20-25% of the hunters contacted each year were novice sage grouse hunters, even though total number of hunters remained constant.

Table 3. Sage grouse season length and bag limits, North Park, Colorado, 1973-82.

Year	Season length (days)	Limits	
		Daily	Possession
1973	3	2	4
1974	3	2	4
1975	9	2	4
1976	9	3	6
1977	16	3	6
1978	16	3	6
1979	16	3	6
1980	16	3	6
1981	23	3	6
1982	30	3	6

Table 4. Sage grouse hunter and harvest statistics, as determined from check station data in North Park, Colorado, 1974-82.

Year	Hunters checked	Birds harvested	Birds/hunter
1974	730	785	1.1
1975	738	551	0.7
1976	595	459	0.8
1977	353	385	1.1
1978	350	480	1.4
1979	521	982	1.9
1980	567	794	1.4
1981	523	695	1.3
1982	535	574	1.1

Timing of Harvest.—Wing collections from 1977 through 1982 were recorded by date to examine the effects of longer seasons on time distribution of the harvest (Table 6). These data indicate that longer seasons attracted hunters throughout the entire season and spread the harvest over time. Over 5% of the total wings collected in 1982 were received in the last 7 days of the 30-day season.

Questionnaire Surveys.—All sage grouse hunters were required to obtain a free permit from 1974 through 1977 for accurate estimation of their hunting activities. In addition, the state-wide small game harvest survey provided independent estimates of hunter numbers and harvest.

Number of permits issued fluctuated from 1,093 to 1,541 and decreased after 1975, even though bag and possession limits were increased in 1976 as was season length in 1977 (Table 7). Interviews with hunters at check stations in all years indicated that compliance with the permit regulation was excellent (< 5% of the hunters contacted did not have permits). The initial increase in season length from 3 to 9 days may have influenced hunter participation. However, total harvest did not increase. We conclude that increased bag and possession limits and season length only slightly affected hunter activities

Table 5. Previous sage grouse hunting experience of sage grouse hunters, North Park, Colorado, 1974-82.

Year	Normally hunt in North Park		Normally hunt elsewhere		First-time sage grouse hunter	
	N	%	N	%	N	%
1974	183	68.3	20	7.4	65	24.3
1975	432	64.9	47	7.0	187	28.1
1976	366	64.8	40	7.1	159	28.1
1977	211	64.9	32	9.8	82	25.2
1978	251	73.2	26	7.6	66	19.2
1979	307	65.7	73	15.6	87	18.6
1980	360	63.5	100	17.6	107	18.9
1981	340	67.6	48	9.5	115	22.9
1982	346	68.5	56	11.1	103	20.4

Table 6. Time distribution (%) of sage grouse wings received, North Park, Colorado, 1977-82.[a]

Period	1977	1978	1979	1980	1981	1982
First weekend	67.3	61.9	73.2	68.6	71.6	60.7
First week	6.2	14.2	4.7	5.2	7.5	3.9
Second weekend	13.1	6.5	11.3	11.5	8.3	13.4
Second weed	5.2	7.9	5.2	4.8	2.1	3.0
Third weekend	8.2	9.5	5.6	9.3	5.8	6.8
Third week		SEASON	CLOSED		2.3	2.4
Fourth weekend		SEASON	CLOSED		2.3	4.4
Fourth week			SEASON	CLOSED		3.9
Fifth weekend			SEASON	CLOSED		1.5
N wings	632	724	1,081	939	1,032	776

[a] Unequal effort for wing collections because of check stations during the opening weekend and the following Sunday.

(number of hunters, hunter days, days/hunter) and had no measurable effect on total harvest.

The state-wide small game survey (unpubl. rep., Colo. Div. Wildl., Denver) overestimated hunter numbers by 29% and sage grouse harvest by 85% in North Park compared to data collected in this study from 1974 to 1977. The state-wide survey data show an increasing trend in hunters and total harvest in North Park from 1978 through 1982. Neither check station nor band recovery data support these trends. Current annual estimates in the park are 900 hunters and 1,100 total birds killed. These estimates are based on the ratio of hunters contacted at check stations during 1974-77 with total hunters estimated from the questionnaire survey of all hunters. Both check station and questionnaire survey data provided similar findings on birds/hunter (Tables 4 and 7). This indicates that the questionnaire survey accurately reflected hunter activities. We conclude that no marked change has occurred in hunter numbers or sage grouse harvested from 1974 to 1982 in North Park.

Table 7. North Park, Colorado, sage grouse hunter questionnaire data, 1974-77.

Category	1974	1975	1976	1977
N permits issued	1,184	1,541	1,258	1,093
Response, %	90.7	88.3	87.0	85.0
N hunters	966	1,187	979	845
% hunters	81.6	77.0	77.8	77.3
% successful	53.0	38.8	33.5	46.4
N hunter days	1,587	2,116	1,682	1,664
Days/hunter	1.6	1.8	1.7	2.0
N sage grouse retrieved	1,121	1,000	797	1,010
Sage grouse/hunter	1.2	0.8	0.8	1.2
Unretrieved sage grouse	72	75	50	60
Total harvest	1,193	1,075	847	1,070
Crippling loss, %	6.0	7.0	5.9	5.5

Harvest Rate

The direct recovery rate (i.e., sage grouse banded and recoverd in the same year) was assumed to be the harvest rate because less than 1% of all recoveries were from mortalities other than hunting. Recovery rates of yearling males were highest (10-year average = 10.9%), followed by adult males (8.8%), and all hens (8.4%, pooled because of small sample sizes). The harvest rate for all birds varied from 7 to 11% with no apparent pattern (Fig. 1). Regardless of season length and bag and possession limits, hunters removed a negligible portion of the fall population of sage grouse.

DISCUSSION

Increasing season lengths and bag and possession limits had no measurable effect on number of male sage grouse counted on leks the following spring, hunter numbers, total harvest, and harvest rates. Previous studies have reported harvest rates of 6.8% (Dalke et al. 1963), 10.7% (Gray 1967), 11.5% (June 1963b), 23% (Autenrieth 1981), 24% (Jarvis 1973), and 25% (Patterson 1952). None of these studies evaluated the impacts of hunting on sage grouse, and most were of short duration.

Data on allowable harvest rate are lacking for sage grouse although Hickey (1955) suggested that gallinaceous birds could be harvested at a rate equal to 50% of their annual mortality rate. If the annual turnover rate of sage

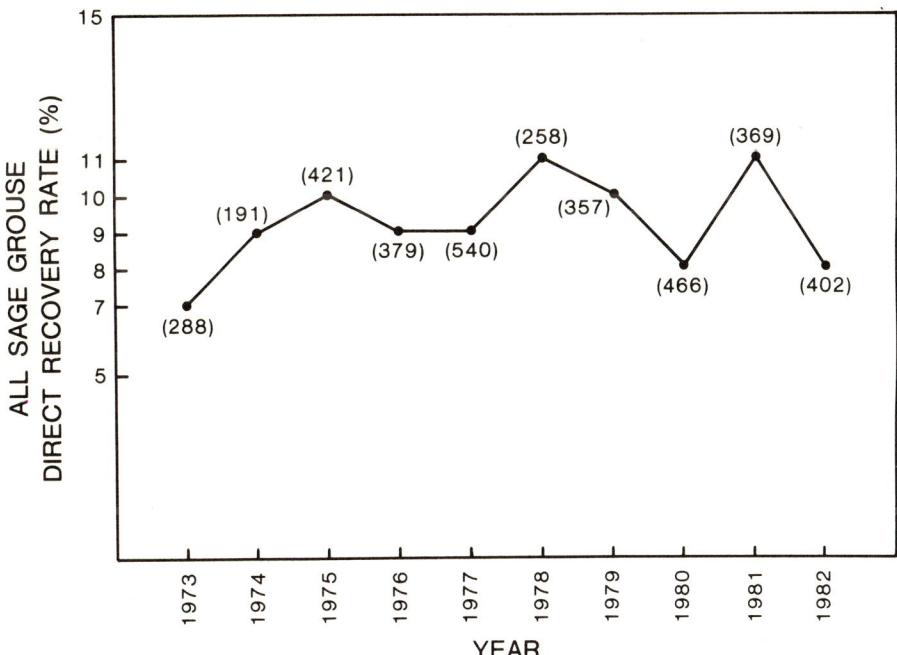

Fig. 1. Direct recovery rates of sage grouse, North Park, Colorado, 1973-82. Sample sizes (number banded) are in parentheses.

grouse averages 40% (females)-50% (males) (C. E. Braun, unpubl. data), then 20-25% of the fall population could be removed without hunting mortality becoming additive. This level was not approached in North Park.

The sage grouse population in North Park, if reflected by average number of males/lek, increased during 1973-83. It is unlikely the population would have increased more if the season had remained restricted because harvest rates did not markedly change during 1973-82. The most important factor affecting sage grouse populations is quality of sagebrush habitat. Nesting success and production of young are directly related to habitat quality (Klebenow 1969, Wallestad and Pyrah 1974). Both factors are important in affecting fall population size and, hence, hunter success. Thus, harvest management is less important than management of sagebrush-dominated rangelands to provide diversity of age, height, and canopy-cover classes of sagebrush interspersed with forbs and lightly grazed wet meadows.

MANAGEMENT IMPLICATIONS

The available data from North Park do not support the assumption that hunting in September-October adversely affects sage grouse populations. Liberalization of hunting regulations should not result in reduced population size if good quality sagebrush habitat is available. Season length can be at least 30 days with bag and possession limits set at reasonable and attainable levels. Sage grouse hunting regulations should be standardized for a period of years since there is no need to indicate a precision of knowledge that most wildlife agencies cannot achieve. Sage grouse have value other than for hunting. They may be a reliable barometer of sagebrush habitat quality and offer a spectacular view during the spring display period. Thus, wildlife agencies should consider all possible recreational uses that do not negatively impact overall population size. By encouraging appreciation of nonconsumptive and consumptive uses of this resource, it may be possible to prevent further losses of sagebrush ecosystems.

LITERATURE CITED

ALDRICH, J. W. 1963. Geographic orientation of American Tetraonidae. J. Wildl. Manage. 27:529-545.

AUTENRIETH, R. E. 1981. Sage grouse management in Idaho. Idaho Dep. Fish and Game Wildl. Bull. 9. 238pp.

―――, W. MOLINI, AND C. BRAUN, eds. 1982. Sage grouse management practices. West. States Sage Grouse Comm. Tech. Bull. 1. 42pp.

BECK, T. D. I. 1977. Sage grouse flock characteristics and habitat selection in winter. J. Wildl. Manage. 41:18-26.

―――, R. B. GILL, AND C. E. BRAUN. 1975. Sex and age determination of sage grouse from wing characteristics. Colo. Div. Wildl. Game Inf. Leafl. 49 (rev.). 4pp.

BRAUN, C. E., T. BRITT, AND R. O. WALLESTAD. 1977. Guidelines for maintenance of sage grouse habitats. Wildl. Soc. Bull. 5:99-106.

CALL, M. W. 1979. Habitat requirements and management recommendations for sage grouse. U.S. Dep. Inter. Bur. Land Manage. Tech. Note. 37pp.

DALKE, P. D., D. B. PYRAH, D. C. STANTON, J. E. CRAWFORD, AND E. F. SCHLATTERER. 1963. Ecology, productivity, and management of sage grouse in Idaho. J. Wildl. Manage. 27:811-841.

EMMONS, S. R., AND C. E. BRAUN. 1984. Lek attendance of male sage grouse. J. Wildl. Manage. 48:1023-1028.

ENG, R. L. 1955. A method for obtaining sage grouse age and sex ratios from wings. J. Wildl. Manage. 19:267-272.

GIESEN, K. M., T. J. SCHOENBERG, AND C. E. BRAUN. 1982. Methods for trapping sage grouse in Colorado. Wildl. Soc. Bull. 10:224-231.

GRAY, G. M. 1967. An ecological study of sage grouse broods with reference to nesting, movements, food habits, and sagebrush strip spraying in the Medicine Lodge Drainage, Clark County, Idaho. M.S. Thesis, Univ. Idaho, Moscow. 200pp.

HICKEY, J. J. 1955. Some American population research on gallinaceous birds. Pages 326-396 *in* A. Wolfson, ed. Recent studies in avian biology. Univ. Illinois Press, Urbana.

HOFFMAN, R. W., AND C. E. BRAUN. 1975. A volunteer wing collection station. Colo. Div. Wildl. Game Inf. Leafl. 101. 3pp.

JARVIS, J. M. 1973. The Parker Mountain sage grouse study. Proc. West. Assoc. State Game and Fish Comm. 53:345-352.

JUNE, J. W. 1963*a*. Western states sage grouse workshop. Wyo. Game and Fish Comm., Cheyenne. 69pp.

———. 1963*b*. Wyoming sage grouse population measurement. Proc. West. Assoc. State Game and Fish Comm. 43:206-211.

KLEBENOW, D. A. 1969. Sage grouse nesting and brood habitat in Idaho. J. Wildl. Manage. 33:649-662.

PATTERSON, R. L. 1952. The sage grouse in Wyoming. Sage Books, Inc. Denver, Colo. 341pp.

PYRAH, D. B. 1960. Eden Valley chicken seasons. Wyo. Wildl. 24(1):26-29.

U.S. DEPARTMENT OF COMMERCE. 1979. Climatological data: annual summary, Colorado. Natl. Oceanic and Atmos. Admin. 84(14). 14pp.

WALLESTAD, R., AND D. PYRAH. 1974. Movement and nesting of sage grouse hens in central Montana. J. Wildl. Manage. 38:630-633.

WILEY, R. H., JR. 1973*a*. Territoriality and non-random mating in sage grouse, *Centrocercus urophasianus*. Anim. Behav. Monogr. 6:85-169.

———. 1973*b*. The strut display of male sage grouse: a "fixed" action pattern. Behavior 47:129-152.

———. 1974. Evolution of social organization and life history patterns among grouse. Q. Rev. Biol. 49:201-227.

———. 1978. The lek mating system of the sage grouse. Sci. Am. 238(5):114-125.

WITTENBERGER, J. F. 1978. The evolution of mating systems in grouse. Condor 80:126-137.

THE ADDITIVE EFFECT OF HUNTING MORTALITY ON THE NATURAL MORTALITY RATES OF GROUSE

A. T. BERGERUD, Biology Department, University of Victoria, Victoria, British Columbia V8W 2Y2, Canada

Abstract: The controversy surrounding the effects of public hunting on upland game bird populations focuses on whether hunting is additive to natural mortality or natural mortality is compensatory to hunting mortality. Data based on 4 indices indicate that hunting is mostly additive to natural mortality losses that occur between autumn and spring. These indices are: a comparison of mortality rates of banded birds between hunted and unhunted populations (5 populations, 5 species), a comparison of the fall population size and subsequent spring populations across an array of densities (12 populations, 6 species), a comparison of mortality rate and fall numbers (10 populations, 6 species), and a comparison of clutch size regressed on natural mortality rates of adults (25 populations, 9 species). By the last method, a significant departure from the regression line greater than that expected suggests additive hunting mortality. The view that hunting is compensatory is generally based on comparing populations with different harvest levels after the birds have redistributed themselves the next spring or later. The Fretwell-Lucas (1969) habitat model argues that birds may select habitat for advertising or nesting based on habitat suitability minus the negative density dependent effects of competing for such preferred sites. Birds from unhunted areas should fill voids in optimum habitat created from hunting. In the future if hunting increases so that entire populations are accessible and birds are removed from all areas, more examples of hunting lowering the size of subsequent breeding populations will be documented. Although hunting is additive to natural overwinter mortality, if densities are greatly reduced, females may benefit by having more space between nests and reduced predation of clutches, resulting in compensatory breeding success.

KEY WORDS: Additive hunting, Mortality rates, Grouse, Harvest.

The history of hunting vs. preservation has passed through several stages. There was a time in pioneer days when there was no thought of conservation; hunters killed whatever they desired. Possibly the most extreme example was the destruction of 3-4 million buffalo (*Bison bison*) in only 4 years (1871-74) (Hornaday, cited in Roe 1951). However, even as early as 1708, New York state had a closed season in the summer for ruffed grouse (*Bonasa umbellus*) to protect young and females (Bump et al. 1947). The protection attitude increased and was discussed by Leopold (1933:211) who realized that populations of game birds could be overharvested: "The virtual disappearance of both quail hunting and bird dogs from shot-out quail states is a case in point."

Then the pendulum began to swing. Wildlife biologists argued that surpluses of game birds were available for fall harvest. In 1930, the first major study of the life history and ecology of ruffed grouse began in New York; it is known as Bump et al. (1947). It is perhaps a reflection of where conservationists have not gone, but no other grouse study in North America has equalled this one. Their object was to find the means of assuring the future for ruffed grouse. Bump et al. (1947:370) reported that 17% of the preseason population was harvested and concluded: "The general effect of man's hunting on grouse as currently practiced is not detrimental..."

At about this time Errington and Hammerstrom (1935) found little difference in subsequent populations between hunted and unhunted bobwhite quail (*Colinus virginianus*) populations. In the mid-1940's, a cyclic low in ruffed grouse approached the Midwest; Minnesota and Wisconsin closed their season, whereas Michigan saw it through. When the seasons reopened in 1948, Minnesota and Wisconsin had not improved their numbers of grouse relative to Michigan. The hypothesis was supported that cycles were natural ecological events not caused by hunting; the new belief was that one could not stockpile game.

The compensation principle was ushered in during the 1950's. Allen (1954:131) said, "If we fail to take a hunting harvest, Nature does it for us. It is quite possible, and usual, for the hunter to get in ahead of natural mortality factors and convert the annual *surplus* (my italics) of game to his own use merely by taking it before something else happens to it." DeStefano and Rusch (1982) recently said, in questioning the compensatory principle, that "Generations of students digested the principle and many biologists came to accept the idea that most game animals present in summer and fall would succumb to late fall and overwinter mortality and that fall hunting would mainly harvest these surplus animals that would die of natural causes." We have built our principles on an unsound foundation. Romesburg (1981:293) said, "Like the Kaibab deer herd, progress in wildlife science may be headed for a crash under the weight of unreliable knowledge."

Now one can detect the winds of change. Kubisiak (1982) and Gullion (1983) reported the overharvest of intensely managed ruffed grouse populations in Wisconsin and Minnesota. DeStefano and Rusch (1982) pointed out that grouse may move from unhunted to hunted areas in fall and spring partially obscuring or alleviating the hunting effect on certain population segments and recommended a re-examination of the ideas of compensatory mortality as applied to ruffed grouse.

This paper deals primarily with whether hunting is additive to the natural mortality that occurs between fall and spring populations. Hickey (1955) pointed out that, when we compare population size between 2 adjacent hunting seasons, there is the possibility of compensatory natural mortality, and there could be compensatory reproduction. Either compensatory reproduction and/or mortality could explain the lack of decline in heavily hunted populations between adjacent fall populations.

THEORIES OF POPULATION REGULATION

One can recognize 2 overwinter scenarios for natural mortality rates—they can vary substantially between winters, or they can be relatively constant. The first scenario implies density dependence, the second density independence. Only if winter mortality was density dependent and varied in response to fall numbers and competition for requisites would natural mortality be compensatory to hunting mortality. Hunting, by reducing numbers, would therein reduce competition, and the survivors would have an increased chance of living to breed in the spring.

Four common density dependent hypotheses explain changes in numbers (Fig. 1). (H_1), the threshold-of-security hypothesis, specifies that winter cover is inadequate to shelter fall populations; numbers above the threshold are vulnerable to predation or dispersal. Spring populations are more constant than fall populations. (H_2), the winter-bottleneck hypothesis, specifies that the availability of winter food is variable and commonly in short supply. Birds starve, and the magnitude of the loss varies with winter severity and with numbers. (H_3), the predator-switchover hypothesis, states that mortality rates are lower when grouse are rare or buffers are common, and as grouse populations increase, predators may switchover to grouse, hence winter mortality increases. (H_4), the territorial or self-regulation hypothesis, argues that breeding space is in short supply. Birds establish territories in the fall or spring, and those that are unable to successfully compete for space are surplus and doomed to die. These 4 hypotheses predict variable winter mortality rates dependent upon the requisite postulated in short supply: H_1—cover, H_2—food, H_3—buffers, and H_4—space. Natural mortality could be compensatory to hunting mortality if any of these hypotheses was generally true.

The threshold-of-security hypothesis dates back to Errington's (1945) study of bobwhite quail in Prairie du Sac, Wisconsin, 1929-44. He noted that spring populations were quite constant and hypothesized that habitats had well-fixed capacities to protect animals; animals in excess were not safe from predators and either died or disappeared. The test implication is that spring populations should be relatively constant in size compared to fall numbers (Fig. 1).

David Lack (1954) argued the view that birds face a density dependent shortage of winter food. Allen (1954) in the same year spoke of the "winter-bottleneck", in which the winter carrying capacity is less than the total number of birds alive in fall after breeding. Such a theory is clearly compatible with a compensatory role of natural mortality.

The switchover model also dates back at least to Lack's 1954 book on the natural regulation of numbers. He reasoned that when snowshoe hares (*Lepus americanus*) declined, northern predators would switch to alternative prey, such as grouse. Later, based on the advice of J. J. Hickey and L. B. Keith, he rejected the hypothesis (Lack 1966). Keith (1963:131) showed that hares peaked before grouse in 9 declines, hares and grouse declined together in 5 examples, and grouse preceded hares down in numbers 11 times. Later, Keith (1974) revitalized the hypothesis, suggesting that grouse could be driven down by switchover even though the local hare populations were not in perfect synchronization and predators might, through numerical responses, concentrate where hares and grouse were still common. Rusch et al. (1978) found support for this hypothesis for a ruffed grouse decline in Manitoba when predators took more grouse after hares disappeared.

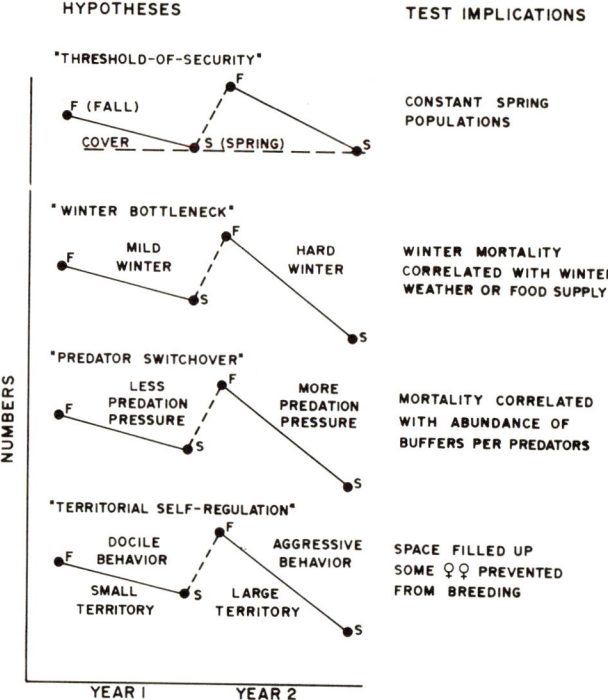

Fig. 1. Hypotheses to explain the regulation of grouse numbers that depend on density-dependent natural winter mortality.

A controversy has lingered since the 1950's as to whether territorial behavior actually limits breeding numbers or if it acts primarily as a spacing mechanism and means of assessing density (Lack 1954, 1966, 1968, Wynne-Edwards 1962, Watson and Moss 1970, Wittenberger 1981). The territorial-limitation hypothesis is most strongly argued for red grouse (*Lagopus scoticus*) (Watson and Moss 1970, 1972) but has also been applied to blue (*Dendragapus obscurus*) and spruce grouse (*Canachites canadensis*) (Zwickel 1972, Boag et al. 1979).

In the red grouse model of population regulation, behavior of birds in the fall and early winter changes between years. Territory size, in turn, determines stocking and population density (Watson and Moss 1972). Birds that do not procure territories are surplus and face a short life expectancy. This model implies that populations are always at a socially induced carrying capacity based on spacing, since behavior determines territory size, leaving surpluses available for hunting.

If one accepts any of these 4 hypotheses that predict density dependent winter mortality, then one can feel comfortable with the hypothesis that natural mortality is compensatory. If one believes in contrast to these hypotheses that winter mortality rates are largely density independent (Bergerud 1970), then one has little theoretical basis to view natural deaths as compensatory and should choose the alternative that hunting mortality is additive to natural mortality.

EVIDENCE OF ADDITIVE ROLE OF HUNTING

Data from Banded Birds

The only irrefutable test of whether hunting is additive to natural mortality is to compare the annual mortality rates of banded adults between areas with different exploitation levels. The birds used in the comparisons should have taken part in breeding activities and thus would be expected to show philopatry, and their absence can be equated with mortality.

Fred Zwickel banded blue grouse at Comox Burn, Vancouver Island from 1962-65 and again from 1969 to 1977 (Zwickel and Bendell 1967, Zwickel et al. 1983). During the first period, hunting was light, but pressure increased in the later period (Zwickel 1982). Mortality rates of banded females were significantly greater during the second period (Fig. 2). Zwickel (1982:1060) said, "This selective removal of females has apparently increased the mortality rate of females..." This study had a built-in control; most male blue grouse migrate before the hunting season. The male mortality rates did not significantly increase between 1962 and 1965 vs. 1969-77 (Fig. 2), indicating that hunting was the cause of the changes in mortality between periods.

Clait Braun banded white-tailed ptarmigan (*Lagopus leucurus*) in the high mountains of Colorado from 1966 to 1969 (Braun 1969, Braun and Rodgers 1971). Birds in 2 populations, Crown Point and Mt. Evans, were hunted in the fall, whereas ptarmigan in Rocky Mountain National Park were not hunted. The life table data Braun (1969) presents indicate that the 2 hunted populations had mortality rates approximately double that of the unhunted populations (Fig. 3). In this example, hunting appears completely additive. At Mt. Evans 51% of the population was harvested. If we assume that the remaining 49% alive at the end of the season died at the natural mortality rate (46% for females), then 49% × 46% = 23% and 23% plus 51% harvested equals 74%, compared to the observed total mortality of 76% (Fig. 3). Braun (1969:86) felt hunting increased the annual mortality rate 15% at Crown Point and approximately 27% at Mt. Evans. He said, "Perhaps hunting mortality was not entirely replacive and was partially additive." These populations were maintained by immigration from surrounding areas (Braun and Rodgers 1971).

The Hammerstroms, Frederick and Fran, banded prairie chickens (*Tympanuchus cupido*) in central Wisconsin from 1949 to 1965 (Hammerstrom and Hammerstrom 1973). The hunting season was closed, except in 1951. The 2 cohorts exposed to this hunting harvest had higher mortality rates than later cohorts not hunted (Fig. 4). The Hammerstroms concluded (1973:36), "It would seem that the hunting season increased normal mortality by about 25%."

Gordon Gullion has been banding ruffed grouse males for the past 25 years in central Minnesota, 1956-83 (Gullion and Marshall 1968, Gullion 1981,

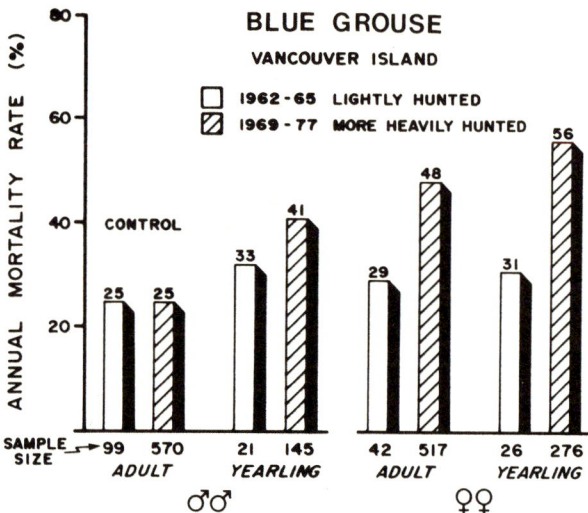

Fig. 2. Comparison of the annual mortality rates of blue grouse at Comox Burn, Vancouver Island, between a lightly hunted period, 1962-65, and a heavily hunted period, 1969-77, (Zwickel et al. 1983).

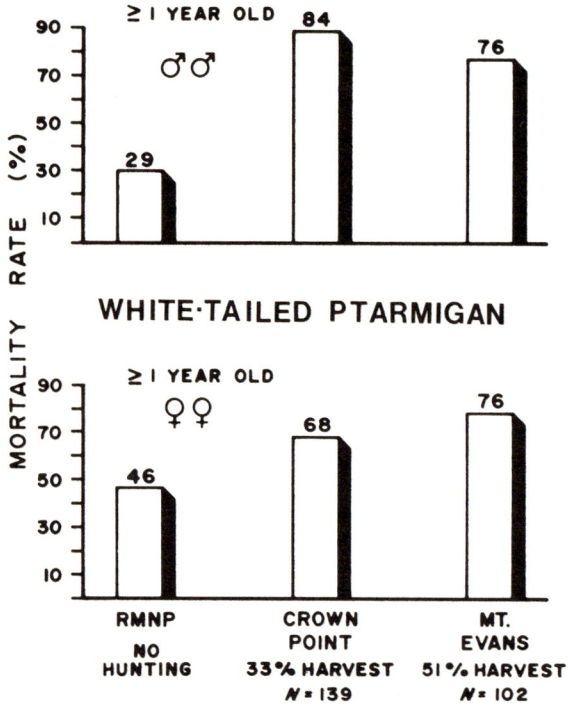

Fig.3. Comparison of annual mortality rates of white-tailed ptarmigan between a population not hunted in Rocky Mountain National Park and 2 areas heavily hunted, Crown Point and Mt. Evans, Colorado (Braun 1969, Braun and Rodgers 1971).

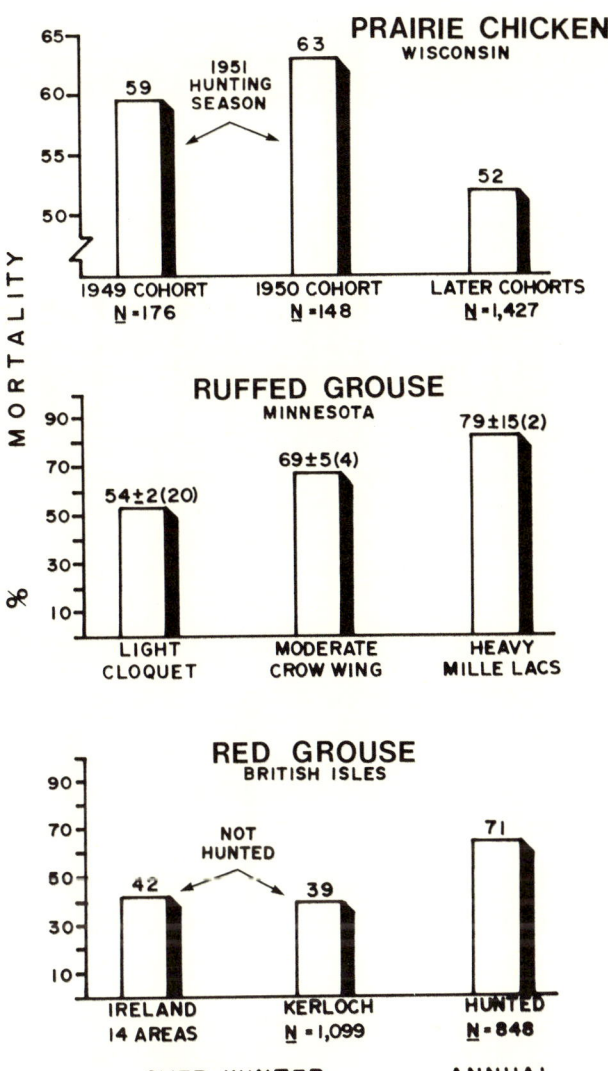

Fig. 4. Comparison of mortality rates for prairie chickens, ruffed grouse, and red grouse compared between populations with different hunting pressure. Only the overwinter mortality rate is shown for the red grouse populations at Kerloch and Ireland (Jenkins et al. 1963, 1967, Gullion 1970, 1981, 1983, Hammerstrom and Hammerstrom 1973, Little 1978, Watson and O'Hare 1979).

1983). Terry Little (1978) also banded males nearby in Crow Wing County, 1970-74. These 3 study areas in Minnesota were Mille Lacs, Crow Wing, and Cloquet. Cloquet is a refuge, but birds are harvested when they move outside (Gullion and Marshall 1968). The birds at both Crow Wing and Mille Lacs had significantly greater mortality rates than Cloquet (Fig. 4). The mortality figures from Cloquet are similar to losses reported for other ruffed grouse populations lightly hunted in North America (Dorney and Kabat 1960, Davies 1973, Boag 1976).

For the Mille Lacs Region, Gullion (1983:21) concluded: "This population depression appears to be the result of excessive hunter harvest each fall. Evidently too many potential breeders are being removed by hunting." Mille Lacs is being intensively managed, whereas the surrounding areas have lowered densities, which reduces the potential of ingress to fill vacancies created by hunting (see Kubisiak 1982).

David Jenkins and Adam Watson began studies of red grouse in 1956, and the work still continues under the direction of Watson and Robert Moss. In the first paper they reported a 71% mortality rate of banded adults that were hunted on their moors (Jenkins et al. 1963). The overall mortality rate of banded adults on hunted moors in Scotland was 67% ($N = 828$) (Jenkins et al. 1963), and they concluded that natural mortality was compensatory: "Shooting exploited part of the surplus, and natural mortality mostly eliminated other birds that could not obtain or hold territories" (Jenkins et al. 1963:375). Watson has not altered his view in 19 years (Moss et al. 1982).

Two largely unhunted populations of red grouse are reported in the literature; 1 is at Kerloch, Scotland and the other in Ireland. The overwinter mortality figures for these populations based on comparing fall populations with spring numbers (no banded birds available) were Kerloch 39% (1962-65) and Ireland 42% mortality (1969-71) (Fig. 4) (data from Jenkins et al. 1967, Watson and O'Hare 1979). The Kerloch birds also had an overwinter loss of 41% in the years 1966-71 (data from Moss et al. 1975). Red grouse have high survival rates over the summer; hence the losses between fall and spring should only slightly underestimate the losses for the entire year. The comparisons of the overwinter mortality rate of 41% for 2 unhunted populations vs. the annual mortality rate of 67-71% for heavily hunted populations indicate that, contrary to Moss et al. (1982), hunting is additive in red grouse.

The Correlation between Fall and Subsequent Spring Numbers

Another approach to decide if hunting is additive to natural overwinter mortality is to compare changes in numbers between fall and the next spring across an array of total numbers. If overwinter mortality responds compensatorily to fall numbers, then there should be a density dependence in the spring numbers. On the average, a smaller percentage of the population should die overwinter when fall numbers are low than when fall numbers are high. The winter bottleneck, threshold-of-security, and territorial-behavior-limitation hypotheses predict that there are surplus numbers in fall. It does not matter whether these birds are harvested; there is only so much food, cover, or territorial space, and they will die anyway until the carrying capacity is reached.

The additive hypothesis predicts that fall numbers drive spring numbers. If in 1 year the population is higher in the autumn than in a second autumn, then spring numbers should also be higher in the first year than in the second spring; i.e., the extrinsic environment for each population provides a relatively constant mortality rate. There is no fixed carrying capacity or bottleneck. For example, spruce grouse in Michigan die annually at 53% regardless of numbers (data from Robinson 1980), whereas spruce grouse in Alberta die annually at about 32% (Boag et al. 1979). These natural mortality rates are distinct for each population and density independent, taking a relatively constant proportion; thus, natural mortality should be additive to hunting losses.

I compared the number of birds in the fall of year 1 with the number of birds in the same population the next spring (year 2) for 12 populations. Most workers didn't count their birds in the fall but rather estimated fall numbers based on spring counts of breeding birds and the addition of juvenile birds still alive in August. Juvenile bird totals are generally based on mean brood sizes and the percentage of hens successful in raising at least 1 chick. Some authors have data on the mortality of adults over summer, and others do not.

For each of the 12 populations, I fitted by eye a line of constant mortality (nearest 5%) through the scatter diagrams of spring numbers plotted on previous fall numbers. These lines of constant mortality fit the scatter diagrams reasonably well (Figs. 5 and 6). Neither the sharp-tailed grouse (*Pedioecetes phasianellus*) population in South Dakota nor the rock ptarmigan (*Lagopus mutus*) population in Scotland showed a completely linear relationship. In the case of rock ptarmigan, a curvilinear regression resulted from 2 years with extremely high fall numbers. These linear regressions are consistent with the hypothesis of the density independence of overwinter losses. Spring populations rise and fall in response to changes in numbers the previous fall. These constant-rate changes, regardless of fall numbers, do not support the view of compensatory overwinter natural mortality. Birds in a specific population after a heavy harvest will still die at a similar rate as would a larger number of birds alive in a year of no hunting.

Mortality Rates Compared with Fall Numbers

A third technique in the additive vs. compensatory hypotheses for grouse is to compare annual mortalities with fall numbers by correlation analysis. The hypothesis of compensatory mortality would predict mortality rates to be positively correlated with numbers in fall. These comparisons are not precise since annual mortality is usually measured from spring to spring, whereas the densities are based on fall numbers; some adults die between spring and fall. Still a substantial proportion of the annual losses of grouse occurs after the fall counts and before the next summer.

There was no significant positive correlation between fall numbers and mortality rates for any population (Table 1). The only significant correlation was a decrease in the annual mortality rate for a cyclic ruffed grouse population at Rochester, Alberta, with an increase in numbers (Table 1). When there were more birds in this population, they lived longer. Again,

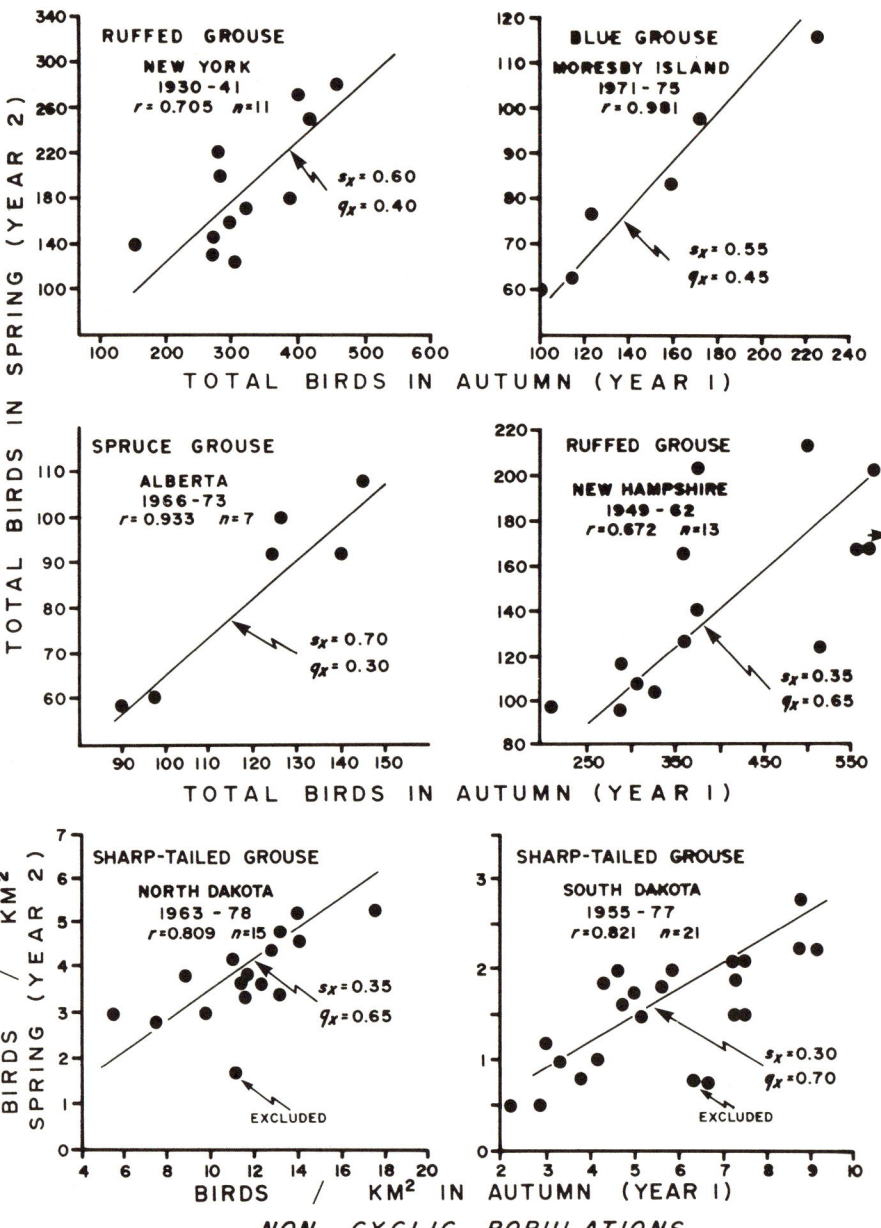

Fig. 5. The regression of spring numbers on previous fall numbers for 6 populations of noncyclic grouse (Bump et al. 1947, Allison 1963, Kobriger 1975, 1981, Linde et al. 1978, Boag et al. 1979).

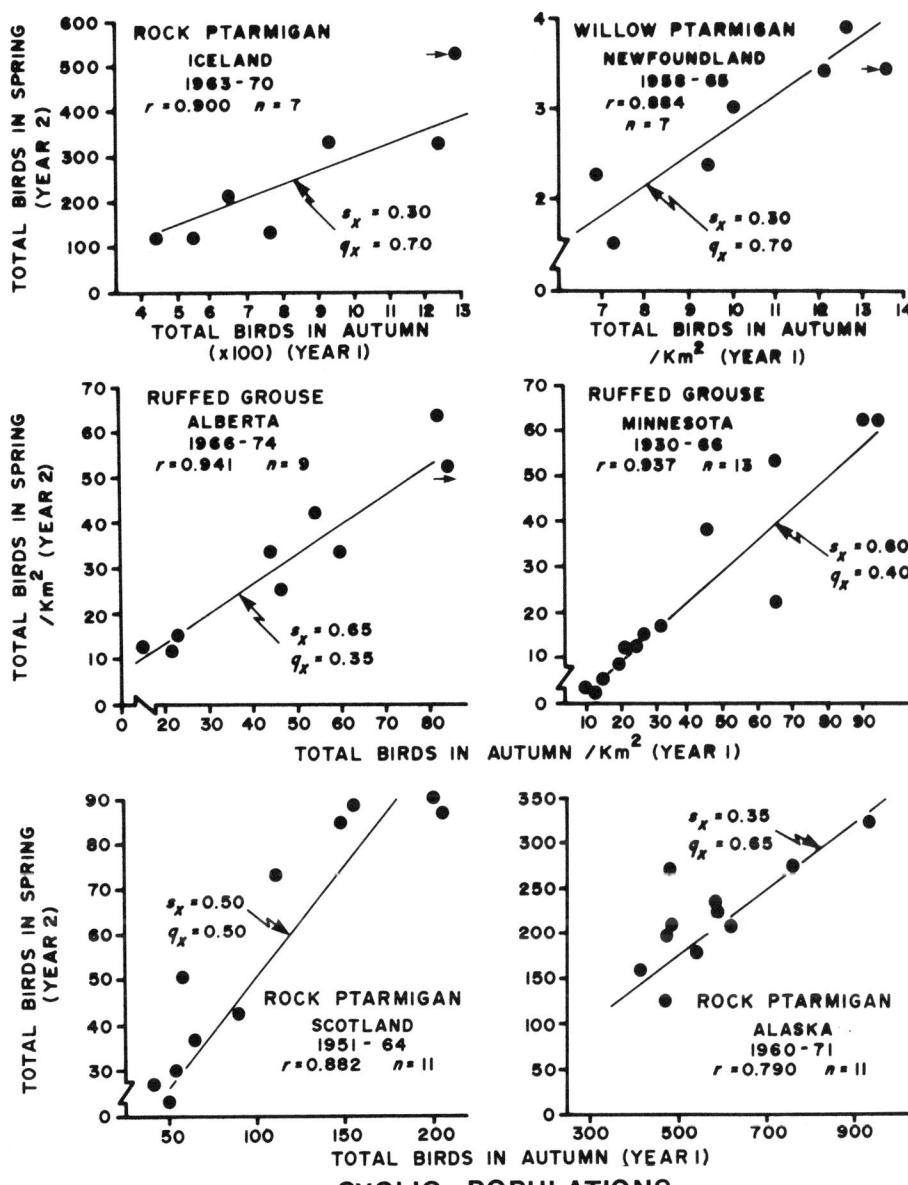

Fig. 6. The regression of spring numbers on previous fall numbers for 6 populations of cyclic grouse (King 1937, Watson 1965, Bergerud 1970, Gullion 1970, Gardarsson 1971, Weeden and Theberge 1972, Rusch, unpubl. data).

Table 1. Reported annual mortality rates for several species of grouse.

Grouse group and species	Mortality rate ± SE (years)	Coefficient of variation	Correlation with density	References
Forest grouse				
Ruffed grouse				
British Columbia	49 ± 5 (6)	27		A.T. Bergerud, unpubl. data
Alberta	65 ± 4 (8)	18	−0.84[b]	D. H. Rusch, unpubl. data
Minnesota	54 ± 5 (7)	24	0.25	Gullion 1970
Spruce grouse				
Michigan	53 ± 6 (4)	23	0.64	Robinson 1980
Alberta	32 ± 3[a] (5)	20	0.15	Boag et al. 1979
Blue grouse				
Moresby Island	26 ± 3 (5)	25	0.42	A.T. Bergerud, unpubl. data
Comox Burn	43 ± 4 (5)	17	−0.42	Zwickel et al. 1977, 1983
Steppe grouse				
Sharp-tailed grouse				
South Dakota	73 ± 5 (4)	14	0.56	Robel et al. 1972
Montana	74 ± 3 (4)	8		Brown 1967
Prairie chicken				
Wisconsin	54 ± 3[a] (10)	17		Hammerstrom and Hammerstrom 1973
Tundra grouse				
Rock ptarmigan				
Iceland	45 ± 8[a] (7)	46	0.04	Gardarsson 1971
Alaska	59 ± 3[a] (9)	20	0.56	Weeden and Theberge 1972
White-tailed ptarmigan				
Colorado	24 ± 3 (3)	21	−0.50	May 1975
Montana	29 ± 5 (3)	28		Choate 1963

[a] Values based on total breeding birds in year 1 vs. adults in year 2; the others based on banded birds.
[b] $P < 0.01$, others n.s.

a large body of data provides statistics contrary to that predicted by compensatory natural mortality.

Clutch Size Compared with Mortality Rates

Most would agree that the clutch size of a population is an evolved life history characteristic not liable to rapid change. Also, there is general agreement that clutch size and natural mortality rates of adults are positively correlated in birds (Lack 1954, Wynne-Edwards 1962). There is disagreement as to the cause and effect of this relationship. Lack (1954, 1966, 1968) argued that clutch size was fixed and mortality the dependent variable; birds die from starvation. Wynne-Edwards (1962) felt that mortality was the independent variable, and clutch size was a density dependent need to regulate populations. The view of Williams (1966) largely reconciled the 2 conflicting views. Clutch size was largely fixed by natural selection, but it was influenced by lifetime maintenance optimization and hence influenced by longevity. In my view natural adult mortality is independent of clutch size (Bergerud, unpubl. data). If this is true, it is valid to compare clutch size and adult mortality rates in a correlation-regression analysis.

The clutch size can be used to gauge if hunting has inflated natural annual mortality rates. I regressed clutch size on annual mortality rate for 25 grouse populations (Fig. 7). The regression was essentially linear for populations with clutch sizes from 4 to 8 eggs (Fig. 7). The only populations with mortality rates greater than 65% were also the ones heavily hunted. I suggest that there are no populations of grouse with natural mortality rates of adults greater than 65% and that populations with higher rates have an additive hunting mortality component.

Three populations that received considerable harvests, in which small clutch sizes are documented, are red grouse in Scotland, blue grouse in Comox Burn, Vancouver, Island, and spruce grouse in Alaska (Jenkins et al. 1963, 1967, Ellison 1974, Zwickel 1975, Zwickel et al. 1983). The regression of mortality on clutch size for the 7 populations with the lowest clutch sizes (Fig. 7) (all lightly hunted) is $Y = -6.76 + 7.112X$. When the representative clutch size is substituted for red grouse (7.2 eggs), the expected natural mortality is 45%, for blue grouse (6.4 eggs) 39%, and for spruce grouse (7.6 eggs) 47% mortality. However the reported mortalities of these hunted populations are red grouse 71%, female blue grouse 50%, and spruce grouse 61% (Jenkins et al. 1963, Ellison 1974, Zwickel et al. 1983). The observed natural and hunting mortalities of these populations are 26, 11, and 14%, respectively, greater than the predicted values based on clutch size. Hunting mortality appears additive in all 3 populations, with red grouse having a very large additive component.

NATURAL MORTALITY FACTORS

Potential mortality factors for grouse are starvation, disease, accidents, and predation. I have been unable to find 1 *bona fide* example of density dependent starvation in the North American literature. Yet, grouse biologists spend more time studying food habits than any other endeavor (based on categorizing all the articles appearing on grouse in the Journal of Wildlife Management through 1983). Birds could be predisposed by food shortages and actually be killed by predation; still a number of radio-tracking studies do not suggest that birds weaken before dying. Actually, several grouse populations either maintain their weight or gain weight over winter (Redfield 1973, May 1975, Beck and Braun 1978, D. Mossop, pers. commun.).

The role of disease in the natural death of grouse is no better clarified today than in 1963 when Herman (1963) reviewed the literature. The major example of substantial deaths attributed to disease is the red grouse (Herman 1963, P. Hudson, pers. commun.). Their populations in the British Isles live in high densities where predators have been reduced; the prevalence of disease there may relate to these artificially high numbers.

Predation is the primary cause of grouse mortality. In a review of the literature I tabulated 1,514 grouse deaths; 58% died from raptor predation and 28% by mammals, primarily the red fox (*Vulpes vulpes*). Eight percent

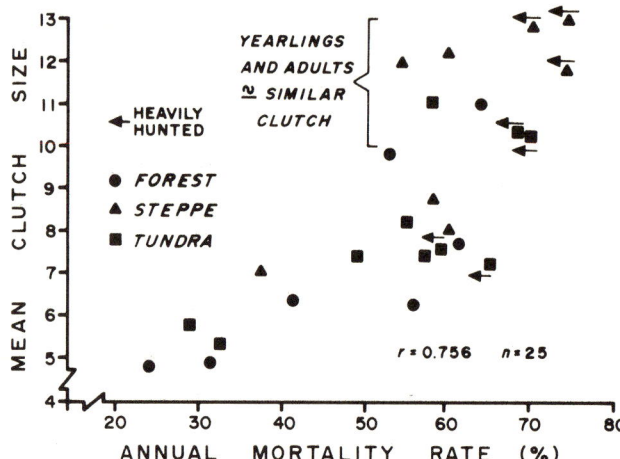

Fig. 7. The clutch sizes of grouse for 25 populations regressed on the annual mortality rates of adults.

of the deaths resulted from accidents. If hunting is additive, then it is additive to overwinter mortality caused by predation.

There is not much information on the numerical and functional responses of predators to changes in grouse abundance. Two major predators, the great-horned owl (*Bubo virginianus*) and red fox, have winter territories and are spaced (Errington et al. 1940, Sargeant 1972, Pils and Marten 1978, Petersen 1979). Goshawks (*Accipiter gentilis*) are also widely scattered, although winter territories may overlap (Newton 1979). This species may also be spaced, with hunting ranges corresponding in size to the abundance of prey (primarily grouse).

The only grouse investigation that has quantified winter losses is the red grouse investigation at Kerloch and the High and Low areas of Scotland (Jenkins et al. 1963, 1964, 1967). The chief predators of these populations were the golden eagle (*Aquila chrysaetos*), fox, and hen harriers (*Circus cyaneus*). In the unhunted Kerloch population, spring grouse numbers were correlated with fall numbers (Fig. 8), suggesting a constant overwinter mortality rate. The percentage of this population killed over winter by predators was not correlated with changes in spring numbers between years (Fig. 8). In the hunted High and Low study areas in Scotland, the grouse killed by predators increased linearly with the post-hunting population (Fig. 8). The number of raptors seen was also positively correlated with post-season grouse numbers. In these study areas, as at Kerloch, the percentage of the population found dead in the winter was not correlated with changes in spring numbers (Fig. 8).

The evidence then from these studies suggests that these predators altered their numerical response in an attempt to maintain homeostasis in functional response; they attempted to optimally forage. If there were more grouse in

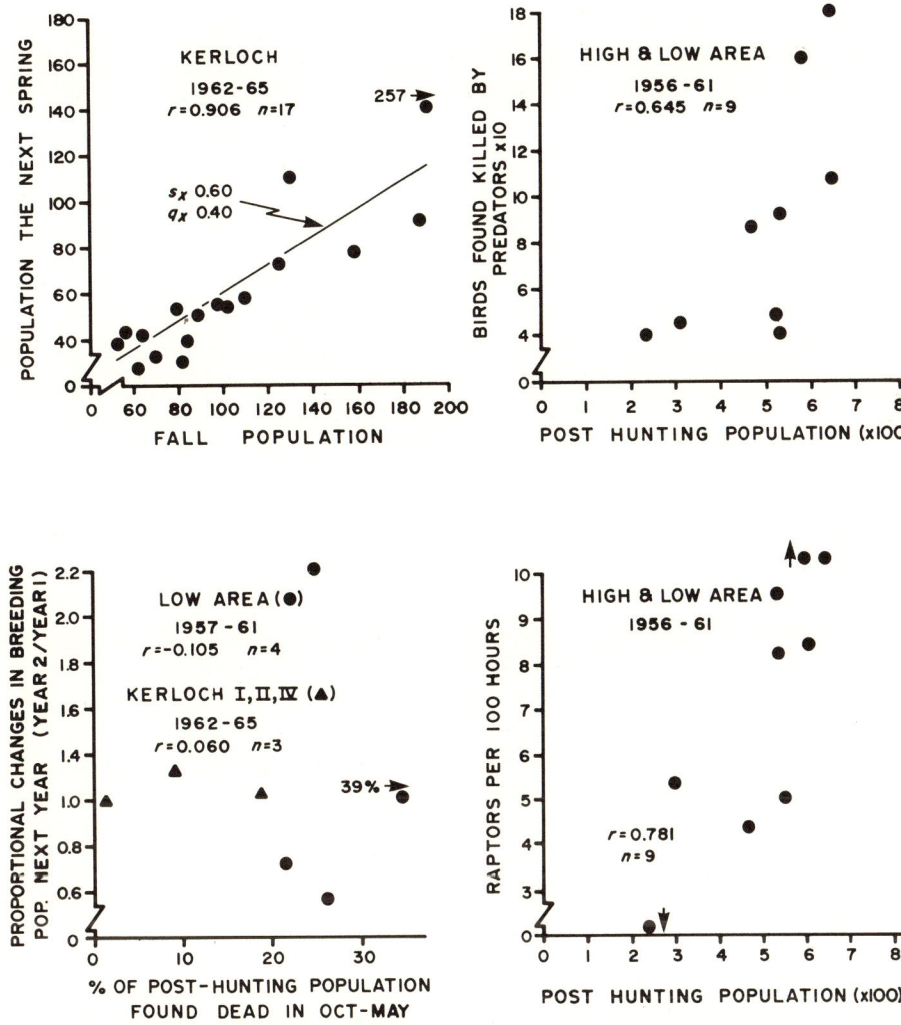

Fig. 8. (Upper left) The regression of spring numbers on previous fall numbers for the unhunted Kerloch population of red grouse. (Upper right) The birds found dead on the High and Low study areas (Scottish red grouse) were correlated with the abundance of the post-hunting population; predation was density independent. (Lower right) The number of raptors increased when red grouse were more common. (Lower left) The proportion of the post-hunting population found dead in winter did not influence changes in breeding numbers for the Low and Kerloch study areas (Jenkins et al. 1963, 1964, 1967).

the winter of year 1 than year 2, then predators might have spaced closer together in year 1 than year 2. Such spacing would result in rather constant winter losses of grouse, regardless of total numbers; thus this natural mortality becomes additive to hunting mortality.

THE COVER-SPACE TRADEOFF

The most important fitness decision a male grouse has to make is where to "advertise" to attract females and breed. The most important fitness decision for the female is where to locate her nest. If she makes the wrong decision and a predator finds her nest, she may lose her lifetime opportunity to propagate her genes. Commonly, grouse in many populations have a life expectancy of only 1-2 breeding seasons. The female cannot afford to be wrong many times.

Both males and females must evaluate both space and cover in deciding where they breed. But this is not an ideal free choice (*sensu* Fretwell and Lucas 1969). Other birds also are seeking good cover to advertise and to locate nests with reduced predation risk.

There is, in fact, a tradeoff between cover vs. space. A female can select the best cover, but other females will also select this cover. The nests of such females will be closely spaced, facilitating the searching image of predators, especially canids. The tradeoff is that a female can select an area of secondary nesting cover in which she will have less competition for such sites and thus will enjoy greater space from other females (Fig. 9).

Blue and spruce grouse females space their nests (Herzog and Boag 1978, Sopuck 1979). Ruffed grouse adults were also uniformly spaced in spring along transect lines (Rusch and Keith 1971). All the ptarmigan have their nests spaced because monogamous females generally nest in the territories of males who are themselves spaced. The spacing of females of the lek species—sage grouse (*Centrocercus urophasianus*), prairie chickens, and sharp-tailed grouse—is not known and is difficult to investigate. Nest habitat is now so discontinuous that females may of necessity nest near each other to optimize patchy cover. Still, these species spread into new habitats when they increase if not fenced-in by agriculture, which means that some type of spacing is in place.

If birds are removed from optimum cover by hunting or in removal experiments (cf. Zwickel 1972), yearlings in secondary locations should move to the more optimum locations where competitors have been reduced in number (Fig. 9). They can improve the odds for their natural fitness by such a move; good cover can compensate for reduced space (Fig. 9).

The movement of these birds between 1 hunting season and the next spring census will, in fact, appear to maintain the numbers of the hunted population, and one could erroneously conclude that compensatory natural mortality has occurred. In fact, the birds may have redistributed themselves.

The evidence for benefits of this cover-space tradeoff is that we do see compensatory reproduction when breeding numbers are reduced. The galliforms commonly display inversity: summer rates-of-gain are greater when densities are lower than when birds are more abundant.

Two grouse populations that showed improved nesting success with reduced densities were spruce grouse at Gorge Creek, Alberta and ruffed grouse in New York State (Fig. 10). The females at Gorge Creek definitely spaced their

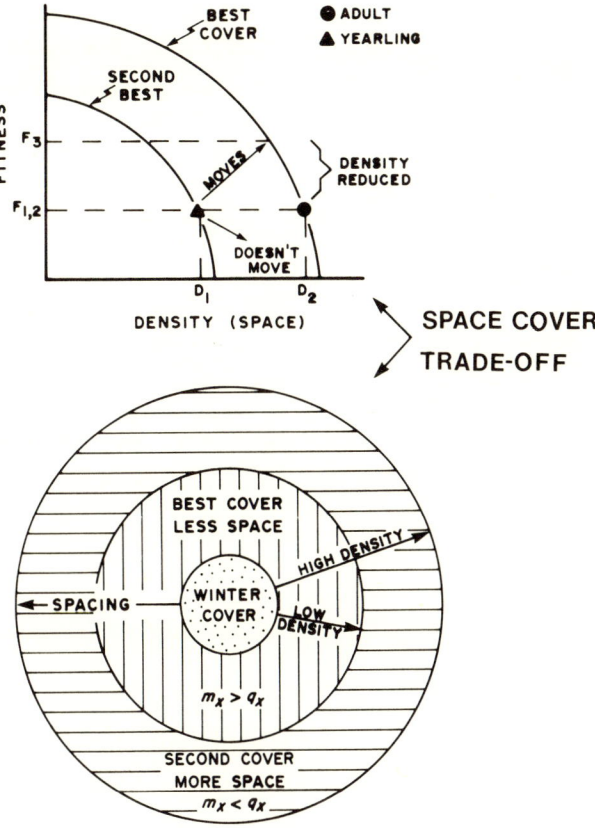

Fig. 9. (Above) The cover-space tradeoff within years between the best and second best cover for advertising and nesting. If the density in the best cover is reduced by hunting (or in a removal experiment) so that the better cover now more than compensates for the reduced space (greater density) a yearling, not localized, that would have bred in the second best cover with more space, should move to the best cover to improve its fitness. (Below) The cover-space tradeoff between years contrasted between low and high densities. When numbers are low the birds space away from winter cover using only the best breeding cover (space is not a problem); recruitment (m_x) is greater than mortality (q_x) and the population increases. The next year, with a higher population, in order to maintain space some yearlings must move to secondary cover which may reduce total recruitment (m_x), and the population is more likely to decline than in the first year, other extrinsic factors being equal.

nests (Herzog 1977), and the females in New York probably avoided each other (Bump et al. 1947). The spruce grouse yearlings moved farther than the adult hens, presumably to seek the best tradeoff in the cover-space option remaining in the face of adult competition (data from Herzog 1977).

Another example of the cover-space tradeoff is the pheasant population (*Phasianus colchicus*) in Wisconsin studied by Gates and Hale (1974, 1975). In the spring, cocks seeking advertising locations, moved out of dense winter cover. They apparently selected advertising sites near where females would

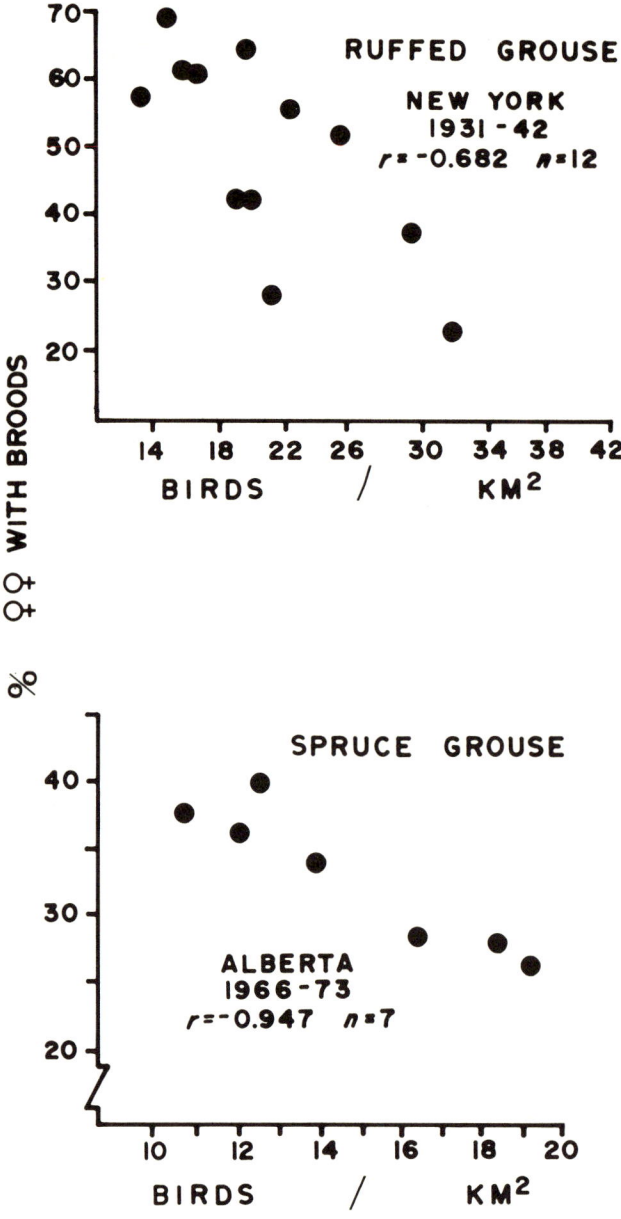

Fig. 10. The nesting success of spruce and ruffed grouse hens (based on the percentage of females with broods) regressed on total spring numbers (Bump et al. 1947, Boag et al. 1979).

later nest (cf. Dumke and Pils 1979). This spacing facilitated their breeding opportunities. Then, the adult females moved to prelaying ranges where they searched for nest sites. These ranges appeared spaced (Gates and Hale 1974). Lastly, the yearling females started their search for the best combinations of nesting cover and space. Since the best nesting sites were already selected by adults, and yearlings and adults showed mutual avoidance, yearlings generally had to disperse farther.

As the pheasant population increased, yearling females compromised cover to maintain space and had reduced nesting success in second-choice habitats (cf. Gates and Hale 1975). However, they might have had even poorer success and also compromised the nest sites of adult females if they had not sought space but instead nested adjacent to established hens. It is this cover-space tradeoff that I believe is a sufficient but not a necessary cause of inversity and compensatory reproduction in relation to breeding densities.

CONCLUSIONS

The reports of the depressing effects of hunting are now just starting to filter in, especially for ruffed grouse in places where they have lost much of their space (Kubisiak 1982, Gullion 1983). As hunters continue to harvest birds from the outback, there will be more depressed populations since buffer zones will no longer be available to provide the colonizers to rebuild numbers in heavily hunted habitats.

Although hunting is additive to overwinter mortality, it is probably not completely additive to the mortality that occurs in the breeding season. If densities are reduced by hunting, when birds space themselves in the spring to advertise and search for nesting sites, the density dependent effect of competition for optimum safe sites will be reduced, and birds can select the very safest sites to nest and advertise, resulting in compensatory natural mortality.

The generalization I propose is that hunting mortality will be additive to natural mortality whenever the natural mortality occurs at the time birds are not spaced, such as in winter when they seek safe feeding sites in conifers, as do spruce and blue grouse, or travel in winter flocks, as do ptarmigan and prairie grouse. The hypothesis of why natural overwinter mortality is additive to hunting losses is that natural mortality is caused mainly by predators, and the most important of these predators are themselves spaced in winter in their efforts to optimally forage.

I can see no operational significance to the word overhunting; hunting does reduce populations. Some populations may not appear to be affected because of the shifts of breeding birds trying to improve their fitness; further, some hens may have improved nesting success at reduced densities. Still, fall hunting is additive and reduces the size of spring breeding populations.

LITERATURE CITED

ALLEN, D. L. 1954. Our wildlife legacy. Funk and Wagnalls, New York, N.Y. 422pp.
ALLISON, D. G. 1963. Basic features of the New Hampshire ruffed grouse census. J. Wildl. Manage. 27:614-616.
BECK, D. I., AND C. E. BRAUN. 1978. Weight of Colorado sage grouse. Condor 80:241-243.
BERGERUD, A. T. 1970. Population dynamics of the willow ptarmigan (*Lagopus lagopus alleni* L.) in Newfoundland, 1955-1965. Oikos 21:299-325.

BOAG, D. A. 1976. Influence of changing grouse density and forest attributes on the occupancy of a series of potential territories by male ruffed grouse. Can. J. Zool. 54:1727-1736.

———, K. H. MCCOURT, P. W. HERZOG, AND J. H. ALWAY. 1979. Population regulation in spruce grouse: a working hypothesis. Can. J. Zool. 57:2275-2284.

BRAUN, C. E. 1969. Population dynamics, habitat, and movements of the white-tailed ptarmigan in Colorado. Ph.D. Thesis. Colorado State Univ., Fort Collins. 189pp.

———, AND G. E. RODGERS. 1971. The white-tailed ptarmigan in Colorado. Colo. Div. Game, Fish and Parks. Tech. Bull. 27. 80pp.

BROWN, R. L., 1967. Sharptail grouse population study. Mont. Dep. Fish and Game. Fed. Aid Proj. 91-R-8. Job II-E. 16pp.

BUMP, G., R. W. DARROW, F. C. EDMINSTER, AND W. F. CRISSEY. 1947. The ruffed grouse life history, propagation, management. N.Y. State Conserv. Dep. Holling Press., Inc. Buffalo, N.Y. 915pp.

CHOATE, T. S. 1963. Habitat and population dynamics of white-tailed ptarmigan in Montana. J. Wildl. Manage. 27:684-699.

DAVIES, R. G. 1973. A study of demography and behavior of ruffed grouse in British Columbia. M.S. Thesis. Univ. Victoria, Victoria, B.C. 99pp.

DESTEFANO S., AND D. H. RUSCH. 1982. Some historical aspects of ruffed grouse harvests and hunting regulations in Wisconsin. Trans. Wis. Acad. Sci. 70:27-35.

DORNEY, R. S., AND C. KABAT. 1960. Relation of weather, parasitic disease, and hunting to Wisconsin ruffed grouse. Wis. Conserv. Tech. Bull. 20. 64pp.

DUMKE, R. T., AND C. M. PILS. 1979. Renesting and dynamics of nest site selection by Wisconsin pheasants. J. Wildl. Manage. 43:705-716.

ELLISON, L. N. 1974. Population characteristics of Alaskan spruce grouse. J. Wildl. Manage. 38:383-395.

ERRINGTON, P. L. 1945. Some contributions of a 15-year local study of the northern bobwhite to a knowledge of population phenomena. Ecol. Monogr. 15:1-34.

———, AND F. N. HAMMERSTROM. 1935. Bobwhite winter survival on experimentally shot and unshot areas. Iowa St. Coll. J. Sci. 9:625-639.

———, F. HAMMERSTROM, AND F. N. HAMMERSTROM. 1940. The great horned owl and its prey in north-central United States. Iowa St. Coll. Agric. Exp. Sta. Bull. 277:757-850.

FRETWELL, S. D., AND H. L. LUCAS, JR. 1969. On territorial behavior and other factors influencing habitat distribution in birds. I. theoretical development. Acta Biotheoretica 19:16-36.

GARDARSSON, A. 1971. Food ecology and spacing behavior of rock ptarmigan (*Lagopus mutus*) in Iceland. Ph.D. Thesis. Univ. California, Berkeley. 382pp.

GATES, J. M., AND J. B. HALE. 1974. Seasonal movement, winter habitat use and population distribution of an east-central Wisconsin pheasant population. Wisc. Dep. Nat. Resour. Tech. Bull. 76. 55pp.

———, AND ———. 1975. Reproduction of an east-central Wisconsin pheasant population. Wisc. Dep. of Nat. Resour. Tech. Bull. 85. 70pp.

GULLION, G. W. 1970. The ruffed grouse in northern Minnesota. Dep. Entomol., Fish. and Wildl., Univ. Minnesota FW67-49. 37pp.

———. 1981. Non-drumming males in ruffed grouse population. Wilson Bull. 93:372-382.

———. 1983. Rejuvenation and maintenance of forest habitats for the American ruffed grouse. Proc. Int. Symp. on Grouse. World Pheasant Assoc. 2:11-25.

———, AND W. H. MARSHALL. 1968. Survival of ruffed grouse in a boreal forest. Living Bird 7:117-167.

HAMMERSTROM, F., AND F. HAMMERSTROM. 1973. The prairie chicken in Wisconsin. Wisc. Dep. Nat. Resour. Tech. Bull. 64. 52pp.

HERMAN, C. M. 1963. Disease and infection in the Tetraonidae. J. Wildl. Manage. 27:850-855.

HERZOG, P. W. 1977. Dispersion and mobility in a local population of spruce grouse (*Canachites canadensis* Franklinii). M.S. Thesis. Univ. Alberta, Edmonton. 98pp.

———, AND D. A. BOAG. 1978. Dispersion and mobility in a local population of spruce grouse. J. Wildl. Manage. 42:853-865.

HICKEY, J. J. 1955. Some American population research on gallinaceous birds. Pages 326-396 *in* A. Wolfson, ed. Recent studies of avian biology. Univ. Illinois, Urbana.

JENKINS, D., A. WATSON, AND G. R. MILLER. 1963. Population studies of red grouse (*Lagopus lagopus scoticus* Lath.) in northeast Scotland. J. Anim. Ecol. 32:317-376.

———, ———, AND ———. 1964. Predation and red grouse populations. J. Appl. Ecol. 1:183-195.

———, ———, AND ———. 1967. Population fluctuations in red grouse (*Lagopus lagopus scoticus* Lath.). J. Anim. Ecol. 36:97-122.

KEITH, L. B. 1963. Wildlife's 10-year cycle. Univ. Wisconsin Press, Madison. 201pp.

———. 1974. Some features of population dynamics in mammals. Int. Congr. of Game Biol. 11:17-58.

KING, R. T. 1937. Ruffed grouse management. J. For. 35:523-532.

KOBRIGER, G. D. 1975. Correlation of sharp-tailed grouse population parameters. N. Dak. Outdoors 38:10-13.

———. 1981. Prairie grouse population data. N. Dak. State Game and Fish Dep. Report B-318. 30pp.

KUBISIAK, J. F. 1982. The impact of hunting on ruffed grouse populations. Ruffed grouse workshop. Traverse City, Mich. 18pp.

LACK, D. 1954. The natural regulation of animal numbers. Clarendon Press, Oxford, U.K. 343pp.

———. 1966. Population studies of birds. Clarendon Press, Oxford, U.K. 341pp.

———. 1968. Ecological adaptations for breeding birds. Methuen, London, U.K. 409pp.

LEOPOLD, A. 1933. Game management. Charles Scribner's Sons, New York, N.Y. 481pp.

LINDE, D. A., M. MUCK, H. H. PIETZ, AND L. ROTH. 1978. Grouse management surveys, 1978. S. Dak. Dep. Game, Fish and Parks. Game Report 80-6. 23pp.

LITTLE, T. W. 1978. Populations, distributions, and habitat selection by drumming male ruffed grouse in central Minnesota prior to clear-cutting. Ph.D. Thesis. Univ. Minnesota, Minneapolis. 141pp.

MAY, T. A. 1975. Physiological ecology of white-tailed ptarmigan in Colorado. Ph.D. Thesis. Univ. Colorado, Boulder. 311pp.

MOSS, R., A. WATSON, AND R. PARR. 1975. Maternal nutrition and breeding success in red grouse (*Lagopus lagopus scoticus*). J. Anim. Ecol. 44:233-244.

———, ———, AND J. OLLASON. 1982. Animal population dynamics. Chapman and Hall, London, U.K. 80pp.

NEWTON, I. 1979. Population ecology of raptors. Buteo Books, Vermillion, S. Dak. 399pp.

PETERSEN, L. 1979. Ecology of great-horned owls and red-tailed hawks in southeastern Wisconsin. Wisc. Dep. Nat. Resour. Tech. Bull. 111. 63pp.

PILS, C. M., AND M. A. MARTEN. 1978. Population dynamics, predator-prey relationships and management of the red fox in Wisconsin. Wisc. Dep. Nat. Resour. Tech. Bull. 105. 56pp.

REDFIELD, J. A. 1973. Variations in the weight of blue grouse (*Dendragapus obscurus*). Condor 75:312-321.

ROBEL, R. J., F. R. HENDERSON, AND W. W. JACKSON. 1972. Some sharp-tailed grouse population statistics from North Dakota. J. Wildl. Manage. 36:87-98.

ROBINSON, W. L. 1980. Fool hen. Univ. Wisconsin Press, Madison. 221pp.

ROMESBURG, H. C. 1981. Wildlife science: gaining reliable knowledge. J. Wildl. Manage. 45:293-313.

ROE, R. G. 1951. The North American buffalo. Univ. Toronto Press, Toronto, Can. 957pp.

RUSCH, D. H., AND L. B. KEITH. 1971. Ruffed grouse vegetation relationship in central Alberta. J. Wildl. Manage. 35:417-429.

———, M. M. GILLESPIE, AND D. I. MCKAY. 1978. Decline of ruffed grouse population in Manitoba. Can. Field. Nat. 92:123-127.

SARGEANT, A. B. 1972. Red fox spatial characteristics in relation to waterfowl predation. J. Wildl. Manage. 36:225-236.

SOPUCK, L. G. 1979. Movements and breeding biology of blue grouse in relation to recruitment, reproductive success, and migration. M.S. Thesis. Univ. Alberta, Edmonton. 96pp.

WATSON, A. 1965. A population study of ptarmigan (*Lagopus mutus*) in Scotland. J. Anim. Ecol. 34:135-172.

―――, AND R. Moss. 1970. Dominance, spacing behavior, and aggression in relation to population limitation in vertebrates. Symp. British Ecol. Soc. 10:167-218.

―――, AND ―――. 1972. A current model of population dynamics in red grouse. Proc. Int. Ornithol. Congr. 15:134-149.

―――, AND P. J. O'HARE. 1979. Red grouse populations on experimentally treated and untreated Irish bog. J. Appl. Ecol. 16:433-452.

WEEDEN, R. B., AND J. B. THEBERGE. 1972. The dynamics of a fluctuating population of rock ptarmigan in Alaska. Proc. Int. Ornithol. Congr. 25:90-105.

WILLIAMS, G. C. 1966. Natural selection, the costs of reproduction, and a refinement of Lack's principle. Am. Nat. 100:687-696.

WITTENBERGER, J. F. 1981. Animal social behavior. Duxbury Press, Boston, Mass. 722pp.

WYNNE-EDWARDS, V. C. 1962. Animal dispersion in relationship to social behavior. Oliver and Boyd, Edinburgh, Scotland. 653pp.

ZWICKEL, F. C. 1972. Removal and repopulation of blue grouse in an increasing population. J. Wildl. Manage. 36:1141-1152.

―――. 1975. Nesting parameters of blue grouse and their relevance to populations. Condor 77:423-430.

―――. 1982. Demographic composition of hunter-harvested blue grouse in east-central Vancouver Island, British Columbia. J. Wildl. Manage. 46:1057-1061.

―――, AND J. F. BENDELL. 1967. Early mortality and the regulation of numbers in blue grouse. Can. J. Zool. 45:817-850.

―――, J. A. REDFIELD, AND J. KRISTENSEN. 1977. Demography, behavior and genetics of a colonizing population of blue grouse. Can. J. Zool. 55:1948-1957.

―――, J. F. BENDELL, AND A. N. ASH. 1983. Population regulation in blue grouse. Pages 212-225 *in* F. L. Bunnell, D. S. Eastman, and J. M. Peek, eds. Symposium on natural regulation of wildlife populations. Proc. No. 14. Forest, Wildl. and Range Exp. Station, Moscow, Idaho.

ABSTRACTS

INTENSIVE FARM MANAGEMENT OF WAPITI BANDS WITH RELOCATION OF YOUNG MALES INTO NEW HUNTING PRESERVES

G. H. MOORE, Invermay Agricultural Research Center, Private Bag, Mosgiel, New Zealand

Abstract: The annual cycle of management and production from farmed bands of wapiti-type deer (*Cervus elaphus*) is important. An enclosed breeding band of wapiti permits selective breeding through single-sire mating and preferential feeding of young females to maximize reproductive rates. Such a system could be economically profitable from sale of surplus females, velvet antlers from the stud bulls, tourism, slaughter of the cull stock for meat, and sale of young males to establish hunting preserves. The concept of male-only stocked hunting preserves was derived by stocking of areas with bull calves from the enclosed farming operations. In female-free areas, these bulls may later disperse widely over the rut in search of females. Inappetence of the bulls during the rut could lead to autumn-saved feed for winter. Lower liveweight losses in bulls through absence of mating activities could reduce winter mortality of bulls and increase the harvest of trophy heads.

GAME HARVEST MANAGEMENT AS APPLIED TO A GAME RANCHING PROGRAM

COLIN E. RUDMAN, Brandtkoppen, Sapkamma 6235, South Africa

Abstract: The Uitenhage Valley Bushveld is an area of dense, indigenous brush, grassveld, and cactus plants called "noors" and has an average annual rainfall of 305 mm. The area harbors the densest kudu (*Strepsiceros* sp.) population in Africa with an estimated 28,000 animals on 170,000 ha. In 1980, I erected a 2.4-m-high fence around approximately 6,500 ha of land in this area on which to run kudu and angora goats. Kudu were selected to complement the goats because they are indigenous, they utilize 2-m-high vegetation well, and they are very attractive as trophy and meat producing animals. A stocking ratio of 3 angoras:1 kudu was decided as optimum; thus, I opted to maintain approximately 400 kudu on the site. A total of 920 kudu were recorded in the initial helicopter count, so 512 were harvested within 2 months to achieve the desired population. The herd is maintained at this level by harvesting, by helicopter and night shooting, a number about equal to the annual increment. Shooting from a helicopter has the advantage of selective culling but the disadvantage of inflicting stress and bruising on the animals and damage to the fence. Night shooting from specially equipped vehicles results in reduced stress and damage to animals and fences, permits harvesting during cooler temperatures, and results in 100% head shots. Approximately 95% of the harvest is sold to local venison, biltong (jerky), and sausage factories. Mature bulls are hunted for trophies.

CONSERVATION AND MANAGEMENT OF BLACKBUCK AND GAZELLE

S. M. MOHNOT, Department of Zoology, Jodhpur University, Jodhpur 342001, India

Abstract: The blackbuck (*Antilope cervicapra rajputanae*) and the Indian gazelle or chinkara (*Gazella gazella bennetti*) are found in the Great Indian Desert in perhaps the largest concentrations in the world. These populations have now reached beyond the carrying capacity of the habitat. The population sustains itself in spite of overpopulation, adverse climatic conditions, and famine. The sample survey around Vishnoi villages of the Fitkasani-Kankelav area of Jodhpur district covered an area of 288 km^2 and yielded about 2,670 blackbucks and 2,217 chinkara. Surprisingly, these animals are not only protected by law by the Vishnois, who are strict vegetarians, but are allowed to feed in the crop fields and are even supplemented during the hottest months of May and June. Because of the sociological barriers existing in the local area, the only harvest management strategy that can be deployed is translocation of live animals to vacuum areas to reduce pressure on the existing resources.

A SUMMARY OF NEW YORK'S WILD TURKEY MANAGEMENT PROGRAM SINCE 1950

JAMES GLIDDEN, NYSDEC, Bureau of Wildlife, Wildlife Resources Center, Delmar, NY 12054

Abstract: The wiid turkey (*Meleagris gallopavo silvestris*) has been successfully re-established in New York since 1950. Initial efforts were directed toward stocking farm-reared birds. This technique failed to produce significant results. The technique was discontinued in favor of the wild-trap-and-transfer method in 1959. Wild turkeys now occupy over 52,000 km^2 of the state; approximately 2,100 km^2 of range remain unoccupied. Fall hunting began in 1959 with an estimated take of 250 birds. Spring hunting began in 1968 with an estimated take of 130 gobblers. Hunters now report taking over 7,300 birds annually. The calculated annual take is approximately 7,900 birds. With the success of the re-establishment effort comes the challenge of optimizing recreational utilization of the resource. This aspect of wild turkey management is now being emphasized. Strategic objectives have been adopted to guide the program through the next decade. These call for quadrupling the take while minimizing problems that might result from excessive hunting pressure. To this end, wild turkey population, harvest, and hunting pressure indices have been developed for each of 4 range classes.

RESPONSE OF GRAY AND FOX SQUIRREL POPULATIONS TO DIFFERENTIAL HARVEST INTENSITIES

CHARLES E. DAVIS, Department of Wildlife and Fisheries Sciences, Texas A&M University, College Station, TX 77843
CHARLES S. SMITH, College of Veterinary Medicine, Kansas State University, Manhattan, KS 66502
SAMUEL L. BEASOM, Caesar Kleberg Wildlife Research Institute, Texas A&I University, Kingsville, TX 78363
WENDELL G. SWANK, Department of Wildlife and Fisheries Sciences, Texas A&M University, College Station, TX 77843

Abstract: An evaluation was made of the effects of differential fall and spring hunting pressure on gray squirrel (*Sciurus carolinensis*) and fox squirrel (*S. niger*) natality, juvenile survival, and population levels on the Gus Engeling Wildlife Management Area in east Texas during 1973-77. Pretreatment data, collected on the 2 study areas during the initial 2 years, involved unregulated public hunting during the regular spring and fall hunts administered by the Texas Parks and Wildlife Department on the area. During subsequent seasons hunting effort was regulated so that the kill on 1 study area was approximately 100% greater than on the other area. The heavy hunting pressure appeared to result in a reduced squirrel population level during some, but not all, of the experimental hunts. Natality and juvenile survival differed between seasons but not between areas. It is apparent that compensatory reproductive success does not occur in these species in this location, so the possibility exists of reducing local squirrel populations by heavy hunting pressure.

HUNTER PARTICIPATION IN THE
MANAGEMENT OF A HERD OF TROPHY ELK

JOHN A. ANDERSON, "Glendonald", Albury, South Canterbury, New Zealand

Abstract: The fundamental aim of the New Zealand Deer Stalker's Association shall be that the organization and management of big game hunting in New Zealand shall be carried out by sportsmen—in other words, the self-regulation of hunting by hunters. This report records the efforts of sportsmen to manage a sympatric herd of cervids, wapiti (*Cervus elaphus nelsoni*) and red deer (*C. elaphus*), occupying a rangeland suffering from overuse in a remote corner of a national park. Geologically the area is deeply dissected with glacially carved U-shaped valleys terminating in deep fiords and narrow razor-edged dividing ridges rising to and occasionally exceeding 2,000 m and densely clad in indigenous rain forest. There have been successes, failures. revelations, and problems associated with wildlife management when this conflicts with and is at the mercy of insecurity of political policy and commercial motivation. A management plan was designed with the aims and objectives of: (1) containing the existing, expanding cervid population, (2) establishing population dynamics and appropriate harvest strategies, (3) effecting a reduction of the cervid population to the degree and in such a manner that it could subsequently be contained at a level that no longer constituted a threat to the indigenous flora, (4) sustaining intensive pressure on the red deer and putative hybrid segment of the population so that crossbreeding no longer constituted a significant threat to the expressed objective, namely, a trophy herd of elk, (5) making use of the inherent inability of the male of the species to reproduce in the absence of the opposite sex and using this as a tool of management in modifying explosive population trends induced through herd reduction, (6) inviting maximum hunter participation in the formation of the management plan, in its implementation in the field, in the collection of field autopsy data, and in special research projects, (7) upgrading the herd so that it could sustain a yield of high quality trophy elk commensurate with environmental limitations and having regard for other values at stake, and (8) harvesting mature bulls as a trophy crop only after these animals had the chance to sire the greater part of the reproductive segment of the herd in the year of harvest.